Place, Space, and Landscape in Medieval Narrative

Place, Space, and Landscape in Medieval Narrative

Edited by Laura L. Howes

Tennessee Studies in Literature

Volume 43

The University of Tennessee Press / Knoxville

"Tennessee Studies in Literature," a distinguished series sponsored by the Department of English at The University of Tennessee, Knoxville, began publication in 1956. Beginning in 1984, with Volume 27, TSL evolved from a series of annual volumes of miscellaneous essays to a series of occasional volumes, each one dealing with a specific theme, period, or genre, for which the editor of that volume has invited contributions from leading scholars in the field.

Inquiries concerning this series should be addressed to the Editorial Board, Tennessee Studies in Literature, Department of English, The University of Tennessee, Knoxville, Tennessee 37996-0430. Those desiring to purchase additional copies of this issue or copies of back issues should address The University of Tennessee Press, 600 Henley Street, 110 Conference Center Building, Knoxville, Tennessee 37996-4108.

Library of Congress Cataloging-in-Publication Data

Place, space, and landscape in medieval narrative / edited by Laura L. Howes. — 1st ed.
    p. cm. — (Tennessee studies in literature ; v. 43)
Includes index.

ISBN-13: 978-1-57233-586-8 (hardcover)
ISBN-10: 1-57233-586-6 (hardcover)

1. Literature, Medieval—History and criticism. I. Howes, Laura L.

PN671.P53 2007
809'.02—dc22   2006035365

Contents

Laura L. Howes

Introduction

In describing six mammoth sculptures by Richard Serra, the art critic Calvin Tompkins articulates the experience of walking near and into Serra's steel "torqued spirals":

> Because the encircling walls are never plumb (they either bend in or bend out from the vertical at all points), you have alternating sensations of confinement and expansion as you walk into them. The weight of Corten steel on either side makes the walk fairly frightening, but then, emerging at last into the open space at the center, you get a jolt of euphoria, space rushing away from you on all sides and the whole vast form becoming buoyant and seemingly weightless.
>
> (52)

Tompkins goes on to discuss Serra's shaping of space—"Serra has said . . . that what he is doing is not creating static objects but shaping space"—and he includes his own surprising response to the works as "intense sensations of joy and delight" (52).

Surely medieval men who designed and built cathedrals were also engaged in "shaping space" to produce certain effects on the people who would encounter those buildings, even though they did not articulate it in exactly the way we do. When we compare Tompkins's description with a description of walking inside Amiens Cathedral by Stephen Murray and James Addiss, we begin to sense the importance of space to sensory experience of the world and to human emotive experience: "the spaces gradually and progressively reveal themselves in a set of transformations of the initial order. . . . [T]he visitor, whose movement energizes the spaces, transform[s] reality" (50, 65). Walking through, or standing in, certain places produces feelings of joy, of ecstasy, of fear, or of foreboding, as these descriptions suggest.

Indeed, space exerts its pressure upon us. Architects know this, Richard Serra knows this. And the premodern authors who walked and built and wrote knew this. Despite the claim that "there was no such thing as 'space' for medieval people . . . [and that] our modern abstract notion of space . . . is a postmedieval category" (Camille 9), "space" remains a useful theoretical construct, particularly as it is defined by Michel de Certeau. In contrast with "place," which identifies static relationships, the concept of "space" is defined by movement and by human experience (Certeau 97; Kobialka 128–29). Medieval men and women moved through urban and agricultural spaces, around gates and through fields and gardens, into and out of cathedrals and small homes, just as we do. Traveling from one town to another on foot or by horse, then as now, engages the traveler's body in reaction to the landscape and impresses his or her mind with perceptions of the places passed over and through.[1]

A body's occupation of static space also impresses with particular force in many medieval narratives. A heightened awareness of enclosed spaces, of locked towers, of small, private rooms, gardens, or closets within these tales suggests the noteworthy nature of isolation in medieval society, with its appeal for illicit pleasure or fear of outlaw activity. In addition, historical places and the specificity of narratives that allude to them or make use of an audience's knowledge of these actual places become newly significant when discovered and aid interpretation of otherwise enigmatic passages. Larger landscapes and cityscapes figure in several works, often depicted in the play of political power or the exploration of public identity. Even the skyscape of heaven may come into play as a specifically meaningful space into which the human activity of sin presses and effects change.

The essays gathered here contribute to an ongoing investigation of place and spatial relationships in medieval culture. It joins *Medieval Practices of Space* (Hanawalt), *Text and Territory: Geographical Imagination in the European Middle Ages* (Tomasch and Gilles), *Inventing Medieval Landscapes* (Howe and Wolfe), and many journal articles in mapping the diverse ways in which medieval culture theorized space, used actual spaces, and incorporated a sense of place into their writings.[2] All of these explorations depend on the foundational work of Henri Lefebvre, Gaston Bachelard, Michel de Certeau, Edward S. Casey, and others. Indeed, following Foucault, John Ganim writes here, "Why should space be regarded as inert and dead . . . and time be valorized as dialectical, dynamic, and creative?" An attention to spatial relations, to the representation of historical places, and to the nuances of interaction between people and their landscapes restores us to a mode of thought sometimes lost or occluded in analyses of medieval narrative.

John Ganim opens this collection by briefly surveying the history of scholarship on English medieval literary landscapes and, beyond that, engaging recent theoretical approaches to landscape, by both medievalists and modernists. In an interesting twist, "as we have become aware of the importance, even the priority, of representation and mediation" in our understanding of the natural world in which we live, writes Ganim, postmodern critics have come to view *medieval* representations of the natural world with greater affinity, not due to the medieval world's mimetic capabilities but due to our appreciation of the medieval use of "explicit signage" regarding landscape, place, and space. Ganim finds the groundwork for these newer approaches in the seminal 1973 study by Derek Pearsall and Elizabeth Salter, *Landscapes and Seasons of the Medieval World,* which argued for a kind of semiotics of medieval landscape, an iconographic language, in literature and in art. Despite this early attention to space, Ganim finds that medieval ways of representing space are routinely seen as "originary, incipient, or prototypical," the medieval period itself still a stage whose importance derives from what comes after. Thus Ganim highlights the work of several scholars here who attend to the medieval city and its civic pageants, without recourse to later developments, and thus without reading backward, as it were, to medieval landscapes as sites of contested political power in their own right and to postcolonial studies which find medieval religious visionary landscapes dependent upon a Western fantasy of exotic places, dangers, and spiritual awakenings. Ganim's wide-ranging survey touches on many distinct points, creating bridges where we might not have noticed them before: Maurice Halbwachs's notion of collective memory, Mary Carruthers's study of mnemonics, Martin Stevens's and Nicholas Davis's work on medieval English mystery plays, and current cinematic representations of the Middle Ages.

In the first group of essays, Lisa H. Cooper's "Making Space for History: Galbert of Bruges and the Murder of Charles the Good" finds imagined space giving shape to historical narrative. Galbert of Bruges's chronicle of the murder of Charles the Good figures city and castral locations as theatrical spaces, fully articulated by Galbert, even though he was not physically present at the historical moments he narrates: the murder itself and the subsequent enclosure of the besieged murderers in the count's castle and church. Perhaps most startling, though, is Galbert's representation of the murderers' minds, treated as interior spaces which Galbert can occupy and describe as if a mere recorder of events.

William R. Askins, in "A Camp Wedding: The Cultural Context of Chaucer's *Brooch of Thebes,*" turns his attention to a specific place and a historical moment: the illicit marriage of John of Gaunt's daughter, Elizabeth, to John Holland, in Plymouth, Devonshire, as they prepared to embark to Spain with the Lancastrian retinue in the spring of 1386. This is the specific occasion, Askins argues, for Chaucer's paired poems, "The Complaint of Mars" and "The Complaint of Venus," which may well form two parts of a single poem, *The Brooch of Thebes,* an epithalamium in the Latin tradition. Dense with historical detail, Askins's piece succeeds in restoring to this poem the specificity of what—and whom—it celebrates and commemorates, and in so doing underscores the importance of grounding poetic works in their moment and place.

Lawrence Warner, in his "Adventurous Custance: St. Thomas of Acre and Chaucer's *Man of Law's Tale,*" similarly details the specific associations of Chaucer's

Man of Law's Tale to a particular London landmark—the Church of St. Thomas of Acre—showing how a historical place becomes a window onto late-fourteenth-century connotative meaning. As Warner considers the uses made of St. Thomas of Acre on the Cheap in Chaucer's time, the associations with merchant adventurers and crusading impulses, he opens a host of associations to us that normally lie dormant in modern readings of the tale.

Turning from historical to fully imagined spaces, Thomas J. Heffernan, in "'The sun shall be turned to darkness and the moon to blood': How Sin and Redemption Affect Heavenly Space in an Old English Transfiguration Homily," engages the space beyond earth—the heavens—as a place where theological meaning resides. The "skyscape" and its ordering reflect the moral status of humans, according to Judeo-Christian apocalyptic tradition, which is well represented in an Old English Transfiguration homily. In that text, Heffernan shows that human sin is deemed "the cause of the loss of the sun's original brilliance." The heavens thus resonate with, and react to, the material world of human existence. Here, space with significance to human behavior, with ties to human activity and sin, expands from the earth we tread to the vastness of the cosmos.

Also exploring imagined and theorized space, Michael Calabrese, in his "Controlling Space and Secrets in the *Lais* of Marie de France," finds Marie de France's opening assertion of the need to reveal her poetic gift and to speak obscurely in her *Lais* begins a pattern of simultaneous exposure and concealment for herself as a poet and for a series of lovers within the tales she tells. While successful in creating a "safe space" for herself, from which she can write, Marie delineates a host of variations on the theme in her *Lais*: "the very search for safety that animates Marie's 'Prologue' animates the stories themselves," writes Calabrese, "and the poet's conflict with slander and envy is replicated anew in each fictive world she summons out of 'Briton.'" Safety, for deserving lovers, comes with safe places that exclude the envious and allows the lovers to keep their secret. In fact, Calabrese discovers that those who use physical space well "thrive and find security," while those "overcome by foul lust and envy . . . suffer when space betrays them." Enclosed spaces examined by Calabrese include a well-caulked ship, a hollow rock, rooms with locked doors, towers, bathtubs, tombs, a bejeweled box, and, finally, the cloister. The range of Marie's safe and unsafe spaces in the *Lais* and her attentiveness to all manner of exits and entrances provide Calabrese with ample evidence that "space and the complex drama of entering, sealing, and revealing is central to an understanding of Marie, her moral universe, and her art."

Kenneth Bleeth's "Chaucerian Gardens and the Spirit of Play" argues for the significance of play and other garden activities to the worlds beyond the garden's walls and thus details imagined garden spaces as they evolve into spaces with larger social and political meanings. Far from being cut off from the realities of the world outside, as Boccaccio's secluded retreats are in the *Decameron*, gardens in Chaucer demonstrate that playful activities have real-world consequences. In addition, the apparent protections provided courtly play within secluded gardens—in the Knight's, Merchant's, and Franklin's tales, as well as in the *Troilus*—prove illusory, according to Bleeth's formulation, and finally cannot isolate the gardens' users from social and historical pressures they have sought to avoid or defer.

In the volume's final section, Gregory Kaplan, in "Landscapes of Discrimination in *Converso* Literature of Early Inquisitorial Spain," finds landscapes that symbolically represent a sense of social alienation for their central characters. Several authors writing in the 1490s who were "New Christians," that is, Jewish converts to Christianity during the Spanish Inquisition, encode allusions to their sense of socioreligious inferiority in the landscapes of their works, well before the state imposition of censorship in 1558. Diego San Pedro, Rodrigo Cota, and Fernando de Rojas, all converted Jews, use setting to represent the uncertain social environment of the *conversos*. By means of a trial-by-combat, a garden setting, and even an urban streetscape, these authors depict "an atmosphere in which all converts were viewed with skepticism, regardless of whether they were actually practicing Judaism in secret." Kaplan's historically savvy analysis of several narratives from this period demonstrates the deep anxieties of *converso* authors as they cleverly disguise these anxieties within landscape descriptions.

Kari Kalve's contribution, "'Truthe is therinne': The Spaces of Truth and Community in *Piers Plowman* B" considers the predominance of outdoor amorphous spaces in the poem, in contrast to the handful of enclosed spaces, such as Mede's bower and Betty the Brewer's tavern. In fact, Kalve finds, Langland generally privileges open spaces as places of healthy community activities, and he portrays enclosed interior spaces as dangerous to an individual wishing to avoid sin. Even the barn of Unity, which promises protection from the Antichrist at the poem's end, gives way under pressure to a dispersal of its inhabitants which in the end will save them. Will's desired goal, the tower where Truth resides, which is introduced in the poem's "Prologue," is the only interior space with a potentially positive effect. But that space exists beyond the grasp of humans, Will finds, at least until death. Indeed, the only positive interior space available to the Truth-seeker is the inner space of individual conscience. Kalve ties this attitude toward private space to late medieval concern over privacy as detrimental to the common good and argues that Langland's spirituality is firmly based in the exercise of public rites and in communal spaces.

Catherine S. Cox, in "Eastward of the Garden: The Biblical Landscape of *Sir Gawain and the Green Knight*," explores the intertextual associations of wandering and exile in *Sir Gawain and the Green Knight*, drawing upon Jewish midrash and Christian exegetical traditions of Cain in the "land of Nod," or the land of wandering. A landscape more biblical and Hebraic than Augustinian and patristic informs Sir Gawain's experience of sin and of punishment, argues Cox. Identifying the burial mound where Gawain meets the Green Knight as a place that suggests the death and rebirth of baptism and the acceptance of a new identity, Cox finds Gawain marked, like Cain, with a sign of penitence when he returns to Camelot from that transformational spot.

Sylvia Federico's "The Place of Chivalry in the New Trojan Court: Gawain, Troilus, and Richard II" examines the places where chivalry is exercised and displayed in two Ricardian works. With the reputation of Richard's court as one of refinement and domestic pleasure, Federico argues, the issue of what knights do and where they do it concerned Richard's detractors, among them Thomas of Walsingham and Adam of Usk. Negative aspects of a chivalric court were, in fact, exacerbated with reference by Richard and his coterie to London as the "new Troy." That is, "allusions to Troy reflected poorly on the king and his court; instead of noble grandeur and knightly valor, Richard's appeals to Trojan history reinforced the reputation of his court as one of foreignness, arrogance, treachery, deceit, and sexual perversion." Significantly, both Gawain and Troilus fail as chivalric figures: "Chivalric pursuit, in both instances, leads to a crisis, even a disintegration, of identity." Following Edward S. Casey, Federico further argues for the two knights' bodies as places, locations that carry signs of their failure and, in Gawain's case, shame. While their bedroom exploits and tests come to define them, it is finally "the chivalric body" itself that fails in each poem. These failures resonate with public concerns for the body politic, for the deviant behavior of Richard II, and for the possibilities for chivalric valor in such a world.

And finally, Robert W. Hanning, in "Before Chaucer's *Shipman's Tale:* The Language of Place, the Place of Language in *Decameron* 8.1 and 8.2" turns his analytic lens on two of Boccaccio's novelle, one set in an urban cityscape, which signals an attention to commercial and gender relations, the other set in a provincial country landscape, which perpetuates stereotypes about rural folk and which examines, by means of specific *loci,* relations among rural parish clergy, the peasantry, and powerful institutional interests of church, government, and commerce. In *Decameron* 8.1, the introduction of commerce into the privacy of the conjugal bedroom suggests that "a woman in business, profiting from her body, is more of a threat to male hegemony" than simple adultery would be, and male verbal trickery catches the wife, the would-be entrepreneur, in her "bedroom-turned-marketplace," causing her to further her husband's fiscal interests after all. Hanning also notes that the "place" of language—the specific circumstances in which words are spoken— enable one character to fool others without his uttering a single lie. In 8.2, both rural *loci*—country church and peasant's home—lack the resources necessary to keeping their inhabitants out of dishonorable situations. An overlay of comic *double entendres* that seeks to ameliorate the reader's recognition of material poverty and the compromises poverty necessitates finally cannot fully cover over the "priest's institutionally supported coercion, and Belcolore's continued deprivation of her wedding clothes" to the city's pawn shop. In these novelle, city and country settings signal relationships of power, between men and women in 8.1 and, more broadly, between rapacious institutions and defenseless individuals in 8.2.

In each of these chapters, then, analyses of space—its many uses and modes of representation within narrative—map a variety of ways medieval narratives encoded meaning. In some, lost historical associations, crucial to an informed reading, are uncovered. In others, a new way of theorizing space—even seeing bodies and minds as spaces to be imagined or marked—leads to interpretations that add significantly to our understanding of medieval narrative art. In still others, broadly political and ideological concerns find expression in the spatial world. The layout of space or the conception of the land as governed by specific literary or religious associations signals a way of reading those spaces that held meaning to a contemporary audience. In all cases, these chapters open new space for further contributions to the investigation of the medieval spatial imagination.

This volume has benefited from the support of the Tennessee Studies in Literature Board, especially Dorothy Scura and Don Richard Cox; from the careful attention of two anonymous readers for the board; and from my department at the University of Tennessee, which granted me a John C. Hodges research leave in fall 2003. To them all, and to the contributors whose work graces this volume, I offer my sincere thanks. The support of my family has also been crucial. To my daughter Mary, my husband Charlie, and my parents—at whose house I checked many citations using the Colgate University Library—my gratitude is endless.

Notes

1. An extended essay by Rebecca Solnit on walking posits a correspondence at every turn between walking and thought. She writes: "The mind is also a landscape of sorts and . . . walking is one way to traverse it" (Solnit 6) and "exploring the world is one of the best ways of exploring the mind, and walking travels both terrains" (Solnit 13).
2. See, for example, Gerhart; Rollo-Koster; Tomasch, "*Mappae Mundi;*" Howes.

Works Cited

Bachelard, Gaston. *The Poetics of Space*. Trans. Maria Jolas. Boston: Beacon, 1964.

Camille, Michael. "Signs of the City: Place, Power, and Public Fantasy in Medieval Paris." Hanawalt and Kobialka 1–36.

Casey, Edward S. *The Fate of Place*. Berkeley: U of California P, 1997.

De Certeau, Michel. *The Practice of Everyday Life*. Trans. Steven F. Rendall. Berkeley: U of California P, 1984.

Foucault, Michel. "Of Other Spaces." *Diacritics* 16 (1986): 22–27.

Gerhart, Mary. "Who Is Hildegard? Where Is She—On Heaven?" *Experiences of Place*. Ed. Mary N. MacDonald. Cambridge: Harvard UP, 2003. 115–45.

Hanawalt, Barbara A., and Michal Kobialka, eds. *Medieval Practices of Space*. Medieval Cultures, vol. 23. Minneapolis: U of Minnesota P, 2000.

Howe, John and Michael Wolfe, eds. *Inventing Medieval Landscapes: Senses of Place in Western Europe*. Gainesville: UP of Florida, 2002.

Howes, Laura L. "'The Slow Curve of the Footwalker': Narrative Time and Literary Landscape in Middle English Poetry." *Soundings: An Interdisciplinary Journal* 83.1 (2000): 165–81; rpt. in *Inventing Medieval Landscapes: Senses of Place in Western Europe*. Eds. John Howe and Michael Wolfe. Gainesville: UP of Florida, 2002. 192–207.

Kobialka, Michal. "Staging Place/Space in the Eleventh-Century Monastic Practices." Hanawalt and Kobialka 128–48.

Lefebvre, Henri. *The Production of Space*. Trans. Donal Nicholson-Smith. Oxford: Blackwell, 1991.

Murray, Stephen, and James Addiss. "Plan and Space at Amiens Cathedral with a New Plan Drawn by James Addiss." *Journal of the Society of Architectural Historians* 49 (1990): 44–66.

Pearsall, Derek, and Elizabeth Salter. *Landscapes and Seasons of the Medieval World*. London: Elek, 1973.

Rollo-Koster, Joëlle. "The Politics of Body Parts: Contested Topographies in Late-Medieval Avignon." *Speculum* 78.1 (2003): 66–98.

Solnit, Rebecca. *Wanderlust: A History of Walking*. New York: Penguin, 2000.

Tomasch, Sylvia. "*Mappae Mundi* and 'The Knight's Tale': The Geography of Power, the Technology of Control." *Chaucer's Cultural Geography.* Ed. Kathryn L. Lynch. New York: Routledge, 2002. 193–224.

Tomasch, Sylvia, and Sealy Gilles, eds. *Text and Territory: Geographical Imagination in the European Middle Ages.* Philadelphia: U of Pennsylvania P, 1998.

Tomkins, Calvin. "Man of Steel." *New Yorker* 5 Aug. 2002: 52–63.

John M. Ganim

Landscape and
Late Medieval Literature
A Critical Geography

Over the past twenty years, a significant body of work in very different fields—art history, geography, and urban theory—has produced new and highly charged understandings of such apparently objective terms as "space" and "landscape." The totalizing impulses of grand theory have given way to partial and provisional tactics, as expressed in the diction of the discourses of our moment: negotiations, situations, positions, location, borders, margins. Underlying this change is one of the shifts in the very ground of research in the humanities and cultural studies over the past few decades, from observations governed everywhere by the question of time to a perspective governed everywhere by the question of space. This shift was one of the categories enumerated in Lyotard's *Postmodern Condition,* but it is evident in the changes in the way we think and the way we talk about what we think, from the phenomenological and existential languages of the 1950s and early 1960s to the structuralist and poststructuralist languages of intellectual discourse today. Why should space be regarded as inert and dead, asked Foucault a quarter century ago, and time be valorized as dialectical, dynamic, and creative? Foucault was crystallizing a position that had been forged a decade earlier, in the early 1960s, in the work of Lefebvre. Lefebvre elevated the analysis of space to the same position as other materials of history, analyzing its politics, its ownership, its relations to power. And those keywords I just mentioned—negotiations, situations, positions, location, borders, margins—are by and large within the semantics of space. What I seek to do here is to suggest some of the ways that studies of

English medieval literary landscapes have taken part in these developments and other ways in which they might.[1]

For almost a century, the study of medieval literary and visual landscapes has been a enterprise of apology. The apparent failure of medieval culture to register a comprehensive record of space and nature, to even appreciate space and nature as categories, has driven a subtle and learned body of explanation. In the past few decades, however, a new and surprising reversal has occurred, calling into question our own contemporary understanding of the natural world and its representations. As W. J. T. Mitchell suggests, "Nature itself threatens to become what it was for the Middle Ages: an encyclopedic illuminated book overlaid with ornamentation and marginal glosses, every object converted into an image with its proper label or signature" ("Language of Images" 359).[2] The tone of Mitchell's observation is ambivalent. On the one hand, postmodern nature has become a network of signs instead of an unmediated experience of the sublime; on the other hand, the very obviousness of this signage means that we can no longer retreat into nature as an escape from culture. What we had to excuse in medieval literary and visual landscape now appears to resemble our own landscapes, as we have become aware of the importance, even the priority, of representation and mediation. The medieval concern with the limits of the visual to represent reality has become an analogue to the critique of the tyranny of the visual in contemporary thought. The medieval "way of seeing" landscape, place, and space has become newly important as a result, not because of its mimetic accuracy but because of its explicit signage, because it asks us to respond intellectually as well as emotionally, conceptually as well as "naturally."

The medieval landscape that Mitchell finds in our national parks, with their commentaries and guided paths, was best described about thirty years ago by Derek Pearsall and Elizabeth Salter, in their *Landscapes and Seasons of the Medieval World,* who crystallized a scholarly consensus with such sensitivity and intelligence that it has since remained both a starting point and ending point. Landscape in medieval literature and art was not a product of observation or invention. Rather, details of background and representations of space were designed to further the rhetorical purpose of the text or the image, to be "read" as a clearly understood sign. Even the lusher profusion of background and setting in later medieval literature and art served the purpose of a theological purpose, included not for their own sake but for what they reveal about the larger spiritual significance of the created world. Pearsall and Salter implicitly argued against a romantic understanding of the landscape of medieval literature and art at the same time that they evocatively explicated the very different visual and poetic effects of a system of enclosed references. In retrospect, it is easy enough to read Pearsall and Salter as proposing a semiotics of landscape in medieval literature and art.

A number of other, more rigid understandings of medieval literary landscapes had been proposed earlier. The most influential of these were certain chapters in Ernst Robert Curtius's *European Literature and the Latin Middle Ages.* For Curtius, the stereotypical settings of medieval narratives were almost always the result of the imitation of certain motifs from classical antiquity, which had become rhetorical *topoi*. The most characteristic of these type-scenes, according to Curtius, was the *locus amoenus,* the paradisiacal landscape of so many allegories and love poems (192–201). After Curtius, it was impossible to assume that a landscape or background description in medieval literature was drawn from life. It was more likely to be an imitation or allusion to a previous literary work or tradition.

Curtius had developed many of his ideas throughout the 1930s and 1940s. At the same time, similar approaches were being developed in art history, resulting in a shift from interest in technique and expression to an interest in iconography. Panofsky, Gombrich, and others shifted the ground of art historical study from questions of perception and mimesis. Its significance is significance: the meanings generated by the replications of traditional conventions with the subtlest variations on those conventions. By now, this approach has grown into a consensus shared by an impulse toward emphasizing theological continuity (especially based on exegetical writings) as well as a more recent radical transformation of semiotics in poststructuralism. Yet it should be remembered that such a widespread consensus is the result of a long scholarly and theoretical rejection of a previous model. This earlier model grew out of romanticism and emphasized style, expression and individual and cultural perception. The rejection of the sweeping racial and historical assumptions of Worringer and others was the result of a programmatic attack on their methodology and their implicit politics by scholars such as Gombrich. An inchoate, emotional, and teleological interpretation of style, largely dependent on Hegelianism, was replaced by an intellectual and logical understanding of representation in which obscurities are to be solved as if they are puzzles or hidden codes.

One of the most elaborate and detailed attempts to consolidate this transformation and to account for it in terms of literary and cultural periods is Chris Fitter's *Poetry, Space, Landscape.* Fitter is interested in the relation of literature, specifically poetry, to landscape, and his assumption is that the poetry of certain periods reflects changing attitudes toward natural and manmade space and its perception. The subtitle of Fitter's book is *Towards a New Theory,* but the book is more an anatomy than a theory, all for the better. Fitter defines his approach as "socio-historical," tracing the development of an interest in landscape (or, more specifically, "landskip," as Fitter borrows an eighteenth-century nomenclature), which peaks from the seventeenth through the nineteenth centuries but can be found from classical antiquity onward. Indeed, the definition of landscape that Fitter employs privileges an eighteenth-century sensibility: "an organized visual field," "localized . . . description," and "exact optical effects" (Fitter 9). Fitter's own preconditions for the appreciation of landscape ("managerial," "comparative," "quotidian," "possessive," and "rational" interests in space [Fitter 10]) provide a heuristic frame of more use to the author than his readers but allow him to cover an enormous historical range without excessive simplification. Similarly, his suspiciously quadpartite definitions of perception, "ecological," "cosmographic," "analogical," and "technoptic" (Fitter 11), however awkward in outline, provides Fitter with some way of defining similarities among different historical periods. He argues convincingly, if belatedly, against sociobiological "habitat" theory and against the mythic understanding of space popularized by

Mircea Eliade and others (though oddly there is no discussion of the somewhat more current and influential anthropological theories of Turner on "liminal" spaces).

Fitter connects the increasing interest in landscape in later medieval literature to new economic forms and new economic expansion. "Gothic landscape-consciousness" (Fitter 156), as he puts it, seeks a command over nature consistent with Christian doctrine, a scholastic concern with uncovering a systematic logic behind material forms, and a newly exuberant sense of luxuriance in natural fecundity. Gothic art lacks an interest in perspective, which limits its ability to project a landskip, but the preconditions for such a projection can be found in fourteenth-century art and literature, in the Limbourg brothers and in Lorenzetti. Their sense of management and ownership of a specific place, the new interest in travel and military and commercial adventure to regions outside western Europe (found metaphorically in Dante and Petrarch), and a concomitant interest in diurnal representation of home scenes, even the beginnings of a rationalization of space, all mark the emerging interest in landskip that will eventually cohere in the seventeenth century. The earlier medieval sense of a civilized outpost in an unshaped and hostile surrounding of waste or forest is replaced by a virtual urbanization of the countryside itself (Fitter 156–232).

For his examination of medieval and early Renaissance literary landscapes, Fitter defers to Pearsall and Salter. And Pearsall and Salter were consistently original, even brilliant, in their descriptions and interpretations. Late medieval calendar art and literature, for instance, limits its vistas to land worked by the hand of man. "No one can study the Calendar pictures of the Middle Ages without seeing evidence of an instability of viewpoint," they write. "The status of landscape is frequently in doubt" (129). The horror and mystery of the forest of medieval romance is, by the twelfth century, "somewhat dated" (53), reflecting a relic of deforestation. If Pearsall and Salter were limited at all by their moment, it was reflected in a certain ambivalence toward the highly constructed scenes they described and analyzed, and there remained a palpable sense of relief in their writing when a medieval landscape seemed to include a mimetic and empirical picture. So too does Fitter seem to valorize what he himself sees as a historically limited sense of landskip. Auden's famous and equally ambiguous lines from "Bucolics" ("Am I / To see in the Lake District, then, / Another bourgeois invention like the Piano" [3.23–25]) serves as an epigraph to the book, as does a citation from Lukács, and like Lukács, Fitter would seem to argue that a fully developed form, even from a reactionary point of view, can include more levels of reality than a more radical schematic. The result, however, is a certain teleology that returns us to the sense of historical development, along Hegelian lines, that iconology first defined itself against.

That is, even with this enormously sophisticated apparatus, we find ourselves in some ways returning to a position of apology for medieval literary and artistic forms of landscape (or other forms), reading them as originary, incipient, or prototypical. New approaches to understanding of space and place in medieval and Renaissance literary studies, however, suggest ways out of this impasse. In the study of medieval literature, for instance, the traditional stress on the incipiently bourgeois city in literary history as the locus of cultural progress has been questioned. The "Brenner thesis," captured most clearly in the title of Robert Brenner's article, "The Agrarian Roots of European Capitalism," has propounded the agricultural countryside as the continually dynamic force in the English economy through the eighteenth century. The literary impact of this transformation is just being measured and is perhaps also exemplified best in what David Wallace titles the "absent city" (156–81). In early Renaissance scholarship, the richest examinations of urban culture have been those of processions and pageants, exploring the ways in which the late medieval and early modern city imagined itself through its civic rituals, and how, to some extent, the city was organized around those rituals. Perhaps the most fully realized synthesis of these directions has been Louise Fradenburg's important study of the ways in which Edinburgh and its ruler imagined themselves as mutually defining. As Raymond Williams's memorable description of *The Country and the City* argued, the opposition of city and country itself obscures powerful forces at work in both, and the legacy of his study has been felt in both Victorian and eighteenth-century studies, though there is no reason why the questions he asks cannot be projected upon the medieval and early modern past.

In addition, what much recent work in other periods suggests is that the representation of the natural world in medieval literature can be seen as a "landscape of power," as suggested in the title words of several influential books, such as W. J. T. Mitchell's *Landscape and Power* and Sharon Zukin's *Landscapes of Power.* Indeed, a powerfully conceived set of developments within the field of geography (first urban and then rural geography) has allowed us, even obliged us, to interpret landscapes in the broadest sense of the term as allegories of power.[3] But we also must consider the languages of chorographic, geographic, and topographic description in medieval and early modern literary texts and how these languages mediated the experience of both the natural and built environment through language. As Richard Helgerson has so convincingly demonstrated in *Forms of Nationhood,* the interest in descriptions of the land in Renaissance literature is part and parcel of a new interest in national and literary identity, what Benedict Anderson had called *Imagined Communities.* In *England the Nation,* Thorlac Turville-Peter has taken an important step toward an understanding of late medieval literature in these terms, investigating the national consciousness of similar evidence from the thirteenth and fourteenth centuries, including chronicles, maps, and civic texts.

Conceptions and "practices" of space in the Middle Ages provide some of the most frequent and concrete examples in *The Production of Space,* Henri Lefebvre's influential elevation of the category of space to the stature of the categories of history, language, and the visible as one of the projects of modern thought. Indeed, one of the most lucid accounts of what Lefebvre actually means by his famously difficult triad of the interaction of "spatial practice," "representational space," and "spaces of representation" is a late medieval picture. "Spatial practice," according to Soja, includes actual travel on local roads between villages, monasteries, and castles as well as between towns and the great pilgrimage sites. "Representational space" is the largely Aristotelian and Ptolemaic universe so fully developed and Christianized in Aquinas and Dante. "Spaces of representation" is something like a dialectical interaction between these conceptions and practices, resulting in imagining, say, the road to Santiago de Compostela as an analogue of the heavenly way from Cancer to Capricorn, itself thought of as the route taken by souls as they are born and fall to earth.[4]

In a spectacular image, Lefebvre describes the soaring "inversion of space" (256) in the Gothic cathedral, where the literally and conceptually "cryptic" space of an older monastic culture suddenly rises up into the light and air. The physical presence of the newly dominant cathedral concentrates the diffuse and interrupted space of the medieval town. Lefebvre offers an arresting critique of Panofsky's famous description of the Gothic cathedral in *Gothic Architecture and Scholasticism* (Lefebvre 257–61). For Panofsky, the cathedral is the physical embodiment of the great scholastic synthesis, offering a relation of purpose and form that is equivalent to the unity of language and thought in the *Summa*. Lefebvre does not dismiss Panofsky's analysis as an extension of a loose appeal to the zeitgeist. Indeed, he argues that Panofsky does not go far enough. The new interest in the created world, articulated in Suger and the School of Chartres, but also in Abelard, in the art program and the form of the Gothic cathedral, says Lefebvre, results in an irreversible interest in clarifying and acknowledging the world in its totality (255–57). This new interest in the physical world, explicitly represented through the visual as well as through the intellectual understanding, is part and parcel of the new economy of the late Middle Ages, with its energetically acquisitive "space of accumulation" (Lefebvre 263). For Lefebvre, the focusing of urban space in the Gothic cathedral and its vertical domination is not simply a matter of spiritual and intellectual expression, or even of a new interest in understanding and accounting for the material world, but is a precondition for the absolutist state which will eventually dominate both the universal church and the free medieval city (260–61).

Postcolonial studies have also rendered newly important the political and cultural significance of space, exposing colonial historiographies as masks for conquest. The conquest of North America was frequently justified by its emptiness, by Europeans' understanding that an uncultivated (in their terms) land was theirs for the taking and the remaking, an assumption that has underwritten colonial and nationalist expansions to the present day. This distinction between an unpopulated waste or wilderness and humanly shaped landscape has been traced to medieval attitudes toward nature, in both postcolonial and ecological accounts (Thomas 25–50). In English history, such attitudes toward the wildness of Wales, Scotland, and Ireland can be found as early as the Norman Conquest, and even earlier. While the Crusades are often described as the origin of Western expansionism and colonial conquest, the actual spatial and geographic experience was sufficiently complex and disorienting as to require the full apparatus of postcolonial theory. The concentrated wealth and cultural achievement of the Islamic East, the levantine outposts, the infamous squabbling and internal treacheries, all these sometimes rendered the crusader armies, even in the eyes of their Christian brethren, as barbarian invaders, and contact with the East resulted in profound cultural transformations—and uncertainties—in the West. The romances simplify this experience, approving analogous institutions (courtly, literary, chivalric) and demonizing dissimilar ones (chiefly religious belief). The landscape of the imaginative literature of the Crusades is a layering of sacral spaces, abstract fields of battle, and cities under siege. The landscape of the expository literature of the Crusades may be no less fictional, but it is one of the most remarkably detailed chorographic discourses of the medieval period, particularly, but not exclusively, of urban description. The result for the description of the domestic landscape in literature is a certain orientalization of the Western literary landscape, in which the fevered intensity of apocalyptic *descriptio* is energized by the actual contact, however mediated by literary preconceptions, of the Holy Lands. From the *Roman de la Rose* through *Pearl*, visions of earthly and divine paradises are filtered through orientalized fantasies. An older interpretation of romances, especially grail romances, as interiorized and local displacements of failed Crusades, however arguable, suggests an interesting territorial fantasy in which the local, only partly civilized landscape functions as a setting for a spiritual test.

Since the desert fathers and spiritual practices of early Christianity, landscape had functioned also as a setting for a spiritual test, serving as an ascetic discipline itself. The long, early medieval trope of *Homo Viator* represented earthly existence as an alienated journey through the land of unlikeness. Pilgrimages, both to the Holy Land and to local shrines, also included a specific vision of landscape. As in the landscapes of quest romance, the scenery along the way represents challenges and obstacles to a final goal. In arguably relevant description, such as the *Book of Margery Kempe,* landscape, seascape, and geography, despite the apparent desire for movement and travel on the part of Margery, are represented as obstacles to a goal, though that is the basic structure of even the nongeographical aspects of Margery's account. Once arrived, however, the pilgrim's landscape is as much mnemonic and imaginary as it is material. By the late Middle Ages, the evidence of many of the sites of Christian history existed more in memory than in physical settings.

As a test case for some of these ideas, we may turn to the medieval English mystery plays. It is widely accepted that the medieval mystery cycles in England attempted to give shape to sacred history as it was understood by its audience. I would point out that that shape was spatial as much as it was temporal. The places of performance operated also as memory locations, recalling the freight of Christian doctrine and Christian history in space as well as time. The mystery plays superimposed an imaginary geography upon the late medieval city, and in so doing recreated a memory of the originary geography of the Holy Land itself. As a result, the mystery cycles find themselves implicated in, and partly explained by, the processes of what Maurice Halbwachs first identified as collective memory (39–40).

The classic study of memory in late medieval and early modern literature has been Francis Yates's *Art of Memory.* Because of Yates's special interest in the Renaissance theater and the theater itself as a metaphor (one that gets taken literally) for the art of memory, her study is still consistently cited in studies of the drama. At the same time, Yates's interest in the hermetic aspects of memory systems, and her tendency to imitate the associational logic of the very systems she describes, has limited broader applications of her brilliant if idiosyncratic investigations. Recently, however, Mary Carruthers's magisterial work, *The Book of Memory*, has reintegrated the study of mnemonics into a more orthodox history of rhetoric and philosophy. Carruthers's book has already been widely cited in studies (some of them as far from her focus as romantic poetry) which stress the functional, technical, and ethical uses of memory in literature. The rhetorical emphasis of these studies fits comfortably with the code-based techniques of both semiotics and of computer technology itself, an analogy not lost on scholars like Carruthers, who is able to link traditional scholarly histories with new insights into the uses and contexts of familiar literary texts.

At the same time, historians and literary scholars of more recent periods have produced studies and defined areas of cultural practice with very different stresses on the processes of memory. The various diasporas of the twentieth century, occasioned by war, genocide, the breakdown of colonial structures, and economic immigration, have created an entire literature of memory, accepting the postmodern critique of continuity at the same time that it seeks desperately to reconstitute such a continuity. An entire subgenre of memoir and memoir-based fiction has developed, identifiable by allusions to memory and synonyms of memory in its titles. Meanwhile, the historiography of the developed nation-states has turned its attention to the ways in which those nations have in fact constructed national memory. Particularly in France, the study of public commemoration, of how the past has been reconstituted and even reshaped through ceremonies, texts, and rituals (or even, in the case of Vichy, films) that purport to remember it, has become an important scholarly enterprise. In the United States, similar studies have investigated the ways in which various wars and historical crises—Vietnam, the Civil War, the Kennedy assassination—have been commemorated and how those commemorations have been shaped by the politics of the moment. In England, the very sources of some traditions in a society that values tradition have been exposed as more recently constructed, even invented.

These studies of public memory are indebted to the sociology of Maurice Halbwachs, whose most important essays on the subject have recently been translated and published as *The Collective Memory*. Halbwachs argued that we organize our past experience in socially sanctioned ways. Over time, the various institutions of society—the family, religion, economic organizations, and so on—constitute group identity by fostering shared memories within those groups. Moreover, the shape of that past is often formed by the pressures of the present moment, through whose concerns memories are selected and interpreted. Halbwachs was particularly interested in the relation between memory and identity in religion, particularly in medieval Christianity. In an extension of Renan's interest in syncretism, Halbwachs highlighted the ways in which early Christianity imagined its founders and foundations in an ahistorical, atemporal vacuum, effectively obliterating its pre-Christian (Jewish and other) predecessors, but in so doing allowing a constant rememorialization of its origins from the point of view of the present. Halbwachs argued that mysticism, only apparently in defiance of orthodox dogma, in fact reproduced this process on an individual level and was therefore tolerated by the church. For our purposes, however, Halbwach's most useful investigation is into "The Legendary Topography of the Gospels in the Holy Land" (193–235).

In 1983, Nicholas Davis suggested some ways in which the medieval mystery plays may have been influenced by mnemonic discourses ("Art of Memory" 5).[5] Davis located a passage in the notorious "Tretise on Miracles Pleyinge" imputing to the supporters of the mystery plays the argument that live dramatic performance better fixes in the memory of its audience "the wille of God and his mervelous werkis" than, say, painting. Behind this argument, suggests Davis, is the entire tradition of classical and medieval mnemonics, most widely circulated in the pseudo-Ciceronian *Rhetorica ad Herennium,* which is here being "recruited" to serve as dramatic theory (Davis, "English Mystery Plays"). It is possible that the staging of the mystery plays, according to Davis, was designed to surround spectators with striking images, scenes, and figures advocated by the author of the *Ad Herennium.* Processional drama in the fourteenth century, with its evidence for pageant wagons being drawn past the spectators, seems almost a literal performance of the virtual prescription of the *Ad Herennium*'s emphasis on imaginary *loci.* The *Ad Herennium,* especially influential in the fourteenth century, can be regarded, says Davis, as a "'blueprint' for medieval dramatic performances" ("Art of Memory" 3).

By staging the mystery plays in the streets and squares of the medieval town, their producers were engaged in an act of commemoration. Most specifically, that commemoration was a reprisal of Christian history as it was understood by medieval theology and expanded upon in discursive forms such as sermons, world chronicles, and, perhaps, the visual arts. More generally, it was a commemoration of the passion of Jesus as underlined in the circumstantial association of the plays with the Feast of Corpus Christi. The plays offer a deritualized commemoration of the Eucharist (though some scholars would argue that the mass had acquired a fully dramatic effect much earlier in any case) underlined in their striking representations of Christ's body and the dramatic actions surrounding it.

These more generally historical and transhistorical effects, however, are projected on to a specific geographic site, and that site becomes something equally specific but otherwise. The corner or street or square becomes "as if" the site in the geography of the Holy Land where the action of the play is supposed to take place. In most cases, these locations have the status of shrines. That is, a virtual mapping of the geography of the Holy Land—itself something of a fiction of memory—is superimposed on the medieval city, which mimetically becomes that geography, and the audience members become something like pilgrims, not only observing in and participating in the dramatic action but also imaginatively visiting those sites.

Such a transformation of the city during the production of the plays is one developed at length in one of the classic studies of the mystery plays, Martin

Stevens's *Four Middle English Mystery Cycles: Textual, Contextual and Critical Interpretations*. Of the Skinners' pageant of the Entry into Jerusalem, Stevens writes:

> At the same time that the procession of the Entry into Jerusalem imitates the civic liturgical procession, it also mirrors another kind of procession, the royal entry. York throughout the Middle Ages was noted for its splendid civic shows with which it greeted visiting royalty. The prescribed route of the royal entry processional was, interestingly, very much the same as that of the Corpus Christi play, and when, therefore, Jesus is greeted in the course of the Skinners' pageant with the accustomed royal entry ceremony as the King of Kings in the streets of York, the spectators saw him take possession of their city much as they had secular kings and queens. There was no more powerful a link to be found between present-day York and historic Jerusalem than this dramatic setting provided. Indeed, the setting of the Skinners' play puts a whole new focus on everything that has transpired and everything that will transpire in the cycle. The Passion is taking place here and now. The characters are Yorkshire people. The place is York. And yet the spectators in the streets gradually recognize that they are really in Jerusalem.
>
> (52)

Stevens's point is not only that the Holy Land is recreated in York but also that the physical layout of York and the traditions of the city actually influence the dramaturgy and the staging of the cycle plays themselves, and that the York cycle is more ideologically and formally urbanized than the other extant cycles.

The specific geographic imagination always implicit in biblical drama is made explicit by the setting of the cycle plays in the city. It is difficult to do more than speculate on the reasons for this. Certainly one reason is to identify the medieval town, increasingly both secure and anxious about its own identity, with Jerusalem, the closest site on earth to the heavenly city of which it is a type. Related to this is the political and social agenda of the mystery plays, their attempt to merge various social sectors of the city into one body, unifying the body politic by the dramatic representation (and torture of) the sacred body of Christ.[6]

It may also be that this superimposition of the medieval English city into Jerusalem may have been determined by the crisis of the Holy Land itself. In the late fourteenth and fifteenth century, the promise of the Crusades grew increasingly distant and unlikely as more and more land was lost to the Turkish incursions. At the same time, a Ghost Dance ideological formation of the Crusades was articulated by such figures as Philippe de Mézières. It may only be a coincidence, but may also be more than that, that England mounts performances in which the spaces of the city become as if the places of the Holy Land at a time when the possibility of pilgrimage and reconquest grows increasingly unlikely. The mounting of the mystery cycle becomes an early simulacrum of geographic original, transforming the medieval city into a simulacrum, a virtual theme park of the Holy Land itself. Such an analogy is by no means frivolous, as the analysis of modern urbanists and architectural historians demonstrates.

I have suggested elsewhere that geographic and spatial theories have to some extent inherited the explanatory burden once borne by film theory (Ganim 363). But almost certainly the current interest in landscape is related to the place of cinema as one of the dominant forms of modernism. We can turn to cinematic representations of medieval works and medieval worlds as a hidden barometer of our own understandings, even scholarly understandings, of medieval landscapes. Our own collective memory is now recorded on film, indeed, is film itself. Medieval cinematic landscapes are in fact allegories of our own compound and complex scholarly representations of the Middle Ages.[7] Three examples will serve as a demonstration: John Boorman's *Excalibur,* still viewed in late-night cult screenings in the United States, probably because of its appeal to a New Age fanaticism; Eric Rohmer's obscure *Perceval le Gallois;* and Robert Bresson's brooding *Lancelot du lac,* the latter two now more the province of film historians. Nor is such an appeal to cinematic evidence trivial. As the production history of these films indicate, a considerable amount of serious scholarly research on landscape and imagery were incorporated into the art design of these films. Boorman's *Excalibur* is as much a comment on neoromantic and Victorian reimaginings of the Middle Ages as a contribution to them.

Rohmer's *Perceval* alludes to medieval miniatures and illuminations, and at the same time it incorporates an aesthetic of animation that is inseparable from modern popular understandings of this art. On the face of it, *Perceval* seems unimaginably far from the cinema of the New Wave that Rohmer has been associated with. Yet Rohmer had been planning the film for nearly fifteen years before it actually was completed. In fact, in its explicit identification of filmic narrative with the visual arts of the Middle Ages, *Perceval* fits squarely into the program advocated by Rohmer's younger and more radical associates, such as Godard and Truffaut. Where they would allude to cinema history as a way of emphasizing the constructed rather than mimetic quality of filmic representation, Rohmer alludes to medieval miniature arts in his sets. For these filmmakers who grew out of *Cahiers du Cinéma* and then went on to make film history themselves, the easy escape into an identification with character and setting in traditional film was to be resisted. Rohmer achieves this distance by rendering the medieval landscape as it appears in medieval visual arts, or at least how a modern imagination recreates those arts. The same few portable trees represent the ubiquitous forests of Chrétien's romance. The gestures and postures of characters imitate the iconographic poses of figures in stained glass and manuscript illuminations. Distance and perspective are purposely obscured, so the relation between objects and figures on screen approximates the symbolic and stylized spatial relations of medieval landscapes and figures. More radically than almost any other filmmaker outside of experimental and surrealist traditions, Rohmer severs the stubborn fidelity of the camera to everyday time and space.

This challenge to perspective and cinematic verisimilitude, while conventional in filmic dream sequences, is rarely carried out as completely as it is in *Perceval le Gallois.* It is not surprising that Rohmer, always interested in ethical and religious themes, would choose a spiritual quest as his subject. It is surprising that the New Wave director most wedded to character and to the poetry of the everyday would engage in such formal experimentation, however cloaked in medieval guise. In fact, Rohmer ends up translating the sacramental mysteries of the grail quest as the quiet epiphanies of everyday life—psychological, erotic, personal—thus rendering his medieval characters akin to the slightly lost seekers of his explicitly moral modern films. The Perceval who understands so little of the significance of his actions and choices is the perfect mirror of Rohmer's modern subjects. Rohmer offers his medieval landscape as a continually meaningful alternative to the modern Waste Land. But it is no accident that the modern landscape of alienation should have been definitively portrayed by another conservative modernist, T. S. Eliot, nor that both Eliot and Rohmer should end up imagining a Middle Ages of enigmatic and impenetrable signification.

Perceval, unlike in most modernist readings of the grail, remains fundamentally optimistic, and Rohmer communicates the enchantment of Chrétien's tone. In *Lancelot du Lac*, which Robert Bresson completed and released a few years earlier (1974), the disenchantment of the grail continuations (Bresson borrows from *La Mort le roi Artu*) finds a corollary in postmodern disenchantment. Bresson, equally experimental, takes an almost opposite approach to visualizing the medieval landscape. The grail moment has passed; Lancelot backslides on his promise and his vision, and by yielding to his desire for Guinevere, he sets in motion the final destruction of the kingdom. Bresson's camera points downward, his armored figures march listlessly across paths and through forests, emphasizing the physicality and earthliness that has doomed the court to failure. Where the limpidity and buoyant unreality of Rohmer's sets communicated the simplicity of Perceval's perspective (and also a certain interpretation of the clarity of medieval faith), Bresson opts for visual obscurity, shadows and a claustrophobic dramatic situation. The sound track is made up of armor crashing, decapitated bodies falling to the earth, horses rushing eerily out of the forest, and a ritualistic and incantatory dialogue. The infinite forests and landscapes of betrayal in Bresson's *Lancelot* call up the military and political struggles and defeats of the two world wars as well as France's colonial retreats. Cinematic representation has become in many ways our own form of collective memory, and it is arresting how often, in the nineteenth and twentieth centuries, we have turned to medieval landscapes as vehicles for our own desires and anxieties. As a new millennium marks an almost visually imaginable distance from the year 1000, we now embark on revising the Middle Ages from a period in time to a simulation in space.

Notes

1. A number of studies of medieval urbanism and space in French, German, Latin, and Italian literature have important implications for this larger development (Frugoni, Kugler, Fumagalli, Zumthor). For the study of space in Middle English narratives, Sarah Stanbury, employing feminist critiques of private and public space, has published a series of groundbreaking articles from 1987 to 1994.

2. Mitchell's iconological critique is by an large a rejection of the classic study by Kenneth Clark, *Landscape into Art.* A turning point in the consideration of landscape as aesthetic pleasure is the response to Clark's description of Gainsborough's "Mr and Mrs Andrews" in John Berger's *Ways of Seeing,* originally the script of his BBC series and an answer to Kenneth Clark's own restatement of his reading in his television series, *Civilization.*

3. On landscapes as allegories of power, see Soja, *Thirdspace* (86–96) and *Postmodern Geographies* (149–55); Gregory; Harvey (226–39); and Cosgrove (39–68). For a critical overview,

see Soja, *Thirdspace* (1–23). Interestingly, these studies often acknowledge the pioneering status of literary studies of landscape in English eighteenth-century and romantic poetry and painting. See, for instance, Fabricant, and for a pioneering study in art history, Bermingham.

4. Lefebvre's triad of "lived," the "conceived" and "perceived" spaces is reinterpreted by Edward Soja in what he calls *Thirdspace* (53–82).

5. Since then two other important but quite different discussions of medieval mystery plays and the theme of memory have appeared. Beckwith ("Present of Past Things") considers the revival of the York cycle since 1951 as part of a ritual of historical memory that rewrites the past for present social purposes, as an "invented tradition" following Hobshawm and (critically) Nora. Enders explores the pervasive staged violence of the mystery plays and relates it to how individual and collective memories rewrite painful or violent events, real and staged.

6. One of the most influential studies of the plays as a ritual of civic and theological union is Mervyn James, "Ritual, Drama and Social Body in the Late Medieval English Town." The potentially multiple, exclusionary, and contested meanings of urban space and somatic imagery is emphasized, however, in studies by Beckwith (*Christ's Body*) and by Rubin.

7. There is a well-developed body of scholarship on medieval films, especially the ones mentioned in this paragraph. Among the most important articles are Burns, "Nostalgia Isn't What It Used to Be," and Williams, "Eric Rohmer and the Holy Grail." Scholarship in the area of films on medieval themes is greatly enhanced by Harty, *Reel Middle Ages,* and by the Arthurian on-line resources coordinated by Alan Lupack at the Rossell Hope Robbins Library at the University of Rochester. Some recent studies include Umland and Umland and Harty's *King Arthur on Film.* Mancoff contains a number of stimulating articles on Arthurian film. The indispensable journal *Studies in Medievalism,* previously edited by Leslie J. Workman and now edited by T. A. Shippey, has pioneered serious scholarly study of medievalism in popular culture, including film.

Works Cited

Anderson, Benedict. *Imagined Communities: Reflections on the Origin and Spread of Nationalism.* London: Verso, 1983.

Aston, T. H., and C. H. E. Philpin, eds. *The Brenner Debate: Agrarian Class Structure and Economic Development in Pre-Industrial Europe.* Cambridge: Cambridge UP, 1985.

Auden, W. H. "Bucolics." *Collected Poems.* Ed. Edward Mendelson. New York: Random House, 1976. 426–35.

Beckwith, Sarah. *Christ's Body.* London: Routledge, 1994.

——. "The Present of Past Things: The York Corpus Christi Cycle as a Contemporary Theater of Memory." *Journal of Medieval and Renaissance Studies* 26 (1996): 355–79.

Berger, John. *Ways of Seeing.* London: Penguin, 1972.

Bermingham, Ann. *Landscape and Ideology: The English Rustic Tradition, 1740–1860.* Berkeley: U of California P, 1986.

Brenner, Robert. "The Agrarian Roots of European Capitalism." Aston and Philpin 213–327.

Burns, E. Jane. "Nostalgia Isn't What It Used to Be: The Middle Ages in Literature and Film." *Shadows of the Magic Lamp: Fantasy and Science Fiction in Film.* Ed. George Slusser and Eric S. Rabkin. Carbondale: Southern Illinois UP, 1985. 86–97.

Carruthers, Mary. *The Book of Memory.* Cambridge: Cambridge UP, 1990.

Clark, Kenneth. *Landscape into Art.* London: Murray, 1949.

Cosgrove, Denis. *Social Formation and Symbolic Landscape.* London: Croom Helm, 1984.

Curtius, Ernst Robert. *European Literature and the Latin Middle Ages.* Trans. Willard Trask. New York: Pantheon, 1953.

Davis, Nicholas M. "The Art of Memory and Medieval Dramatic Theory." *EDAM Newsletter* 6 (1983): 1–3.

——. "The English Mystery Plays and 'Ciceronian' Mnemonics." *Atti del IV Colloquio della Société internationale pour l'étude du théâtre médiéval: Processo in paradiso e in inferno, dramma biblico, technologia dell'allestimento scenico,* Viterbo, 10–15 July 1983. Ed. Maria Chiabo. Viterbo, Italy: Centro studi sul teatro medioevale e rinascimentale, 1984. 75–84.

Eliade, Mircea. *Cosmos and History: The Myth of the Eternal Return.* New York: Harper, 1959.

Enders, Jody. *The Medieval Theater of Cruelty: Rhetoric, Memory, Violence.* Ithaca: Cornell UP, 1999.

Fabricant, Carole. *Swift's Landscape.* Baltimore: Johns Hopkins UP, 1982.

Fitter, Chris. *Poetry, Space, Landscape: Towards a New Theory.* Cambridge: Cambridge UP, 1995.

Foucault, Michel. "Of Other Spaces." *Diacritics* 16 (1986): 22–27.

———. *Power/Knowledge.* Trans. C. Gordon. New York: Pantheon, 1980. 63–77.

Fradenburg, Louise. *City, Marriage, Tournament Arts of Rule in Late Medieval Scotland.* Madison: U of Wisconsin P, 1991.

Frugoni, Chiara. *A Distant City: Images of Urban Experience in the Medieval World.* Trans. William McCuaig. Princeton: Princeton UP, 1991.

Fumagalli, Vito. *Landscapes of Fear: Perceptions of Nature and the City in the Middle Ages.* Trans. Shayne Mitchell. Oxford: Blackwell for Polity, 1994.

Ganim, John M. "Recent Studies on Literature, Architecture, and Urbanism." *MLQ* 56 (Sept. 1995): 363–79.

Gombrich, E. H. *Norm and Form: Studies in the Art of the Renaissance.* London: Phaidon, 1966.

Gregory, Derek. *Geographical Imaginations.* Oxford: Blackwell, 1994.

Halbwachs, Maurice. *On Collective Memory.* Trans. Lewis Coser. Chicago: U of Chicago P, 1992.

Harty, Kevin J., ed. *King Arthur on Film: New Essays on Arthurian Cinema.* Jefferson, N.C.: McFarland, 1999.

———. *The Reel Middle Ages: American, Western and Eastern European, Middle Eastern and Asian Films about Medieval Europe.* Jefferson, N.C.: McFarland, 1999.

Harvey, David. *The Condition of Postmodernity.* Oxford: Blackwell, 1989.

Helgerson, Richard. *Forms of Nationhood: The Elizabethan Writing of England.* Chicago: U of Chicago P, 1992.

Hobshawm, Eric, and Terence Ranger, eds. *The Invention of Tradition.* Cambridge: Cambridge, 1983.

James, Mervyn. "Ritual, Drama and Social Body in the Late Medieval English Town." *Society, Politics and Culture: Studies in Early Modern England.* Ed. James Mervyn. Cambridge: Cambridge UP, 1986. 16–47.

Kugler, Hartmut. *Die Vorstellung der Stadt in er Literatur des deutschen Mittelalters.* Munich: Artemis, 1986.

Lefebvre, Henri. *The Production of Space.* Trans. Donald Nicholson-Smith. Oxford: Blackwell, 1991.

Lukács, Georg. *History and Class Consciousness: Studies in Marxist Dialectics.* Trans. Rodney Livingstone. Cambridge: Massachusetts Institute of Technology P, 1971.

Lupack, Alan. "The Camelot Project at the University of Rochester." Begun in 1995, updated June 23, 2006. <http://www.lib.rochester.edu/camelot/cphome.stm>.

Lyotard, Jean François. *The Postmodern Condition.* Trans. Geoff Bennington and Brian Massumi. Minneapolis: U of Minnesota P, 1984.

Mancoff, Debra N. *The Arthurian Revival: Essays on Form, Tradition and Transformation.* New York: Garland, 1992.

Mitchell, W. J. T. "Editor's Note: The Language of Images." *Critical Inquiry* 6 (1980): 359–62.

———, ed. *Landscape and Power.* Chicago: U of Chicago P, 1994.

Nora, Pierre. "Between Memory and History: *Les Lieux de Memoires.*" Trans. Marc Roudebush. *History and Memory in African-American Culture.* Ed. Genevieve Fabre and Robert O'Meally. New York: Oxford UP, 1994. 284–300.

Panofsky, Erwin. *Gothic Architecture and Scholasticism.* Cleveland: World, 1968.

Pearsall, Derek, and Elizabeth Salter. *Landscapes and Seasons of the Medieval World.* London: Elek, 1973.

Rubin, Miri. *Corpus Christi: The Eucharist in Late Medieval Culture.* Cambridge: Cambridge UP, 1991.

Soja, Edward W. *Postmodern Geographies.* London: Verso, 1989.

———. *Thirdspace: Journeys to Los Angeles and Other Real-and-Imagined Places.* Oxford: Blackwell, 1996.

Stanbury, Sarah. "The Body and the City in *Pearl*." *Representations* 48 (1994): 30–47.

——. "Space and Visual Hermeneutics in the Gawain-poet." *Chaucer Review* 21 (1987): 476–89.

——. "Women's Letters and Private Space in Chaucer." *Exemplaria* 6 (1994): 271–85.

Stevens, Martin. *Four Middle English Mystery Cycles: Textual, Contextual and Critical Interpretations.* Princeton: Princeton UP, 1987.

Thomas, Keith. *Man and the Natural World: Changing Attitudes in England, 1500–1800.* Oxford: Oxford UP, 1983.

Turner, Victor. *Dramas, Fields and Metaphors: Symbolic Action in Human Society.* Ithaca: Cornell UP, 1974.

——. *The Ritual Process.* Ithaca: Cornell UP, 1977.

Turville-Peter, Thorlac. *England the Nation: Language, Literature and National Identity, 1290–1340.* Oxford: Clarendon, 1996.

Umland, Rebecca A., and Samuel J. Umland. *The Use of Arthurian Legend in Hollywood Film.* Contributions to the Study of Popular Culture, 37. Westport: Greenwood, 1996.

Wallace, David. *Chaucerian Polity.* Stanford: Stanford UP, 1997.

Williams, Linda. "Eric Rohmer and the Holy Grail." *Literature/Film Quarterly* 11 (Apr. 1983): 71–82.

Williams, Raymond. *The Country and the City.* London: Chatto and Windus, 1973.

Worringer, Wilhelm. *Form in Gothic.* New York: Schocken, 1964.

Yates, Francis. *The Art of Memory.* Chicago: U of Chicago P, 1966.

Zukin, Sharon. *Landscapes of Power: From Detroit to Disney World.* Berkeley: U of California P, 1991.

Zumthor, Paul. *La Mesure du Monde: Représentation de l'Espace au Moyen Âge.* Paris: Éditions du Seuil, 1993.

The Specificity of Place

Lisa H. Cooper

Making Space for History
Galbert of Bruges and the Murder
of Charles the Good

When Charles the Good of Flanders was murdered at Bruges by four of his barons in 1127, the city became a theater of chaos, its tragedy a spectacle for all the world to see. This at least is how Galbert of Bruges, who kept a daily chronicle of the tumultuous events that followed, understood what was happening around him, and it is also how he represented what he saw:

> Anno milleno centeno vicesimo septimo . . . circa mane, dum pius comes Brugis in ecclesia . . . in oratione decumberet. . . . [E]x pia consuetudine eleemosynarum suarum largitiones pauperibus erogabat, fixis oculis ad legendos psalmos et manu dextra porrecta ad largitiones eleemosynarum. . . . [C]omes more suo officiose et aperte legendo orabat. Tunc tandem post tot consilia et juramenta et securitates inter se factas . . . comitem . . . gladiis confossum et saepius transverberatum, mortuum dimisere.

> (In the year one thousand one hundred and twenty-seven . . . about dawn, the count at Bruges was kneeling in prayer. . . . Following his pious custom he was giving out alms to the poor, with his eyes fixed on reading the psalms, and his right hand outstretched to bestow alms. . . . [T]he count, according to custom, was praying, reading aloud obligingly; then at last, after so many plans and oaths and pacts among themselves, those wretched traitors . . . slew the count, who was struck down with swords and run through again and again.)[1]

As the count lay unburied in his own chapel and mayhem spread through the castellany and city, some fled Bruges as fast as they could. Others, however, entered the town to either participate in or attend the show. According to Galbert, more than two weeks later people still "tum pro praeda, tum pro vindicta, tum magis pro auferendo consulis funere, tum pro admiratione omnium quae ibidem fiebant, in suburbium confluxerant" (poured into the town . . . some for loot, some for vengeance, others to steal the count's body, some out of sheer wonder at everything that was going on there) (§45: Rider 95; Ross 183). The ensuing contest for control of the county turned Flanders into a kind of bloodstained theater, filled with what Galbert saw as a series of performances that his narrative would not only preserve but actually reenact for his readers.[2]

It is clear from his work's preface that Galbert was concerned not only to attend to the kind of careful record keeping that appears to have been part of his profession[3] but also to affect his audience with his account. In the preface, Galbert tells us that we should come to his record just as the wondering bystanders came to Bruges. "Rogo . . . et moneo, si cui . . . hujus opusculi exiguus manipulus ad manus venerit" (I ask and admonish anyone who happens upon . . . this little handful of a book), he appeals to us, "non derideat et contemnat sed nova admiratione quae scripta sunt . . . admiretur" (not to make fun of it or condemn it but to read with fresh wonder what is written down) ("Prologue": Rider 3; Ross 80). There is more, however; we are also to approach the text prepared to believe that what it displays to us is, as Galbert calls it, "rerum verita[s]" (the truth of things). But historiography, like narrative of any kind, is always governed by more or less conscious principles of selection that, as Hayden White among others has shown, usually serve to tighten the "plot" of history (10). So despite Galbert's claim in a later chapter—"ordina[vi] secundum rerum eventum descriptionem praesentem" ([I] set in order the present account of events as they happened) (§35: Rider 81; Ross 164)—his chronicle is certainly not unmediated *veritas*. Instead, it is a record of cultural performance and social drama both prescripted and spontaneous, both real and, more intriguingly, actively imagined.[4] While the seeming realism of Galbert's chronicle has led all but his most recent readers to examine *De multro* more as a collection of useful facts about twelfth-century Flanders than as a literary achievement,[5] it is Galbert's ability to render spectacle in words, to shape both cultural performance and social drama to his own narrative ends, that produces the impression of mimesis.[6] Galbert himself tells us that his account is neither perfectly omniscient nor objective: "Neque quid singuli agerent prae confusione et infinitate notavi," he writes, "sed hoc solum intenta mente notavi quod in obsidione communi edicto et facto ad pugnam et ejus causam congestum est" (I have not set down individual deeds because they were so numerous and so intermingled but only noted carefully what was decreed and done by common action throughout the siege, and the reasons for it), adding that this much "quasi me invitum, ut scripturae commendarem, coegi" (I have forced myself, almost unwillingly, to commit to writing) (§35: Rider 81; Ross 164).

Volition aside, Galbert does appear to have consciously crafted his text so that it would work as verbal theater. As he puts it, in the same passage just quoted, his chronicle is itself a kind of place within which we both read and see: "quod videtis et legitis in arto positus fidelibus transcripsi" (I transcribed for the faithful what you see and read) (§35: Rider 81; Ross 164).[7] Galbert's emphasis here upon his narrative's potential to work as a kind of stage for action reanimated in, and by, language is perhaps not particularly surprising, given that intensely public modes of cultural performance were as much facts of life in twelfth-century Flanders as they were across twelfth-century Europe. Even before the murder of Count Charles, Galbert's was a world full of rituals, including but not limited to acts of homage and the swearing of oaths, reliquary processions, the wars and tournaments of counts and kings, legal hearings, and public punishment for private as well as public offense.[8] This matrix of publicly performed life could not help but influence the way Galbert perceived events and the way he approached the writing of history. As Gabrielle Spiegel has observed, medieval historiography

> was . . . receptive to being shaped by structures already residing in the social reality which the historian perceived as the focus of his narrative. . . . Depending on the chronicler's point of view, his ideological perspective, his traditional or innovative historical vision, such "[perceptual] grids" came to him more or less naturally from the world in which he was embedded and . . . provided the structural principles which guided his work. ("Genealogy" 46)[9]

Galbert's perceptual "grid" was a largely performative one, shaped by the rituals of the world in which he lived, and his chronicle provides a good deal of evidence that that grid grew ever more theatrical as events in Flanders wore on. As the world fell apart in Bruges, the city's inhabitants participated in a veritable proliferation of planned and spontaneous performances—more oaths, more processions, more violence.[10] Galbert's account records these in scrupulous detail, but it also works to render the dramatic more so, shapes the nontheatrical into theater, and, most importantly, makes the unseen visible. All this it achieves largely through its careful attention to physical space of all kinds and to the conflict of energies and desires within the arenas that interested the self-appointed chronicler most.[11] Galbert's descriptions of buildings, walls, public squares, fields, roads, and local as well as national boundaries form a kind of frame over which the action of his narrative is stretched; the movements of individuals through (and sometimes over) these practically concentric circles of space create patterns, albeit slightly haphazard ones, of centripetal and centrifugal force throughout the daily record. Galbert's narrative habits appear to have been shaped not just by the performative but also by the way performances of all kinds resounded within the spaces that meant the most to him—the land of Flanders, the city of Bruges, and the castral palace and chapel of St. Donation. In Galbert's chronicle these places and spaces became, if not quite actors, then certainly carefully delineated settings for the dramatic reenactment of a troubled time. In addition, as Galbert used his imagination to peer into places in which he had not himself been present in order to describe what had happened within them, he seems to have been led almost inevitably to a view of the human conscience—particularly, and peculiarly, of Charles's betrayers—as but one space among others. The minds of some of the figures whose deeds he portrays in graphic detail become spaces within which the historiographer positions himself and from which he tells part of his story—as if his images of others' thoughts were part of the "truth of things" rather than projections of his own imaginings.[12]

However, the preface of Galbert's record (which he added to the front of his daily chronicle at least three months after Charles's death) opens not within the sanctum of any one mind but with a bird's-eye view of the whole of Flanders and its tragically emptied center.[13] In his opening lines, Galbert locates Count Charles within a geography of twelfth-century princely power, establishing him as a transcendent presence within and beyond the borders of his land:

> Cum inter regnorum principes, quos circa nos cognovimus, summum gloriae ac laudis sibi ascribendi studium per militiae facinora enituisset et eisdem affectus consimilis ad bene regendum inesset, minoris potentiae et famae principabatur imperator Romanorum Henricus . . . ac . . . rex Anglorum . . . comes Karolus, Flandarium marchio, naturalis noster dominus et princeps, qui quidem militiae fama et generis nobilitatus regio sanguine, septennis in comitatu pater et advocatus ecclesiarum Dei praeerat.

> (At a time when we saw the rulers of neighboring kingdoms displaying the greatest zeal in winning glory and praise for themselves by knightly exploits as well as a disposition for ruling well, Count Charles, marquis of Flanders, exceeded in fame and power the emperor of the Romans, Henry . . . and . . . the king of the English. . . . As our natural lord and prince, renowned for his knightly valor and royal blood, he had presided over the county for seven years like a father and protector of the churches of God.)

> ("Prologue": Rider 3; Ross 79)

Charles's valor worked to the honor of Flanders, a territory to which he was bound by both duty and blood. The chronicler recalls that the count "matre oriundus quae terrae Flandrensis comitum de sanguine processerat, ea affinitate cognationis a puero in patria nostra altus est usque in virile robur corporis et animi" ([was] born of a mother who was descended from the blood of the counts of the land of Flanders, [and] because of this relationship grew up from boyhood to manly strength of body and mind in our fatherland).[14] Practically fostered by Flemish soil as well as by a Flemish mother, Charles soon achieved a reputation that traveled well beyond the limits of his homeland, for according to Galbert, he attained "famam bonam et gloriam sui nominis penes regnorum potentes" (glory for his name among the rulers of the earth) (§1: Rider 5; Ross 81–82). Despite this renown, the most crucial evidence for Galbert of Charles's right rule seems to have been the count's beneficent actions within territorial boundaries to which he clearly paid close attention. That Charles "[c]epit . . . de pacis reformatione disponere, leges et jura regni revocare, ita ut paulatim pacis statu *undecumque* correcto" (took . . . measures to strengthen the peace, to reaffirm the laws and rights of the realm [so] that little by little public order was restored *in all parts*) and that the count spread "justitiae et pacis securitat[em] . . . *per terminos regni*" (the security of peace and justice . . . *throughout the limits of the realm*) (§1: Rider 5, 7; Ross 83; emphasis added) is for Galbert as much proof of Charles's goodness as is the fact that the count decided twice over not to leave his home for the proffered crowns of empire and Judea.[15] Galbert praises Charles for staying in Flanders and animating it from within through good deeds befitting one who "[s]ciebat enim esse dominus, pater, advocatus, pius, mitis, exorabilis, ad honorem Dei et decorem ecclesiae idoneus" (knew how to be lord, father, advocate, to be pious, gentle, compassionate, an honor to God and an ornament to the Church) (§6: Rider 17; Ross 95–96). So exquisitely did Charles fulfill his duties in each of these capacities that his goodness and his might, like his fame, practically overflowed the very borders of the realm. To further emphasize the spread of Charles's bravery and virtue up to and past the limits of Flemish territory, Galbert insists that when "[comes] secularis militiae facinora acturus foret, non habebat hostes circa terram suam sive in marchiis sive in confiniis et terminis suis" ([the count] wanted to perform deeds of knighthood, he had no enemies around his land, either in the marches or on the frontiers and borders) (§4: Rider 13; Ross 91–92).

The preface of *De multro* (that is, the introduction and first fourteen chapters of the modern edition) stands as a kind of monument to Count Charles. Its encomium is in fact practically a tomb made out of words, for if Charles is the text's first hero, he is also, as Galbert of course knew by the time he added this first section to his work, about to disappear from its pages.[16] And as if he were preparing his readers for that absence, and for the very different kind of narrative they would encounter as they read further, Galbert begins in the preface to shift attention to the men who were to take the count's place in the forward-moving action of his chronicle: the traitors, those relatives, friends, and associates of the Erembald clan whose members Count Charles had been preparing to claim as his serfs and that was headed by Bertulf Erembald, provost of the castral church of St. Donation.[17] Slowly the preface, with those traitors, withdraws from the broad expanse of Flanders into the "cameram" (inner room) in which the betrayal was first planned (§11: Rider 27; Ross 109). The action then moves quickly to another secluded space and to the making of a second, deadlier pact that sets the following dawn as the time for the count's death. The plan, Galbert emphasizes, is made in "silentium noctis" (the silence of the night), its plotters concocting, "[s]ecuri . . . in tenebris" (safe in the darkness), a secret business Galbert further notes was "contra morem" (contrary to custom) (§11: Rider 29; Ross 110–11). In the very next chapter we are shown (for the first time, but not the last) how Charles's murder, the crime that provided the impetus for Galbert's writing in the first place, was carried out by these men who emerged from the darkness to wreak havoc in the center of Bruges.

The murder of the count of Flanders, done with Bertulf the provost's knowledge and consent but carried out by knights belonging to and in the service of the Erembald clan, was a very real, very ghastly, and probably very gory event. But Galbert uses his preface to transform what must already have been a rather spectacular happening into an even more emphatically dramatic and suspenseful narrative. For Galbert told his tale of Charles's death not once but twice, and it is in this narrative duplication that we can glimpse some trace of the chronicler's intentions as to the impact he hoped his work would have. Galbert first described the murder on or soon after the day of its occurrence (2 March 1127), although that first account now appears as §15 of the text's modern edition. In that account, written first but perhaps revised later, Galbert makes clear that Charles's death is not only the climax of a scripted plot, one that occurred "post tot consilia et juramenta et securitates" (after so many plans and oaths and pacts) (§15: Rider 37; Ross 119), but also a sacrificial performance on the part of the victim. Although it is hard to imagine what the good Count Charles really did when the traitors burst into his chapel, Galbert presents him as one ready to the play the martyr's part:

> In supremo ergo articulo vitae et mortis accessu vultum dignissime atque regales ad coelum manus inter tot verbera et ictus gladiatorum, quantum potuit, converterat, sicque suum Domino universorum spiritum tradidit et se ipsum Deo obtulit sacrificium matutinum.

> (In the final moment of life and at the onset of death, he had most nobly lifted his countenance and his royal hands to heaven, as well as he could amid so many blows and thrusts of the swordsmen; and so he surrendered his spirit to the Lord of all and offered himself as a morning sacrifice to God.)

> (§15: Rider 37; Ross 119)

The depiction seems formulaic, and it is a formula we might expect, for Charles's martyrdom has been deftly foreshadowed by the earlier prefatory narrative that, as I noted above, imagines the count as ever willing to sacrifice himself in one way or another for the good of Flanders.

Sometime between May and September 1127, Galbert, in adding a preface to his record, decided to describe Charles's murder a second time. He was clearly well aware, however, that because of its placement at the head of his chronicle, this second description would be the first his readers would encounter, for he went to some length to offer them the drama with which he wanted them to engage as if they themselves had been present. Whereas the chapter written on or about the day of the murder itself (§15) begins with the count already in his chapel hearing mass, the preface sets the scene of the crime outside as well as inside the chapel, allowing us to learn of a morning "obscura valde et nebulosa, ita ut hastae longitudine nullus a se discernere posset rem aliquam" (so dark and foggy that you could not distinguish anything a spear's length away), of the watching serfs of the enemy, and of the count's anxiety during the previous night. From the courtyard where the count's early morning progress to prayer is spied upon, Galbert moves us back in time to the count's bedroom so that we see him "modo in altero cubans latere modo residens in stratu" (now lying on one side, now sitting up again on the bed). Then we, with the waiting serfs, watch until we know that Charles has ascended "in solarium ecclesiae" (into the gallery of the church). Finally we, as if with "ille furibundus Borsiardus et milites et servientes ejus" ([t]hat raging Borsiard and his knights and servants), burst into the chapel. At this point Galbert interjects an expression notably absent from the account written on the day of the murder itself: "Et ecce!" ([A]nd behold!) Opening the curtains as if for our viewing (dis)pleasure, he shows us "comitem prostratum suo more juxta altare" (the count prostrate before the altar) (§12: Rider 29; Ross 112). We hold our breath, but the death blow never comes. For here Galbert digresses, telling us not of a sword stroke and mayhem but of Charles's pilgrimage to Jerusalem some years earlier. His aside, which removes us both temporally and geographically from the crisis at hand, also glosses over the moment of death; at the end of the interruption, we are told only that "tam gloriosi principis martyrium vita [susceperat]" (the life of such a glorious prince had undergone martyrdom) and that the count was greatly mourned (§12: Rider 31, 33; Ross 113). In other words, we do not get to see Charles die in the preface, for he expires between the lines. We have to keep reading if we want the full story, as Galbert must have hoped his readers would. As Joseph Roach has observed, "All violence is performative, for the simple reason that it must have an audience—even if that audience is only the victim, even if that audience is only God" (41). But the count's murder received, and continues to receive, a large audience; first accidentally "attended" by all those present in the chapel gallery, it is then performed again by Galbert's chronicle for every new set of readers, who are transformed by the text's careful plotting into a new set of anxious spectators—or, to speak less metaphorically, readers whom carefully calculated narrative suspense drives from the preface's truncated account of the death to the satisfaction (as it were) of the fuller, more immediate, and bloodier description provided three chapters later.[18]

It is not completely clear just what sort of a work Galbert believed he was writing as he was writing it, or what kind of a work he thought he had written once he had reached the point at which he added the preface. He claims there that "[t]anti quidem principis mortem descripturus" (I set out to describe the death of such a great prince), but he also insists on the importance of the death's aftermath, adding that "memoriae fidelium scribendo commendavi peregrinum mortis ipsius eventum" (I committed to writing for the memory of the faithful the strange outcome of his death) ("Prologue": Rider 3; Ross 79–80). He further promises his reader that "ha[e]c passi[o]" (this . . . passion) contains a "vera et certa descripti[one] et vitae et mortis [comitis]" (true and reliable account of [the count's] life and death) (§14: Rider 35; Ross 117). The first two days of the chronicle certainly do return rather obsessively to an image of Galbert's dead lord "[j]acebat . . . cruentum . . . solum," "cruentum et solum jacebat" (lying bloody and alone), "jacebat occisus," and "occisus jacebat" (lying slain) (§15: Rider 37; Ross 119; §21: Rider 51; Ross 134; §17: Rider 41; Ross 124, 125). But the record is not, in the end, about Charles's life or death (although it certainly is about his death's outcome).[19] Nor is Galbert's text, unlike other contemporary accounts, either a list of postmortem miracles by, or a collection of laments for, the dead count.[20] While Galbert notes how a cripple was healed by Charles's agency, he chooses neither to emphasize this "miracul[um]" (miracle) as did his contemporaries (§22: Rider 55; Ross 139–40) nor to refer to the discovery of Charles's apparently uncorrupted body as a miracle at all.[21] And the drama of Charles's anxiously awaited interment itself competes for our attention with what Galbert specifically calls the "spectaculum" (spectacle) of the death of a townsman who had aided the conspirators and that occurred on the same day as the funeral (§77: Rider 130; Ross 246).

Finally, the one *planctus* Galbert describes appears in a passage that is less about Charles than it is about the lament itself as a kind of locationally specific performance. Galbert writes that it was only once he could see his lord's tomb that Fromold

Junior, one of the count's notaries, was able "ex longo desiderio et ardenti animo vota Deo pro salute domini sui consulis offerre, lachrimis et cordis contritione sacrificium mactare, et gaudio gaudere pro inspectatione loci in quo dominus suus humatus quiescebat" (to do what . . . he had long and ardently desired, to offer prayers to God for the salvation of his lord . . . to make a sacrifice in tears and contrition of heart, and to rejoice greatly in the sight of the place where his lord, buried, was resting in peace) (§64: Rider 117; Ross 224–25).[22] Fromold's grief finds effective release only once he finds, quite literally, the proper place for its expression; his sorrow and his joy are as much about an experience of place as they are about personal loss.

Both Charles's body and his tomb create emotion and action—they are, especially in Galbert's account, places where things happen. Michel de Certeau has defined hagiography as narrative that "revolves around the place" of its hero (living or dead), and in these terms we might see the passages I have just discussed as hagiographic interludes (281). But Galbert's narrative practice actually prevented the creation of a *passio;* even the most cursory reading of *De multro* reveals that it does anything but correspond to the generic label Galbert tried to give it. A daily chronicle, which must by definition focus on the new and the different if its writer is to continue with the task, cannot be a hagiography since, as de Certeau has observed, hagiography "focus[es] its portrayal of the hero around constancy, the perseverance of the same" (277). Galbert's daily record, with which he seems to have persevered as an almost instinctive response to his simultaneous fascination with and revulsion at the chaos following the murder, was a careful day-to-day observation of events, and his recording of supreme inconstancy and continual change transformed any aspiration to hagiography into something else entirely—or simply prevented its emergence.[23] Count Charles, alive or dead, is already in Galbert's first chapter and certainly from that point forward less an actor than an object around which others perform. His tomb becomes part of a stage set and his body a prop, a still center from which action taken in the chapel spreads through Bruges and beyond the borders of Flanders—not to mention through the 122 chapters of Galbert's chronicle. News of the "infamia traditionis" (infamy of the betrayal), writes Galbert, spread immediately from its site "in castro Brugensi" (in the castle of Bruges) so that "in Londonia civitate . . . secundo die postea . . . perculit cives" ([it] shocked the citizens of London . . . on the second day afterwards) and "turbavit" (disturbed) the people of Laon shortly thereafter (§12: Rider 33; Ross 113). He adds, as if embarrassed, that the merchants fled the marketplace of nearby Ypres, "secum infamiam nostrae terrae ferentes et ubicumque divulgantes" (bearing with them word of the disgrace of our land and spreading it everywhere) (§16: Rider 41; Ross 124).

Despite his apparent distaste for the spread of scandal, Galbert continued to take notes with the intention of turning Bruges's shame into narrative. Perhaps he saw his tablets full of notes as themselves places within which his city's "disgrace" could be contained;[24] perhaps what Galbert was after was a kind of control in language that he lacked over events. He suggests as much in his preface, drawing a direct connection between the chaos of Bruges, the panic of its people, and his own self-discipline in a passage worth citing in full:

Neque equidem locum et temporis oportunitatem, cum animum in hoc opere intenderem, habebam, quandoquidem noster locus eodem tempore sollicitabatur metu et angustia adeo ut, sine alicujus exceptione, tam clerus quam populus indifferenti periclitaretur occasu et rerum suarum et vitae. Ibi inter tot adversa et angustissimos locurum fines, cepi mentem fluctuantem et quasi in Euripo jactatam compescere et juxta scribendi modum cohibere. In qua animi mei exactione illa caritatis scintillula suo igne fota et exercitata omnes virtutes spirituales cordis funditus ignivit et subsequenter hominem meum, quem a foris timor possederat, scribendi quadam libertate donavit.

(And, in fact, I did not have a favorable time or place when I turned my mind to this work, because our place at that time was so disturbed by fear and anxiety that the clergy and people without exception were threatened continually with loss of life and property. It was, therefore, in the midst of many calamities and in the most constrained circumstances that I began to compose my mind, as unquiet as if it were tossed about in Euripus, and to subdue it to the discipline of writing. In this distress of mind, a little spark of love, warmed and animated by its own fire, set aflame all the spiritual strength of my heart and consequently endowed my bodily self, which had been seized by fear, with the freedom to write.)

("Prologue": Rider 3; Ross 80)

This rather amazing image of a mind soothing itself with words, replacing "noster locus" (our place) with rhetorical *loci,* is the closest Galbert comes to giving us a personal motive for his work. But on the whole he was much less interested in himself than he was in the men who had killed Charles the Good, and, in fact, in the entire clan of the rebellious Erembalds and their associates. While Galbert praises the notary Fromold Junior for accepting exile rather than a treaty with the killers, asserting that "[g]ravissimum enim est viro cum inimico concordem esse et contra naturam, cum omnis creatura sibi inimica, si possit, effugiat" (it is a most grievous thing for a man to be in accord with his enemy, and against nature, for every creature flees what is inimical to itself, if it can) (§24: Rider 59; Ross 143), he took the opposite tack in his own writing about these particular enemies. He spends much of the first part of the chronicle depicting their activities with care and speculating frequently as to their motives and emotions. As the tide of public opinion in Bruges began to turn against the Erembalds, "suburbani nostri loci aperte introierunt ad consilia dominorum illorum, praepositi scilicet et castellani et nepotum suorum nefandorum, et secreta consiliorum ipsorum." (the townsmen of our place openly entered into the councils of their lords, that is, the provost and castellan and their wicked nephews, and tried to find out their secret decisions.) (§25: Rider 61; Ross 144–45).

Galbert, in his writing rather than in council, also attempted to pry open the "secreta" of the conspirators who took over the count's castle and church but quickly found themselves trapped inside, besieged by Charles's more faithful barons and the burghers of Bruges. Galbert reports the traitors' increasing entrapment within the castle walls and their feelings about the straits in which they found themselves as intermingled and indeed as corresponding facts. At first he only comments that "[q]uanto ergo timore et dolore laborarent traditores illi . . .

supersedere longum erat." ([i]t would take too long to tell with what sorrow and fear those traitors were afflicted.) (§26: Rider 65; Ross 149). But when the traitors are attacked from three sides by a crowd of united citizens, Galbert begins to portray the besieged in clear spatial and psychological retreat. He projects an image of their emotions while adroitly mapping the gradual stages of their self-protective but ultimately self-destructive enclosure:

> In tertio vero ponte, qui in orientali parte jacebat a castro et usque ad portas castri se tenebat, fortissimus congressus fiebat adeo ut, non tolerantes pugnae acerbitatem, illi qui intro stabant frangerent pontem et portas super se clauderent. . . . Vellent nollent quidem, agitati sunt infra castrum miseri illi, quorum magna pars vulnerata est, et simul exanimati metu et dolore atque lassitudine pugnae defatigati.

> (On a third bridge, which lay on the eastern side of the castle, such a fierce combat was going on that those who were inside, not able to bear the violence of the attack, broke the bridge and closed the gates on themselves. . . . Whether they liked it or not the wretches inside the castle were full of anxiety; a great part of them were wounded and at the same time dispirited by fear and sorrow, and faint from the weariness of fighting.)

> (§28: Rider 69; Ross 153)

Galbert's images of the cornered traitors emphasize the extent to which the besieged rebels played a part in their own downfall; the detail and the clarity with which he depicts their increasing physical isolation seems almost deliberately designed to emphasize the moral gulf they were responsible for placing between themselves and their countrymen. Galbert articulates in no uncertain terms the finality of their self-isolation: "portas castri terrae et lapidum et fimorum comportationibus introrsum humaverant ab immo usque in summum . . . ita nullus aditus relictus est inimicis vel exitus obsessis" (they had blocked up the gates of the castle on the inside from bottom to top with loads of dirt and stones and dung . . . so that no means of getting in was left to the attackers and no way of getting out to the besieged) (§36: Rider 83; Ross 166). While the traitors may have thought they were safe behind their improvised blockade, their hopes proved futile, and they were forced to retreat from the castle into the church of St. Donation through the passageway that Galbert takes care to explain connected the two buildings (§41: Rider 91; Ross 175). There, remarks the chronicler with an evident relish of the moment's poetic justice, they found themselves "sine velle ipsorum cum domino suo consule clausi" (through no desire of theirs . . . confined with their lord the count) (§43: Rider 93; Ross 180). Galbert later imagines the killers to have used the count's tomb as a dining table, painting a scene clearly meant to demonstrate their utter depravity:

> occiso comite Karolo, Borsiardus et sui sceleris participes more paganorum et incantatorum . . . acceperunt cyphum plenum cervisiae et panem, considentes circa sepulchrum, posuerunt potum illum et panem in mensa sepulchri, edentes et bibentes super beati comitis corpus ea fide ut nullo modo illum quis vindicaret.

> (after Count Charles was killed, Borsiard and his accomplices in the crime . . . followed the custom of pagans and sorcerers. Taking a vessel full of beer, and bread,

they all sat around the tomb and placed that drink and bread on top of the tomb as if it were a table, eating and drinking over the body of the dead count in the belief that no one could in any way avenge him.)

(§90: Rider 140; Ross 263)[25]

Galbert presents this banquet, at which he was not present, as if he had seen it with his own eyes; his description transforms the chapel into a stage set for devilry and the traitors' behavior, not to mention their misplaced confidence in their own security, into a performance to which only Galbert and his readers are privy. This he does in order to emphasize the degree to which the traitors polluted the space they invaded—something he makes explicit in his comment that after the conspirators took shelter within it, nothing in Saint Donation "sancta et integra maneret sed turpi et informi deformitate horribilior staret quolibet carcere" (retained its holy and untouched appearance but everything looked defiled and deformed, more horrible than if it were a prison) (§43: Rider 94; Ross 180). But Galbert also shows us what that same space, in turn, did to the traitors. In an entry that follows their defeat and surrender, Galbert revisits the gradual stages of their retreat, compressing more than six weeks into a single brief passage to show "quomodo Deus traditores illos in paucitatem redegerit et genere *et loco*" (how God had laid those traitors low, reduced them in respect to family *and place*). He writes that "soli Deo relicta est vindicta" (vengeance was left to God alone), a God who

statim coartavit eos et timore concussit ut non auderent extra vicum loci nostri prodire, sed magis consiliati sunt villam et suburbium nostrum sepire et circumfodere sicut supra memoravimus. Statim die octavo post mortem consulis per obsidionem in castro clausi, deinde cum castrum fuisset invasum a nostris, in turrim fugati, magis coartati sunt. Deinde in carcerem trusi, in tantum artati sunt ut non possent simul omnes sedere, nisi tres aut quatuor ad minus stetissent. Tenebrae, calor et fetor et sudor inficiebant illos et desperatae vitae horror et incertae mortis futurae turpitudo.

(at once confined them and struck them with fear so that they did not dare to go out beyond the inhabited area of our place but decided instead to enclose the area and our town by palisade and ditch, as we have told above. On the eighth day after the count's death they were forthwith shut up in the castle by the siege; then when the castle was invaded by our men, they fled to the tower where they were more confined; finally thrown into prison, they were in such close quarters that they could not sit down at the same time unless at least three or four stood up. Darkness, heat, stench, and sweat undid them, and the horror of hopeless life and the shame of uncertain death to come.)

(§75: Rider 127–28; Ross 243; emphasis added)

Causal connections are here overshadowed by symbolic ones. The passage suggests not that the traitors were defeated because they were trapped (as was in fact the case), but that that entrapment was a blow dealt by God for their original misdeeds. This punishment, Galbert implies, was as much psychological as literal: God trapped the criminals through their fear, ensuring that they would be destroyed by the very space in which they had committed their crime.

Galbert uses spatial imagery to convey more than the changing fortunes and minds of the besieged. Most notably, in addition to tracing the progressive enclosure and fading confidence of the traitors in parallel strokes, he also personifies the castral church of St. Donation, in and around which all this activity took place.[26] After its canons, in an attempt to save its contents, are shown on 17 March stripping St. Donation of its furnishings in a symbolically charged, catastrophically inverted reliquary procession, Galbert tells us that the church "[s]tabat . . . sola et deserta" (stood alone and deserted) with the body of the dead count at its heart (§35: Rider 81; Ross 163). Only two chapters later (and part of the record for the same day), St. Donation is no longer just a container for a corpse and the hideout of scoundrels; it has taken the place of the good Count Charles, who once brought "justitiae et pacis securitate" (the security of peace and justice) to his realm (§1: Rider 5; Ross 83):

> Stabat autem ecclesia beati Donatiani aedificata in rotundum et altum. . . . Unde honestatis suae fulgore praeeminebat velut regni sedes, et in medio patriae securitate et pace, jure et legibus undique terrae partibus salutem et justitiam demandans.
>
> (There stood the church of Saint Donation, built round and high. . . . From this place it dominated the scene in the splendor of its beauty like the throne of the realm; in the midst of the fatherland it called for safety and justice everywhere in the land through security and peace, right and laws.)
>
> (§37: Rider 86; Ross 167)

Saint Donation becomes both an actor and a stage, for it is both the living, speaking symbol of the more glorious Flemish past and, as the siege wears on, the increasingly profaned theater of the present.[27] It is a place from which the props of the everyday are removed in the tragic procession referred to above in which the canons

> scrinia et feretra sanctorum et reliquarum suarum emiserunt. . . . Cortinas et aulearia quoque tapeta, cappas palliatas et sericas, vestes sacras et librorum aggerem, et utensilia templi . . . [et] [d]e redditibus comitis brevia et notationes. . . .
>
> (brought out the reliquaries and biers of the saints and their relics . . . vessels, tapestries and hangings, woolen and silken cowls, sacred vestments, and a pile of books and church utensils . . . [and] the accounts and records of the revenues of the count. . . .)
>
> (§35: Rider 79; Ross 162–63)[28]

And St. Donation is also a place into which the rather extraordinary enters, most memorably in the form of a battering ram used by the besiegers to pierce its walls and reach the traitors, practically destroying the building in the process of saving it. Galbert's description of this forced entry is an outstanding example of the way in which he makes the naturally dramatic more spectacular than real spectacles intended as such, and an even better example—perhaps the best—of the dramatic role that spatial description plays in the chronicle as a whole. Galbert himself refers to the event as a kind of violent performance, a "labor tundendi" (work of ramming) that although "fuit a meridie inceptus . . . post vesperam finitus" (begun at noon . . . was not finished until after evening had come) (§62: Rider 115; Ross 222). Having characterized St. Donation as a living, speaking being only a month earlier, now Galbert describes how those who ought to have cherished the church most shattered its walls in an act reminiscent of the murder of Count Charles, who, we remember, was "gladiis confossu[s] et saepius transverberatu[s]" (struck down with swords and run through again and again) (§15: Rider 37; Ross 119):

> . . . retro a muro et pariete templi reducto per laqueos ariete quantum extensis brachiis suspensi possent, uno impetu et uno clamore arietis ruinum et casum valde ponderosum virium suarum fortitudine et maximo conatu templo appulere. Ex cujus singula percussione maximus lapidum cumulus in terram corruit donec tota maceries et paries in eo loco quo contusus est perforaretur.

> (. . . having pulled the ram back from the church wall by means of the nooses as far as they possibly could with outstretched arms, all together, with one impetus and one cry, they drove the great mass and weight of the ram against the church with their maximum strength and effort. At each blow a great heap of stones fell to the ground until the whole area of the wall was perforated in the place where it was pounded.)

> (§62: Rider 114–15; Ross 221–22)

Galbert's relationship to the chapel space whose violation he here imagines and describes in such detail was, it seems, intimately connected to his sense of responsibility for his role as witness and record keeper. For it is in the chapter recording the stripping of St. Donation, clearly the sacred center of his world, that Galbert introduces himself by name and discusses his work methods for the first time.[29] And although he tells us only that he took notes "in tanto tumultu" (in the midst of such a great tumult) and that he transcribed those notes in rare moments of peace, his signature reinforces the fact that all the performances and spaces described in the text are part of his own performance as historiographer attempting to encompass *veritas rerum* in words. Such all-inconclusiveness comes with a price, if indeed that is what it should be called—that is, the disappearance of the chronicler from his own pages. It is striking that in contrast to the degree of specificity with which he locates both besieged and besiegers within and without the walls of castle, church, and city, Galbert never locates himself except to tell us, here, that he and his tablets had no place: "locum scribendi ego Galbertus non habe[bam]" (I, Galbert . . . had no . . . place for writing). Indeed, we never know where Galbert was during any of the events he describes—we know only that he created his record "inter tot noctium pericula et tot dierum certamina" (in the midst of so much danger by night and conflict by day) (§35: Rider 81; Ross 164). This lack of a "place for writing" Galbert transforms into literary license; unlike every other figure in his record, Galbert is impossible to locate because he is, in a sense, everywhere.[30] Gabrielle Spiegel has noted in her study of thirteenth-century historiography that the withdrawal of the writer from his text is often an attempt to lend it the appearance of transparency (*Romancing* 220), an observation frequently made of the nineteenth-century novel but rarely about medieval histories, whose writers are more frequently accused of inserting themselves too boldly into their narratives. While we cannot know whether Galbert refrained from speaking of himself out of modesty or design, it is certainly the case that his absence has the effect of making us feel present at the scenes he describes and more confident than we might otherwise be as to their completeness. Even more interesting is the fact that the more distant Galbert was from the places he describes and the people he probes, the more penetrating and the more omniscient his chronicle becomes. We saw an example of this phenomenon above, in his descriptions of the besieged as a group, for of course Galbert was nowhere near the traitors as they underwent their slow and claustrophobic defeat. However, it is to Galbert's representation of a single person that I would like, in conclusion, to turn, for his characterizations of the provost Bertulf Erembald can show us how Galbert's attention to spatial detail and to the depiction of drama in various interiors led him to think of the mind as but one more space that could be laid open by the historiographer's piercing and omniscient eye.

From the very beginning of his record keeping, Galbert seems to have felt the need to explain what Bertulf thought and felt as well as what he did. The provost's were feelings to which Galbert almost certainly did not have access; nevertheless, in an early chapter, he claims that Bertulf, rather than working quickly to protect Charles's favorite Fromold Junior from attack on the day of the murder, "ibat . . . non celeri gressu, sed nimis tardo, utpote ille qui parum de [Fromoldo] curaret, quem valde suspectum habebat" (went, not with a quick step . . . but very slowly, inasmuch as he was little concerned about Fromold, whom actually he held in great suspicion) (§19: Rider 47; Ross 130). Here and elsewhere Galbert reads the provost's external movements through space as signs of an inner state: the provost walked slowly because he cared little, but later that same day, apparently stricken by fearful guilt, he was anxiously "in domo sua cum canonicis suis deambulabat, excusans se verbis quantam potuit" (walking up and down in his house with his canons, absolving himself as well as he could in words) (§20: Rider 49; Ross 132). Next, unsettled by the vehemence with which the people of Bruges refused to allow Count Charles's body to be removed to Ghent, the provost, Galbert tells us, "ibat et redibat, consulens cum traditoribus" (kept coming and going, talking things over with the traitors) (§22: Rider 55; Ross 140). Nevertheless, when Bertulf found himself standing next to Charles's hastily built tomb, he "deflebat tunc tandem consulem quam rationis ductu recognovit patrem fuisse universae regionis Flandriarum, et talem illum planxit qualem quidem recognoscere obstinato animo indignabatur" (at last wept for the count whom he acknowledged by the dictates of reason as having been the father of the whole region of Flanders . . . even though he could not bear to recognize [him as such] . . . in his obstinate mind) (§23: Rider 57; Ross 141).[31] In each of these passages, Galbert explains Bertulf's actions by reference to both the spaces through which he moved and the feelings to which those spaces must (he assumes) have given rise and which the provost's movements then reflect—except, of course, for the passage in which Bertulf weeps. The description of the provost crying before his lord's sepulcher is especially notable because of the way in which what Galbert says he believes to be true of Bertulf's thoughts (he was firm in his treachery) directly contradicts what Bertulf's tears would otherwise appear to suggest (he was repentant for his crime). In other words, Galbert had begun to feel as free to read Bertulf from the inside out as from the outside in, as if the man were transparent, open to interpretation and thus to condemnation by the chronicler who could see right through him.

The description of the provost in the tacked-on preface, on the other hand, constructs an image of a mastermind whose deceptive character is suggested by—even made analogous to—his spatial violations. Galbert, writing in retrospect, shows us Bertulf and his nephews looking for "locum et oportunitatem" (a place and an opportunity) for murdering Charles. They force a standoff between themselves and the count by attacking the house of one Thancmar, whom the count supported:

> Quem [Thancmarum] quidem obsedit circumquaque in loco, quo se vallaverat, et tandem collecta manu invasit validissime obsessos, et claustra portarum confringens, detruncavit pomeria et sepes inimicorum suorum. Absens tamen et quasi nihil fecessit, consilio et dolo omnia fecit. Omnem benevolentiam a foris praetendebat et inimicis dicebat sese dolere quod nepotes sui tot lites, tot homicidia peragerent, quos quidem omnia nefaria animaverat. . . .

> (They besieged Thancmar on all sides in the place where he had entrenched himself, and finally with a considerable force strongly attacked those within. Breaking the bolts of the gates, they cut down the orchards and hedges of their enemies. Though the provost did not take part and acted as if he had done nothing, he actually did everything by direction and deception. He pretended in public that he was full of good will and told his enemies that he grieved to see his nephews engaged in so much strife and killing, although he himself had incited them to all these crimes. . . .)

> (§9: Rider 21 and 23; Ross 103–4)

Here Galbert shows us that Bertulf's words do not match his intentions or his deeds; his example of the man's duplicity highlights the degree to which the violent, illicit penetration of space is caused by and reflective of the provost's "dol[us]" (deception). Making an external show ("a foris") of the best of intentions, the provost instead tells lies, collects weapons, and finally holds a vulgar celebratory feast in the dead of night in the middle of the building that, as we have seen above, Galbert held dear as the most holy place in Bruges.

The arrogance Galbert attributes to Bertulf here and elsewhere in the preface is unmatched by that of any other figure in the record.[32] But in the chronicle itself, once Galbert notes that Bertulf's relatives and associates "pugnaturos se fore contra universum mundum amodo intellexerant" (had . . . learned that they would have to fight against the whole world), a realization that comes while the besieged take refuge behind a wall that "circumxinxerat et domum praepositi et dormitorium fratrum et claustram et pariter omne illud castrum" (encircled the house of the provost and the dormitory of the brothers and the cloister and likewise the whole castle) and "quem tandem obtinere sibi praesumpserant" (which they expected to hold on to until the end) (§37: Rider 86; Ross 168), his portrait of Bertulf begins to shift in emphasis even as it becomes bolder in its assumptions as to what the provost was thinking and feeling. Now Galbert gives us a Bertulf who comes to a parley "vultu tristiore et omisso majestatis suae rigore et superbia, mente consternatus" (sad in countenance and no longer stern and proud in his dignity) (§38: Rider 87; Ross 169), as if he knows the fate that is to overtake him. The very next time we read of him, Bertulf has escaped from the tight enclosure of the site of the murder just as the rest of the traitors have been forced into the church, but his fate is just as hideous as theirs. Open space, Galbert emphasizes, is in Bertulf's case just as perilous as cramped quarters. He relates how the betrayer found himself betrayed by one former friend who, "tamen ipsum transductum in desertum locum, scilicet Mor, solum reliquit, expositum inimicis suis et derelictum fugae, cum tamen in loco illo sibi ignoto nesciret quo fugeret et quem fugeret" (after leading him to a wasteland called Mor, abandoned him, exposed to his enemies and forsaken in his flight since in that unfamiliar place he did not know where he should flee or to whom) (§42: Rider 92; Ross 177). Bertulf is now utterly alone and unprotected in a wide-open space above which Galbert positions both himself and his readers, encouraging us to imagine, with him, the state of the provost's mind as he flees from cover to cover: "Et vere gravissime vir ille dolebat, qui pridem omnibus imperitabat. . . ." (He must have been in a state of profound grief, that man who had recently lorded it over everyone. . . .) With an expression we have seen once (and only once) before, Galbert directs us to look down upon the scurrying criminal: "Ecce! solus et infra terminos suos exul solus pererrabat" (Behold! he wandered alone, a solitary exile within his own boundaries!) (§46: Rider 97; Ross 186).[33] Where once we, with his killers, had been directed by the same phrase to "behold" the text's first martyr, Count Charles, in the moments just before his death (§12), now we gaze down upon the body and into the mind of a traitor upon whom Galbert's narrative works its own particular form of retribution for the text's initial crime.

Charles was made a martyr by the opening chapters of the chronicle; now Galbert makes a martyr—of sorts—of the man he held largely responsible for Charles's death.[34] First Galbert forces Bertulf into the position of a penitent, reading his shoeless state (probably caused by the haste of his flight) as a form of deliberate self-flagellation: "sicut audivimus . . . nudis pedibus penam peccatorum suorum sponte perpessus ibat ut tanto peccatori Deus indulgeret, quod contra consulem pium deliquerat" (as we have heard, he went on his way with bare feet, suffering voluntary punishment for his sins so that God might forgive such a great sinner the crime he had committed against the pious count) (§46: Rider 97; Ross 185–86). Bertulf is captured, but practically off stage, for Galbert never narrates his arrest. Instead, he moves his readers directly to the scene of Bertulf's execution, a scene which in effect serves as a kind of climax in the chronicle. Despite the fact that the record was to be continued for many months to come, nothing that comes after the entry for 11 April 1127 quite matches Bertulf's final moments in narrative intensity. Galbert makes the provost's death extraordinary in his chronicle in part by insisting that it was so in life; he comments that "[t]antus erat tumultus, clamor et concursus . . . circa captivum unum hominem ut non possimus aequiparare eum" ([t]here was so much tumult and clamor . . .

around that one captive that there is nothing to which we can compare it) (§57: Rider 107; Ross 209). Here, following the pattern he had developed in the course of more than a month of writing, Galbert first locates Bertulf's body—no longer isolated but instead all too hemmed in by a furious crowd:

> Et sicut aiunt, saltando, choreas ducendo, diversis applausibus praeibant et consequebantur praepositum, trahentes eum funibus longioribus a dextris ejus et sinistris ita ut ordo trahentium in longum et ab invicem in latum procederet, ut sic ab omnibus olim vir ille dignus et potentissimus verecunde et ingnominiose derideretur.

> (It is said that they went before and followed after the provost, leaping, dancing, applauding in various ways, and pulling him with long ropes from the left and right so that the line of pullers could move alternately forwards and sidewise; in this way that man, once so respected and powerful, could be insulted shamefully and ignominiously by everyone.)

(§57: Rider 107; Ross 209)

"[S]icut aiunt"—with these words, Galbert makes clear that he was not present at the execution, which indeed took place in Ypres while Galbert was in Bruges. But although he even admits in the next chapter that he is reporting what he was told later by a witness, Galbert proceeds in his description as if he had in fact been at Ypres, and does so skillfully that, as Jeff Rider notes, he manages "to convey the impression that he, and we, are there" ("Journal" 75–76). First Galbert describes what he, Galbert, believes Bertulf might have been doing as he was dragged through the streets, stoned, and taunted by the mob:

> [I]lle . . . mortis suae supplicium eminus expectabat, ante cujus mentis faciem poterant ad memoriam merito reduci omnia quae egerat si aliquod vivendi spatium turba in ejus mortem corruens praestitisset. Poterat quidem reminisci, si debuit, quomodo. . . . in templo Dei praelationem usurpasset. . . .

> ([H]e saw the punishment of death approaching him; and he could with justice have called up before his mind's eye everything he had done, if the mob, rushing him headlong to his death, had granted him any time to live. He could indeed have remembered, if he had wished, how . . . he had usurped the prelacy in the Church of God. . . .)

(§57: Rider 107; Ross 209)

But in the middle of this description of the repentance which Galbert clearly wished to believe the provost would have experienced had he been given "vivendi spatium"—literally, "the space of living," an expanse of time large enough to permit such thoughts to travel through his no less spatially imagined "faciem mentis" and "memoriam"[35]—Galbert suddenly becomes less tentative. He tells us not what the provost *could* have done, but what he, Galbert, thinks Bertulf *did* do. This is an extraordinary moment in an already extraordinary passage, for while Galbert merely continues his sentence, he also takes up a position within Bertulf's mind so that we, with him, can watch the provost's last thoughts:

> [E]t nunc tandem catholicum et de regum stirpe progenitum nobilissimum principem Karolum . . . morti tradiderit qui sicut inter sui supplicii angustias profitebatur.

... [N]isi fallor, Deum ... invocabat, sine strepitu vocum sed in secreto mentis sibi invocaverat, semper adjutorem.

([A]nd now finally he was admitting in the agony of his punishment that he had betrayed to death ... the most noble and Catholic prince Charles. ... [U]nless I am mistaken, he was invoking the aid of God; not with his voice but in the depths of his soul he called upon him. ...)

(§57: Rider 107–8; Ross 209–10)

Galbert cannot quite elide the rather ironic discrepancy between the penitent thoughts he places here in Bertulf's mind ("in secreto mentis") and his report of the scornful way the condemned man actually responded to his tormentors; nevertheless, he continues to position Bertulf in the martyr's role, telling us that he died with his "brachia in crucem extensa" (arms stretched out like a cross), his body ripped to pieces as it hung "sub acerrimae mortis tenebris" (in the shadow of the most bitter death) (§57: Rider 108–9; Ross 211). This execution was almost certainly as spectacular as Galbert's narration of it, but here Galbert's language exerts itself to aid the executioner in dressing Bertulf in the role of Christ—his road to Calvary ended, his body torn apart on a makeshift cross.[36] Although Galbert used his preface, we recall, to insist that his text was to be the story of the *passio* of Count Charles, here he uses the cristological matrix—with what may have been meant as the sharpest of ironies, for Galbert clearly saw no saint in Bertulf[37]—in order to help him depict, in a moment of heightened drama, a conscience he at least hoped was repentant and which, if not, was largely unimaginable. Just as he makes one of his most innovative narrative leaps, that is, Galbert finds himself forced to turn to a scriptural model of explanation, a tactic that Stephen Nichols has shown is the prevalent mode of much earlier medieval historiography.[38] But what is important here is less that Galbert must imagine Bertulf's conscience through a model, and more that he bothers to imagine it at all. Bertulf, a man whom Galbert clearly believed deserved to die, is in the moment of his death brought to resonant life by the chronicler's daring to leap from the exterior perspective of the crowd into the imagined interior, the *secretum*, of the provost's mind.[39]

This move from objective description to subjective exploration is one Galbert cannot make, it seems, without reference to his own subjectivity: "nisi fallor," Galbert cautions us, in a rare moment of self-reference.[40] The martyrdom of Count Charles, itself performed as ritual by its victim and as neatly patterned upon an established model as one could wish, required no such qualification by its narrator. Charles's death was objectively readable theater and practically ready-made dramatic narrative; his death provided Galbert with both motivation to write and a central site from which to unfold and imagine succeeding events as they occurred. With Bertulf's death, however, Galbert chooses to read further than he can see, to look into the depths of the provost's soul for a regret not evident in his external bearing.[41] Bertulf's admittedly dramatic death thus briefly becomes tragic soliloquy, a soliloquy which is, moreover, a fictionalized interior monologue imagined by its creator and "heard" only by its readers. It is worth noting that Galbert begins the passage in which Bertulf's death occurs with a discussion of the omniscience of God, "cui nihil resistit, cujus auctoritate dictum est: nihil occultum, quod non reveletur" (whom nothing can resist, by whose authority it is said, "There is nothing hidden which will not be revealed") (§57, referring to Matthew 10:26: Rider 107; Ross 208). Galbert, then, is a bit like God, possessing by virtue of his narrative the authority to penetrate the space of Bertulf's mind and bring to light what lies hidden within it. Throughout the chronicle, as we have seen, Galbert felt free to imagine drama within spaces in which he could not have been present. Perhaps it is not, in these terms, a very large leap from a description of Charles's murder to a depiction of the villain Bertulf's repentance before God. Both moments require an imaginative penetration of space—the one architectural, the other psychological—on Galbert's part; both involve a stretching of historical "fact" beyond the limits of "objective" reality. But whereas the description of Charles's martyrdom in his chapel probably bears some relationship to actual events, the scene of Bertulf's repentance is less a record of Bertulf's actions than it is a trace of Galbert's performance as a reader of events and a writer of history. The narrative space in which Galbert gives Bertulf time to call upon God is a stage not for Bertulf but for the play of Galbert's imagination. It is a space—like many others in medieval historiography—in which the matter of fact joins forces with what we now think of as the material of fiction, a space in which the historian makes of an event what he feels he must for the sake of *rerum veritas,* the truth of things.

Notes

It gives me great pleasure to thank Robert M. Stein for introducing me to Galbert of Bruges and for encouraging my work on Galbert's chronicle ever since. I presented an earlier form of this chapter at the International Congress on Medieval Studies at Kalamazoo, Michigan, in 1998 in a session sponsored by the Chronicle Society and chaired by Dr. Lister Matheson; thanks are due to Linda Georgianna, Nancy Partner, and Gabrielle Spiegel for their enthusiastic responses and useful comments there. I am most grateful to Jeff Rider for sending me his important study of *De multro* while it was still in manuscript and for his enthusiastic organization of further work on Galbert by myself and others. Finally, I thank my fellow former members of Columbia University's Medieval Guild—particularly Heather Blurton, Andrea Denny-Brown, Mary Agnes Edsall, and Geoff Rector—for their cheerful willingness to hear so much about Galbert for so long.

1. §15: Rider 35, 37; Ross 118–19. All Latin citations are from Rider; English translations are from Ross. I will cite quotations in the text, as I do here, by chapter (§) and by the corresponding pages of Rider's and Ross's editions.

2. My argument both accords with and develops a point made by Rider in his article "Galbert of Bruges' 'Journal.'" Rider further examines the many literary devices and designs of Galbert's chronicle in his *God's Scribe,* which reached me in manuscript shortly after this chapter was completed in December 1999. My arguments about Galbert's use of space as a means to both structure and enliven his narrative agree in many places with Rider's own observations. While I could not take every similarity into account, in these notes I have done my best to indicate the places where our readings coincide most significantly. Rider highlights Galbert's ability to make the most of the dramatic potential of events ("Galbert of Bruges' 'Journal,'" esp. 74–75, 82); see also *God's Scribe* 87–141 and *passim.*

3. Although Ross's translation of Galbert's only signature in the text reads "I, Galbert, a notary" (§35: Ross 164), the phrase "ego Galbertus notarius" is a variant present in three of the manuscripts and is rejected by Rider in his edition. Rider proposes that Galbert was a cleric connected to Count Charles's fiscal administration and that he was neither a notary nor a canon of the castral church of St. Donation. For a detailed discussion of Galbert's

probable background and position, and for a description of the manuscripts of *De multro,* see the relevant sections of Rider's comprehensive introduction to the Latin text (*De multro* xiii–xix and xxix–xl) and Rider, *God's Scribe* 16–28.

4. I draw the terms "cultural performance" and "social drama" from the work of anthropologist Victor Turner. Turner distinguishes between the cultural performances by which normative social life is regulated and the heightened activity he calls social drama, occurring when crisis rips the fabric of that social life apart. Social drama, argues Turner, reveals the performative nature of public life while intensifying its sociodramatic nature (74–75, 90–93).

5. See, for example, Dhondt; Van Caenegem, "Law and Power" and *Galbert van Brugge;* Ganshof, "Le roi," "Trois mandements," and "Les origines." For a very useful historiography of the reception of *De multro* to the present day, see Rider, *God's Scribe* 1–8 and bibliography.

6. Rider argues convincingly for Galbert's book as a "thoroughly revised" text whose artfulness has gone unrecognized: "The *De multro* is not . . . a true journal but a journalistically organized history" (*God's Scribe* 9). For Rider's suggested chronology of the stages of Galbert's revisions, including the addition of events of which he must have learned after the fact, see *De multro* xx–xxviii and *God's Scribe* 29–49, as well as Appendices 6 and 7 (226–30).

7. This phrase suggests that Galbert intended that his words produce *enargeia,* a "bringing-before-the-eyes" of what he had seen as well as of what he had not. On the concept of *enargeia* and its use and development within the rhetorical tradition, see Eden 71–75. That Galbert was trained to some extent in that tradition and that he was highly aware of the power of rhetoric is made clear at several points in his preface. He claims to have avoided rhetorical flourish in his description of Charles's death: "non elaboravi elopquentiae ornatum seu diversorum colurum distinguere modo" ("I did not seek to embellish it with eloquence of to display the modes of different styles") (*De multro* "Prologue": Rider 3; Ross 80). In another striking passage, he reflects upon the spread of legal rhetoric and its (in his view) ultimately corrupting influence (§1: Rider 7; Ross 84). On that passage, see Partner 40–41.

8. For a reading of Galbert's record as the representation of a fatal clash of different kinds of law and legal processes, see Van Caenegem, "Law and Power."

9. For an earlier formulation of a similar idea, see Bakhtin and Volosinov 409.

10. The events of 1127–28 in Flanders in fact form an almost perfect example of the four-stage process of social drama schematized by Victor Turner: breach, crisis, redress, and reintegration. Redress, according to Turner, is characterized most often by formal performances like legal processes or by collective rituals much like those engaged in by the citizens of Bruges during this period. See Turner 74–75 and 93.

11. Galbert's text, I would argue, is in this sense part of the development studied by Spence, who argues that the rise of the vernacular and of a new sense of an inner self in twelfth-century narrative are not only parallel but also interrelated events, predominantly because both are spatial phenomena. Particularly relevant to my reading of Galbert here is Spence's remark that "the irruption of the subjective present is possible as soon as space has become the predominant paradigm. . . . It is only because time becomes measured in spatial terms by the twelfth century that the present can take on the dimension necessary for its subjective literary development" (15). Galbert's text is of course written in Latin, not the vernacular, but Spence herself locates the beginnings of the shift she traces in the Latin writings of Abbot Suger on St. Denis, begun about twelve years after Galbert ended his chronicle, circa 1140–41.

12. It is not at all clear for whom Galbert was writing; part of what makes the text so fascinating is that he appears to have begun simply out of a need to write rather than with thoughts of potential patronage—as was first suggested by Van Caenegem in *Galbert van Brugge en het recht* (cited by Rider, "Galbert of Bruges' 'Journal'" 68). On Galbert's imagined audience and his changing attitude toward it, see Rider, *God's Scribe* 74–76 and 192–98.

13. The preface of *De multro,* which consists of the "Prologue" and first fourteen chapters of the modern edition, was almost certainly written at least three months after Charles's death, sometime during the period of relative stability (May–September 1127) that followed the execution of those condemned of his murder and the election, under the pressure of Louis VI of France, of William Clito, son of Robert Curthose of Normandy, to the county seat. The order in which Galbert appears to have composed and revised his work is complex but has been clearly outlined by Rider in his introduction to the text and analyzed in his more recent study. As Rider and others have argued, Galbert's revisions and additions to the chronicle reveal his commitment to shaping a coherent narrative from ongoing chaos; the preface alone, as I will discuss below, is testament to Galbert's desire to create much more than a daily transcript of events in Bruges.

14. Charles was the son of Adele, daughter of Robert the Frisian, count of Flanders (1071–93); Robert married Adele to Canute IV of Denmark (1080–86). See Rider, *De multro* xi and Ross 13, 15, and 81 n.1.

15. §4: Rider 11, 13; Ross 90–93. On the offer to Charles of the kingdom of Jerusalem (in 1123) and his candidacy for holy Roman emperor (in 1125), see Rider *De multro* xi and n. 2 and *God's Scribe* 180–90. Rider also notes the "intimate, physical association between Charles and peace in Flanders" (*God's Scribe* 58).

16. On the order in which the preface and the rest of the narrative were composed and revised, see note 7, above.

17. §7: Rider 17, 19; Ross 96–100. On Bertulf, the Erembald family, and their legal status, see Ross 97–99 n. 5–10; Rider, *God's Scribe* 62–66 and the further bibliography at 239 n. 3.

18. Rider also cites this passage as evidence of Galbert's manipulation of narrative for dramatic effect (*God's Scribe* 127–28).

19. It is, of course, also about Charles's absence; however, we should note that Galbert's record focuses more on what fills that absence than on the void it creates. For example, even the story of Charles's death is immediately followed by an equally detailed and dramatic account of the killing of the castellan of Bourbourg and his sons, deaths given almost as much textual weight as Charles's more politically significant murder (§16: Rider 37–39; Ross 120–21).

20. The most important contemporary record of the murder is that of Walter of Thérouanne, who wrote his *Vita Karoli* at the request of his bishop. Another important source is Herman of Tournai's *Liber.* For parallels between Galbert's work and Walter of Thérouanne's, see Rider, *God's Scribe* (Appendix 5, 221–25); although he admits the evidence is inconclusive, Rider believes that Galbert was directly influenced by his reading of Walter's *Vita Karoli.* Quite a number of verse and prose laments were written shortly after Charles's death; on these, see Smet, "Bij de latijnsche" and "Poésies latines" in the appendix to Pirenne's edition of Galbert's text. A new edition of Walter's *Vita Karoli* and the Latin poems, edited by Jeff Rider, is forthcoming in the Corpus Christianorum, Continuatio Mediaevalis series. In a forthcoming article, I argue with Mary Agnes Edsall that a fabliau in B.N. MS Fr. 837 is also to be included among the texts that respond to the murder of Charles the Good; see our "History as Fabliau and Fabliau as History."

21. On the healing of the cripple, see Walter of Thérouanne §30 and §31 and Herman of Tournai §29; cited by Ross 140 n. 9. On the discovery of Charles's uncorrupted body, all Galbert has to say is that while the brothers of the church had feared that Charles's body would stink when they prepared it for its more ceremonious interment, they smelled "nihil fetoris" (nothing bad) when they opened the temporary tomb and unwrapped the body (§77: Rider 129; Ross 246). Ross notes that Walter calls this a miracle (Ross 246 n. 3). In his "Death from a Trivial Cause," also forthcoming, Stein discusses Galbert's approach to such moments in the larger context of what he calls the chronicler's "direct, conscious, and legibel refusal to read the signs" as they were intended by their often aristocratic authors; I thank him for sharing this article with me in advance of its appearance.

22. Galbert may be paraphrasing a *planctus* actually written by the notary Fromold Junior of whom he speaks here, although Rider posits that the passage could well be his own invention (*God's Scribe* 122).

23. Spence makes a similar observation about the relationship of Abelard's generic marking of the *Historia calamitatum* to its form, remarking that while he might have hoped, through the use of the term *historia*, "to suggest that his story is to be understood against a scriptural background, as with other *historiae*, he soon loses that thread as the story of his particular trials takes over and the text becomes solely and explicitly a space for articulating his own troubles" (57). Rider suggests that Galbert first intended to describe the events at Bruges and then changes his mind, deciding instead to write a *passio Karoli* and revising his initial *descriptio* accordingly (*God's Scribe* 50–54).

24. Galbert refers to his method of note taking and ordering in §35 in a passage I discuss below; on Galbert's use of wax tablets and a suggestive hypothesis regarding his later transference of notes to parchment, see Rider, *God's Scribe* 29–34 and 37–49.

25. On the possibility that the traitors may have been following a Saxon custom of appeasing the dead, see Kervyn de Lettenhove 385–86, cited by Ross 263 n. 4. At two other points, Galbert instead reads the candle the traitors placed on the tomb as a sign that the traitors were attempting to honor their dead lord (§60 and §64). Ross practically suggests that the candle was simply there to provide light (217 n. 8). Galbert's depiction of this scene is also discussed by Stein.

26. For a schematic reconstruction of St. Donation, which is not longer extant, see Mertens (Ross 318–20). Mertens excavated the site in 1955. Also see Rider (*De multro* App. 5) for both a ground plan and three-dimensional section of the church. In *God's Scribe*, Rider refers to what he calls the chronicle's "romance" of St. Donation (139).

27. Murray notes that St. Donation, even before Charles's death, was "keeper of the dynastic memory of the counts of Flanders" (141).

28. For a strikingly similar description of the stripping of the count's castle by looters, see §41.

29. Ross suggests that this sense of personal trauma at the stripping of the church led Galbert to name himself at this point (66).

30. Rider refers to this phenomenon as Galbert's "central marginality" (*God's Scribe* 27). Spence notes a similar simultaneous self-erasure and presence in Suger's description of St. Denis. For Spence, Suger's absence is in fact a telling mark of his bodily presence within the church, a presence which becomes the building's "organizing principle" in the narrative (35–36). Galbert's absent presence in his record, in contrast, is less that of a focal point for a single structure than an overseeing eye that can peer into every structure, including the mind.

31. Ross asks if Galbert's "attitude toward Bertulf begin[s] to soften here" (141 n. 6), indicating that she believes it does. I would argue less for a "softening" than for a shift in Galbert's own perspective—that is, he wants to believe that the provost regrets his deeds, and so he recreates Bertulf in that image. However, I would argue that that shift does not begin here, but in §38, which I discuss below.

32. See especially §8, in which Galbert relates Bertulf's arrogant response to Count Charles's claim against the Erembalds. On Galbert's portrait of Bertulf as a whole, see also Rider, *God's Scribe* 125–26.

33. Ross translates "Et ecce" here as "Consider him now."

34. It should be noted, however, that Galbert shifts responsibility for Charles's murder quite a number of times, at least in part because it was, in the end, so hard to untangle the knotted threads of multiple motivations surrounding the count's death. Bertulf bears much of the blame and is certainly made by Galbert into the text's star scapegoat; see, however, §45 and §113, where the nephews of one of the count's men receive the blame; §70, in which Galbert assigns the murder to the working out of God's vengeance; and §116, where Galbert blames the land and people of Flanders for a deeply rooted iniquity that lay beneath the whole sequence of horrific events (on which see Rider, *God's Scribe* 177).

35. Rider also notes Galbert's spatial approach to human psychology, and points to these phrases, among others, as evidence for that approach (*God's Scribe* 120–24 and 288 n. 27). On the medieval understanding of human memory as a spatial system, see the now-standard work on the subject by Carruthers.

36. Crucifixion was a rare method of execution in medieval Europe despite its innumerable depictions in medieval art; however, it did occasionally occur. For the suggestion that Bertulf was indeed crucified on the order of the King of France, see Merback 198 and references. Rider discusses the relationship of this depiction of Bertulf's death to the Gospel accounts of the crucifixion of Christ in *God's Scribe* 108–11. As Rider notes, Galbert may have been influenced by Walter of Thérouanne's more explicit reference to Christ in his description of this event (§38: 554, 35–49; quoted in *God's Scribe* 111).

37. Nichols, especially 9; cited and discussed by Spence 26–27.

38. There is perhaps another reason behind this dramatic rendering of Bertulf's inward repentance. Fashioning the provost in the image of a penitent sinner works as a kind of textual exorcism of the malevolence Galbert attributes to him and his associates and on which he blamed the (fortunately temporary) destruction of Bruges and Flanders. In fact, Galbert used his description of Bertulf's death as a model for that of the other traitors, whom he shows confessing openly to their crimes and welcoming their deaths in §84; none of these, however, are described from the inside out as Bertulf is. It may be that Galbert felt his narrative had a role to play in the ritual cleansing of evil, working in language a purification comparable to that of St. Donation by its canons and the bishop (§76 and §78). On the medieval concept that the "good death" of a criminal (including the confession of guilt and an admission of repentance) was capable of purging the communal evil that had arisen through his or her crime, see Merback 142–50.

39. Spence distinguishes between writing that adheres to the scriptural model and that which "starts to recognize and incorporate sin and transgression" and which, as a result, opens "room for the self" (14). This passage would seem to fall somewhere in between the two poles identified by Spence, since Bertulf's recognition of his sin as well as his punishment adheres to the scriptural pattern, but Galbert's hesitancy reveals his sense that his knowledge of Bertulf may be relative, that Bertulf's self may be, in fact, unreadable.

40. In a much later chapter, Galbert virtually admits that his image of Bertulf's penitence was fully imagined, telling us, "De ipsius vero pena et non de penitentia quidquam audivimus" (We have heard of his punishment but nothing about his penitence) (§84: Rider 136; Ross 256).

41. Although it is possible, as Rider notes, that Galbert saw Charles's murder ("Galbert of Bruges' 'Journal'" 75), Ross finds it unlikely; she claims that none of the writers of the major accounts of this killing were eyewitnesses to it (119 n. 11).

Works Cited

Bakhtin, Mikhail, and V. N. Volosinov. "Discourse in Life and Discourse in Art (Concerning Sociological Poetics)." Trans. I. R. Titunik. Rpt. in *Contemporary Literary Criticism: Literary and Cultural Studies*. 2nd ed. Ed. Robert Con Davis and Ronald Schleifer. New York: Longman, 1989. 392–410.

Carruthers, Mary J. *The Book of Memory: A Study of Memory in Medieval Culture*. Cambridge: Cambridge UP, 1990.

Cooper, Lisa H. and Mary Agnes Edsall. "History as Fabliau and Fabliau as History: The Murder of Charles the Good and Du provost a l'aumuche." *Galbert of Bruges and the Historiography of Medieval Flanders*. Eds. Jeff Rider and Alan V. Murray. Forthcoming.

De Certeau, Michel. *The Writing of History*. Trans. Tom Conley. New York: Columbia UP, 1988.

De Smet, J. M. "Bij de latijnsche gedichten over den moord op den Glz. Karel den Goded Graaf van Vlaanderen." *Miscellanea historica in honorem Alberti de Meyer*. 2 vols. Louvain: Bibliothèque de l'Université, 1946.

——. "Poésies latines sur le meurtre de comte Charles le Bon." *Histoire du meurtre de Charles le Bon, comte de Flandre (1127–28) par Galbert de Bruges suivie de poésies lataines contemporaines publiées d'après les manuscrits*. Ed. Henri Pirenne. Paris, 1891.

Dhondt, Jahn. "Medieval 'Solidarities': Flemish Society in Transition, 1127–28." *Lordship and Community in Medieval Europe*. Ed. and trans. Frederic L. Cheyette. Huntington: Robert E. Krieger, 1975. 268–90.

Eden, Kathy. *Poetic and Legal Fiction in the Aristotelian Tradition*. Princeton: Princeton UP, 1986.

Galbert of Bruges. *De multro, traditione et occisione gloriosi Karoli comitis Flandriae*. Ed. Jeff Rider. Corpus Christianorum, Continuatio Mediaevalis, 131. Turnholt: Brepols, 1994.

Ganshof, F. L. "Les origines du concept de souveraineté nationale en Flandre." *Revue d'histoire du droit* 18 (1950): 135–58.

——. "Le roi de France en Flandre en 1127 et 1128." *Revue historique de droit français et étranger*. 27 (1949): 204–28.

——. "Trois mandements perdue de roi de France Louis Vi interessant en la Flandre." *Annales de la société d'émulation de Bruges* 87 (1950): 117–33.

Herman of Tournai. *Liber de restauratione monasterii S. Martini Tornacensis*. Ed. G. Waitz. *Monumenta Germaniae Historica, Scriptores* 14. Hannover, 1883. 284–89.

Kervyn de Lettenhove, J. M. B. C. *Histoire de Flandre*. Vol. 1. Brussels, 1847.

Merback, Mitchell B. *The Thief, the Cross, and the Wheel: Pain and the Spectacle of Punishment in Medieval and Renaissance Europe*. Chicago: U of Chicago P, 1999.

Mertens, Joseph. "The Church of Saint Donation at Bruges." Ross 318–20.

Murray, James M. "The Liturgy of the Count's Advent in Bruges, from Galbert to Van Eyck." *City and Spectacle in Medieval Europe*. Ed. Barbara A. Hanawalt and Kathryn L. Reyerson. Minneapolis: U of Minnesota P, 1994.

Nichols, Stephen G. *Romanesque Signs: Early Medieval Narrative and Iconography*. New Haven: Yale UP, 1983.

Partner, Nancy. "The New Cornificius: Medieval History and the Artifice of Words." *Classical Rhetoric and Medieval Historiography*. Ed. Ernst Breisach. Kalamazoo: Medieval Institute Publications, 1985.

Rider, Jeff. "Galbert of Bruges' 'Journal': From Medieval Flop to Modern Bestseller." *Verhalende Bronnen: Repertoriëring, editie en commercialisering*. Ed. Luod Milis, Véronique Lambert, and Ann Kelders. Studia Historica Gandensia Series No. 283. Ghent: Stuclia Historica Gandensia, 1996. 67–93.

——. *God's Scribe: The Historiographical Art of Galbert of Bruges*. Washington, D.C.: Catholic UP, 2001.

Roach, Joseph. *Cities of the Dead: Circum-Atlantic Performance*. New York: Columbia UP, 1996.

Ross, James Bruce, trans. *Galbert of Bruges: The Murder of Charles the Good*. Medieval Academy Reprints for Teaching 12. New York: Harper and Row, 1967.

Spence, Sarah. *Texts and the Self in the Twelfth Century*. Cambridge: Cambridge UP, 1996.

Spiegel, Gabrielle M. "Genealogy: Form and Function in Medieval Historical Narrative." *History and Theory* 22.1 (1983): 43–53.

——. *Romancing the Past: The Rise of Vernacular Prose Historiography in Thirteenth-Century France*. Berkeley: U of California P, 1993.

Stein, Robert M. " Death from a Trivial Cause: Events and Their Meanings in Galbert of Bruges's Chronicle." *Galbert of Bruges and the Historiography of Medieval Flanders*. Eds. Jeff Rider and Alan V. Murray. Forthcoming.

Turner, Victor. *The Anthropology of Performance*. New York: PAJ Publications, 1987. 72–98.

Van Caenegem, R. C. *Galbert van Brugge en het recht*. Mededelingen van de Koninklijke Academie voor Wetenschappen, Letteren en Schone Kunsten van België, Klasse der letteren 40.1 (1978). Trans. "Galbert of Bruges on Serfdom, Prosecution of Crime, and Constitutionalism." *Law, Custom, and Social Fabric in Medieval Europe: Essays in Honor of Bryce Lyon*. Ed. Bernard S. Bachrach and David Nicholas. Kalamazoo: Western Michigan U, 1990. 89–112.

——. "Law and Power in Twelfth-Century Flanders." *Cultures of Power: Lordship, Status, and Process in Twelfth-Century Europe*. Ed. Thomas N. Bisson. Philadelphia: U of Pennsylvania P, 1995. 149–71.

Walter of Thérouanne. *Vita Karoli comitis Flandriae*. Ed. R. Köpke. *Monumenta Germaniae Historica, Scriptores* 12. Hannover, 1856. 537–61.

White, Hayden. "Narrativity in the Representation of Reality." *Critical Inquiry* 7.1 (1980). Rpt. in *The Content of the Form*. Baltimore: Johns Hopkins UP, 1987. 1–25.

William R. Askins

Ʌ Camp Ⱳedding
The Cultural Context of Chaucer's
Brooch of Thebes

Though a sense of space is central to a reading of Chaucer's *Brooch of Thebes,* the current view of the first part of this poem, "The Complaint of Mars," is that it is concerned primarily with outer space, the astronomical transits it describes. Its second part, "The Complaint of Venus," is usually located wherever its readers please, one declaring that it is "artificial" and "unreal," another that it might as well have been made in France. I subscribe of course to the view of Rodney Merrill and others that "Mars" is not an independent poem, that it is the first panel in a diptych, the second, "Venus," and the whole, as the manuscripts and the illumi-nation in MS Bodley Fairfax 16 suggest, a single piece, *The Brooch of Thebes.*[1] The emphasis on the heavens in "Mars" has led many readers to deny that the poem has anything to with the mundane, the world through which the poet moved, to claim that "Mars" at least is but a witty treatment of adultery, a piece which toys with the idea that adultery is writ in the stars. Such readings, however, square with neither the claim of Mars himself that what distresses him "is no feyned mat-ter" ("Mars" 173) nor the ways in which Chaucer's contemporaries responded to astronomical and astrological texts. In his recent comments on Richard II's interest in astrology, Nigel Saul notes that his tastes were widely shared in aristocratic circles, that there was a "ready market" in astrological works among "well-to-do clergy and the aristocracy" which appealed to their desire "to fathom the uncertainties and unpredictability of the times in which they lived" (324–25). These uncertainties were not imagined. They were driven by the vicissitudes of history and, in the case of Richard II, the collection of astrological and geomantic tracts presented to him in the 1390s, MS Bodley 581, opens with a political treatise which, as I have pointed out elsewhere, makes distinct reference to the political difficulties he experienced in the late 1380s (Askins 104–5). My argument is that *The Brooch of Thebes* was similarly shaped, that it can be situated with some precision within Chaucer's world and has its own political orientation, and that it is the Lancastrian poem John Shirley said it was in the notes he pinned to his copies of the poem in the fifteenth century (Brusendorff 261–68). Chaucer, I believe, composed this poem on the occasion of a wedding which took place in a specific place, Plymouth, Devonshire, in the spring of 1386, and it may well be the first epithalamium in the English language.

Framed diptych of Jupiter, Mars, and Venus for Chaucer's *Brooch of Thebes*. MS. Fairfax 16, fol. 14v. Reprinted by permission of the Bodleian Library, University of Oxford.

Admittedly, attempts to read the topical references in this poem have not inspired confidence. All sorts of furtive couples have been proposed as models for Venus and Mars, and these proposals have been marked by egregious fictions and historical anomalies which have rightly prompted a chorus of dissent. However, of these readings, the best remains that of George Cowling. Taking his cue from Shirley, Cowling argued that Mars and Venus were apt representations of the character of John Holland and Elizabeth of Lancaster, the second daughter of Blanche and John of Gaunt. The young Holland was a celebrated athlete and notorious rakehell. He murdered two men before he married Elizabeth and the second killing outraged his half-brother, Richard II, who swore to hunt him down like a common criminal. Holland lost everything he owned and, faced with a sentence of exile, lived the life of the outlaw in Lancashire for a least six months, between July 1385 and January 1386. For her part, Elizabeth of Lancaster, described as a "vivacious adolescent" (Goodman 280), was probably about twenty when her relationship with Holland took a serious turn. Certainly lively and attractive, her voice and her legs were praised by her contemporaries who pronounced her the best singer and the best dancer at the court of Richard II, this when she was in her thirties (Reeves 143; Goodman 364). When she took up with Holland, she turned her back on the husband Richard II and her father had provided her, John Hastings, Earl of Pembroke, and, though this may have happened because her intended, Hastings, was but a child, the child more likely at issue was the one she carried the day she married its father.

Though George Cowling traded in similar information, he mistold the rest of this tale and opened the door to the improbable second guessing to which I have referred. His sense of the dynamics of the Lancastrian *familia* was uncertain, and he was especially unsure about one of its members, the one historical person to whom *The Brooch of Thebes* refers, the poet Oton de Grandson. Like Skeat before him, Cowling believed that Grandson did not arrive in England until 1392 (*Chaucer* 112). But the French poet, as Haldeen Braddy and Arthur Piaget subsequently pointed out, may have journeyed to England in 1369 in the company of those who had witnessed the wedding of Chaucer's first patron, Lionel, in Italy. Grandson first received an annuity from John of Gaunt in 1374, as did Chaucer, spent most of his adult life attached to the house of Lancaster, and, as Anthony Goodman notes, "often attended the duke" (202). Circumstances suggest that Grandson might well be considered a Lancastrian poet and Cowling's claim that Chaucer first read his poems in manuscript in the 1390s is unlikely to say the least (*Chaucer* 112).[2] Confusion about the whereabouts of Grandson also led Cowling to believe that the "Complaint of Venus" was composed well after "Complaint of Mars," that Chaucer frittered away his idle hours mulling over the marriage of Holland and Elizabeth of Lancaster, as if he had nothing else to worry about. This seems as unwarranted as his view that Holland's marriage "surprised and scandalized the good ladies of the period" (110), a charge which is intrinsically suspect and for which there is absolutely no evidence. The tale Cowling started to tell needs to be told anew.

Though modern historians and the Chaucerians who have followed them have tirelessly repeated the notion that the Holland marriage was a "scandal," contemporary witnesses beyond the confines of Westminster do not corroborate this view, not that font of gossip, Froissart, not even the most acid of English chroniclers, Thomas Walsingham. The only one of Chaucer's contemporaries to discuss this affair in any detail was the Westminster chronicler who, as we shall see, was well positioned to know about it. Having noted that Elizabeth was betrothed to John Hastings, "a child of tender age," the Westminster chronicler says that John Holland subsequently "fell violently in love with her at first sight and pursued his wooing night and day until at last his constantly renewed campaign of enticement led to such folly that by the time her father [John of Gaunt] left for the coast [of England] she was with child" (192–93). What is most critical about this description of their affair is the chronicler's own sense of space, his droll note about where it transpired. When Elizabeth of Lancaster was seduced by John Holland, she lived not in her father's house but had been "introduced into the royal court to study the behavior and customs of courtly society" (192–93). She was, the text suggests, an excellent student, Richard's court, a fine academy. The narrative within "The Complaint of Mars" indicates that the lovers worry that they will be discovered by Phoebus and some scholars who have subscribed to a topical reading of the narrative have suggested that Phoebus is meant to represent John of Gaunt. The view that Lancaster, an accomplished adulterer himself, would have been angry with his daughter or her lover has little to recommend it, and since their affair was consummated within the household of Richard II, the comments of the Westminster chronicler reflect upon the Ricardian court rather than the house of Lancaster. It would follow that the depiction of Phoebus in "The Complaint of Mars" is meant to represent the king. Elsewhere, John Gower explicitly associates Phoebus with Richard II, and Chaucer does so implicitly, both of them responding to the king's heraldic paraphernalia, his solar badge, the sunburst (Saul 440; Wallace 257). If John of Gaunt was upset by his daughter's seduction, his anger would have been directed toward his nephew, the king, against whom he held a number of other grievances.

The political crises of the mid-1380s are commonly discussed in the light of the troubled relationship between John of Gaunt and Richard II and the relationship between Elizabeth of Lancaster and John Holland is simply one of its elements. Though he was half-brother to the king and would prove to be one of his most loyal subjects in the 1390s, John Holland's allegiances during the 1380s were firmly with the duke of Lancaster and, in turn, Lancaster was devoted to Holland. Their close relationship prompted Holland's murder of the Carmelite friar, the Irishman who had accused Lancaster of compassing the death of Richard II in 1384 (Saul 131; Goodman 100). Holland's subsequent murder of Ralph Stafford during the Scottish campaign of 1385 infuriated Richard II, not only because the young Stafford was a favorite of his but also because the murder was precipitated by a quarrel between Holland's cronies and a member of the queen's household, one of her Bohemian retainers (Froissart 2: 50). Nor is there any indication at all that John of Gaunt, at his end, was troubled by the liberties Holland had taken with his daughter. Indeed, it was Lancaster who convinced Richard II to pardon Holland's homicide (Knighton 338–39), shortly after the much-delayed funeral of the mother of the king and the murderer, Joan of Kent, in January 1386, and there is a great deal of evidence which suggests that, as Anthony Goodman puts it, Lancaster "had a soft spot for John Holland and rehabilitated his fortunes" (98).

Nor can the marriage of Holland and Lancaster's daughter be dismissed as the inevitable result of the actions of two impulsive, privileged young persons with too much time on their hands. Their personal fates were clearly determined by the politics of the moment. Richard's decision to pardon Holland may have been prompted by his knowledge that soon he would be rid of both his violent half-brother and his contentious uncle since, as the Westminster chronicler notes, on the day he did forgive him, 2 February 1386, it was common knowledge that Holland was bound for Spain with Lancaster and his army (158–61). At first glance, it might seem that Holland's seduction of Elizabeth of Lancaster was an act of defiance, a response to Richard's threat to send him into exile. Something similar might be said of Elizabeth. Like the young man her lover had murdered, Ralph Stafford, Richard II favored the boy she repudiated, John Hastings, took him into his household after Elizabeth spurned him, provided him with a new wife, and then watched him die at seventeen, the victim of a horrible accident on the playing field at Woodstock (*Westminster Chronicle* 408–11). At his end, the father of the bride pulled his own strings, and, when the young couple married, the ceremonies were held beyond the king's grasp, while the wedding party was on the verge of boarding a ship under the aegis of another king, the self-styled king of Castile and Leon, John of Gaunt himself. Lancaster, furthermore, did not ask Richard for permission to marry his daughter to Holland, nor was he given it.

Because Chaucer frequently deals with the issue of marriage in his work, his readers are familiar with a great deal of scholarship which focuses on the ecclesiastical aspects of marriage contracts and it goes without saying that from this point of view alone the relationship between Holland and Lancaster's daughter was irregular. However, rather less attention has been paid to the medieval view of marriages performed without the king's leave. The feudal rights of medieval English kings included their control over the marriages of their feudal tenants and such related matters as wardship and dower, the political aspects of which are the subject of an important study by Scott Waugh. Drawing much of his evidence from thirteenth-century sources, Waugh describes a number of ways in which feudal families resisted the king's prerogatives in these areas, one of which was to marry without the king's consent, an act which could result in fines, forfeiture and even imprisonment (215–18). For the fourteenth century, the marriages of Elizabeth of Lancaster provide one of many illustrations of how this system worked. In the early 1380s, Lancaster purchased marriages for his children from the king, John Hastings for Elizabeth in 1380 and Mary Bohun for Henry Bolingbroke in 1381. The return on these investments in both cases was access to the wealth to which these heirs were entitled, and in the case of John Hastings, John of Gaunt was granted wardship of the Pembroke estates by the king (Goodman 280). Chaucer himself was quite familiar with these arrangements since he had served as a mainpernor for William Beauchamp when he had been appointed custodian of the Pembroke estate in 1378 (Crow and Olson 279–81). However, when Elizabeth rejected Pembroke and married Holland, these formalities were not observed and no such arrangements are in evidence. Elizabeth proved her father's daughter when Holland was executed in 1400 in response to the overthrow of Richard by her brother, now Henry IV. At this point, she promptly married another well-known athlete, Sir John Cornwall, again without license from the king, and her new husband was immediately slapped into the Tower of London (Reeves 143). Brother or not, Henry regarded Elizabeth's marriage to Cornwall as not simply an affront but a challenge to his royal prerogatives, and, in 1386, Richard II would have felt the same way about her marriage to Holland and would have known that Lancaster had encouraged this sleight. It is this political subtext which informs the narrative portion of "The Complaint of Mars," the anxiety and the dread that Mars and Venus feel in the face of "jelous Phebus" ("Mars" 140). If this were simply a rehash of the classical story, one would expect a jealous Vulcan rather than a jealous Phoebus, but, as readers of the poem have frequently noted, the cuckolded husband is nowhere to be found. Vulcan, that is to say, John Hastings, had never consummated his marriage. He was but thirteen years old.

If hard feelings between the duke of Lancaster and the king of England provide a subtext for *The Brooch of Thebes,* its context is, as I have suggested, the crusade of 1386. When Holland and Elizabeth were married at Plymouth in May or June 1386, they were surrounded by the army John of Gaunt had assembled there while he waited for the ships and the winds that would carry them all to Spain, and a fuller sense of his preparations for this campaign sheds light, I believe, on the setting into which *The Brooch of Thebes* was introduced.[3]

Though Lancaster had toyed with the idea of a Spanish campaign for some time, his plans gathered momentum as the distance between himself and the king widened in the mid-1380s. Urban VI had authorized Lancaster and his ecclesiastical representatives to finance this "crusade" through the sale of indulgences. These were first offered publicly in London at the cathedral of St. Paul on 18 February 1386 with the usual sermon and ceremony (Armitage-Smith 305). On the very next day, 19 February, a number of Lancaster's dependents, including Philippa Chaucer, were inducted into the confraternity at Lincoln cathedral, and while Chaucerians have not read this event within this historical context, the confraternity at Lincoln cathedral was dedicated to furthering crusading efforts and it can be assumed that the services were accompanied by a sermon not unlike that heard at St. Paul's (Crow and Olson 91–93). The children of Philippa Chaucer's sister, Katherine Swynford, were inducted into the Lincoln confraternity on the same day, and it is known that the mistress John of Gaunt had publicly repudiated nonetheless lent him five hundred marks for his Spanish adventure (Goodman 116). This event was followed by more like it, for example, the induction of Constance of Castile and her retinue into the confraternity of St. Albans (Goodman 106). Similar fund raising efforts continued throughout the early part of 1386, as is suggested by the mention in *The Westminster Chronicle* of the pilgrimages undertaken by John of Gaunt "in the east, south, and north of England" through March of this year (164–65).

Philippa Chaucer's involvement with the Lancastrian crusade did not end, I would argue, with the ceremonies at Lincoln. In the spring of 1386, Lancaster seems to have believed that he would spend the rest of his life ruling Spain. At Plymouth, he gathered not only his soldiers but also artisans, embroiderers, and minstrels. A number of well-wishers and family members, including Henry Bolingbroke, also traveled to Plymouth, returning to their bailiwicks once the anchors were raised. With Lancaster went all the women in his *familia:* his wife, Constance of Castile, their daughter, Catherine, his daughters by Blanche, Philippa as well as the newly wed Elizabeth, and Blanche Morieux, the illegitimate daughter he had had with one his *domicellae,* Marie de Saint Hilaire (Armitage-Smith 459–60). There is no doubt that these women took with them their *domicellae,* and, as I will explain, good reason to believe that Philippa Chaucer was among them. For the voyage to Spain, Constance and her household required a separate ship, a ship of their own (Froissart 2: 166), and when they reached their destination, according to the chronicler of St. Denys, it would appear that Elizabeth, pregnant when she married Holland at Plymouth, delivered a still-born daughter, this but the beginning of the horrors Lancaster's retinue would encounter in Spain (Armitage-Smith 459).[4]

In the course of describing Lancaster's movements through Spain, continental chroniclers like Froissart and Fernao Lopes continually take notice of the women who accompanied him and their *domicellae.* Froissart notes that when Lancaster and his entourage first moved to their headquarters at Santiago da Compostella, the women who were with him and their *demoiselles* rode in his van, surrounded, he says, by "four hundred spears" (2: 172). Thereafter, there are frequent references to Constance of Castile and her train moving across northern Spain or riding to Portugal to celebrate the marriage of Philippa of Lancaster to its king.[5] When they were not with Lancaster, the women stayed wherever John of Gaunt was headquartered at the moment, guarded, says Froissart, by an old friend of Geoffrey Chaucer, Lewis Clifford (2: 222). More typically, however, they traveled with the army and they were with it when Lancaster's crusade stopped dead in its tracks in May 1387, undone not by Spanish schismatics but by dysentery and plague (Goodman 126). With hundreds of his men dying, Lancaster, himself ill, disbanded his army and, according to the Portuguese chronicler Lopes, also dismissed his wife's *domicellae,* replacing them with Spanish women. The *domicellae,* Lopes continues, then attempted to leave Spain by land, traveling across the country with John Holland and Elizabeth of Lancaster, through the Pyrenees to Bayonne (Lopes 282–83; Goodman 140–41). This long march was itself an ordeal, and according to Froissart, hundreds more died along the way (2: 290–91). John Holland and Elizabeth of Lancaster survived, but if Philippa Chaucer was with them, she did not.

Despite the evidence that Constance of Castile's household accompanied her to Spain and despite Anthony Goodman's note that Philippa Chaucer was close to the duchess and the most highly paid of her *domicellae* (363), Chaucer's biographers have insisted that she was not with Constance in the spring of 1386, that she lived with Katherine Swynford at Kettlethorpe, Lincolnshire (Howard 341; Pearsall 141). As always, there is the question of evidence. According to both Donald Howard and Derek Pearsall, the warrant for the claim that Philippa

Chaucer resided at Kettlethorpe is a single reference to the payment of her annuity for 1378–79 through Lancaster's receiver, the sheriff of Lincoln. However, as Crow and Olson note (88), she could have been living at one of Lancaster's Lincolnshire manors, and, were Philippa with Katherine, it seems odd that she would have subsequently received New Year's gifts along with the rest of the Lancastrian *domicellae* in 1380, 1381, and 1382. Furthermore, it should be noted that during the season in question, the spring of 1386, both Philippa and her husband received their annuities on 22 June, not from a Lancastrian official in Lincolnshire but from one of John of Gaunt's lawyers, William Barwell, the sheriff of Worcestershire (Crow and Olson 78). It would appear, then, that Philippa Chaucer had journeyed west. That she had done so with Lancaster's retinue is indicated by the sense of Gaunt's itinerary, provided by the Westminster chronicler, who remarks that "on 25 March this year [1386] the duke of Lancaster . . . set out for the west and after visits to holy places in the area fetched up at Plymouth" (164–65). Philippa, then, would have passed through Devonshire with John of Gaunt's household, riding by the banks of the river Plym to its mouth, her husband, the poet, in tow.

Geoffrey Chaucer was at this point in his life certainly free to accompany his wife to Plymouth. His duties at the port of London were in the hands of deputies, and his absence from his post there in the spring of 1386 is reflected in several records which specifically indicate, first, that accounts from the port of London had not been received when they were due, 30 April 1386, and, second, that the poet's name had been omitted from these same accounts when they were returned to the Exchequer on 26 June (Crow and Olson 239–40).[6] Chaucer had also served as justice of the peace in Kent since 1385, but once more there is a break in his service, indeed, the only break in his service, between April and September of this same year (Crow and Olson 355). When the April sessions of the peace commission in Kent concluded, Chaucer received a prest or advance on his annuity from the Crown, travel funds perhaps, perhaps a sign that he anticipated not having access to his usual sources of income (Crow and Olson 119–20). During the months of May and June 1386, while Gaunt and his retinue milled about Plymouth, there is no record which indicates Chaucer was in London or Kent and no reason to believe that he was not at Plymouth, perhaps to bid his wife farewell, perhaps to play the role he played at the beginning and end of his artistic career, that of the Lancastrian poet. There he would have also taken leave of his oldest son, Thomas Chaucer, then in his late teens or early twenties, one of the many young men who took up Gaunt's crusade (Roskell 3: 153), what one chronicler called "the bloom of the nation's chivalric youth" (Usk 14–15).

My claim, then, is that if readers of "Mars" must follow the stars, they need consider too the paths of those who once walked the earth and gathered at Plymouth in the spring of 1386. The available evidence suggests that Geoffrey Chaucer as well as his wife and son witnessed the wedding of Holland and Lancaster's daughter and that afterward wife and son sailed to Spain. If this were the case, then this was the last time Chaucer saw his wife alive, a possibility which may or may not underscore the anxiety which marks the separation of Mars and Venus described in *The Brooch of Thebes*. It more certainly lends a note of pathos to the seemingly gratuitous remark Chaucer makes in the envoy to this poem, the claim that he has grown old ("Venus" 76), a response in keeping with the prospect of his son's doing what he had himself done twenty years earlier, journey to Spain. What is absolutely certain is that the annuity to Philippa Chaucer stopped in the summer of 1387 (Crow and Olson 83–84), and the context for this, as I have noted, is provided by Armitage-Smith, who remarks that "after the deadly summer of 1387 many a well-known name falls out of the roll-call of the Lancastrian retinue" (326). Though the implications of Philippa Chaucer's death in Spain might call for a separate chapter and I have no wish to summon up the specter of psycho-analysis, common sense, I submit, suggests that the death of a man's wife in a far-away place would affect him differently than the immediate experience of it, and that the loss of his wife in such a manner might help explain the attention Chaucer would subsequently pay to women and marriage in *The Legend of Good Women* and *The Canterbury Tales,* texts she may haunt, the presence, as it were, of an absence.[7]

To return to the list of guests at the Holland wedding, there is again the matter of Oton de Grandson. Though Grandson returned to his native Savoy in 1386 on the news of his father's death, his father died on 10 July, the day after Gaunt left England, and it is not unlikely that he too could have witnessed the marriage of Lancaster's daughter that spring and that he would have heard first hand the homage Chaucer pays him in the poem in question. That he might have participated in the ceremonies himself, assisted perhaps by Lancaster's minstrels, is nothing more than a wicked guess, but at least it is not implausible. The season certainly witnessed several written tributes to John of Gaunt. Despite the murder of the Carmelite friar by Holland in 1384, the Carmelites, led by Lancaster's confessor, Walter Diss, were the strongest ecclesiastical supporters of his crusade and pro-vided headquarters for him at their house in Plymouth while he readied his army (Armitage-Smith 306–7). It was there that the Carmelites might have presented to Lancaster the *Kalendarium* dedicated to him and composed by one of their own, Nicholas of Lynn, a text which, as is well known, Chaucer read.[8] A second text prepared in anticipation of Lancaster's crusade was the *Life of the Black Prince* by the Chandos Herald, then attached to the household of John of Gaunt's youngest brother, Thomas of Woodstock (Herald of Sir John Chandos liv). After describing how the Black Prince and his army gathered at Plymouth before the invasion of France in 1355, this poem dwells on the Iberian campaign of 1366, events which transpired twenty years before the poem's composition. Because it exaggerates the role the young John of Gaunt played in that campaign and because it refers specifically to a crusade, J. J. N. Palmer has argued convincingly that it was a piece of propaganda expressly written for the crusade of 1386, for the return of John of Gaunt to the Iberian peninsula. The Chandos Herald had of course participated in the Spanish campaign of 1366–67, and so had Geoffrey Chaucer. It might be said that *The Brooch of Thebes* bears witness to these "Lancastrian" texts, all of them in circulation by 1386, and that it echoes them all: the plaintive Valentine poems of Grandson, the *Kalendarium* and its technical vocabulary, the *Life of the Black Prince* and its formulaic chivalric language.

There are of course a number of chronological issues raised by reading Chaucer's complaints within the context of Lancaster's stay at Plymouth in the spring of 1386. As to the year, Johnstone Parr and Nancy Ann Holtz have argued that the astronomical transits described in "Mars" clearly refer to the skies of 1385, but they have also cautioned that it does not follow that "Mars" was necessarily composed in that year. Others, Hamilton Smyser, for example, have been less certain about the astronomical "data" in the poem, and scholars like J. D. North (142) and Henry Angsar Kelly (125) contend that the poem was composed in 1386. As to the day, the commonplace that the poem was designed to celebrate Valentine's Day, perhaps 14 February, perhaps, pace Kelly, 3 May, is itself open to argument. Though the opening reference to Valentine's Day in the poem is unequivocal, the description of the birdsong the poet heard is presented in the past tense, has the distinct characteristic of a remembered experience. When the poet shifts tenses and announces that he will play the songbird ("Mars" 22), it does not necessarily follow that the "solemn feast" to which he refers is Valentine's Day instead of the wedding I have in mind. Too, though recent studies of the relationship between Chaucer and Grandson by Helen Phillips and John Scattergood have focused entirely on "The Complaint of Venus," I would suggest that Chaucer begins to pay homage to Grandson in the *aubade* which opens "The Complaint of Mars," one Lancastrian poet nodding toward another, and that this is another element which binds these poems together. Furthermore, though Kelly's complex argument regarding the dating of Valentine's day is extremely valuable and cannot be ignored, it is worth noting that one of Lancaster's new books, the *Kalendarium* of Nicholas of Lynn, identifies 14 February as the feast of St. Valentine (70) and that when Elizabeth of Lancaster's older sister, Philippa, married the king of Portugal the year following, 1387, the nuptials were celebrated on 14 February (Armitage-Smith 320–21). Within the Lancastrian household, then, 14 February may have been a date of some moment, and given the many years Grandson spent in Lancaster's employ, this hardly seems surprising. It is only when readers assume that *The Brooch of Thebes* is a Ricardian poem that they are required to do a great deal of fishing through astronomical and ecclesiastical calendars. Furthermore, there have been no attempts, to my knowledge, to establish even the possibility that the Ricardian court celebrated Valentine's Day in either February or May. There is a fascinating entry in *The Westminster Chronicle* to the effect that in February 1386, Richard II "at his own expense married some of the queen's [Bohemian] countrywomen to [English] men of rank," but the chronicler does not indicate that this group wedding took place on the feast of St. Valentine (160–61). The entire question requires further study, beginning perhaps with an examination of the Wardrobe Rolls. For now, there is nothing inherently implausible about my own claim that *The Brooch of Thebes* was composed in the late spring of 1386.

The clearest indication that this piece is the occasional poem John Shirley said it was is the poet's suggestion that he is imitating the bird he heard one Valentine's Day. The songbird frequently served Chaucer and contemporary poets as a representation of the court poet, and though later, in a dark hour, Chaucer might have savaged the very idea in his tale of the caged crow dismantled by Phoebus, *The Manciple's Tale,* there is none of that bitterness here.

The clearest evidence that this poem was meant for a wedding is the most straightforward, the vows which Mars and Venus exchange. Hard on the heels of his claim that he will serve her in good times and bad, "wele or wo," Mars avers that he will be "hir treuest servant and hir knight" until the day he dies ("Mars" 182–88). Venus of course echoes this in her complaint, assuring Mars that she will be his forever ("Venus" 15) and declaring that she will "love him best" until her "ending day" ("Venus" 55–56). The image in MS Bodley Fairfax 16 which I have previously mentioned provides a pictorial representation of this exchange of vows, both Venus and Mars holding one hand aloft, plighting their troth. This oath taking hardly seems consistent with the many dark readings of "Mars," readings which have claimed that the relationship between Mars and Venus is ludicrous or undignified. While many of those who gathered at Plymouth for this wedding would have known the tale of Venus and Mars, the classical analogues, as it were, on the day that Holland married Lancaster's daughter, every last witness would have also known that their relationship had been illicit, adulterous in the eyes of the church, illegal in the eyes of the Crown, that the marriage had been consummated well before the ceremony, and that the bride carried the evidence. To such an audience it would have seemed not that Chaucer was denigrating the relationship of Mars and Venus but that he was elevating the relationship of Holland and his bride, associating it with an enduring fiction, fixing it in the stars, and investing this apotheosis with enough light touches to keep it from being overbearing, to humanize it. Too, if *The Brooch of Thebes* does take a backward glance at *Troilus and Criseyde*, as some have suggested, the poet may be revising the tragic thrust of that poem rather than rearticulating it.

But what evidence is there that *The Brooch of Thebes* specifically refers to the Holland marriage? This wedding, as I have said, took place in a martial environment, bride and groom surrounded by thousands of soldiers bound for Spain. John of Gaunt had appointed Holland constable to this army, and at one point in the poem, Mars turns to men he describes as "men of my division" and begs them not to belittle his commitment to Venus ("Mars" 272–77).

I would submit that this is a local reference, that it imagines Holland turning to the young soldiers in his presence and asking them not to take his relationship lightly, a classic bit of wedding folklore, the groom taking leave of his smirking bachelors. Even more important is the vocabulary which marks not only the complaint of Mars but also that of Venus. Because the Holland marriage was illegal, it is fitting that these complaints should be laced with legal language, the vocabulary of contracts. The stanza which opens the actual complaint of Mars ("Mars" 155–62) is couched in the language of the legal complaint, thrice mentioning the plaintiff's "cause" and drawing attention to the "order" or arrangement of the complaint as though Mars were a medieval lawyer, bound to present his petition in the precise manner prescribed by common law. The several stanzas which follow show a similar familiarity with this vocabulary, and, when Venus addresses Love directly in the second and third sections of her complaint, she too resorts to the language of the law. Starting with her remark that it is "covenable" that Love should exact such a high price from men, one hears Venus appeal to a higher "legal" authority, the God of Love, and echo a complex of legal jargon like that which shaped the complaint of Mars, yet another element which knits these complaints together.[9]

On a more general level, Chaucer's poem should be regarded within the tradition of the medieval Latin epithalamium and not merely because it invokes at its beginning, as that tradition dictates, the twittering paradise of Venus. Here, comparison with a more celebrated example of the genre might prove useful.

Readers of Edmund Spenser's "Epithalamium" will observe that that poet specifically rejects the idea that his wedding day should be marked by complaint and that, by and by, he even erases the anxiety of his bride (not to mention that of the Irish tenants whose culture he attempts to appropriate). The fundamental reason for that is that Spenser's piece is a monologue which celebrates his wedding in the tradition of the Greek wedding poem rather than the Latin. The spirit and the form of Chaucer's piece are of course quite different. Marked by apprehensive sentiments as well as a sense of affirmation, it is cast as a dialogue, and it is this central feature of his poem which is rooted in the medieval Latin epithalamium, characterized, as its students have indicated, by multiple voicing, by dialogue and sometimes debate, by the rudiments of drama (Wilson 35–57).

This feature of the poem is also represented by the images of Mars and Venus in MS Bodley Fairfax 16. While they are discrete, the images separated by frames, Mars and Venus nonetheless appear to be engaging in an exchange which breaks the boundaries suggested by the frames, dialogue underscored by the hands they raise, the left hand of Mars mirroring the right hand of Venus. As is typical of the Latin epithalamium (consider for example Catullus 64), the poet then replicates the drama of the wedding ceremony. He begins by playing the wedding singer or master of ceremonies and describes the ecstasy the lovers felt when first they met ("Mars" 29–77) and the sorrow which followed at their separation ("Mars" 78–153). He then drops the astronomical conceit and gives voice to the anguish of the groom ("Mars" 153–271). Mars asks for compassion from the witnesses, "hardy knyghtes," "treue ladies," and "lovers in fre," and concludes his complaint by heralding the entrance of the bride ("Mars" 298), who has been, as it were, offstage. When she appears in the person of Venus, she acknowledges her devotion to the groom ("Venus" 1–24), seconds his account of the difficulties they have faced ("Venus" 25–48), and concludes with pledges to love him nonetheless ("Venus" 49–72).

The poem also acknowledges the presence of John of Gaunt. Whatever one makes of the invocation of Saint John in the *aubade* which opens "The Complaint of Mars," the description of the brooch of Thebes confounds its beauty with the beauty of the Venus and attributes both to "he that wroghte hir" ("Mars" 267). George Cowling's suggestion that this is a reference to the father of the bride seems reasonable ("Complaintes" 409). We notice that this brooch is set not with the emeralds to which Statius refers in the *Thebiad* but with rubies and pearls (or "stones of Inde"; 2.277), and by way of corroborating Cowling's insight, it should also be noted that Lancaster, as might be expected, showered his daughters with jewelry, Christmas gifts, presents for the New Year, pieces described in the household accounts which survive. Because they mention the occasional silver bauble presented to Philippa Chaucer, these documents have been partially reprinted in *The Chaucer Life-Records* (Crow and Olson 88–93). The full text of these accounts in *John of Gaunt's Register* reveal that in addition to the jewelry he distributed on holidays, when it came to wedding presents, Lancaster was partial to rubies of the kind which, according to Chaucer and Chaucer alone, ornament the brooch of Thebes. One of these was presented to Elizabeth herself on the occasion of what the document calls her "marriage" at Kenilworth in 1380, this her betrothal to John Hastings (152). The same document mentions gifts to the minstrels and heralds who were present at that ceremony as well as gifts to the poet Grandson and even John Holland. An entry in the register for 1381 indicates that Lancaster also presented jewelry set with rubies to Mary de Bohun when that child was married to his son, Henry Bolingbroke, the year after Elizabeth's betrothal (179). The household accounts for 1386 have not survived, but if they had, something like the brooch of Thebes might be mentioned in them, and while readers might object that the consideration of such mean documents is inimical to the reading of poetry, might object that the claim that this poem is an occasional piece strips the work of any meaning, save for those long dead who, one summer's evening in 1386, sailed past the Eddystone Rocks, it seems to me that the opposite might be true, that it is only by examining as carefully as we can the space into which a poem is introduced that we can begin to see what it is that art celebrates: the significance of the lives of individuals, the forces which shaped their fates, the roads they traveled, the trinkets they clutched, vows broken and kept.

Notes

1. Though convention dictates the citation of the text in *The Riverside Chaucer,* I prefer the presentation of the text in the edition of John Hurt Fisher (Chaucer 683–89) and have cited this edition instead. The line numbers in both editions are in any case the same and I have referred to the texts separately as "Mars" and "Venus" in keeping with the practice of all editors. The illustration to this poem in MS Bodley Fairfax 16 to which I several times refer is also reproduced in Brusendorff (plate 3). I am grateful to Robert W. Hanning, Sandra Pierson Prior, Robert Stein, Sealy Gilles, Joan Haahr, and Ann Schotter for providing me with an audience for this paper, one evening at Columbia University, and grateful too to Lisa Ransom Askins and Edward McGinley for having taken this poem to heart and exchanged their own vows.

2. Readers might look askance at my suggestion that Oton de Grandson was a Lancastrian poet, especially since Anthony Goodman has recently said that "there is no evidence that any of his poems were written for the duke" (37). His own evidence for this claim, as it turns out, is Haldeen Braddy's monograph on the poet, a source which deserves to be regarded with skepticism at the least (Kelly 65). Whether or not one accepts the notion that the "Isabel" whose name is frequently stitched into Grandson's Valentine poem refers to Lancaster's sister-in-law, Isabella Langley (Braddy 72–79), Grandson was associated with the house of Lancaster for more than twenty years and the recipient of a generous annuity from John of Gaunt, not to mention an array of gifts. Specific texts like "La complainte de lan nouvel" could very well have been composed for the lavish celebrations with which Lancaster greeted the New Year, especially when the poem is marked, as this one is, by intertextual references to Chaucer's *Book of the Duchess* (Braddy 57–61; Wimsatt 87). The plain truth is that the relationship between Grandson and the Lancastrian *familia* has never been studied with care, that Braddy's monograph is riddled with error, that Arthur Piaget's

study was driven by a great deal of jingoism, and that the sheer quantity of evidence available warrants a fresh appraisal of the question.

3. Nigel Saul claims that Elizabeth and Holland were married 24 June 1386, two weeks before Lancaster sailed to Spain (149). While there is nothing implausible about this date, Saul offers no evidence for it and he may have confused the date of her wedding to Holland with that of her betrothal to Pembroke: 24 June 1380.

4. Anthony Goodman speculates that it was Constance of Castile who gave birth to a daughter when Lancaster's ships landed in Spain but admits that there is no evidence to corroborate his claim (126). The view of Armitage-Smith that the child at issue was his granddaughter by Elizabeth seems more defensible and independent authorities attest to her pregnancy.

5. For references to these *domicellae* in Spain, see Froissart 2: 166, 2: 171, 2: 221, 2: 223–24, 2: 291 and Lopes 224–37, 244–45, 282.

6. In his valuable essay on Chaucer's work at the custom house, Thomas Garbaty says that Chaucer personally testified to the accuracy of its accounts "even in 1384–1386" (98), but this is not true for the spring of 1386.

7. Though I once shared my sense of the circumstances surrounding the death of Philippa Chaucer with one of the poet's biographers, he rejected the idea and I might have abandoned it myself had I not stumbled across the several papers which Jesús Luis Serrano Reyes has published on his web site. This scholar's claims about the Chaucers in Spain are based on *The Chaucer Life-Records* and, for the most part, the chronicle of Pedro Lopez de Ayala, and while I am skeptical of some of them, the independent evidence I have cited corroborates his claim that Philippa died in Spain, a view with which I agree for reasons I hope are not entirely self-serving.

8. Though he agrees that it was composed in 1386, Sigmund Eisner asserts that Nicholas of Lynn worked on the *Kalendarium* after Lancaster went to Spain (2). He offers no evidence that this was the case, and if Lancaster did not see the text until he returned to England in 1389, the dedication of the book to the "King of Castile and Leon" and the text itself would have been terribly out of date.

9. Some but by no means all of the legal vocabulary in the complaints of Mars and Venus is discussed in Alford under the appropriate entries for the following terms in the "Complaint of Mars": "cause" (158), "pleyn" (158), "reherse" (162), "depraven" (207), and "chevise" (289). And in "The Complaint of Venus": "covenable" (25), "resonable" (35), "ordynaunce" (38), "fraunchise" (59), and "assay" (62).

Works Cited

Alford, John. *Piers Plowman: A Glossary of Legal Diction*. Woodbridge: D. S. Brewer, 1988.

Armitage-Smith, Sydney. *John of Gaunt*. London: Constable, 1905.

Askins, William. "The Tale of Melibee and the Crisis at Westminster: November 1387." *Studies in the Age of Chaucer: Proceedings* 2 (1986): 103–12.

Braddy, Haldeen. *Chaucer and the French Poet Graunson*. Port Washington: Kennikat, 1968.

Brusendorff, Aage. *The Chaucer Tradition*. Oxford: Clarendon, 1925.

Chaucer, Geoffrey. *The Complete Poetry and Prose of Geoffrey Chaucer*. Ed. John Hurt Fisher. New York: Holt, 1989.

Cowling, George H. *Chaucer*. London: Methuen, 1927.

———. "Chaucer's Complaintes of Mars and of Venus." RES 2 (1926): 405–10.

Crow, Martin, and Clair Olson, eds. *The Chaucer Life-Records*. Oxford: Clarendon, 1966.

Froissart, Jean. *Chronicles*. Trans. by Thomas Johnes. 2 vols. London: Bohn, 1857.

Garbaty, Thomas J. "Chaucer, Customs and the Hainault Connection." *Studies in the Age of Chaucer: Proceedings* 2 (1986): 95–102.

Goodman, Anthony. *John of Gaunt: The Exercise of Princely Power in Fourteenth-Century England*. London: Longman, 1992.

The Herald of Sir John Chandos. *Life of the Black Prince*. Ed. Mildred Pope and Eleanor Lodge. Oxford: Clarendon, 1910.

Howard, Donald. *Chaucer: His Life, His Works, His World.* New York: Dutton, 1987.

John of Gaunt's Register: 1379–1383. Ed. Eleanor Lodge and Robert Somerville. 2 vols. London: Camden Society, 1937.

Kelly, Henry Angsar. *Chaucer and the Cult of Saint Valentine.* Leiden: Brill, 1986.

[Knighton, Henry]. *Knighton's Chronicle: 1337–1396.* Ed. and trans. G. H. Martin. Oxford: Clarendon, 1995

Lopes, Fernao. *The English in Portugal: 1367–87.* Trans. Derek W. Lomax and R. J. Oakley. Warminster: Aris and Phillips, 1988.

Merrill, Rodney. "Chaucer's Broche of Thebes: The Unity of The Complaint of Mars and The Complaint of Venus." *Literary Monographs* 5 (1973): 3–61.

Nicholas of Lynn. *Kalendarium.* Ed. Sigmund Eisner. Athens: U of Georgia P, 1980.

North, J. D. "Kalenderes Enlumyned Ben They." *Review of English Studies* n.s. 20 (1969): 131–54.

Palmer, J. J. N. "Froissart et le Heraut Chandos." *Le Moyen Age 88* (1982): 271–92.

Parr, Johnstone, and Nancy Ann Holtz. "The Astronomy-Astrology in Chaucer's The Complaint of Mars." *Chaucer Review* 15 (1981): 255–66.

Pearsall, Derek. *The Life of Geoffrey Chaucer.* Oxford: Blackwell, 1992.

Phillips, Helen. "The Complaint of Venus: Chaucer and de Graunson." *Medieval Translator* 4 (1994): 86–103.

Piaget, Arthur. *Oton de Grandson.* Lausanne: Société d'histoire de la Suisse Romande, 1941.

Reeves, A. C. *Lancastrian Englishmen.* Washington, D.C.: UP of America, 1981.

Roskell, J. S. *Parliament and Politics in Late Medieval England.* 3 vols. London: Hambledon, 1983.

Saul, Nigel. *Richard II.* New Haven: Yale UP, 1997.

Scattergood, John. "Chaucer's Complaint of Venus and the 'Curiosite' of Graunson." *Essays in Criticism* 44 (1994): 171–89.

Serrano Reyes, Jesús Luis. *Chaucer and Spain.* 14 Feb. 2000 <http://jlserrano@arrakis.es>.

Smyser, Hamilton. "A View of Chaucer's Astronomy." *Speculum* 45 (1970): 359–73.

Usk, Adam. *The Chronicle of Adam Usk: 1377–1421.* Ed. and trans. C. Given-Wilson. Oxford: Clarendon, 1997.

Wallace, David. *Chaucerian Polity.* Stanford: Stanford UP, 1997.

Waugh, Scott L. *The Lordships of England: Royal Wardships and Marriages in English Society and Politics, 1217–1327.* Princeton: Princeton UP, 1988.

The Westminster Chronicle, 1381–1394. Ed. and trans. L. C. Hector and Barbara F. Harvey. Oxford: Clarendon, 1982.

Wilson, E. Faye. "Pastoral and Epithalamium in Latin Literature." *Speculum* 33 (1948): 35–57.

Wimsatt, James. *Chaucer and the Poems of "Ch."* Bury St. Edmunds: D. S. Brewer, 1982.

Lawrence Warner

𝕬dventurous Custance
St. Thomas of Acre and Chaucer's
Man of Law's Tale

*From the new triumph of the new martyr
himself, the Church now gives new thanks.*

**—Bosham 1412: sermon on
Becket's feast day, 1180s**

*Read all the lives and passions of the holy
martyrs and you will not find any martyr who
wished to kill his persecutor. It is a new kind of
martyr who wishes to kill another.*

—Liber de poenitentia 213: 893

The last decades of the twelfth century in Western Christendom witnessed a fundamentally new conception of the act of sacrifice that was at the heart of their faith, according to which Christ's passion established the model of martyrdom by which future saints could achieve their bliss. Herbert de Bosham's celebration of his mentor St. Thomas of Canterbury's new martyrdom appears as nothing more than an identification of Becket's actions as ritualistic in nature, new in history but ancient in signification. But the spread of the archbishop's legends in the decades following his martyrdom in 1170 and canonization in 1173 was attended by the development of another new form of martyrdom for the cause, of which his example was quickly appropriated. This is the creation of the "crusade martyr," who no longer passively suffers for the faith but goes down fighting, and killing, and about whom the Benedictine author of the second epigraph above, writing in about 1190, is so dismayed.[1]

At precisely this moment, the "newness" of Thomas's martyrdom dovetailed with the "new kind of martyrdom" lamented by the Benedictine moralist, for Becket was called into the service of the Third Crusade in the Far East, most prominently in the form of the Order of St. Thomas of Acre. Chroniclers attributed the founding of this crusading order to either Henry II, who took the cross as part of his penance for the murder of Becket, or Richard I, who was saved, by an apparition of St. Thomas, from shipwreck as he arrived in the Holy Land for the crusade of 1190 (Forey; Watney 1–9). Knowledge of this is crucial to our understanding of the cult of Becket in Chaucer's London, the focus of this chapter, for in 1227 Becket's sister granted the order the site of his birthplace on the Cheap, which remained the Church of St. Thomas of Acre (or Acon) and "one of the most celebrated religious institutions in London" (Robertson 139) until the Reformation. The military aspects of the Order of St. Thomas of Acre had by then long since been abandoned—it now followed the rule of St. Augustine—and its headquarters in the East had relocated to this London site, whose master was calling himself head of the whole enterprise in 1379 (Forey 502). In 1383, its founding was commemorated by a visitation of Robert, bishop of London, at which the grant of 1227 was displayed (Watney 9), and that same year the rebuilding and enlargement of the church commenced (Robertson 39).

The Christian transformation of holy passion into violent aggression in the later Middle Ages was accompanied by another, similar shift, which would have even broader consequences for Chaucerian historical consciousness, and in which St. Thomas of Acre again plays a major role. This shift concerns the idea of the "adventurer," in the classical concept of which "an individual can be nothing other than completely *passive,* completely *unchanging,*" as Bakhtin noted (105). But a "new conception of the adventurer" arose in the Middle Ages, one with an "essential hallmark that distinguishes it from the classical conception," according to Michael Nerlich: "that adventures are undertaken on a *voluntary* basis, they are *sought out* (*la quête de l'aventure,* 'the quest for adventure'), and this quest and hence the adventurer himself are glorified" (5). The most vibrant "adventurers" of the fourteenth century were no longer knights on a quest, but, rather, the merchants whom Chaucer knew so well throughout his lifetime. What attracted merchants to this ideology of adventure was not only the traditional appeal of romance on the high seas, which they could appropriate in figuring their own voyages, but also the fact that the term *aventure* connoted "risk" or "chance," which they so fervently sought out. Thus Chaucer's friend Gower asserts that the law allows "that he who can lose in a venture (*en aventure*) should also be allowed to gain from it when his fortune brings it about"; therefore we should not blame that honest merchant who wants to risk his money, "son argent *aventurer*" (25,202–7).[2] An alchemist in Chaucer's *Canon's Yeoman's Tale* claims that his peers, like the merchants, "moste putte oure good in aventure" (VIII [G] 946; cited by Carus-Wilson xii);[3] perhaps it is no surprise that Chaucer's own Merchant shows an interest in such risk, having Damian burn so hotly with desire for May that "he putte his lyf in aventure" (IV[E] 1877).

The tensions between passion and action, legendary and new martyrdom, unchanging adventure and nautical risk, are the forces that generate Chaucer's *Man of Law's Tale*. This pious collection of stanzas dramatizes the adventures of both one of his most passive heroines, Custance in her rudderless boat, and the merchants and crusaders who sail the Mediterranean. Its careful rhyme royal form evokes a sense of timelessness, to be sure; but the *Man of Law's Tale* refracts such large-scale military and mercantile movements by means of local and material connections with the Church of St. Thomas of Acre. I suggest that in this tale Chaucer sought to produce a narrative form of *aventure* in which the mercantile and the military are inextricably fused. Through the tale's associations with the church on the Cheap, our poet seeks to identify his own storytelling as a participant, as the martyrdom of Becket had become, in the redemption of the Holy Sepulcher.

While no records associate Chaucer directly with the church, we can confidently place a number of his associates there. At least two of them remain (unless the burial grounds were dug up when the Mercers' Hall was built on the site), for those whose final resting places were in St. Thomas of Acre included (see Watney 174) Richard Goodchild (d. 1390), citizen and cutler, Chaucer's agent in settling the Cecily Champain affair (*Chaucer Life-Records* 346–47), who had made a bequest to the church (*Calendar of Wills* 281; Watney 32), and Thomas Gernon, sheriff, who, together with our poet, was among those granted livery of mourning for Joan of Kent (*Chaucer Life-Records* 104). Among the most illustrious supporters of the church were the Cavendishes, under whose powerful influence Chaucer might well have fallen: the will of Thomas Cavendish, one of many of the family buried there, leaves a bequest to a brother named John, perhaps the chief justice who heard the case of trespass brought against Chaucer by Thomas Stondon in 1379—and who was beheaded by rebels in Bury St. Edmunds during the Rising of 1381.[4]

These were not the only figures in Chaucer's milieu whom we can definitely locate in St. Thomas of Acre. The Man of Law is another. In identifying him as "A Sergeant of the Lawe, war and wys" (I [A] 309), Chaucer signals that Custance's narrator was a member of the Order of the Coif, as it came to be known, the highest order of his profession, from which the justices of the King's Bench, including the ill-fated John Cavendish, were selected. In Richard II's reign (1377–99), a total of twenty-two new sergeants of the law were "created": eight in January 1383, another by Michaelmas 1387, eight at Michaelmas 1388, and five in October 1396 (Baker 158–59). The prestige and cost of the creation ceremonies were enormous. In 1396, the king himself helped procure the provisions for the feast; Sir John Fortescue, in his mid-fifteenth-century treatise "In Praise of the Laws of England," remarks that on the day of their creation, the sergeants "are to hold, among other solemnities, a feast and entertainment such as are held at the coronation of a king, which lasts for seven days" (71; see Baker 99). After the feast, the sergeants processed to St. Paul's, where Becket's parents were buried, stopping en route to make an offering at the shrine at St. Thomas of Acre (Baker 101, 309).

The new sergeants' procession to St. Thomas of Acre was but one example of
the church's service as a focal point of civic London. On major feast days throughout the year, the mayor and aldermen met after dinner at the chapel on the
Cheap for devotional services, usually proceeding from there to St. Paul's. John
Carpenter's *Liber Albus* (1419) gives a detailed account of the most elaborate such
procession, which took place annually when the mayor was inaugurated. After
he hosted a banquet,

> it was custom for the new Mayor to proceed from his house to the church of Saint
> Thomas de Acon, those of his livery preceding him; and after the Aldermen had
> there assembled, they then proceeded together to the church of Saint Paul. . . . They
> then moved on to the churchyard, where lie the bodies of the parents of Thomas,
> late Archbishop of Canterbury; and there they also repeated the *De profundis, etc.*,
> in behalf of all the faithful of God departed, near the grave of his parents before
> mentioned. After this, they returned through the market of Chepe (sometimes
> with lighted torches, if it was late) to the said church of Saint Thomas, and there
> the Mayor and Aldermen made an offering of one penny each. . . .
>
> (Carpenter 23–24)

Of the victualler Perkyn Revelour, Chaucer's Cook remarks, "whan ther any
ridyng was in Chepe, / Out of the shoppe thider wolde he lepe" (IV[E] 4377–78),
so delectable a sight were these ceremonies (see Wallace 183). Langland, too, as
James Simpson has suggested, might have inscribed such processions into his
portrayal of the Paraclete's descent upon Piers and his fellows (109–10).[5]

In the civic imagination, as in the city's geography, then, St. Thomas of Acre
had a place parallel, if not equal, to that of St. Paul's Cathedral. While their physical proximity certainly made the association convenient, "the strong emphasis
placed on the memory of St. Thomas Becket, London's chief citizen, is especially
significant" to these processions (Robertson 77). A sixteenth-century reformist
document describes the sergeants' creation ceremonies as an "old popyshe pyl-
gremage or offringe to St Thomas of Acon in the nether ende of Chepesyde,"
which, its author attests, by his own day had been replaced by simple prayers
(Baker 309). The reference to pilgrimage is not far off the mark. Indeed, if we are
to see the journey from Southwerk to Canterbury as a figure "Of thilke parfit
glorious pilgrymage / That highte Jerusalem celestial" (X [I] 50–51), so too can
we see in these civic processions to St. Thomas of Acre a means of ceremonially
identifying London with the Holy Land, over which St. Thomas kept watch by
means of his English crusade order.

Because they were located on or near the Cheap, St. Paul's and St. Thomas
of Acre had ties to London's mercantile communities that were even closer than
were their connections to the politicians and lawyers. If our Benedictine com-
mentator was unsure about the status of the new kind of martyr that arose with
the crusade, Chaucer's Sergeant of Law is unabashed in his celebration of the new
"adventurers" that appeared in the same era. Through him and his tale Chaucer
explores the material and intellectual connections between the taking of the cross
and the adventuring of merchants. The Sergeant himself has close ties with the

mercantile communities that aligned themselves with the Becket cult: as Chaucer tells us, he "often hadde been at the Parvys" (I [A] 310), a reference to the pillars inside St. Paul's Cathedral, where he conducted business dealings (Baker 101–4; Wallace 197–98). On the Cheap near St. Thomas, an even larger variety of trade took place, for chandlers, cutlers, and spicers sold their wares alongside the more prominent groupings of the drapers and the mercers (Keene 8–9). The church itself served as a site where debts were settled, as in a certain Thomas's agreement to pay two hundred pounds to William of Holbeche at St. Thomas in 1361 (Forey 302). Moreover, many crafts and guilds—the city's carpenters from as early as the 1330s (Wright 131), its bakers by 1382, and the mercers by 1391 (Sutton, *Mercery* 73–74)—held their meetings on its grounds.

This latter association came to dominate the identity of Thomas of Acre, for the annual elections of the mercers' wardens took place there, where the Company, chartered as such by Richard II in 1394, had a hall, a chapel, and a chest for keeping records (Keene 13; Watney 36). And those records, as Linne Mooney has discovered, were written by none other than Chaucer's scribe, Adam Pinkhurst (Mooney 106–12). Moreover, for eight days in April 1385, Pinkhurst was co-owner of a property adjoining St. Thomas of Acre, which was sold back to its previous owners and "later accorded to the Mercers for their sole use within the hospital" (Mooney 110; see also 101 n. 15, 109). Mooney remarks that "it seems possible that Pinkhurst had a foothold at the hospital as well and conducted his scribal work out of it" (111). The earliest records of the fifteenth-century Company of Merchant Adventurers would become wholly mixed with Pinkhurst's records in that chest; indeed, that company's material origins in the church were so widely known that they would be commemorated in the name by which its branch in the Netherlands was often called, the Fraternity of St. Thomas beyond the Sea (Carus-Wilson 150; Sutton, "Merchant" 28–32).

It is appropriate, then, that the Man of Law's subsequent tale of adventurous Custance follows upon a prologue in which he fantasizes that fortune always smiles on the "riche marchauntz" he apostrophizes: "Youre bagges been nat fild with ambes as, / But with sys cynk, that renneth for youre chaunce; / At Cristemasse myrie may ye daunce!" (II [B1] 122, 124–26). Indeed, the Sergeant's fascination with merchant adventuring explains his own luck in having a tale at all. Merchants, he claims, "been fadres of tidynges / And tales, bothe of pees and of debaat"; "many a yeere" ago one brought him tidings of Custance (II [B1] 129–30, 132). The Sergeant's tale thus issues from, and is aimed at, those who would come to be known as the Fraternity of St. Thomas beyond the Sea, those merchants centered on the Cheap at the church devoted to the martyr, most prominent among whom were the mercers.[6] Our narrator further tips his hat to this powerful guild by opening the tale with an account much more elaborate than that in his sources:[7]

> In Surrye whilom dwelte a compaignye
> Of chapmen riche, and therto sadde and trewe,
> That wyde-where senten hir spicerye,
> Clothes of gold, and satyns riche of hewe.

Hir chaffare was so thrifty and so newe
That every wight hath deyntee to chaffare
With hem, and eek to sellen hem hire ware.
(II [B1] 134–40)

In identifying this company as mercers via the reference to "spicerye, / Clothes of gold, and satyns riche of hewe," this stanza offers information not in the parallel passages of Chaucer's sources.[8] Trevet's Anglo-Norman *Chronicle* refers simply to "heathen merchants from the great Saracen land carrying much diverse and rich merchandise" ("marchaunz paens hors de la grant Sarizine, aportauntz trop diverses et riches marchaundises" [18–20]). Gower's tale in the *Confessio Amantis* subordinates, both grammatically and thematically, the merchants and their wares: Constance is so full of faith that she has converted "the greteste of Barbarie, / Of hem whiche usen marchandie" (599–600). Chaucer thus goes out of his way to inscribe mercery into the opening stanzas of the *Man of Law's Tale,* in part surely to celebrate the "adventuring" of the rising merchant class of London.[9] More important, though, this reference serves to call forth to Chaucer's Ricardian audience the crusading force of the cult of Becket, most obviously represented by the name and history of the mercers' home, St. Thomas of Acre.

Before we turn to this violent aspect of the Becket legendary, it is worth noting the clear, if often overlooked, point that crusading is a governing force of the Constance legend, which compels much of the approach of our poet, in particular, toward the Muslims. While Chaucerians have expended much energy demonstrating the ways in which the *Man of Law's Tale* is what the narrator says it is not—one of the "cursed stories . . . / Of swiche unkynde abhomynacions" (II [B1] 80, 88) as those of Canacee or Apollonius of Tyre (e.g., Dinshaw 88–112)—few have treated the fact that, as Joerg Fichte has recently noted, the "Constance story which Trevet included in his Anglo-Norman *Chronicles* bears all the marks of a crusading tale" (239). And merchant adventuring plays a central role in the crusading ethos of the tale. Both Trevet and Chaucer discarded the motif of the incestuous father from the "calumniated queen" tale (Schlauch, *Chaucer's Constance* 62–70), relating instead the conversion of the Sultan via the merchants' tidings of Constance. The account in the Anglo-Norman history, much fuller than those in the tales of his Ricardian followers, firmly establishes the crusading impulse of the marriage negotiations: the Sultan signs a treaty that grants the Romans "free passage to travel freely for trade"; moreover, "he surrendered the city of Jerusalem to the lordship of the Christians to live in" ("fraunch passage do aler fraunchement e marchaunder" [55–56]; "la cité de Jerusalem abandona a la seignurie des Cristiens pur enhabiter" [59–60]). A number of crusading texts with similar episodes could have inspired Trevet to include this account of Muslim-Christian negotiations: the early-thirteenth-century romance the *King of Tars,* William of Tyre's narration of one "Constance" in his *History of Deeds Done beyond the Sea,* or the 1229 treaty between the Holy Roman Emperor Frederick II and the sultan of Egypt, in which, "without striking a blow, the excommunicate Emperor won back the Holy Places of Christendom" (Runciman 187).[10]

The identification of the company's trade as mercery is not the only difference between Chaucer's account and those of Trevet and Gower. The *Man of Law's Tale* also underscores, in an innovative manner, the crusading spirit that his early source had first put forth. These mercers, unlike their literary forebears, remain wholly separate from the Christianity embodied in our heroine, leaving in their wake a violence that issues in the tale's particular crusading energy, directed against all who embrace what the Sultan's advisers call "oure lawe sweete / That us was taught by Mahoun, oure prophete" (I [B1] 223–24). Both Trevet and Gower have Constance convert the merchants, but in the *Man of Law's Tale*, "the commune voys of every man" (II [B1] 155) that expresses Custance's goodness and beauty has no effect on their spiritual lives:

> And al this voys was sooth, as God is trewe.
> But now to purpos lat us turne agayn.
> Thise marchantz han doon fraught hir shippes newe,
> And whan they han this blisful mayden sayn,
> Hoom to Surrye been they went ful fayn,
> And doon hir nedes as they han doon yoore,
> And lyven in wele; I kan sey yow namoore.
>
> (II [B1] 169–75)

Here it remains for the Sultan alone to convert; the "other," embodied in the exotic and sensual merchants, remains intact, venturing off to other lands. Never to be seen or heard from again, these Syrian mercers are constant in a way that threatens the unity endorsed by Trevet and Gower, who make all who accept Constance convert to her faith, and all who reject her die painful deaths.

The Syrian merchants' non-assimilation into Christendom contradicts Chaucer's original source in a way that brings the crusading ethos directly to bear on the Mediterranean journeys of the *Man of Law's Tale*. In Trevet's version of the story, the Christianized merchants are the agents for the Sultan's own conversion, leading to his ensuing treaty with the Romans as part of his marriage negotiations. This treaty, as mentioned earlier, granted Christian merchants full trading rights in the East (as well as access to tourist attractions like Bethlehem and Nazareth) and put Jerusalem in Christian hands. If Trevet invokes the crusading ethos in order to dispel it immediately, Gower refuses even to acknowledge its existence.

Chaucer's approach differs from both of his models. Unlike Trevet, he refuses to indulge fantasies of the recapture of the Holy Land, and by attending so carefully to the Syrian mercers and refusing to have them convert, he aligns his tale with crusading and mercantile energies wholly absent from Gower's tale in the *Confessio Amantis*. Indeed, the hostilities upon which the crusade ethos was founded generate crucial elements of his tale's plot. Thanks to the Sultan's mother, all the Christian wedding guests and the would-be groom himself "Been al tohewe and stiked at the bord" (II [B1] 430), Custance being sent forth to venture (passively, unchangingly) alongside the active merchants at large. In response, her father, having learned about "The slaughtre of cristen folk, and dishonour / Doon to his dogther by a fals traytour" (II [B1] 956–57), launches a full-scale attack on the Syrians:

> For which this Emperour hath sent anon
> His senatour, with roial ordinance,
> And othere lordes, God woot, many oon,
> On Surryens to taken heigh vengeance.
> They brennen, sleen, and brynge hem to meschance
> Ful many a day; but shortly—this is th'ende—
> Homward to Rome they shapen hem to wende.
>
> (II [B1] 960–66)

Here again, Chaucer here draws much greater attention than do his sources to the Emperor's revenge, putting it into the declarative voice of the narrator rather than having the senator relate the episode to Custance, as in Trevet (460–72) and Gower (1178–86). He thus presents crusading as a form of Christian *aventure* that answers the risks undertaken by the Syrian mercers, the "merchant adventurers" who live or die by the role of the dice. Their "tidings" of Custance turn out to be much more adventurous, much riskier, for the Sultan and indeed all the Syrians than for themselves: while the Syrian mercers wander the seas in search of more tales and winnings, the Emperor's senator extends the *meschance* to the entire Muslim people of Syria—no "sys cynk" for them.

Chaucer thus portrays this proto-crusade, as do the chronicles of the First Crusade, as an endeavor guided by divine providence, not subject to the vicissitudes of chance. The wanderings of Custance proceed under the watchful eye of the lord of Fortune: "No wight but God" kept her from death (II [B1] 476), "No wight but Crist" fed her (II [B1] 501), for "The wyl of Crist was that she sholde abyde" (II [B1] 511).[11] She is, as V. A. Kolve so beautifully shows (297–358), the embodiment of the Ship of Church, cast about by *aventure* (II [B1] 465) yet finally having "scaped al hire aventure" (II [B1] 1151). David Wallace, pointing to the Syrian merchants, remarks that "this dominant image is not an uncontested one; there are other ships at sea" (184); his corrective applies equally to our understanding of Custance's own ship as well. For even as a figure for the Ship of Church, Custance need not be reduced to allegory: insofar as she traverses the Mediterranean from Northumberland to Syria, she also embodies the Ship of the Church Militant—now literalized, and no longer merely a reference to the spiritual battles in which Christians engage in this world—that will prepare the way for the Church Triumphant. At the end of the tale, Custance reluctantly acknowledges as much, begging her father, "Sende me namoore unto noon hethenesse" (II [B1] 1112). Chaucer's only other use of this last term, in his portrait of the Knight, indicates that the Man of Law's heroine seeks to disavow a region that occupies a specifically crusading register: "And therto hadde he riden, no man ferre, / As wel in cristendom as in hethenesse" (I [A] 48–49; see Fichte 238–39 on this appearance of the term).

Merchant ships were as crucial to the material history of crusading campaigns as they would be to the tidings of Custance. The commercial fleets of Genoa, Venice, and Pisa "played a vital role in transporting men and supplies to the Holy

Land, and also in capturing the seaports which ensured the future preservation of communications with western Europe," notes J. R. S. Phillips. "Most of the major ports, . . . and many of the lesser ones . . . were taken with the assistance of the ships of one or other of the Italian cities" (44; see also Atiya 169–73). The West's crusading and mercantile impulses were crystallized in the original home of the Order of St. Thomas of Acre: for the century in which it was under Christian control, Acre had been the "command centre of the Latin trade network in the Middle East" (Abulafia 8). This status is commemorated in day two, story nine of the *Decameron,* in which a wife falsely accused of adultery begins her reentry into Italian society at a trade fair at Acre.[12]

Furthermore, this inextricable relationship between the crusade and mercantilism was promulgated in the Becket legendary, in large part due to the presence on the Cheap of St. Thomas of Acre. Both merchant adventurers and crusading leaders, as we have seen, accepted Becket as their patron; these connections were put into powerful narrative form in the popular legend of his birth to a Saracen princess and a London crusader and merchant, Gilbert Becket. Indeed, it might have come into being as a form of etiology, intended to explain to Londoners why the site of the martyr's birth on the Cheap was called St. Thomas of Acre.[13] While Chaucer had no need to rely on this popular story for the bulk of his own tale, it was certainly circulating among those "riche marchauntz" who sold their wares on the Cheap and ventured overseas under St. Thomas's protection. From its appearance in mid-thirteenth-century *Vitae* of the martyr, the legend proliferated in many genres and media: Chaucer would have encountered it in the *South English Legendary* and would certainly have heard it as well from the pulpit, if not also from the mercers on the Cheap.[14]

The tale has crusading overtones from its first words: Gilbert Becket, a good man of London, "took the cross" (*crucem . . . arripuit*) to the Holy Land (29). Although he does so because of a vow of penance and not ostensibly to fight Muslims, this action powerfully suggests a crusading context for his actions, for the term "crusader" derives from *crucesignatus,* man signed with the cross, which the candidate receives via a liturgical rite (Brundage). Subsequent events confirm that Christian-Muslim relations, not just pious pilgrimage, are at stake. Upon the emergence of Gilbert and his serving man Richard from prayer at holy places in Jerusalem, they are taken prisoner by Muslims, remaining in bondage to a certain Prince Amiraud. After a year and a half, Amiraud, having noticed the worthiness of the London merchant, invites him (in chains) to his table for conversation about the customs of the world. The prince's daughter, like Desdemona, is enraptured by the foreigner's tales, and one day in private she asks Gilbert about his religion. Impressed by the passion of his exposition, the Muslim princess declares that she will convert to Christianity if he will marry her, yet before she can ever get a commitment from Gilbert, his companions and he escape and return to London.

At this point the princess takes on the role of Custance alone in her ship, albeit willingly, and in a manner that distances her from the unchanging classical concept of the adventurer: she does not hesitate "to face the innumerable perils of a vast extent of country and of a stormy sea, so long as she might seek for one man, far away and ignorant of her love" (30). Her overriding erotic passion is helped by other adventurers, for she joins "certain pilgrims and merchants who knew her language" (30) who are en route to England, with whom she survives the dangers at sea. Able to say only "London! London!" she makes her way to that city, where "she chanced to pass in front of the house of Gilbert, which was situated in one of the better known and more frequented sections of the city, where now a hospital has been erected in honor of St. Thomas" (30), that is, our Church of St. Thomas of Acre. Richard recognizes her and runs to report this wonder to Gilbert, who gives Richard charge over her. Gilbert proceeds to St. Paul's, where he confers with six bishops, there for important business, about the matter. The bishop of Chichester proclaims that this is the work of God, and that this woman "would be the mother of a son whose sanctity and labors would elevate the Church, to the glory of Christ. The others agree with the bishop in this opinion, and advise that Gilbert should marry her, provided she be baptized" (31). These sacraments are conferred the next day, and that night the former Muslim conceives the future St. Thomas. "On the next day," however, "Gilbert was filled with a great desire to return to the Holy Land"; with his wife's encouragement, "he set out for Jerusalem, where he remained for three and a half years. Afterward he returned and found his son Thomas, a beautiful child, and held in high esteem in the eyes of all" (31–32).

Readers who, like Chaucer (VII 899), are familiar with the Middle English romance *Bevis of Hampton* will recognize its numerous parallels with the legend of the Muslim princess (Brown 57–58). But the *Man of Law's Tale* shares with the Becket legend a number of crucial elements that are lacking even in *Bevis*. First, its startling end: Gilbert's alacrity in leaving his bride the day after their wedding will remind us of the Man of Law's Alla, who, upon begetting a child with Custance, leaves to seek his foes in Scotland, and takes her for safe keeping "to a bisshop, and his constable eke" (II [B1] 716). This romance motif is rare, appearing elsewhere, according to Paul Alonzo Brown, only in *Guy of Warwick* and the later (c. 1400) *Emaré*, another contribution to the fourteenth century's passion for "Constance-sagas."[15] Second is the motif at the core of what Kolve identifies as the poem's dominant image, "The Rudderless Ship and the Sea" (297–358), for in *Bevis of Hampton*, Josian's wanderings in search of Bevis are neither solitary (she is with Saber and the twelve knights) nor nautical (3893–98; see Brown 58). Although the Muslim princess, unlike Custance, achieves a desired destination, their journeys in the Mediterranean have much in common: both rely on merchants as conduits of the respective maidens and both enable a constancy lavishly praised by their narrators. The Latin version of the legend exclaims, "O wonderful beyond measure both the courage and the love of this woman in undertaking such difficulties and hardships!" (30) ("O mirandam nimis hujus mulieris tam audaciam quam amorem tanta difficilia et ardua praesumentis!" [col. 347]). Likewise, the Man of Law praises his heroine's travels: "O my Custance, ful of benignytee, / O Emperoures yonge doghter deere, / He that is lord of Fortune be thy steere!" (II [B1] 446–48). Such use of apostrophe is typical of saints' legends (Paull); in these instances, although neither the princess nor Custance is a saint, both still represent womanly virtue via their constancy and birthing of marvelous sons.

The third similarity is even more compelling than these motifs, for it pertains to a passage unique to Chaucer's version of the tale of Constance. Both the Becket legend and the *Man of Law's Tale* treat the matter of marriage between faiths by similarly dramatizing a bishops' consultation, a figure absent from Trevet, Gower, or *Bevis of Hampton*.[16] In the Becket legend, Gilbert proceeds to St. Paul's, even before the maiden has encountered him in London, to confer with the six bishops. The Man of Law relates a similar circumstance from the Muslim perspective: having "caught so greet plesance / To han hir figure in his remembrance" from the merchants' tidings of Custance (II [B1] 186–87), "This Sowdan for his privee conseil sente" to learn how he might achieve his goal (II [B1] 204):

> Diverse men diverse thynges seyden;
> They argumenten, casten up and doun;
> Many a subtil resoun forth they leyden;
> They speken of magyk and abusioun.
> But finally, as in conclusioun,
> They kan nat seen in that noon avantage,
> Ne in noon oother wey, save mariage.
>
> Thanne sawe they therinne swich difficultee
> By wey of reson, for to speke al playn,
> By cause that ther was swich diversitee
> Bitwene hir bothe lawes, that they sayn
> They trowe that no "Cristen prince wolde fayn
> Wedden his child under oure lawe sweete
> That us was taught by Mahoun, oure prophete."
> (II [B1] 211–24)

Paul Beichner is certainly correct to call attention to the juridical terminology of *disparitas cultus*, disparity of worship, in the phrase "swich diversitee / Bitwene hir bothe lawes," whose uniqueness to the Man of Law's version of the Constance story "reveals the interest in his own legal mind" (70; cf. Fowler 62–63). But as we have seen, our narrator is interested in much more than the law. He directs his tale specifically toward a body of mercantile listeners centered on one church on the Cheap, a maneuver that prompts him to send his heroine along the routes of merchant adventurers and crusaders, both, from England to the Holy Land. Chaucer, to be sure, does not tell the legend of the Saracen princess. But his focus on merchant adventurers, and his appropriation of the legend's central and distinctive motifs, enable him to imbue adventurous Custance with the holiness of St. Thomas himself, patron saint of mercers and crusaders.

By issuing in opposite conclusions, these two counsels about *disparitas cultus* highlight the tense balance between chance and fate so prominent in both narratives. The Sultan charges the members of his counsel "To shapen for his lyf som remedye" (II [B1] 210), but his efforts at shaping fortune are useless, for the death of every man is written "in the sterres, clerer than is glas" (II [B1] 194–96). Nor do the Christians' attempts to "shape" their destinies (II [B1] 249, 253) succeed: "is noon oother ende" (II [B1] 266) but violence and death for all but Custance.

Yet in the early version of the legend of Gilbert, "it chanced," *incedens* (30), that the Muslim princess was standing in front of Gilbert's home on the Cheap when Gilbert's serving man walked by and recognized her, leading to the bishops' declaration that divine providence has guided her for the sake of the church. Despite their differences, however, both instances give rise to expressions of crusading ideology, which so many propagandists understood to be written "in the sterres" (see Warner, "Sign"). Gilbert, having conquered at least one Muslim (the former princess, who has now been wife and Christian for one day), is able to repeat his journey to Jerusalem, from which he returns to the future site of St. Thomas of Acre to find the future protector of Richard the Lion-Hearted being admired by London; and in the *Man of Law's Tale*, the Emperor's inability to shape the Christians' destiny upon his daughter's wedding leads to his vengeful crusade against the Syrians.

This ongoing Chaucerian tension between chance and fate can be directly correlated to the tension in the *Man of Law's Tale* between the two modes of *aventure,* Custance's classical passivity and the medieval willfulness of the Sultan and the Emperor.[17] For the former mode serves not so much to distance the Man of Law's protagonist from knights and merchants as to suggest that the mercantile-chivalric "adventures" against Muslims are actually the work of the lord of Fortune, of the God "That kepte peple Ebrayk from hir drenchynge, / With drye feet thurghout the see passynge" (II [B1] 489–90)—the God, that is, who had led the mercantile and chivalric campaigns against the Muslims in the Holy Land from 1095 to Chaucer's own day.[18]

Chaucer's Sergeant of Law might have enjoyed a sumptuous celebration upon his creation, but his subsequent career would have been (and still remains) fraught with anxiety (Askins). The Man of Law's reputation today is little better than it was among his contemporary enemies, for critics have been quick to indict, among his other errors, his desire for land: "So greet a purchasour was nowhere noon: / Al was fee symple to hym in effect; / His purchasyng myghte nat been infect" (I [A] 318–20).[19] To be sure, the Sergeant's methods are suspect, but his quest for land accords very well with the tale he chooses to tell and the context in which he tells it. Trevet's Sultan, we will remember, offered Jerusalem itself to the Christians in return for Constance's hand. Because such events occurred so rarely in the Crusades, those signed with the cross had to rely on force in their attempts to take what they saw as their "patrimony." This term already implies a legal framework for much crusading ideology; it is central, for instance, in the consolidation of crusading thought offered by Innocent III, source for so many of the Man of Law's verses (Lewis), in the bull *Quia Maior* (1213) and in the decree *Ad Liberandam* (1215) of the Fourth Lateran Council (Tyerman 35–41).

While the Canterbury pilgrims are not on a mission to free Jerusalem, their "patrimony," from the Muslims, their ultimate destination is "Jerusalem celestial," the city to which, crusading propagandists never tired of asserting, the terrestrial city points (e.g., Mézières 71). Their storytelling contest opens with one told by the sole pilgrim to have campaigned "in hethenesse," the Knight, and in the Ellesmere manuscript at least their first grouping of stories culminates in the tale of a journeyer "in hethenesse" told by a Sergeant (Kolve 364–71), himself deemed *miles* for legal purposes (Baker 17–20). Real-life pilgrims to the martyr's shrine, like Erasmus in the early 1500s, saw among his relics "a certayn leden table hauynge grauyd in hym a tytle of saynte Thomas of Acrese,"[20] an appellation that recalled London-based pilgrims both to the markets on the Cheap and to the Holy Land under siege. The Man of Law, in other words, is not alone in seeking to "purchase," for the *Canterbury Tales,* as many have recognized, is driven in large part by a mercantile impulse (Eberle; Georgianna). The converse, we might imagine, obtains as well: while selling their wares on the Cheap, those among the merchants who maintained a pious idealism could hope that their enterprise constituted a form of pilgrimage. They could even hope that, insofar as mercantilism entailed the stewardship of God's bounty (Thrupp 174–80), it participated in the impulse that sought to redeem the Holy Land.

A desire for healing, both physical and spiritual, drives Chaucer's individual pilgrims to Becket's shrine at Canterbury. On a communal level, such a desire attracted the mercers and men of law to the Church of St. Thomas of Acre, an institution that fuelled their vision of the crusade as written in the stars, so natural an undertaking that it need not be spoken, even if it is a fundamental justification for the journey. Thomas Hoccleve, in a stanza from his rhyme royal "Learn to Die," made explicit some of the paradigms that underlie the *Man of Law's Tale,* the legend of the Saracen Princess, and the journeys to St. Thomas of Acre and Canterbury:

> Right as a Marchant stongynge in a port,
> His ship þat charged is with marchandyse
> To go to fer parties / for confort
> Of him self / lookeþ / þat it in sauf wyse
> Passe out / Right so, if thou wirke as the wyse,
> See to thy soule so / or throw hens weende,
> Þat it may han the lyf þat haath noon eende.
> (Hoccleve 212; see Kolve 349)

This bold simile leaves unspoken the fact that, like the pilgrims seeing to their souls en route to Canterbury, merchants tell tales—and that their tidings can effect a single woman's voyage that makes her so lonely that she begs "Sende me namoore unto noon hethenesse," a region as yet unconquered by those who take the cross.

Notes

1. On crusade martyrdom, see, for example, Riley-Smith, "Death on the First Crusade" (he cites this Benedictine treatise at p. 29).
2. Citations of Chaucer, Trevet, Gower, and *Bevis of Hampton* are by line number. This chapter focuses on the Man of Law and his tale as they are presented in the Ellesmere manuscript, accepting that the appearance of *MLPro* and *MLT* after fragment I, and their link with each other, are authorial (see Blake 84–85 for other opinions). Nolan offers a nuanced reading of this performance that takes account of the textual difficulties presented in this portion of the *Tales.*
3. On Chaucerian *aventure* in relation to commerce, see Wallace 205.

4. On the possibility that the Chief Justice is the "John" in Thomas's will, and Thomas's interment at St. Thomas of Acre, see Bickley 2–3; on the will, see *Calendar of Wills* 149 and Watney 35, 173. The documents relating to the action brought against Chaucer are in *Chaucer Life-Records* 340–42. On John Cavendish's beheading during the Rising of 1381, see Maddicott 61–65.

5. Simpson cites *Piers Plowman* B.19.202–12. The Pentecost procession Simpson adduces does not involve St. Thomas of Acre, but most of the others do: see *Liber Albus* 23–27.

6. Beidler even suggests that these stanzas constitute a Chaucerian request, apart from the Man of Law's performance, for funds from merchants, perhaps read aloud at a guild meeting.

7. Most scholars (e.g., Block) have assumed that Chaucer's most direct source was the passage on Constance in Trevet's *Chronicle*. Yet Nicholson has made a strong case that "in the most significant respects, it is fair to say not only that Gower provided Chaucer's most important model, but that it was Gower's tale rather than Trevet's that Chaucer chose to retell" (171).

8. Gower's mercer hawks "silks, satins, imported cloths" (*Mirour de l'Omme* 1.25,292). The term "spicerye" was a catch-all term for many types of wares, not just spices (*Medieval Trade in the Mediterranean World* 108–14), and mercery in earlier centuries had dealt extensively in "spices" proper as well (Sutton, *Mercery* 3, 3n19, 23).

9. See Thrupp, especially 53–60, 234–87, on merchants' political and social prestige.

10. On the possible reliance of Trevet's Constance story upon the *King of Tars*, see Hornstein's two essays: upon William of Tyre, Schlauch, "Historical Precursors," and upon the 1229 Treaty, Wynn.

11. See Kaske 25–32 on this theme in the *Man of Law's Tale*.

12. On these trade fairs, see Atiya 177–82.

13. See Brown 65–67 on the legend's possible connection with St. Thomas of Acre.

14. Brown 28–37 surveys many of its appearances (though not in drama or sermons). On its appearance as late as the sixteenth century in drama, see Davidson 58–59. My essay "Becket and the Hopping Bishops" discusses medieval English preachers' interest in this legend and Langland's allusion to it, and Kelly has now discussed it as part of his survey of materials relevant to the contextualization of the treatment of non-Christians in works like the *Prioress's Tale*. I cite the legend by page number from the translation of the earliest form of the legend, the *Later Quadrilogus*, in Brown; the Latin is from V*ita et Passio Sancti Thomae*.

15. The sole manuscript containing *Emaré*, BL Cotton Caligula A.ii, dates from the early fifteenth century, and the poem's dialect features "indicate a late fourteenth-century Northeast Midlands or East Anglian dialect" (Laskaya and Salisbury). Hanks argues that *Emaré* influenced the *Man of Law's Tale*.

16. In *Bevis of Hampton*, the hero does seek counsel from the patriarch of Jerusalem (Brown 58; see 2582–84), but her Christening is brought about without any clerical consultation about how to proceed concerning the two faiths, which issue is already decided.

17. On his tale's affinities with the genre of the Greek romance, see Schlauch, *Chaucer's Constance* 75n.

18. On the use of the exodus in crusading rhetoric, see D. H. Green 228–71, especially 258–71.

19. See R. F. Green for one such reading. Spearing (101–36) has mounted a comprehensive and convincing assault on the critical tendency to take such readings to the extreme, according to which Chaucer wrote the *Man of Law's Tale* for the purpose of satirizing its teller: "He was truly interested in the possibility of connections between stories and their tellers, and voiced narratives and unreliable narrators are the ultimate outcome of the process he set going; but we must not suppose that Chaucer in the late fourteenth century could make an immediate transition into the world of the dramatic monologue (or would have wished to do so)" (120–21).

20. This is from the "Pilgrimage of Pure Devotion" of 1513, in Erasmus 169. "The inscribed slip of lead seen by Erasmus was evidently such as it was usual to deposit in coffins, in order to identify the corpse in case it should be disturbed" (Nichols 120–21).

Works Cited

Abulafia, David. "The Role of Trade in Muslim-Christian Contact during the Middle Ages." *The Arab Influence in Medieval Europe.* Ed. Dionisius A. Agius and Richard Hitchcock. Reading: Ithaca, 1994. 1–24.

Askins, William. "The Anxiety of Affluence: Chaucer's Man of Law and His Colleagues in Late Fourteenth-Century England." Congress of the New Chaucer Society. Dublin, Ireland. 25 July 1994.

Atiya, Aziz S. *Crusade, Commerce, and Culture.* Bloomington: Indiana UP, 1962.

Baker, J. H. *The Order of Serjeants at Law.* London: Seldon Society, 1984.

Bakhtin, Mikhail. "Forms of Time and of the Chronotope in the Novel." *The Dialogic Imagination: Four Essays.* Ed. Michael Holquist. Trans. Caryl Emerson and Michael Holquist. Austin: U of Texas P, 1981.

Beichner, Paul E. "Chaucer's Man of Law and Disparitas Cultus." *Speculum* 23 (1948): 70–75.

Beidler, Peter G. "Chaucer's Request for Money in the Man of Law's Prologue." *Chaucer Yearbook* 2 (1995): 1–15.

Bevis of Hampton. Ed. E. Kölbing. Early English Text Society, e.s. 46, 48, 65. London, 1885–94.

Bickley, Francis. *The Cavendish Family.* Boston: Houghton, 1911.

Blake, N. F. *The Textual Tradition of the Canterbury Tales.* London: Edward Arnold, 1985.

Block, Edward A. "Originality, Controlling Purpose, and Craftsmanship in Chaucer's Man of Law's Tale." PMLA 68 (1953): 572–616.

Bosham, Herbert de. *De natalitio martyris die.* Patrologia Latina 190: cols 1403–14.

Brown, Paul Alonzo. *The Development of the Legend of Thomas Becket.* Philadelphia: n.p., 1930.

Brundage, James A. "Cruce Signari: The Rite for Taking the Cross in England." *Traditio* 22 (1966): 289–310.

Calendar of Wills Proved and Enrolled in the Court of Husting, London, a.d. 1258–a.d. 1688. Vol. 2. Ed. R. R. Sharpe. London, 1890.

Carpenter, John. *Liber Albus.* Trans. Henry Thomas Riley. London, 1861.

Carus-Wilson, E. M. *Medieval Merchant Venturers: Collected Studies.* London: Methuen, 1954.

Chaucer, Geoffrey. *The Riverside Chaucer.* Gen ed. Larry D. Benson. 3rd ed. Boston: Houghton, 1987.

Chaucer Life-Records. Ed. Martin M. Crow and Clair C. Olson. Oxford: Clarendon, 1966.

Correale, Robert, with Mary Hamel, eds. *Sources and Analogues of The Canterbury Tales.* Vol. 2. Cambridge: D.S. Brewer, 2005.

Davidson, Clifford. "The Middle English Saint Play and Its Iconography." *The Saint Play in Medieval Europe.* Ed. Clifford Davidson. Kalamazoo: Medieval Institute, 1986. 31–122.

Dinshaw, Carolyn. *Chaucer's Sexual Poetics.* Madison: U of Wisconsin P, 1989.

Eberle, Patricia. "Commercial Language and the Commercial Outlook in the General Prologue." *Chaucer Review* 18 (1983–84): 161–74.

Erasmus, Desiderius. *The Earliest English Translations of Erasmus' Colloquia, 1536–1566.* Ed. Henry de Vocht. Louvain: Uystpruyst, 1928.

Fichte, Joerg O. "Rome and Its Anti-Pole in the Man of Law's and the Second Nun's Tale: Cristendom and Hethenesse." *Anglia* 122 (2004): 225–49.

Forey, A. J. "The Military Order of St Thomas of Acre." *English Historical Review* 364 (1977): 481–503.

Fortescue, John. "In Praise of the Laws of England." Trans. S. B. Chrimes. *On the Laws and Governance of England.* Ed. Shelley Lockwood. Cambridge: Cambridge UP, 1997. 1–80.

Fowler, Elizabeth. "The Empire and the Waif: Consent and Conflict in the Laws in the Man of Law's Tale." *Medieval Literature and Historical Inquiry: Essays in Honour of Derek Pearsall.* Ed. David Aers. Cambridge: D. S. Brewer, 2000. 55–67.

Georgianna, Linda. "Love So Dearly Bought: The Terms of Redemption in The Canterbury Tales." *Studies in the Age of Chaucer* 12 (1990): 85–116.

Gower, John. *Mirour de l'Omme. The Complete Works of John Gower.* Ed. G. C. Macaulay. Vol. 1. Oxford, 1899, 1–334.

———. *Mirour de l'Omme* [The Mirror of Mankind]. Trans. William Burton Wilson. Rev. Nancy Wilson Van Baak. East Lansing: Colleagues, 1992.

———. " Tale of Constance." Ed. G. C. Macauley. Correale with Hamel, 330–50.

Green, D. H. *The Millstätter Exodus: A Crusading Epic.* Cambridge: Cambridge UP, 1966.

Green, R. F. "Chaucer's Man of Law and Collusive Recovery." *Notes & Queries* n.s. 40 (1993): 303–5.

Hanks, D. Thomas, Jr. "Emaré: An Influence on the Man of Law's Tale." *Chaucer Review* 19 (1983): 182–86.

Hoccleve, Thomas. *The Minor Poems.* Ed. Frederick J. Furnivall and I. Gollancz. Rev. J. Mitchell and A. I. Doyle. Early English Text Society, e.s. 61, 73. London: Oxford UP, 1970.

Hornstein, Lillian Herlands. "The Historical Background to The King of Tars." *Speculum* 16 (1941): 404–14.

———. "Trivet's Constance and the King of Tars." *Modern Language Notes* 55 (1940): 354–57.

Kaske, R. E. "Causality and Miracle: Philosophical Perspectives in the Knight's Tale and the Man of Law's Tale." *Traditions and Innovations: Essays on British Literature of the Middle Ages and the Renaissance.* Ed. David G. Allen and Robert A. White. Newark: U of Delaware P, 1990. 11–34.

Keene, Derek. "The Mercers and Their Hall before the Great Fire." Introduction. *The Mercers' Hall.* By Jean Imray. Ed. Ann Saunders. London Topographical Society Publication No. 143. London, 1991. 1–20.

Kelly, Henry Ansgar. "'The Prioress's Tale' in Context: Good and Bad Reports of Non-Christians in Fourteenth-Century England." *Studies in Medieval and Renaissance History* 3rd ser. 3 (2006): 73–132.

Kolve, V. A. *Chaucer and the Imagery of Narrative: The First Five Canterbury Tales.* Stanford: Stanford UP, 1984.

Laskaya, Anne, and Eve Salisbury, eds. *The Middle English Breton Lays.* Kalamazoo: Medieval Institute Publications, 1995. "Introduction to Emaré" consulted online. July 4, 2006 <http://www.lib.rochester.edu/camelot/teams/emint.htm>.

Lewis, Robert E. "Chaucer's Artistic Use of Pope Innocent III's *De miseria humane conditionis* in The Man of Law's Prologue and Tale." PMLA 81 (1966): 485–92.

Liber de poenitentia et tentationibus religiosorum. Patrologia Latina 213: cols. 863–904.

Maddicott, J. R. *Law and Lordship: Royal Justices as Retainers in Thirteenth- and Fourteenth-Century England.* Oxford: Past and Present Society, 1978.

Medieval Trade in the Mediterranean World. Ed. Robert S. Lopez and Irving W. Raymond. New York: Columbia UP, 1955.

Mézières, Philippe de. *Letter to King Richard.* Ed. and trans. G. W. Coopland. Liverpool: Liverpool UP, 1974.

Mooney, Linne R. "Chaucer's Scribe." *Speculum* 81 (2006): 97–138.

Nerlich, Michael. *Ideology of Adventure: Studies in Modern Consciousness, 1100–1750.* Trans. Ruth Crowley. Vol. 1. Minneapolis: U of Minnesota P, 1987.

Nichols, John Gough, ed. and trans. *Pilgrimages to Saint Mary of Walsingham and Saint Thomas of Canterbury by Desiderius Erasmus.* Westminster, 1849.

Nicholson, Peter. "*The Man of Law's Tale:* What Chaucer Really Owed to Gower." *Chaucer Review* 26 (1991): 153–74.

Nolan, Maura. "'Acquiteth yow now': Textual Contradiction and Legal Discourse in the Man of Law's Introduction." *The Letter of the Law: Legal Practice and Literary Production in Medieval England.* Ed. Emily Steiner and Candace Barrington. Ithaca: Cornell UP, 2002. 136–53.

Paull, Michael R. "The Influence of the Saint's Legend Genre in the Man of Law's Tale." *Chaucer Review* 5 (1971): 179–94.

Phillips, J. R. S. *The Medieval Expansion of Europe.* 2nd ed. Oxford: Clarendon, 1998.

Piers Plowman: The B Version. Ed. George Kane and E. Talbot Donaldson. Rev. Ed. London: Althone, 1988.

Riley-Smith, Jonathan. "Death on the First Crusade." *The End of Strife.* Ed. David Loades. Edinburgh: T. & T. Clark, 1984. 14–31.

Robertson, D. W., Jr. *Chaucer's London.* New York: Wiley, 1968.

Runciman, Steven. *History of the Crusades.* Vol. 3. Cambridge: Cambridge UP, 1954.

Schlauch, Margaret. *Chaucer's Constance and Accused Queens.* New York: New York UP, 1927.

——. "Historical Precursors of Chaucer's Constance." *Philological Quarterly* 28 (1950): 402–12.

Simpson, James. "'After Craftes Conseil clotheth yow and fede': Langland and London City Politics." *England in the Fourteenth Century: Proceedings of the 1991 Harlaxton Symposium.* Ed. Nicholas Rogers. Stamford: P. Watkins, 1993. 109–27.

Spearing, A. C. *Textual Subjectivity: The Encoding of Subjectivity in Medieval Narratives and Lyrics.* Oxford: Oxford UP, 2005.

Sutton, Anne F. *The Mercery of London: Trade, Goods and People, 1130–1578.* Burlington, VT: Ashgate, 2005.

——. "The Merchant Adventurers of England. Their Origins and the Mercers' Company of London." *Historical Research* 75 (2002): 25–46.

Thrupp, Sylvia. *The Merchant Class of Medieval London.* Ann Arbor: U of Michigan P, 1948.

Trevet, Nicholas. "Of the Noble Lady Constance." Ed. and Trans. R. M. Correale. Correale and Hamel, 296–329 .

Tyerman, Christopher. *The Invention of the Crusades.* Toronto: U of Toronto P, 1998.

Vita et Passio Sancti Thomae. Ch. 2. Patrologia Latina 190: cols. 346–49.

Wallace, David. *Chaucerian Polity: Absolutist Lineages and Associational Forms in England and Italy.* Stanford: Stanford UP, 1997.

Warner, Lawrence. "Becket and the Hopping Bishops." *Yearbook of Langland Studies* 17 (2003). 107–34.

——. "The Sign of the Son: Crusading Imagery in the Cacciaguida Episode." *Electronic Bulletin of the Dante Society of America.* 16 Sept. 2002. "Paradiso." <http://www.princeton.edu/~dante/ebdsa/>.

Watney, John. *Some Account of the Hospital of St. Thomas of Acon, in the Cheap, London, and of the Plate of the Mercers' Company.* London, 1892.

Wright, Laura. "The London Middle English Guild Certificates of 1388–89, ii: The Texts." *Nottingham Medieval Studies* 39 (1995): 119–45.

Wynn, Phillip. "The Conversion Story in Nicholas Trevet's 'Tale of Constance.'" *Viator* 13 (1982): 259–74.

Imagined Space

Thomas J. Heffernan

"The sun shall be turned to darkness and the moon to blood"
How Sin and Redemption Affect Heavenly Space
in an Old English Transfiguration Homily

Apocalyptic thinkers viewed the unanticipated activity of the heavens as an annunciation of divine revelation, a precursor of impending judgment signaling that God's favor or vengeance was at hand. Medieval Christians, like their ancestors in antiquity, believed that the order in the universe was a reflection of the harmony between god(s) and his people. And disorder was a sign of his enmity (Collins 53). God's favor or vengeance was thought to be a response to human will and action, and thus behavior had grave implications for creation since nature usually shared in the deity's wrath: "on your account the earth will be cursed" (Genesis 3.17; Goodspeed). A common midrash (reflecting an oral tradition that influenced Christianity) makes this explicit and implicates the sun and the moon in Adam's sin, claiming that their light dimmed at the moment of human disobedience (Ginzberg 1: 79).

How was creation to protect itself from such wrath? For Jews and Christians the answer was through the observance of the Decalogue and church teaching. These laws were intended to ensure social polity, seek the favor of God and thereby maintain order in the universe. The heavens were a speculum of the divine will. Thus it is that many of the judgments of God against the Israelites are preceded by heavenly portents (Rowland 23–48; Hanson 10). Isaiah proclaimed that the universal judgment will be announced by heavenly omens, "the moon will blush and the sun be ashamed" (Isa. 24:23). Christianity uses many of the same cosmic metaphors in its prophecies of the final judgment. In Matthew, the sun loses its light at Christ's crucifixion: Ἀπὸ δὲ ἕκτης ὥρας σκότος ἐγένετο ἐπὶ πᾶσαν τὴν γῆν (Matt. 27:45). John opens the Book of Revelation with "The revelation (Ἀποκάλυψις) of Jesus Christ which God gave to him to make known to his servants. . . . for the time is at hand . . . and the light of the sun was darkened (καὶ ἐσκοτώθη ὁ ἥλιος)" (Apoc. 1:1–3, 9:2).

Typically, apocalyptic texts are pseudonymous (John being very singular), and they are frequently eschatological, using antic metaphors that portend the approaching final presence (ἐν τῇ παρουσίᾳ) manifest in creation (1 Cor. 15:23). The final revelation is sometimes mediated by a celestial being with a consequent loss of heavenly light at "the coming of the son of man . . . the sun will be darkened and the moon will not give her light (οὕτως ἔσται ἡ παρουσία τοῦ υἱοῦ τοῦ ἀνθρώπου . . . ὁ ἥλιος σκοτισθήσεται, καὶ ἡ σελήνη οὐ δώσει τὸ φέγγος αὐτῆς)" (Matt. 24:27–31).

There is a further tendency in many eschatological apocalypses to portray the present age as corrupt, as having abandoned the law and being resistant to redemption. The authors of eschatological apocalypses breathe deeply of the air of contemptus mundi.[1] It was not the power of the Adamic sin as an isolated ontological fact that was crucial in the cosmic darkening. Rather, it was the ripple-like effect that sin had on creation, a creation over which God had given humans dominion that reflected the limitations of that authority. A certain few medieval texts even argued that the power of human sin is so great that it could diminish the grandest monuments of God's creation, notably the sun and the moon. For example, the Old English (OE) homily in Bodley MS 343 (homily VI/11), composed for the feast of the Transfiguration of Christ, which I will discuss below in more detail, contains virtually all of these characteristics, albeit using restrained language to develop its argument. While it warns of the wrath of Judgment Day, it avoids the visceral depictions of the end times that we see in other Old English homilies, for example, Vercelli II "De Die Iudicii" of approximately the same date ("the death-bearing dragon and the river of blood / & se deaðberenda draca . . . & se blodiga stream"). Bodley 343 tends to avoid harsh condemnations of the present age (Scragg, Vercelli Homilies 58, 11.45–46).

Although the OE Transfiguration homily does indict human desire as the principal cause of sin, it does so without fire and brimstone rhetoric and sets its critique in a broad theological frame: "þonne sceole we nu forlæten unrihtlicæ dædæ & lichamlice lustæs" (Irvine, Old English Homilies 177). Its most notable apocalyptic discussion that illustrates the way certain medieval English monastics conceptualized space is the homily's theologically bold identification of human sin as the cause of the loss of the sun's original brilliance. For this homilist, the materiality, function and the ordering of the skyscape were part of a divine creation that is anthropocentric and answerable to the redemptive soteriology of medieval religious culture.

The heavens were a part of medieval societies' moral universe (Emmerson). There were no neutral, nonmoral dimensions in this universe. All creation was subject to the effects of human volition by virtue of nature's shared ontology. The natural world—animals, gardens, the seas and the heavens—were ipso facto participants in the moral universe. A garden was at once a verdant green refuge, a reminder of prelapsarian paradise and a potential arena for sin; a deer, a gentle animal of the woodland but, (according to the *Physiologus*) an implacable enemy of the devil; the moon, a transfiguring light that guards from the dangers of the night but whose diminished light is a reminder of the Fall. Since humans are a part of this same creation, attributes of the natural world as they appeared in humans—for example, the use of the metaphor of light/good and dark/evil derived from the sun—were signs of moral worth. The OE Transfiguration homily in Bodley 343 is an important statement of these themes. My chapter is divided into three parts: I will begin with a brief discussion of the manuscript, the significance of OE homiletic texts in late-twelfth-century manuscripts and then present an account of the origin and transmission of the idea of sin and the diminished light of the heavens within a universe where all creation is seen as materially related and moral (see Gameson; Weber, *Scribes and Scholars* and "Script and Manuscript"). Lastly, I propose Ambrose's *De bono mortis* as a likely source for the Old English homilist's trope of cosmic darkening.

I

Bodleian Library 343 is a handsome manuscript (s.XII2) that contains eighty-three Old English (s.XII2) texts and sixty-seven Latin, chiefly dominical and sanctorale homilies for the church year, written in the immediate environs of Worcester by a scribe with likely access to the Worcester Library whose dialect has West Midland features (Irvine, *Old English Homilies* li). Ker provides a complete list of the contents and identifies the known Old English exemplars, including the Ælfric and Wulfstan items (Ker, *Catalogue* 368–75).[2] There are seven unique Old English homilies, three of which are anonymous and likely pre-Ælfrician (Irvine, *Old English Homilies* xlvii). My focus is on the anonymous homily for the Saturday before the Second Sunday in Lent, the Transfiguration of Christ.[3] Surprisingly, for such a late copy of pre-Conquest materials, Bodley 343 contains no original twelfth-century compositions, a situation that appears more typical for manuscripts of this period that contain Old English, for example, BL Cotton Vespasian D. XIV (s.xiii med.) (Handley) or Worcester Cathedral F. 174 (s.xiii1) (Ker, *Catalogue* 271–77; Watson 109).

Although reception is not a principal concern of this chapter, it is nonetheless an issue that needs to be addressed briefly, since it likely played a part in the selection and treatment of the theme. What can we say about how this homily was used? Was it read privately, or perhaps preached, and if the latter, to what audience: clerical, lay, mixed? There are no internal cues in the manuscript that point to its use or specify the nature of the congregation, if any. The manuscript, however, contains two folios where the Old English text is glossed (folios 141v–143v), albeit by a fifteenth-century scribe. The glosses then, while of interest, are of little use in determining the utility of the Old English texts in the late twelfth century. While there is ample evidence of scribal glossing of Old English texts in post-Conquest manuscripts, it is difficult to extrapolate from the extant samples of scribal glossing and generalize knowledge of the language to the population at large, even for twelfth-century readers of Old English texts (Bethurum 116–18,

Cameron 218–29, Irvine, *Rewriting OE* 61). Indeed, it is often difficult to gener-alize from a scribe's response to his exemplar. Such response depended on the individual's training, the nature and the quality of the exemplar, the degree of engagement with the exemplar, a scribe's physical ability and repertoire of philo-logical skills (Liuzza 164).

There is some evidence—albeit drawn from a small sample—that suggests certain genres were viewed and therefore treated differently. For example, a com-parison of twelfth-century copies of Ælfric's *Catholic Homilies* with his *Lives of Saints* indicates that the homily form was regarded less canonically than the "life" and therefore scribal idiosyncrasies were more common in the homily (Clemoes; Godden, Ælfric's *Catholic Homilies: Introduction;* Hill; Scragg, "The Corpus"; Zettel). The saint's life was likely viewed as an item of canonical liturgical importance, particularly a saint of the first grade: a text with a verifiable biographical pedigree and a unique historical context. The homily, however, was understood as a teach-ing tool, a commentary that, because it was chiefly pedagogic and situated in a particular historical milieu, might admit of some emendation to suit the context for a new readership (Swan 81; Proud 130).

Indeed, response even was affected by geography. Certain locations were more conservative culturally and linguistically. Worcester is a notable instance—if we can judge by the number of surviving Old English manuscripts from that monas-tic library—and the scriptorium there appears to have maintained an interest in Old English materials longer than elsewhere (McIntyre 198; Ker, *Catalogue* xlix).[4] Some of this variability regarding knowledge of Old English centuries after the Conquest is idiosyncratic since there was clearly no impetus to continue to write in the old tongue. Bodley 343 with a Worcester provenance has two folios, as noted above, where a fifteenth-century scribe has correctly glossed the Old English text, whereas a bilingual text of Chrodegang's *Rule for Canons* (Exeter provenance), MS Corpus Christi College Cambridge 46, contains a title in a thirteenth-century hand that, while it acknowledges the general usefulness of the volume, minimizes the utility of the English texts, "De ordine canonicorum. Martyrologium. liber utilis exceptis omnibus expositionibus in anglico" (Ker, *Catalogue* xliv–xlix, 75). In sum, it is best to be cautious in our decisions concerning use and not assume a wider currency than the evidence warrants.

Yet the presence of sixty-seven short Latin homilies, chiefly dominical, from Lent to Quinquagesima, implies that, despite the anachronistic nature of so much Old English in a manuscript completed almost two centuries after their com-position, Bodley 343 was intended as more than a museum piece relished by antiquarian devotees (Bethurum 106). The Latin of these homilies is unadorned and catechetical, drawing its repertoire of themes from the standard patristic authors used in homilies of this period, for example, Augustine, Gregory, and Bede. The presence of the Latin homilies, the infrequency of marginal annota-tions, the inclusion of such non–homily like items as the "History of the Holy-Rood Tree," and lack of changes in punctuation in the folios that contain the Old English items—characteristics all present in other twelfth-century collections of Old English homilies used for preaching, for example, manuscripts Bodleian 340,

342 and Corpus Christi College Cambridge 162—suggest, I believe, that the English items in this collection were principally used for pious private reading, as an aid in constructing homilies, and only secondarily, if at all, for preaching.[5] While it is true, as Ker, Cameron, Graham, and others have shown, that knowledge of OE was continuous in England during the Middle Ages and beyond, particularly to individuals like Thomas Talbot (c. 1505–58), their judgments are based on scribal annotations in manuscripts, that is, on an individual scribe's reading ability.[6] Since these are homilies and intended, at least ideally, for oral delivery, we must ask what was the ability of congregations (even granting learned congregations) to comprehend spoken OE? Given the rather substantive changes in the language between the late tenth and late twelfth century, notably in the lexicon and in phonology, it seems unlikely that comprehension would have been nuanced, and the effect surely anachronistic, rather like reading in a modern liturgy from Tyndale's translation of the Bible. Indeed, even if we were to conclude that certain congregations in linguistically conservative areas of the country, like that of the West Midlands, might well understand much of these homilies, it is unclear how an evangelical ministry would have been strengthened while preaching linguistically anachronistic homilies two centuries old? Despite the well authenticated evidence for preaching in the vernacular at the end of the twelfth century, it is hard to imagine an audience or an occasion for these homilies save that of private reading or as an aid in homily composition.

II

The themes of the Bodley homilies vary and are of interest in understanding the important exegetical and religious concerns of the day. Homily VI/11 is a unique Old English treatment of the Transfiguration of Christ based on Matthew 17:1–9, a gospel passage of interest because it is not extant in any other Old English homiletic text. In Latin homilaries of the period, it is usually reserved for the Saturday before the Second Sunday in Lent. However, unlike most of the homilies in Bodley 343 the text contains no rubric that would identify the particular liturgy for which the homily was intended. Cross's suggestion, that the homily was intended as a Lenten sermon, likely for the Saturday before the Second Sunday in Lent, rests principally on those passages in Matthew that were used as pericopes on that day (following a tradition dating from Pope Leo the Great). Moreover, the homily follows the homily composed for the first Sunday in Lent (Irvine, *OE Homilies* 146; Cross 138 n. 17). Gatch, discussing the specific occasion of five Lenten sermons of Ælfric, made the useful point that such homilies with slight liturgical association—not unlike Bodley 343 VI/11—might have been used in the Night or Capitular office, or as a refectory reading, or as a *lectio divinia* (Gatch 54–55; Irvine, *OE Homilies* 149). Lastly, although the Transfiguration was widely celebrated in the eastern church before the eleventh century, it was not widely observed in the West until Pope Callistus III ordered its general observance (1457). In short, while the particular day or the service for which the homily was written is speculation, there is a likelihood that it was originally intended for preaching the Saturday before the Second Sunday in Lent.

The homily is a long (268 lines) subtle treatment of the Transfiguration of Christ based on Matthew 17:1–9 with a marked emphasis on eschatology and the final judgment "domes dæg." The author is learned and capable of fine distinctions. For example, in a brief discussion of humanity's vision of the Last Judgment, the homilist asserts that, while both the good and the bad will see Christ on Judgment Day, the bad will see no glory and joy but only the instruments of torture and his wounds: "Ac þa synfulle men sceolen iseon þa wundæ & þa sar onure Drihtne & þær næglæ swage . . . & nænne dæl þæ blisses." Although the homily is principally indebted to Bede's homily "In Quadragesima," the author, when he treats the subject that we shall discuss below, namely, Adam's sin and its relationship to the dimming of the celestial bodies, departs from Bede and appears to follow an unidentifiable exemplar, itself indebted to Pseudo-Isidore's *De Ordine Creaturarum Liber* (likely the work of Adomnán of Iona, c. 700), Jerome's *Commentaria in Isaiam Prophetam*, Haymo of Halberstadt's *Commentaria in Isaiam*, *An Old English Martyrology* (Herzfeld), and, as I will show, Ambrose's commentary on 2 Esdras (4 Esra in the Vulgate) in his *De bono mortis*. The homily does not appear indebted to Ælfric or his school and may well be pre-Ælfrician.

The most important aspect of the homily, as it presents ideas on the landscape and belief, concerns the intimate connection between obedience to God's law and how such obedience affects nature. The homilist argues that Adam's sin dimmed the light of the sun and moon and placed them in a toilsome orbit. The genesis of this extraordinary notion concerning the loss of brightness of the heavenly bodies because of sin is compatible with a medieval Judaeo-Christian geocentric view of the universe. Genesis is explicit in its argument that humans were created in God's image to have dominion over creation. Medieval Christians believed the proof of that was the Incarnation. Many medieval thinkers followed Boethius's argument that human will and behavior, created and foreknown, yet free, affects the rest of creation through a chain of relationships based on the will's obedience to God: "God's universal foreknowledge and freedom of the will/videtur praenoscere universa deum et esse ullum libertatis arbitrium" (5.3.3).

But from whom did the OE homilist inherit this idea of sin's power to dim the sun's light? How did he shape them into his own coherent view of the cosmos? Lastly, what do they reveal about the continuity of English religious thought from the late tenth through the twelfth century? In the most general sense, these ideas and their attendant rhetoric were the common currency of educated Christian exegetes, who were, in turn, indebted to their Jewish and classical heritage. Although the homilist was particularly indebted to Bede's "In Quadragesima" for his presentation of the Transfiguration of Christ, Bede's title indicates that it was not intended for a specific day. From the early seventh century, particularly in Latin documents with an English provenance, "Quadragesima" referred to the Lenten forty-day fast and was not restricted to a specific liturgical festival. Bede's homily's inclusiveness was a wise choice for what appears to be a *quando volueris* OE homily. Although the "In Quadragesima" appears to be the principle source for the OE homily, the homilist freely amplifies, deletes, and deviates from "In Quadragesima" and stresses, more than Bede, the eschatological character of the

Transfiguration and the imminence of Judgment Day. Lastly, and most significantly, the passage concerning sin and the light of the heavens is *not* in Bede.

The particular passage pertinent to a study of medieval ideas of sin, spatial
relations and the natural world contains three significant theological ideas: (1) the
function and harmony of natural creation is contingent on human will, (2) the orbit
of the celestial bodies is the result of their shared complicity in Adam's sin, and (3)
the brightness of the heavenly spheres will be increased on Judgment Day, and
they will cease their toilsome orbits. Following his exegesis of Matthew's presentation of the Transfigured Christ (Matt. 17:1–9; cf. Mark. 9:2–13, Luke 9:28–36, and
2 Pet. 1:16–18), the homilist begins a discussion on the state of the heavens before
and after the creation of Adam and Eve. He reasons that the very planets in the
heavens depend for their luminosity on the covenant made with Adam and Eve.
Before their first sin, the sun, moon and the stars were far brighter than they are
now. The sin of our first parents was, however, so cataclysmic that it diminished
the light of the sun, the moon and the stars and has forced them into a odious orbit
that will not cease until the end of time. The heavenly bodies were not innocent
victims of this terrible rupture in creation but the homilist believed them also culpable. This common belief in their guilt seems to result from some understanding
of a conjunct materiality shared between the human and celestial creation.

But what was the nature of the materiality that was the common inheritance
of humanity and the planets? The canonical scriptures do not provide answers
to this question. There were discussions of such matters in other Jewish sources,
however. Hebrew speculation on the nature of the universe can be found in the
mishna and the copious midrashic literature. The medieval Christian understanding on this relationship of humans and the rest of creation is indebted to Paul. Paul
argued that nature was enslaved by Adam's sin. The natural world now exists in a
state of decadence awaiting Christ's coming at the last judgment. He will restore
primal innocence: " . . . that the creation itself will be set free from its bondage to
decay (τῆς δουλείας τῆς φθορᾶς) and will obtain the freedom of the glory of the
children of God (τῶυ τέκνων τοῦ θεοῦ)" (Rom. 8:21). Paul is obliged to two teach-
ings: the biblical position that all creation is from God and substantially related
and the oral tradition of the Jews that taught nature was a participant in Adam's
sin. The OE homilist, indirectly following this Pauline line of thought, states that
the sun, moon, and stars were obliged to take on the nature of the mortals "menniscen onfon sceoldon" and hence had to suffer this punishment. However, on
Judgment Day, when the just and the unjust are discriminated, the celestial bodies
will receive their full brightness. The moon will have the luminosity formerly of
the sun, the sun will have its light back sevenfold greater, and both will cease their
endless movement. Hence, their culpability is a contingent one. Before proceeding
further with an analysis, let us have the passage before us:

> Hwi sæde þe godspellere þæt 'þæs Hælendes ansyne wære scinendæ and swiþe
> wunderlic iworden, and scean swa synne'? For þan þe ðe Hælend w(o)lde festnen
> and strengæn heore bileafe þe þæt iseȝen, and eac eft alræ þare þe hit ihyrden sec-
> gæn, þæt we alle mihten underȝyten, þæt swa swa his ansyne wearð on beorhtnes
> iturnd, swa beoð alle his halȝæn on wlite and on wuldor ihwærfod on domes

dæʒ swa he him sylf sæde: Soðfeste men scineð swa beorhte swa sunne on heore fæder rice. Leofe men, ær þam þe ðe æreste men Adam and Eua agulten and Gode wreðædon on neorxnawo[n]gæ, ær þan þa tunglæn, sunne and monæ hæfdæn mucele mare beorhtnesse þenne heo nu habbeð; ac syðæn heo gylten þurh unhersumnesse, and God heom weorp of þam mucele murhðe on þisse deaþelic lif hider on middæneard, þa sceolden þa (t)unglæ þæs wite þrowiæn, for þam ðe heo þare menniscen cunde onfon sceoldon, and heo þa for þon worden heoræ beorhtnes muceles dæles benumene. Hit ilimpð þeah on þissere weorlde endunge on domes dæʒ, þæt God ʒyfð heom æft heoræ fulle brihtnesse. Þenne underfehð þe mone þare sunne brihtnesse, and þeo sunne [bið] seofen siðe brihtre þenne heo nu is. Heo moten eac þenne heom resten þæs runes and þæs ʒewinnes þe heo nu ðrowæð. (Irvine, *Old English Homilies* 169–70,11. 73–92)

(Why did the gospel author say that the Saviour's face shone and was so wonderful, and as bright as the sun? Because the Saviour wished to confirm and strengthen the belief of those who had seen [this event], and also of all those who heard it said. So that we all might understand, that as his countenance turned bright so all his saints shall be changed in appearance and in glory on judgment day as he himself said. True men shall shine as bright as the sun in their Father's kingdom. Dear men, before the first humans Adam and Eve had sinned and angered God [while still] in Paradise, before then the stars, sun and the moon had much more brightness than they have now. But after the sin of disobedience, God cast them from that great pleasure into this mortal life here in the world. Then the stars must suffer this punishment because they were obliged to take on the condition of men and therefore they were deprived of a great portion of their brightness. It will happen, however at the world's end, on judgment day, that God will give them their full brightness again. Then the moon will receive the brightness of the sun, and the sun will be seven times brighter than it now is. They may also then rest from the movement and the strife they suffer now [author's translation].)

The passage opens with a singular interpretation of the Transfiguration that Christ revealed his divinity before his death to strengthen faith: "strengæn heore bileafe" (Irvine, *Old English Homilies* 11. 73–6). The rest of the passage (11. 76–92), appears to be loosely derived from a variety of sources, none of which were the probable exemplar. The loss of the sun and moon's light attributable to the sin of the first humans is not found in Bede's "In Quadragesima." Although Cross identified one of the homilist's principal sources as the Pseudo-Isidore's discussion of the sun and the moon ("De sole et Luna," chapter 5 of the *De Ordine Creaturarum*). I believe that an earlier and possibly more widespread exemplar was Ambrose's *De bono mortis*.

However, let us first review the pertinent passage in Pseudo-Isidore. Isidore summarizes the bliss enjoyed by Adam and Eve, their sin and expulsion from paradise, the consequent loss of light of the sun and moon, and the sorrow these heavenly bodies endured as a result of that diminished brightness, "quamvis non sua culpa, sui luminis detrimenta non sine suo dolore pertulerunt."[7] The passage confers sentience on the planets since it implies they experience sorrow "suo dolore pertulerunt." Cross has shown the correspondences between the passage in the OE "Martyrology" for the fourth day of creation (1611) and the homily. However, there are sufficient differences between them that preclude immediate influence (Cross 137, Herzfeld 42–43, Irvine, *OE Homilies* 153). The homily simply says that before Adam's sin the sun and the moon were brighter than after the Fall. The "Martyrology," however, spells out the traditional reading from Isaiah 30.26 that the sun was seven times brighter and the moon had the brightness of the sun. The homilist states that God was angry in paradise: "Gode wreðædon on neorxnawongæ." The "Martyrology" is silent on God's attitude. An idea also not in the "Martyrology" or in Pseudo-Isidore is the concept that the righteous shall be distinguished on Judgment Day by the increased brightness of their countenances, which derives from the good deeds that an individual has done in life. This is an idea that is quite rare in vernacular texts (Irvine, *OE Homilies* 154) and is used only here and once in Ælfric's homily on the Nativity of the Blessed Virgin Mary. Finally, only the homily indicates that the heavenly bodies had to suffer because they shared the nature of the first parents. In the homily, the phrase "þæs gewinnes þe heo nu ðrowæð" does seem to imagine that the sun and the moon are sentient-like, since they have the capacity to suffer.

Such a bestowal of a sentient-like state is an arresting idea with a complex history of transmission, and one that Pseudo-Isidore, for example, apparently wished to defend through his quotation of Paul, whom he cites immediately following: "We know that the whole of creation has been lamenting in pain until now (οἴδαμεν γὰρ ὅτι πᾶσα ἡ κτίσις συστενάζει καὶ συνωδίνει ἄχρι τοῦ νῦν)" (Rom. 8:22). Does Paul literally intend that the sun, moon, and the stars shared in the guilt and pain of our first parents, and was it the intention of the Old English homilist to convey that thought? If so, such a conception of the universe and creation must imply a shared materiality between mortals and the stars, and that the first sin materially damaged all creation. Paul's language suggests such a reading since he uses the word "κτίσις" (a usage that denotes "creature" or "thing created") when he refers to the non-human-created world, for example, the heavenly bodies. It is a puzzle that the OE homilist does not quote or paraphrase Paul, a normative practice in most English homilies, especially since Pseudo-Isidore cites Paul and citing Paul would have conferred the same authority Isidore invoked for the OE homilist. This omission may reflect a lacuna in his exemplar. The OE homilist does nonetheless use the word "cunde" (that is, the nature or the condition of being a creature), which is analogous to Paul's "κτίσις" when discussing the consequent metamorphosis of the planets after the sin of Adam. And the OE homilist actually extends the Pauline idea. The homily claims that acts of the will—in particular, acts that violate the commandments of God—enjoin all creation in the subsequent punishment: "Then the stars must suffer this punishment because they were obliged to take on the condition of men and therefore they were deprived of a great portion of their brightness / þa sceolden þa (t)unglæ þæs wite þrowiæn for þam ðe heo þare menniscen cunde onfon sceoldon, and heo þa for þon worden heoræ beorhtnes muceles dæles benumene" (Irvine, *Old English Homilies* 11. 85–87; see also Jolly and Kabir).

III

Paul's remark in Romans is a gloss on God's curse of creation in Genesis 3:15–18, in particular, the curse directed against material creation: "cursed is the ground because of you." (Gen. 3:17). There were a number of different competing cosmological ideas in first-century Hellenized Palestine concerning the nature of the cosmos and sin's effect on it. The majority of Jewish thinkers believed in a geocentric universe and in a traditional creation narrative derived from scripture and authoritative midrashim. There is little speculative investigation on their part into the structure of the universe. In fact, there is an important early teaching from Rabbi Bar Kappara which seems to prohibit such investigation: "You may speculate from the day that days were created, but you may not speculate on what was before that" (Ginzberg 5: 100 n. 83). Midrashic commentaries from the early centuries of the Common Era use poetic language to explicate creation, some claiming that sun and moon were formed of light, fire, and water. A common midrash says that the "heavens were fashioned from the light of God's garment, and the earth from the snow under the Divine Throne" (Ginzberg 1: 8). Of those Jews who thought to construct a more abstract theory of the cosmos (and they were few), none were more thoughtful than Gamaliel the Elder (d. c. 50), Paul's teacher, who argued that God created the formless matter of Genesis 1 (*Midrash Rabbah* 1: 8 n. 5). Briefly turning to the Greek community, aside from residual believers in Aristarchus of Samos's (c. 200 b.c.e.) heliocentricism, most thinkers who speculated on the nature of the cosmos were also principally geocentric (Lloyd 213). Indeed, Ptolemy, so important for later Christian thought, rejected the position of Aristarchus. Semitic and Greek ideas of creation, however, differed. The Greeks show far less interest in an explication of the creation narrative than in the structure of the universe, while the Jews focus almost entirely on the creation story and ignore the structure.

While early Christians also held some divergent beliefs, they all wrestled with the account in Genesis of God creating from primeval chaos. A view that was to have a long and successful history was that the world was created *ex nihilo* (see Tertullian's *Adversus Praxean* 5.2 and Hildegard's *Scivias*)[8]; and some, like Justin Martyr and Clement of Alexandria (1 *Apology* 59 and *Stromateis* 5.89.5–6; Mondesert), were indebted to a Platonist view (best exemplified in the *Timaeus* and the *Laws*) that God was the "soul of the cosmos" and fashioned it from pre-existent matter (Collins 328; Jacob 72; Wright 26). Gnostic Christians believed that the material world was the degeneration left from a divine pleroma. Augustine, who also tried to reconcile the creation story in Genesis with inexplicable events in nature, proposed that God conceived in his Logos *rationes seminales*. These rational seeds, or potentialities, God then implanted in creatures at their creation and observed them as they later came into being (Daley 131–50).

Paul shared the dominant pharisaical tradition that saw all creation as matter and hence subject to senescence. This notion would have included the sun, moon, and stars since they were created on the fourth day (Gen.1:14). Paul reshaped this idea by attributing creation's senescence to human sin and the subsequent hope of redemption to Christ's second coming: "creation itself will be set free from its bondage to decay" (Rom. 8:21). Despite some differences, the majority of Christian thinkers subscribed to Paul's position that the world was created *ex nihilo* and that salvation was possible through God's grace mediated by Christ and good works (Rom. 4:17). This position was to become normative for the Middle Ages. It is worth noting because of his cultural closeness to Bodley 343 that Ælfric accepts some variant of a Platonist notion mediated through Paul and Augustine that God always had the thought of creation in his mind "se ræd wæs æfre on his rædfæstum geþance" (Crawford 17).

Lastly, let us now turn briefly to a discussion of what some believed to be a unique association of the Transfiguration event in the Old English homily. The homilist associates the idea of good works as a means of meriting salvation (James 2:14) with the light motif of the Transfiguration. The light of the sun and moon that is the light of nature is now a sign of righteousness. The projection of the moral landscape onto created beings is made explicitly here, as is the ontological connection between humanity and the natural world of creation. The transfigured Christ will come on Judgment Day to distribute this celestial light and separate the good from the bad. Although the passage has been thought to follow no known source, I have found a markedly similar idea in chapter 40 of Ambrose's commentary on 2 Esdras in his *De bono mortis*. First, let us look at the Old English passage:

> Swylc biʒ þe mon ærest on domes dæʒe swa mucele wundorlycor and brihtræ þenne he þer scinæð for þene oðerne. For þam swa mycele mare swa ðe mon her on weorlde to gode deþ toforen þam oðre, and swa mucel swa he bið on his dæde bætere þene þe oðre, swa mycele mare mæde and ædlean he sceal underfon æt ure Drihtine on domes dæʒ. (Irvine, *Old English Homilies* 170, 11. 99–104)

> (The righteous man shall shine so much more glorious and brighter on judgment day than the other [the sinner]. Because as much as the one man does more good in this world than the other—as much as he is better in his works than the other—so much more reward and alms shall he receive from our Lord on Judgment Day.)

The passage states that the transfiguring light that manifests the divinity of Christ is present, albeit in differing degrees, on the faces of those just individuals on Judgment Day. The brightness of their countenances is proportional to the good works they have done in life. The homilist illustrates by analogy that just as the sun and the moon shall have their light restored, so too shall Adam's righteous children. This natural light is a part of their original creation that was lost through sin and is now being restored to the planets and the righteous because their guilt was at most participatory because they shared in the "matter" of creation. The righteous humans are having their original light restored because they have lived according to the law and followed the *imitatio Christi*. Thus there is an implicit ontological connection made between the natural order of creation (the sun and moon created on the fourth day) and human beings (created on the fifth day).

Although there are instances in the canonical scriptures where a singular individual's merit (e.g., Abraham's and Moses's) was manifested through a shining countenance or its opposite, none use the light in an eschatological sense as a postmortem measurement of an individual's worth. There was an oral tradition, however, that said that Adam possessed this light before his sin and that on the return of the Messiah he will recover it (Ginzberg index). The noncanonical texts of apocalyptic apocrypha—works like 2 Esdras, the three books of Enoch, the Apocalypse of Peter, and the Ascension of Isaiah—are richer sources for such motifs (Elliott). Of these, Jerome's translation of the composite Judaeo-Christian 2 Esdras (c. 100?–400?) may prove to be the strongest link in the transmission of this motif. Book 7 of 2 Esdras had an importance for Christians and patristic exegetes, like Ambrose, because it discussed the final judgment, the soul's reunification with the body, seven levels of reward for the just, and punishment for the damned (Stone; Hamilton).

Let us examine the connections a bit more closely. Although the idea for the resurrection of individuals on Judgment Day occurs first in Daniel, pseudoepigraphic texts of the early centuries of the common era develop it in detail. Chapter 7 of 2 Esdras makes the earliest attributive comparison between the brilliant light on the faces of the righteous after Judgment and the light of the sun: "their face is to shine like the sun / vultus eorum fulgere sicut sol" and then they will be like the incorruptible light of the stars, "incipient stellis adsimilari lumini, amodo non corrupti" (7:97).[9] Second Esdras also speaks of the Messiah who will liberate his creation from their pain on Judgment Day: "shall we remain in rest until those times arrive in which you shall renew creation, or shall we be crucified at once/si conservabimur in requie, donec veniant tempora illa in quibus incipies creaturam renovare, aut amodo cruciabimur" (7:75). Esdras emphasizes the importance of good deeds—"You after all have a treasure of good works stored up with the Most High / Etenim est tibi thesaurus operum repositus apud Altissimum" (7:77)—and like the Old English homily, joins the merit for good works to the transfiguring divine and natural light, judgment and salvation: "The sixth level will be the revelation that they are to shine like stars, never to fade or die, with faces as radiant as the sun / Sextus ordo, quando eis ostendetur quomodo incipiet vultus eorum fulgere sicut sol, et quomodo incipient stellis adsimilari lumini" (7:97). The Old English homilist, possibly concerned with the growing length of his homily, simplifies this idea: "Swylc biʒ þe mon ærest on domes dæʒe swa mucele wundorlycor and brihtræ þenne he þer scinæð for þene oðerne." Ambrose cites this same passage (albeit not verbatim) from Esdras 7:97: "Denique sexto ordine demonstrabitur his quod vultus earum sicut sol incipiat refulgere et stellarum luminibus comparari / Lastly, the sixth level will be revealed to them that their faces will gleam with the sun's light and be compared with the stars' light" (744). Each person, in order of merit beginning with Christ, "will receive this light and glory to the extent that they deserve it / Erit igitur ordo diversus claritatis et gloriae, sicut erit ordo meritorum" (744). The Old English homilist simply states that the more worthy will receive the greater gift on Judgment Day: "swa mucel swa he bið on his dæde bætere þene þe oðre, swa mycele mare mæde and ædlean he sceal underfon æt ure Drihtine on domes dæʒ." Ambrose, following 2 Esdras, discusses the seven levels (*ordo*) that the just will pass through on their journey to see the face of God: "Ergo qui iusti hanc remunerationem habent, ut videant faciem Dei" (745). The Old English homily repeats a number of times this idea that only the just will see the shining face of the Lord: "& soðfeste men beoð to heofene rice ilædde, þær heo moten þa scinendæ Christes ansyne a ecelice iseon."

Although the Vulgate text of 2 Esdras may have been available to the Old English homilist in a library like that of Worcester—extant copies do exist from the early ninth century—it is more probable that the influence came from commentaries, like that of Ambrose's *De bono mortis*. There are few medieval commentaries on 2 Esdras (See Sims Williams). I have been unable to find another medieval commentary that would have been available to our Old English homilist.

The Old English homily on the Transfiguration illustrates the complex understanding that English monastics of the late tenth century had of the relationship of sin to the natural world. The natural world, the world of the senses, was also a moral one. All creation was ontologically related in its being and thus responsible to God's commandments. Adam's sin infected all creation. Sin-wrought senescence even damaged the heavens. It was human desire that led the will to sin, condemned the flesh to death, and consequently dimmed the brightness of the sun and moon. Although the planets were not directly culpable, their material relationship to humans (Paul's "κτίσις" and the Old English homilist's "þare menniscen cunde") nonetheless made them censurable. Because their shared guilt is only of a contingent nature, however, their brilliance will be restored at the Last Judgment. At that judgment, their brilliant light will also be available to the righteous humans to the degree that their actions in life merited it. The homilist's bold imagination, a truly original religious sensibility, and his intelligent use of sources are some of the reasons this Old English homily was treasured, read, and recopied two centuries after its composition.

Notes

1. The final judgment was necessary, it was argued, to rehabilitate a world presently fallen and beyond redemption. Every aspect of creation, but particularly human language and sexuality, was complicit in the Fall. Augustine goes so far to remark that sin caused human genitalia to be wholly captive to lust (*De civitate Dei* 14.19.30–31); Joachim of Fiore and Hildegard of Bingen, in explicit sexual language, both accuse the church of rejecting Mary for the Whore of Babylon (McGinn 115, 117, and Hildegard 3.11). In his untitled eschatological sermon on the last days, Wulfstan argued that the present age was so vile that the Antichrist surely must be imminent (see Bethurum 136–37; Caie 245–47); Dante writes in *Inferno* that only the last judgment will cleanse creation of the filth that is strangling it (18.113–14); and, lastly, Augustine argued that even nonsentient creation revealed the effects of sin (*De civitate Dei* 21.8.98; see also *De Genesi*).
2. Ker, *Catalogue* 368–75. The manuscript was written in seven booklets, and the quires illustrate that such wear was consonant with a period of being unbound. See also Sisam 250 n. 4: "wr biscopen war wolstane god" on folio 173r. See also Collier and Ramsay.
3. Irvine, *Old English Homilies* xlvii–xlviii. Irvine and Belfour number their homilies differently (Irvine = I; Belfour = B): Ii = Biii; Iii = Biv; Iiii = Bvii; Iiv; 1.2860 = Bvii; Iv = Bx; Ivi = Bxi; Ivii = Bxii. Of these, Pope printed Belfour's 1, 2, both by Ælfric, and 14 (from 1.170). Belfour's numbers 5 and 6 are both anonymous, and their possible textual affiliation is discussed in Irvine, *Old English Homilies* (xxxii–xxxviii). Belfour's number 9 is a reworking of Ælfric's Christmas homily, which begins his *Lives of Saints*. Belfour 13 is the second part of Ælfric's homily for the Ninth Sunday after Pentecost and is number 26 in *Catholic Homilies: Second Series* (see Godden xxvi). Belfour14 (Pope vi) is from Ælfric's *Temporal*

Homilies. The items contained in section (g): no. 77 is a revised version of Ælfric's Christmas homily that begins his *Lives of the Saints;* number 78, anonymous homily for First Sunday in Lent; 79 is the anonymous Transfiguration homily; 80 is possibly a homily for Tuesday in Rogationtide; 81 is a Latin dialogue between student and teacher on Lord's Prayer and the Creed; 82 is the second part of Ælfric's homily for the Ninth Sunday after Pentecost in *Catholic Homilies;* 83 is a narrative on the types of sin represented by three men resurrected from the dead (cf. Pope vi); 84 is Ælfric's second homily for a Confessor (Assmann iv); and 85 is a verse fragment on "The Grave." See also Clemoes and DiNapoli.

4. Irvine, *Old English Homilies* xliii; no. 66 is Wulfstan's "Sermon de baptismate," no. 71 is Wulfstan's "Sermo Lupi ad Anglos," no. 72 is Wulfstan's "Leofæ Men" (Bethurum 6).

5. Ker observes that punctuation was "carefully attended to . . . in many manuscripts of homilies by Ælfric and Wulfstan" (*English Manuscripts* 46).

6. Cameron makes the point that the fifteenth-century reader of the Wulfstan pieces in Bodley 343 "substitutes over ninety obsolete words with their late ME equivalents" (226). See also Ker, *Catalogue* 368.

7. Isidore of Seville 83.923: "Haec enim dum humanis usibus ministrare a Deo creatore destinata sunt, cum homines inculpabiliter vixissent, et sub Creatoris, quo conditi fuerant, lege perseverarent, etiam sui luminis plenitudine decorata ministrabant; cum vero homines, quibus in ministerio sociata primitus rutilabant, propter transgressionem dejecti, paradisi beatitudinem amiserunt, ipsa quoque luminaria, quamvis non sua culpa, sui luminis detrimenta non sine suo dolore pertulerunt, sicut Paulus apostolus contestatur [Rom. 8.22], dicens: 'Quoniam omnis creatura congemiscit, et dolet usque adhuc.'"

8. Hildegard of Bingen: "Terra autem rotunda in celi medio sicut creatio ex nihilo." See Simek 21.

9. The Vulgate edition is used for the citations from 2 Esdras (4 Esdras).

Works Cited

Assmann, von Bruno, ed. *Angelsächsische Homilien und Heiligenleben.* Bibliothek der angelsächsischen Proso 3. Kassel: G. H. Wigand, 1889.

Ambrose. *De bono mortis. Sancti Ambrosii Opera I.* Ed. C. Schenkl. Corpus Scriptorum Ecclesiasticorum Latinorum, no. 32.1, 1897. 701–53.

Augustine. *De civitate Dei.* Corpus Christianorum, Series Latina, 48.14, 2. Ed. B. Dombart and A. Kalb. Turnholt: Brepols, 1955. xi–xxii.

——. *De Genesi ad Litteram.* Patrologia Latina 34: col. 406b.

Belfour, A. O., ed. *Twelfth Century Homilies in MS. Bodley 343.* Pt. 1, *Text and Translation.* Early English Text Society, o.s. 137. London: Kegan Paul, Trench, Trübner, 1909.

Bethurum, Dorothy, ed. *The Homilies of Wulfstan.* Oxford: Clarendon, 1957.

Boethius. *Consolatio Philosophiae.* Ed. James J. O'Donnell. Bryn Mawr: Bryn Mawr College, 1984.

Caie, Graham D. *The Judgment Day Theme in Old English Poetry.* Copenhagen: Nova, 1976.

Cameron, Angus F. "Middle English in Old English Manuscripts." *Chaucer and Middle English Studies in Honour of Rossell Hope Robbins.* Ed. Beryl Rowland. London: George Allen & Unwin, 1974. 218–29.

Clemoes, Peter, ed. *Ælfric's Catholic Homilies: The First Series.* Early English Text Society, supplementary series 17. London: Oxford UP, 1997.

Collier, W. E. J. "'Englishness' and the Worcester Tremulous Hand." *Leeds Studies in English* n.s. 26 (1995): 35–47.

——. "A Thirteenth-Century Anglo-Saxonist." Ed. G. Owen-Crocker. *Bulletin of the John Rylands University Library of Manchester* 79.3 (1998): 149–66.

Collins, John J. Seers. *Sybils and Sages in Hellenistic Roman Judaism.* New York: Brill, 1997.

Crawford, S. J., ed. *The Old English Version of the Heptateuch, Ælfric's Treatise on the Old and New Testament and His Preface to Genesis.* Early English Text Society, o.s. 160. London: Oxford UP, 1922.

Cross, J. E. "'De Ordine Creaturarum Liber' In Old English Prose." *Anglia: Zeitschrift für Englische Philologie* 90 (1972): 132–40.

Daley, B. E. *The Hope of the Early Church: A Handbook of Patristic Eschatology*. Cambridge: Cambridge UP, 1991.

Dante, Alighieri. *Inferno. The Divine Comedy*. Ed. and trans. Charles S. Singleton. Princeton: Princeton UP, 1970.

Di Napoli, Robert. *An Index of Theme and Image to the Homilies of the Anglo-Saxon Church*. Hockwold cum Wilton, Eng., 1995.

Elliott, J. K. *The Apocryphal New Testament*. Oxford: Clarendon, 1993.

Emmerson, Richard K. "The Apocalypse in Medieval Culture." *The Apocalypse in the Middle Ages*. Ed. Richard K. Emmerson and Bernard McGinn. Ithaca: Cornell UP, 1992. 293–332.

Gameson, Richard. *The Manuscripts of Early Norman England (c. 1066–1130)*. Oxford: Oxford UP, 1999.

Gatch, Milton McC. *Preaching and Theology in Anglo-Saxon England: Ælfric and Wulfstan*. Buffalo: U of Toronto P, 1977.

Ginzberg, Louis. *The Legends of the Jews*. Trans. H. Szold. 7 vols. Philadelphia: Jewish Publication Society of America, 1909–38.

Godden, Malcolm, ed. *Ælfric's Catholic Homilies: Introduction, Commentary and Glossary*. Early English Text Society, supplementary series 18. London: Oxford UP, 2000.

———. *Ælfric's Catholic Homilies: The Second Series, Text*. Early English Text Society, supplementary series 5. London: Oxford UP, 1979.

Goodspeed, E. J. *Die ältesten Apologeten*. Göttingen: Vandenhoeck & Ruprecht, 1914.

Graham, Timothy. "Robert Talbot's 'Old Saxonice Bede' Cambridge University Library, MS Kk.3.18 and the 'Alphabetum Norwagicum' of British Library Cotton MSS, Domitian A.IX." *Books and Collectors, 1200–1700: Essays Presented to Andrew Watson*. Ed. James P. Carley and Colin G. C. Tite. London: British Library, 1997. 295–316.

Hamilton, Alastair. "From the Church Fathers to the Renaissance." *The Apocryphal Apocalypse*. Oxford: Clarendon, 1999. 13–30.

Handley, R. "British Museum MS Cotton Vespasian D. XIV." *Notes & Queries* n.s. 21 (1974): 243–50.

Hanson, Paul D. *The Dawn of Apocalyptic*. Philadelphia: Fortress, 1975.

Haymo of Halberstadt. *Commentariorum in Isaiam Libri tres*. Patrologia Latina 116: cols. 713–1086.

Herzfeld, George, ed. *An Old English Martyrology*. Early English Text Society, o.s. 116. London: Kegan, Paul, Trench, Trübner,1900.

Hildegard. *Scivias*. Patrologia Latina 197: 383–738.

Hill, Joyce. "The Dissemination of Ælfric's 'Lives of the Saints': A Preliminary Study." *Holy Men and Holy Women: Old English Prose Saint's Lives and Their Contexts*. Ed. Paul E. Scarmach. Albany: State U of New York, 1996. 234–59.

Irvine, Susan. "The Compilation and Use of Manuscripts Containing Old English in the Twelfth Century." *Rewriting Old English in the Twelfth Century*. Ed. Mary Swan and Elaine M. Treharne. Cambridge: Cambridge UP, 2000. 41–61.

———, ed. *Old English Homilies from MS Bodley 343*. Early English Text Society, o.s. 302. Oxford: Oxford UP, 1993. lvi–lvii.

Isidore of Seville. *De Ordine Creaturarum Liber*. Patrologia Latina 83: cols. 913–54.

Jacob, Louis. "Jewish Cosmologies." *Ancient Cosmologies*. Ed. Carmen Blacker and Michael Loewe. London: Allen & Unwin, 1975. 66–84.

Jerome. *Commentariorum in Esaiam Liber*. Corpus Christianorum, Series Latina, 73.9, 30, 26. Ed. Marci Adriaen. Turnholt: Brepols, 1963.

Jolly, Karen. *Popular Religion in Late Anglo-Saxon England: Elf Charms in Context*. Chapel Hill: U of North Carolina P, 1996.

Kabir, Ananya Jahanara. *Paradise, Death and Doomsday in Anglo-Saxon Literature*. Cambridge: Cambridge UP, 2001.

Ker, Neil R. *Catalogue of Manuscripts Containing Anglo-Saxon*. Oxford: Clarendon, 1990.

———. *English Manuscripts in the Century after the Norman Conquest*. Oxford: Clarendon, 1960.

Liuzza, Roy Michael. "Scribal Habit: The Evidence of the Old English Gospels." *Rewriting Old English in the Twelfth Century*. Ed. Mary Swan and Elaine M. Treharne. Cambridge: Cambridge UP, 2000. 143–65.

Lloyd, G. E. R. "Greek Cosmologies." *Ancient Cosmologies*. Ed. Carmen Blacker and Michael Loewe. London: Allen & Unwin, 1975. 198–224.

McGinn, Bernard, ed. and trans. *Apocalyptic Spirituality*. New York: Paulist, 1979.

McIntyre, E. A. "Early-Twelfth-Century Worcester Cathedral Priory with Special Reference to the Manuscripts Written There." D.Phil., Oxford, 1978.

Midrash Rabbah. Ed. H. Freedman and M. Simon. London: Soncino, 1939.

Mondésert, C., ed. "Clément d'Alexandrie. Les Stromates I." *Soucres chrétiennes* 30. Paris: Éditions du Cerf, 1951.

Pope, John C., ed. *Homilies of Ælfric: A Supplementary Collection*. Early English Text Society, o.s. 259, 260. 2 vols. London: Oxford UP, 1967–68.

Portalié, Eugène, S.J. *A Guide to the Thought of Saint Augustine*. Chicago: Henry Regnery, 1960.

Proud, Joanna. "Old English Prose Saints' Lives in the Twelfth Century: The Evidence of the Extant Manuscripts." *Rewriting Old English in the Twelfth Century*. Ed. Mary Swan and Elaine M. Treharne. Cambridge: Cambridge UP, 2000. 117–31.

Ramsey, Jennifer. "A Possible 'Tremulous Hand' Addition to 'The Grave' in MS Bodley 334." *Notes & Queries*. N.s. 2 (2002):178–80.

Rowland, Christopher. "Apocalyptic and Eschatology." *The Open Heaven: A Study of Apocalyptic in Judaism and Early Christianity*. London: Society for Promoting Christian Knowledge, 1982. 23–48.

Scragg, D. G. "The Corpus of Anonymous Lives and their Manuscript Context." *Holy Men and Holy Women: Old English Prose Saint's Lives and Their Contexts*. Ed. Paul E. Szarmach. Albany: State U of New York, 1996. 209–30.

——. "Source Study." *Reading Old English Texts*. Ed. K. O'Brien O'Keefe. Cambridge: Cambridge UP, 1997. 39–58.

——, ed. *The Vercelli Homilies and Related Texts*. Early English Text Society, o.s. 300. Oxford: Oxford UP, 1992.

Simek, Rudolf. *Heaven and Earth in the Middle Ages*. Trans. Angela Hall. Woodbridge: Boydell, 1996.

Sims Williams, Patrick. *Religion and Literature in Western England, 600–800*. Cambridge: Cambridge UP, 1990.

Sisam, C. "Early Middle English 'Drihtin.'" *Middle English Studies Presented to Norman Davis in Honour of his Seventieth Birthday*. Ed. D. Gray and E. G. Stanley. Oxford: Clarendon, 1983. 244–54.

Stone, Michael Edward. *Fourth Ezra: A Commentary on the Book of Fourth Ezra*. Hermeneia: A Critical and Historical Commentary on the Bible. Ser. ed., Frank Moore Cross. Minneapolis: Fortress, 1990.

Swan, Mary. "Ælfric's Catholic Homilies in the Twelfth Century." *Rewriting Old English in the Twelfth Century*. Ed. Mary Swan and Elaine M. Treharne. Cambridge: Cambridge UP, 2000. 62–82.

Tertullian. *Adversus Praxean*. Ed. A. Kroyman and E. Evans. Corpus Christianorum, Series Latina, 2.1157–1205. Turnholt: Brepols, 1954.

Watson, Andrew G. *Catalogue of Dated and Datable Manuscripts, c. 700—1600 in the Departments of Manuscripts, British Library*. London: British Museum Publications, 1979.

Weber, T. *Scribes and Scholars at Salisbury Cathedral, c. 1075–c. 1125*. Oxford: Oxford UP, 1992.

——. "Script and Manuscript Production at Christ Church, Canterbury after the Norman Conquest." *Canterbury and the Norman Conquest: Churches, Saints and Scholars*. Ed. R. Eales and R. Sharp. London: Hambledon, 1995. 144–56.

Wright, M. R. *Cosmology in Antiquity*. London: Routledge,1995.

Zettel, P. H. "Saints Lives in Old English: Latin Manuscripts and Vernacular Accounts." *Peritia* 1 (1982): 17–37.

Michael Calabrese

Controlling Space and Secrets in the *Lais* of Marie de France

Right from the beginning of her *Lais,* in two prologues, Marie de France makes it clear that her enemies are never far behind, the *gangleür* and *losengier* whose biting slanders constantly snap at the heels of anyone who has distinguished herself. Where, this makes us ask, can the poet and her reputation be safe from such attacks, once she has spoken her mind and expressed her poetic gifts? Marie confronts this problem head on, insisting throughout that there are stories to tell—"they will not stay hidden for long," as she often reports—and that she is the one to tell them:

> Ki Deus ad duné escïence
> E de parler bone eloquence
> Ne s'en deit taisir ne celer,
> Ainz se deit voluntiers mustrer.
>
> (Whoever has received knowledge
> and eloquence in speech from God
> should not be silent or secretive
> but demonstrate it willingly.)[1]
>
> ("Prologue" 1–4)

Marie respects God's gift and will speak openly and fearlessly, but oddly, she must at the same time follow the classical principle of speaking obscurely so as to inspire glosses and sharpen the minds of both author and reader:

Custume fu as anciens,
Ceo testimoine Preciens,
Es livres ke jadis feseient,
Assez oscurement diseient
Pur ceus ki a venir esteient
E ki aprendre les deveient,
K'i peüssent gloser la lettre
E de lur sen le surplus mettre.

(The custom among the ancients—
as Priscian testifies—
was to speak quite obscurely
in the books that they wrote,
so that those who were to come after
and study them
might gloss the letter
and supply its significance from their own wisdom.)

("Prologue" 9–16)

Through this the philosophers and, we presume, the evolving readership throughout time, not only became "plus . . . sutil de sens" (20) but also learned how to
guard themselves from things "that should be avoided" ("de ceo k'i ert a tres-
passer") (22). Marie's opening manifesto thus signals not only her refusal to "conceal" ("celer") what she knows but also, paradoxically, her need to reveal things
"oscurament" in accord with a legacy of learning and glossing that best supports
both tradition and the individual talent ("lur sens") of the ongoing readership.[2]

To accomplish all she sets out to do, Marie must embrace this paradox of at
once unsealing and concealing, both showing (*mustrer*) and hiding (*celer*) together.
Through this she finds safe space for herself in the learned tradition, whose borders will justify and protect her endeavor through time, as it has protected the
ancients before her. For Marie serves at an ancient alter, safe then as it will be for
Pope over five hundred years later, from "sacrilegious hands" (Pope 280). But in
Marie's case the enemies are less hands than mouths, the sniping dogs addressed
in her second "Prologue" preceding the first *lai*, "Guigemar":

Mais quant il ad en un païs
Hummë u femme de grant pris,
Cil ki de sun bien unt envie
Sovent en dïent vileinie:
Sun pris li volent abeissier;
Pur ceo comencent le mestier
Del malveis chien coart, felun,
Ki mort la gent par traïsun.
Nel voil mie pur ceo leissier,
Si gangleür u losengier
Le me volent a mal turner:
Ceo est lur dreit de mesparler!

(But anywhere there is
a man or woman of great worth,

people who envy their good fortune
often say evil things about them;
they want to ruin their reputations.
Thus they act like
vicious, cowardly dogs
who bite people treacherously.
I don't propose to give up because of that;
If spiteful critics or slanderers
wish to turn my accomplishments against me
They have a right to their evil talk.)

(7–18)

The envious force her into the paradox of open obscurity, force her to brave their slander while hiding within a learned obliqueness that they cannot penetrate with their envy. This obscurity, as Augustine and Aquinas had argued for Scripture and as Boccaccio would later for poetry, prevents the unworthy from grasping its truths, for we should not cast pearls before swine, or before curs in this case.[3] With dogged and mordant confidence, then, Marie defies her potential detractors, crafting a safe space from which to exercise her learning free from envy, free from vice and from whatever "grant dolur" ("Prologue" 27) they might bring the anxious poet. The prologues are a success.

But within the *Lais* themselves, Marie's lovers are not always so easily successful, and throughout them Marie wonders where the young lover or the noble knight can be safe from the envy of husbands, fathers, courts, comrades, and anyone who takes pleasure in ruining the happiness of others. Rumor and slander run wild in the *Lais,* as we know, for example, from "Fresne," where a jealous woman accuses her twin-bearing neighbor of having slept with "dui humme" (43). The rumor spread till it was known all over Brittany ("Par tute Bretaine seüe") (52). In varied manifestations, the *Lais* are all about the concealing and revealing of information by, from, and about both the noble and the villainous. I therefore agree with Sarah Spence that though we customarily see "love" as the common theme in the *Lais,* we can make just as strong a case for "envy."[4] Thus the very search for safety that animates Marie's "Prologue" animates the stories themselves, and the poet's conflict with slander and envy is replicated anew in each fictive world she summons out of "Briton." Marie's enemies are the lovers' enemies too, those who snipe and snip at the heals of freedom and of love. Marie will show often in the *Lais* that with a kind of natural law on their side, the lovers will defeat the plans of the envious, just as Marie will defeat the *gangleürs* and follow her muse. The "Prologue" prepares us for this conflict and sets up the forthcoming battles between the intrusive, envious slanderers and the open-hearted lovers who try to honor their own muse, not of poetry but of love. This neither makes Marie a lover nor the lovers poets but rather unifies the struggles between the two, exposing the parallel dangers that hamper each, stemming from the common causes of envy and intrusion.[5] Marie was aware of the constant dangers of slander, exposure, and judgment faced by poets, wives, knights, young lovers, and werewolves, even when they practice *mesure* and love honestly. Thus in her *Lais* she constantly explores the search for a secret, private space where, if only fleetingly, love and honor can be free, if it meets with her high standards, that is, if it deserves a home either in time or in memory.

Much of the *Lais*, thus, is about the search for what Lanval's mythic lady calls a place "U nuls puïst aveir s'amie / Sanz repreoce e sanz vileinie" (165–66) ("where a man might have his mistress without reproach or shame"). And yet the conflict is not so rigidly structured nor contrived, for not all lovers are the same and not all are entitled to the same protection, either by natural or societal law. All Marie's lovers, good and bad, young and old, sympathetic or scurrilous, seek safety from their envious enemies, yet not all find surety and safety, and some even meet death for their efforts, as in "Equitan" and "Bisclavret." Success in love depends on the deft use of secrets and secret places, a control and manipulation of the physical world, the artificial landscape of love. Those who use it well will thrive and find security; those overcome by foul lust and envy will suffer when space betrays them. In some cases, further, secret loves can finally be revealed and publicly enjoyed by the persevering couple. Thus, as Marie takes us through the secret places of love, she simultaneously conducts a moral inquiry of its spatial poetics. And, as is usually the case with Marie, the poetics that emerges is not without its ambiguities and aporias.

Spence notices such ambiguities, studying what she calls the "ever-changing qualities of life of the individual in a changing spatio-temporal frame," which leads to a kind of situational morality in the *Lais*: "What is right for X in situation Y is not right for X in situation Z or for W in situation Y" (*Texts* 124). This fluidity is crucial to the *Lais*, but I agree less with Spence's conclusion that amid all this confusion love asserts itself as a medicine. Spence says of "Guigemar" that "the love between Guigemar and his lady, and the true love Marie writes of in all her stories, is both the cure for envy and the empowerment of *caritas*" (*Texts* 130).[6] Marie is ever playful and ambiguous, for though lovers battle envy, seldom are any characters "cured" of envy in the *Lais*; more often they are cuckolded, mutilated, or killed for their envy. And sympathetic lovers, furthermore, often prosper without displaying anything close to *caritas*. For often space helps the lovers throughout the work—if they are noble, and even if they commit acts of violence and callous vengeance, as Renée L. Curtis has observed.[7] I agree with Spence, therefore, if I may synthesize her different formulations, that there is a force of love that animates the *Lais*, sometimes remotely but sometimes not at all related to *caritas*. And in this chapter I will argue that secrets and space play important roles in serving the aims of this love, when neither *caritas* nor any other abstract virtue is always at hand. To put it differently, and I hope provocatively, space helps the lovers that we and Marie like—those we feel for as victims of envy or of imprisoning encumbrance. Because restraint and space are at the center of all Marie's dramas, love can succeed, and the noble can reclaim their right and honors by using the spatial world deftly, even if treachery and violence are needed.

In order to understand more about the use of space in Marie's romantic universe, I want to trace her depiction of the strategies, games, and devices that lovers employ to protect themselves from exposure and woe, often involving the use of secret spaces and private places, away from the watchful eyes of authority and custom.[8] Marie enacts her study of space variously, and our discussion could embrace all twelve *Lais*, but I will focus on six stories: "Guigemar," "Equitan," "Yonec," "Milun," "Laüstic," and "Eliduc," which collectively display the varied, and sometimes confusingly mercurial, role of space and secrecy in the *Lais*.[9] How, indeed, does Marie use space? Often Marie's theme is escape from confinement, as young lovers combat the imprisonment brought on by jealousy, envy, and old grasping men who try to confine women behind walls, as in "Guigemar," "Yonec," and "Milun." In other instances, specifically enclosed spaces often provide secrecy and security, as in the case of Milun's swan, Bisclavret's hollow rock, Guigemar's well-caulked ship, and the haven of Lanval's lady's tent where he finds freedom from the slander and political persecution of Arthur's court. Further, when finally the real world will not deliver, Lanval flees to yet another, imaginary space and pulls it in around him, finding there inviolable surety that no one can penetrate or expose. On the other hand, spatial poetics can punish vicious lovers who do not take proper secretive precautions and who treacherously misuse space, as in "Equitan" and "Bisclavret." In "Yonec," similarly, the *Jaloux* who treacherously traps a noble lover is himself later killed at the man's tomb by his son, proving that he could not use a spatial trap to kill or confine the force of love and justice. Marie depicts a wholly different kind of private place in "Laüstic," where the bachelor neighbor has an elegant gold vaisselet made for the dead nightingale—a personal memorial to a love and disaster barely averted. "Eliduc," we will see, far from wrapping up the collection neatly or confirming a clear moral paradigm, explodes the issues of the previous poems, in a festival of mock-comic secrecy and lies. "Eliduc" is the longest *lai*, the feistiest, most persistently episodic and picaresque, Marie's final flourish, where the outcome is kept secret from the reader in an extended tease until all the lovers mysteriously retreat into holy orders, safe behind sacred walls.[10] Just as Marie must survive as an artist by controlling both the surface and the hidden treasures within her words, her characters too must control the secrets and the hidden spaces that ensure the survival of love.

Marie launches her collection with "Guigemar," a tale of secrecy and of spaces that ultimately protect and exult its lovers, while the restraints of evil fail and the enclosures of the envious betray their masters. Throughout the *lai*, acts of concealing and revealing, of entering and exiting, and of opening and closing animate the amorous drama, as Marie crafts a complex landscape of spatial poetics. The first intrusion is by Guigemar's hunting dogs, which flush out the white stag, which, in turn, flushes Guigemar himself out of sexlessness and solitude, cursing him and condemning him to both love and to fame (119–21). The stag wishes, finally, to be left in peace ("lais m'aveir pés" [123]). As Marie begins the *Lais*, she wants us to recall the forces of intrusion and persecution with which she began, and so Guigemar's hunting dogs imagistically—if subtly—recall the yelping curs who pursue Marie in her "Prologue." Like Marie, Guigemar cannot hide; he now enters public life, and from now on the dogs will be chasing him, Actaeon-like. So exposed, like the "hummë u femme de grant pris" (8) in Marie's "Prologue," for the rest of the *lai* Guigemar must search for safety and security from his enemies, but at the same time he must do so without withdrawing from the world, for he must bravely confront his amorous, as Marie does her artistic, destiny.

After his wounding, he finds refuge first in one of the central images of enclosed space in the *Lais*, the ship that ferries him to his destiny: "Defors e dedenz fu peiee, / Nuls hum n'i pout trover jointure" ("caulked outside and in—/ no one could discover a seam in its hull") (154–55). Marie's emphasis on the carpentry stresses surety and protection, and her observation that Guigemar did not think boats could land in that harbor (161ff.) underlines this boat's unique abilities to penetrate risky enclosures in pursuit of its odd amorous mission. The boat's appearance, though unexplained, is no accident, because Guigemar does indeed need it to help him circumvent his future lover's imprisonment in the walled garden and tower where she is held by the *Jaloux*, for, as Hanning and Ferrante aptly render it, "the watch he kept over her was no joke" ("Il ne la guardat mie a gas") (218). Since the grove is "clos tut envirun" (220) and the marble walls are "espés e halz!" (222), and the other side of the grove is "clos de mer" (225), this boat is the lovers' only means of subverting these restraints. As we will see so often in the *Lais*, success in love comes to those who, either through craft or magical fortune, can master the spatial poetics of entry and exit, of "conceal" and "reveal."

And once he meets the lady, Guigemar, despite his Hippolytus-like beginning, wants love and knows how difficult is it for a woman to find a man as worthy as herself ("a sa maniere") (521) and to be safe from public scrutiny and invasion. He tells his hesitant savior that when a woman "de bon purpens, / Ki en sei eit valur ne sens" ("of good character, sensible as well as virtuous") (519–20) finds a man of worth, she should not "treat him too disdainfully" ("Ne se ferat vers lui trop fiere") (522) because love only allows a brief period of safety:

> Ainz l'amerat, s'en avrat joie.
> Ainz ke nuls le sachet ne l'oie
> Avrunt il mut de lur pru fait!

> (Rather she should love him and enjoy him;
> this way, before anyone knows or hears of it,
> they'll have done a lot that's to their advantage.)
>
> (523–25)

Here Marie creates not physical but temporal space; love exists in this brief moment, as a coveted secret "before anyone hears of it," before it is revealed and ruptured by the envious. The lady quickly agrees, and the lovers unite, though Marie gives them their privacy and only implies that they enjoyed the sorts of things that people do in this situation: "Bien lur coviege del surplus, / De ceo que li autre unt en us!" (533–34). The poet sets up walls herself, over which she will not peer, but she lets us witness just enough to celebrate a love fulfilled. Yet knowing how fragile such space is, the lovers sense something is wrong and fear that they will be exposed by the husband.

Thus, to protect themselves from the ruin of exposure, the lovers seal off and take control of their own secret spaces, as they essentially enclose each other's bodies for private use through the devises of the knot and the belt that each alone can unravel and unlock and thus "reveal." We might say both these enclosures are "well caulked" like the stout ship; no man can find a seam, that is, no one can penetrate these seals, except the lovers themselves. She makes the knot then puts the belt on none too soon, as Marie underlines the urgency of the pact by having them discovered immediately after they seal their plan:

> Ki la bucle purrat ovrir
> Sanz despescier e sanz partir,
> Il li prie que celui aint.
> Puis la baisë, a taunt remaint.
> Cel jur furent aparceü,
> Descovert, trové e veü
>
> (Whoever could open the buckle
> without breaking it or severing it from the belt,
> would be the one he would urge her to love.
> He kissed her and left it at that.
> That day they were discovered—
> Spied upon and found out.)[11]

(573–78)

Somehow, even before the lock and knot come into play, this plan works like a charm, for the next time space tries to encumber the lovers, it fails to do so. For once the lovers are caught and the Lady is imprisoned by the *Jaloux*, for some reason, the cell is not particularly confining. One day, while apostrophizing her lover,

> Dunc lieve sus;
> Tute esbaïe vient a l'hus,
> Ne treve cleif ne sereüre,
> Fors s'en eissi; par aventure
> Unques nuls ne la desturba.
> Al hafne vint, la neif trova.
>
> (She got up:
> In astonishment she went to the door
> and found it unlocked;
> by good fortune, she got outside—
> no one bothered her
> She came to the harbor, and found the boat.)

(673–78)

The door is not locked, and no one "disturbs" her (an important word in the *Lais*, from the Latin *turba*, a swirl or disturbance but also an assembly); we might say "she went privately" to the magic ship. As one friendly open enclosure frees her, another, well sealed and safe, welcomes her and takes her to her lover.

In this *lai* a genuine love cannot be undone by jealous restraint, for just as the *Jaloux* uses space ineffectively, just so does the hapless Meriaduc, the next man who attempts to enclose Guigemar's love but who, of course, cannot open her belt. Guigemar, claiming the lady and her sealed body as his own, besieges

Meriaduc's castle and kills him, for the last edifice in this *lai* yields, as all others have done, to the will of the lovers. Despite the fortified castle's resistance ("Mes forz esteit, al prendre faillent" [874]), the final assault underlines the charmed spatial life Guigemar and his lady have led. Thus this *lai,* we see, is a series of intrusions, entrances and exits prevented or facilitated, a flow inward and out, the making and the unmaking of what Chaucer will later call "privitee."[12] Marie, as Bloch argues, may at one point participate as the author of the lovers' discovery, betraying and revealing them, but that moment is fleeting, for throughout the *lai* Marie makes sure that the lovers enjoy a series of safe and private spaces (see Bloch 72–73). Ships ferry the lovers; locks and doors open for them at will, while, with a little perseverance, strong castles finally yield to their authority and might. And in the lovers' wake lie the failed, fallen forces of envy: "Le chastel ad destruit e pris / E le seignur dedenz ocis" (879–80) ("the castle he seized and destroyed; the lord inside he killed"; my translation). For although the lovers endure much and live in constant danger, "Guigemar" is a clear triumph for love and a defeat for the dogs of envy and espionage. We cannot find a seam in it.

"Equitan" provides immediate contrasts to "Guigemar," and though the moral framework here may be more broad than in other *lais,* as Hanning and Ferrante note (see their commentary, 69ff.), Marie nonetheless enacts the drama of love and of justice again through a series of physical spaces and enclosures. The focus in this *lai* is not only on how the envious plot against the good but also on the treacherous abuse of secrets and space, the misuse of the arts of concealing and revealing. The lovers here look for all the same things as in "Guigemar": surety, privacy, freedom from control and intrusion, but they do not earn or deserve it. Equitan has merely heard the seneschal's wife praised for her beauty and covets her without seeing her, evidently envious of the love between this "Bon chevalier, pruz e leal" (22) and his wife, "bele durement / E de mut bon affeitement," with "gent cors" and "bele faiture" (31–33). This appetite and covetousness leads to a series of secret, private trysts for the glib king Equitan and his seneschal's all-too-willing wife, all set behind the king's closed doors: "Li us des chambres furent clos" (191; see 185ff.). But finally, the profane secret space of treachery is ruptured, for the adulterous lovers pursue their secret love rather sloppily and without adequate precautions against being exposed, discovered, and revealed. For just as Guigemar's lady's prison door is easily opened, so too is the door guarding these adulterous lovers, letting the truth out and the avenging husband in, in the *lai's* steamy, final scene:

> Pur la cuve, ki devant fu.
> L'us firent tenir e garder;
> Une meschine i dut ester.
> Li senescals hastis revint;
> A l'hus buta, cele le tint.
> Icil le fiert par tel haïr,
> Par force li estut ovrir.
> Le rei e sa femme ad trovez
> U il gisent, entr' acolez.
> Li reis garda, sil vit venir;

Pur sa vileinie covrir
Dedenz la cuve saut joinz piez;
E il fu nuz e despuillez,
Unques garde ne s'en dona:
Ileoc murut e escauda.
Sur lui est li mals revertiz
E cil en est saufs e gariz.

(Because the tub was right before them,
they set a guard at the bedroom door;
a maidservant was to keep watch there.
Suddenly the seneschal returned,
And knocked on the door; the girl held it closed.
He struck it so violently
That he forced it open.
They he discovered the king and his own wife
Lying in each other's arms.
The king looked up and saw him coming;
To hide his villainy he jumped into the tub feet first,
Stark naked.
He didn't stop to think what he was doing.
And there he was scalded to death,
Caught in his own evil trap,
While the seneschal remained safe and sound.)
("Equitan" 284–300)

Some secrets ought not to be kept, and space becomes permeable not to aid the lovers but to expose and in fact destroy them, as the seneschal easily bursts through the young girl's absurd buttressing. Guigemar and his lady had been discovered, but that was a temporary setback to a destined love, whereas here the revelation brings the base to justice. The bathtub serves as the final, ridiculous attempt to conceal what has been revealed in the *lai*, an enclosed space that provides neither privacy nor security but frantic death. Readers are left feeling that the king and the wife got what they deserved not so much for their adultery but for their blundering use of space. Equitan cannot have thought to be safe on the cuckolded husband's bed with only a door and "une meschine" (286) protecting them, and he cannot have thought to be protected by the boiling tub with which he planned to kill his own man. But in his nakedness and shame he was not thinking clearly, and this thoughtlessness here stands in stark contrast to his earlier rhetorical seduction of the wife, in which he artfully reverses their power relationship; as he puts it: "Vus seiez dame e jeo servanz" ("you be the lord and I'll be the servant") (175). Marie thus uses physical space to strip the king, literally and figuratively, down to his essential nature, weak, frightened, shameful, and artless, as he desperately seeks a security that he himself has squandered through his own vice. The tub, no doubt, welcomes him, as the caulked ship does Guigemar, and it too holds water all too well.

Another of Marie's naked men is more thoughtful than Equitan in his use of space and secrets, for though Bisclavret's wife and her lover attempt to betray him, he ultimately masters space in his own struggle for justice. The noble were-wolf is thus in the parallel position of Equitan's seneschal—the victim of secretive betrayal who, finally, by his own control of space and of the art of concealing and revealing, defeats his duplicitous enemies. Bisclavret's own secret, of course, generates the central drama in the *lai:* he is a werewolf who hides his clothes in a hollow rock, an enclosure that protects him, because without his clothes, without concealing himself after a bestial episode, he cannot transform himself back into a man, exposed ("aperceüz") and trapped as a werewolf forever "a tuz jurs" (74–75). He continues to explain to his inquiring wife how his security depends on maintaining his secret and his secret space: "Ja nen avreie mes sucurs / De si k'il me fussent rendu. / Pur ceo ne voil k'il seit seü (76–78) ("I'd be helpless / until I got them back / That's why I don't want their hiding place to be known").

The object that protects him from exposure and enslavement to the werewolf form is the "piere cruose e lee . . . dedenz cavee" (93–94) ("a big stone / hollowed out inside"), a convenient and friendly enclosure left, like Guigemar's ship, unexplained. But the wife coaxes the secret out of him with verbal craft, much as Equitan glibly wins the wife of the seneschal and betrays him. Bisclavret was not anxious to reveal himself because secrets, he knows, preserve not only his humanity but also, therefore, the love he fears to lose: "Mal m'en vendra si jol vus di, / Kar de m'amur vus partirai / E mei meïsmes en perdrai" (54–56) ("Harm will come to me if I tell you about this, / because I'd lose your love / and even my very self"). He begs her, for love, to stay away from his secret space, but by pretending to ask for love's own sake herself (80 ff.), she tricks him into revealing it, all the while planning "Cum ele s'en puïst partir: / Ne voleit mes lez lui gisir" (101–2) ("how she might get rid of him; / she never wanted to sleep with him again"). Her treacherous violation of space, a space her husband imbues with the power to preserve their love, leads ironically to her own downfall, for one revelation leads to another here, and the wife's infidelity is exposed in the process. Bisclavret was simultaneously and unknowingly preserving not only his dark side but hers too, and one could argue that the real monster in the tale is the treacherous wife, who ends up the mutilated mother of deformed, noseless children, as the beast himself is restored to humanity, civilization and honor. Her secret would not stay hidden for long, as Marie might say, because it is extracted from her, not with sly rhetoric but with torture (255ff.) in moments of violence that recall the end of Equitan. And like Equitan, the wife here proves herself no master of the arts of concealing and revealing, for her actions serve only to unmask herself, all too literally as it turns out.

Significantly, Marie draws much attention to the final private space in the *lai,* the inner chambres where Bisclavret changes clothes.[13] The king's councilor advises giving the beast private time and space to allow the proposed retransformation; it all occurs behind firmly shut doors:

> "En tes chambres le fai mener
> E la despoille od lui porter;
> Une grant piece l'i laissums.
> S'il devient hum, bien le verums."
> Li reis meïsmes le mena

> E tuz les hus sur lui ferma.
> Al chief de piece i est alez,
> Deus baruns ad od lui menez.
> En la chambrë entrent tuit trei;
> Sur le demeine lit al rei
> Truevent dormant le chevalier.
>
> ("Have him lead to your chambers
> and bring the clothes with him;
> then we'll leave him alone for a while.
> If he turns into a man, we'll know about it."
> The king himself led the way
> and closed all the doors on him.
> After a while he went back,
> taking two barons with him;
> all three entered the king's chamber.
> On the king's royal bed
> they found the knight asleep.)
>
> ("Bisclavret" 289–99)

The episode reflects the return of privacy, and the proper use of space, in this case the king's own chambers which facilitate and signify the beast's reintegration into society, just as the dense wood and the hollow rock had earlier hidden him and his secret from observation. But now he has moved from that exilic landscape to the king's own bed, in a wonderful reversal of the profane bed in "Equitan." Marie shows in this *lai* that space serves not only deserving lovers but also a just and isolated man, for Bisclavret, like the seneschal in "Equitan," loses his treacherous wife but keeps his honor and his place. The animated spaces in the *Lais* can protect Marie's lovers from treachery and can protect the "Hummë . . . de grant pris" ("Guigemar" 8) too, punishing, in the process, the secretive lovers who sought to benefit from betraying the just. These last two *lais* do not feature a woman imprisoned by an old jealous husband or father but rather a man as the victim of secrecy and lies; yet nonetheless, just as in "Guigemar" and in the other *lais* to follow, Marie manipulates the physical world to alternately rupture and conceal secrets in a series of violations, intrusions and reclamations, exposing the base and protecting her heroes, bringing everyone, finally, to a place of justice.

In "Yonec" we see a similar use of enclosures to mete out justice, this time as a *Jaloux* both imprisons his wife and uses a trap window to ensnare her magical, birdman lover, Muldumarec, the father of the yet unborn title character. As in "Guigemar," "Equitan," and "Bisclavret," the evil once again try to manipulate secret space to further their control over the protagonists, but Marie depicts the marriage here as a particularly severe form of isolation and deprivation:

> De ceo ke ele iert bele e gente,
> En li garder mist mut s'entente;
> Dedenz sa tur l'ad enserreie
> En une grant chambre pavee.
> Il ot une sue serur,

Veille ert e vedve, sanz seignur:
Ensemble od la dame l'ad mise
Pur li tenir mieuz en justise.
Autres femmes i ot, ceo crei,
En une autre chambre par sei,
Mes ja la dame n'i parlast,
Si la vielle nel comandast.
Issi la tint plus de set anz.
Unques entre eus n'eurent enfanz
Ne fors de cele tur n'eissi,
Ne pur parent ne pur ami.
Quant li sires s'alot cuchier,
N'i ot chamberlenc ne huissier
Ki en la chambre osast entrer
Ne devant lui cirge alumer.
Mut ert la dame en grant tristur,
Od lermes, od suspir e plur;
Sa beuté pert en teu mesure
Cume cele ki n'en ad cure.
De sei meïsme mieuz vousist
Que morz hastive la preisist.

(Because she was beautiful and noble
he made every effort to guard her.
He locked her inside his tower
in a great paved chamber.
A sister of his,
who was also old and a widow, without her own lord,
he stationed with his lady
to guard her even more closely.
There were other women, I believe,
in another chamber by themselves,
but the lady never spoke to them
unless the old woman gave her permission.
So he kept her more than seven years—
they never had any children;
she never left that tower,
neither for family nor for friends.
When the lord came to sleep there
no chamberlain or porter
dared enter that room,
not even to carry a candle before the lord.
The lady lived in great sorrow,
with tears and sighs and weeping;
she lost her beauty,
as one does who cares nothing for it.
She would have preferred
death to take her quickly.)

(25–50)

Though the *Jaloux* wanted children to pass on his lineage, Marie hints at his impotence, making this space not only a prison of silence and deprivation but also a dead and sterile place, bound to be ruptured, with the approach of spring, by love, by life, and by procreation. As Ferrante puts it, concerning the *Lais* as a whole, "Possessive love brings sterility, shame, frustration, even death, but generous love heals, brings joy, wealth, and honor in the world" ("French Courtly Poet" 66). The evil and artificiality of her confinement is worsened by the fact that she cannot even hear mass (75–76). Thus, not only does he fail to love and to impregnate her, but he also strips her of her religious rights, cutting her off from both nature and from spirit. From what we have seen so far in Marie's poetics of space, we recognize here a corrupt, even unholy space, watched by the envious eyes of the impotent *Jaloux* and his lordless sister, forces eager to prevent all love and joy from flourishing. The bird lover himself describes their constant surveillance, as he promises his love to return at her will:

> "Mes tel mesure en esgardez
> Que nus ne seium encumbrez.
> Ceste vielle nus traïra,
> E nuit e jur nus gaitera;
> Ele parcevra nostre amur,
> Sil cuntera a sun seignur.
> Si ceo avient cum jeo vus di
> E nus seium issi trahi,
> Ne m'en puis mie departir
> Que mei n'en estuce murir."

> ("But you must make certain
> that we're not discovered.
> This old woman will betray us,
> night and day she will spy on us.
> She will perceive our love,
> and tell her lord about it.
> If that happens,
> If we are betrayed,
> I won't be able to escape.
> I shall die.")

(201–10)

Like Bisclavret, Muldumarec knows that betrayal can lead to doom and thus that a secret is a fragile thing in the world of suspicion, envy and treachery. "Encumbrez" (202) indicates not merely discovery but also dishonor and harassment (*encumbrance*), which will destroy both the love if it is "perceived" and the lover himself. His fears are of course all too justified, as the envious successfully plot his death.

Marie, sworn enemy of the envious, accordingly lashes out at the conspiracy launched against the handsome couple, as she recounts the *Jaloux*'s instructions to his old sister:

"Fetes semblant de fors eissir,
Si la lessiez sule gisir;
En un segrei liu vus estez
E si veez e esgardez
Que ceo peot estre e dunt ço vient
Ki en si grant joie la tient."
De cel cunseil sunt departi.
Allas! Cum ierent malbailli
Cil ke l'un veut si agaitier
Pur eus traïr e enginnier!

("Let her lie alone;
You stay in a hidden (secret) place
And see and look
For what it can be and from whence it comes
That holds her in such great joy."
They broke off their meeting.
Alas, how mistreated will be
Those whom someone wants to spy upon
In order to betray and deceive them!)[14]

(247–56)

The exclamation indicates Marie's hatred, but it also displays how the envious use secrecy to try to undo the lovers, who are of course keeping secrets themselves to protect their love. Marie is thus here crafting a battle for control of both space and of secrecy, with love, and life itself, at stake.

The battle continues when, after the lover is wounded, the lady defies her prison by leaping from the window—a more perilous escape than that of Guigemar's lady through the unlocked door (337), and in may ways "Yonec" is an intensified version of "Guigemar," more dire and violent. She follows the trail of blood through an "entree" in a hill; then to a city "De mur fu close tut entur" (361), but luckily, "La porte aval fu desfermee" (371); she then enters one chamber and then a second and finally a third (382), where she finds her love, dying but able to give her the ring that protects her from her husband's wrath. Just as the lady escapes an enclosure, she at once takes control of space in seeking out her man, leaping out of and penetrating into a series of places. The ring may reflect the renewed power she has over her captor, since she has willed herself free from his encumbering control by planning her and her lover's ultimate revenge. But in any case, all motion out of and through enclosures in this *lai* helps to bring about justice. Those who use space to spy and trap and to kill, making space not only a prison but an animal trap, will suffer for their envy and treachery. Fittingly, the lover's ornate tomb is the *lai*'s final locus; here in front of memorialized space, the son learns the story of his parents and kills his evil stepfather. The lady, fleeing confinement for most of her life, now dies and is placed in the coffin together with her dead lover, in a final act of spatial and romantic justice.[15]

The tomb here foreshadows the jeweled box of the next *lai*, "Laüstic," where the killing of another bird chastens loving neighbors who were toying with dangerous spaces and secrets as they conduct an extramarital flirtation. The description of their situation is rich with the vocabulary of space, enclosure, surveillance, and secrecy that informs and animates the drama here and in so many other of the *lais*:

> Sagement e bien s'entreamerent,
> Mut se covrirent e garderent
> Qu'il ne feussent aparceü
> Ne desturbé ne mescreü;
> E il le poeient bien fere,
> Kar pres esteient lur repere:
> Preceines furent lur maisuns
> E lur sales e lur dunguns;
> N'i aveit bare ne devise
> Fors un haut mur de piere bise.
> Des chambres u la dame jut,
> Quant a la fenestre s'estut,
> Poeit parler a sun ami
> De l'autre part, e il a li,
> E lur aveirs entrechangier
> E par geter e par lancier.

> (They loved each other discreetly and well,
> concealed themselves and took care
> that they weren't seen
> or disturbed or suspected.
> And they could do this well enough
> since their dwellings were so close,
> their houses were next door,
> and so were their rooms and their towers;
> there was no barrier or boundary
> except a high wall of dark stone.
> From the rooms where the lady slept,
> if she went to the window
> she could talk to her love
> on the other side, and he to her,
> and they could exchange their possessions,
> by tossing and throwing them.)
> ("Laüstic" 29–44)

Here neighbors flirt, loving each other "discreetly and well," "conceal[ing] themselves" and "tak[ing] care that they weren't seen or disturbed or suspected," all facilitated by the physical proximity of their homes. Thus, though the woman is "estreit gardee" (49) when her husband is in town, the lovers can communicate through and around the impeding wall. Marie's lovers, as we will see emphasized in "Milun," always find a way, no mater how awkward or bizarre it now seems. The lady's husband thwarts the affair by killing the nightingale, her excuse for waking at night and going to the window to see her lover. At the end of the failed love and failed adultery, we learn that the affable but thwarted lover has enshrined (*enseeler* [155]) the dead nightingale in a lavish, bejeweled box:

Un vaisselet ad fet forgier;
Unques n'i ot fer ne acier,
Tuz fu d'or fin od bones pieres,
Mut precïuses e mut chieres;
Covercle i ot tres bien asis.
Le laüstic ad dedenz mis,
Puis fist la chasse enseeler.
Tuz jurs l'ad fete od lui porter.

(He had a small vessel fashioned,
with no iron or steel in it;
it was all pure gold and good stones,
very precious and very dear;
the cover was very carefully attached.
He placed the nightingale inside
and then he had the casket sealed—
he carried it with him always.)

(149–56)

The killing of the bird, therefore, does not bring justice to evil doers per se but hints at the potential violence that would occur if the married lady and her neighbor were to concretize their illicit love—a love that has no sanction because, in contrast to "Yonec," the lady here has suffered no severe imprisonment or deprivation beyond the basic demands of marriage. The violence here is actually a gift to the lady, who makes it a gift to her would-be lover, a jeweled memorial sublimating their love and representing disaster averted, for as the *Lais* clearly depict, foolish lovers are just as likely to suffer violence as are the envious enemies of love. Thus the box here constitutes not so much the death of love as it embodies a safe space for a love unfulfilled but keenly felt and perpetually remembered. The husband conceals well, for he does not reveal openly his knowledge of the incipient affair, communicating instead in secret signs, just as the wife had when she claimed it was the bird who drew her nocturnal attention. In fact, all three conceal danger craftily, and in the jeweled box the potential for both love and death remain forever hidden. Perhaps, as readers have noticed, no other image in the *Lais* reflects Marie's own art as pointedly as does this elegant box enclosing the tuneful bird.[16] For three lines after describing the sealed, concealing box, Marie reports, in one of her customary celebrations of tale telling, that the story she has just told would not stay hidden for long ("Ne pot estre lunges celee" [158]). Marie thus juxtaposes these images of concealment and revelation (here carried by *enseeler* and *celer*) in "Laüstic" just as she does in her "Prologue," where she will not hide her abilities, although she must offer them forth obscurely, as if in a splendid *chasse*, a bejeweled *integumentum* that hides a secret truth within. For though a sinful love is thwarted, here it can be enclosed, encased, and enshrined within walls, where it remains forever an obscure object of scrutiny that we may gloss, becoming, one would hope, "plus sens" in the process. This *lai* displays well that the labor of gloss, more than the comfort of *caritas*, is Marie's legacy to her readers.

In "Milun" we witness another kind of concealing *integumentum,* as Marie conducts a battle between secrets and intrusions and lovers again use concealed spaces to further their love and to defeat the encumbrances of the envious and wicked. This time Marie offers not a jeweled case but a feathery swan that ferries secret missives between the lovers, well concealed from the lady's husband, a rich and powerful lord. The *lai* recalls "Guigemar" and "Yonec," for here again our protagonists combat surveillance and female constriction, first under the rule of the lady's father and then of the husband. As soon as the love begins, Milun knows that it must be kept secret, because if their *cunseil* were revealed, all will be lost, as he tells a trusty companion: "Amis, fet il, or t'entremet / Qu'a m'amie puisse parler / E de nostre *cunseil* celer" (36–38) ("My friend," he said, "please undertake / to help me to speak to my beloved / and to keep our communications secret"). As in "Yonec," this *lai* revolves around an extramarital birth, which itself betrays the double nature of concealing and revealing. Giving birth is the most powerful kind of revelation, expressing the strength and historicity of a noble love, yet it also provides the ultimate challenge for Marie's masters of concealing secrets. Pregnancies often are "writ," as Shakespeare would put it, "with character too gross" (*Measure for Measure* 1.2.136) on the mother, yet Milun's girl manages to hide both pregnancy and birth from her father with the help of a trusty old servant and friends of Milun who take the child to his sister. No one ever knew. Despite this success, the lady's troubles are not over, for she fears that she will not be able to conceal the unsealing, as it were, of her virginity. Her words before her wedding night depict her awareness of the plight of lovers exactly as we have been tracing it in the *Lais:*

"Lasse, fet ele, que ferai?
Avrai seignur? Cum le prendrai?
Ja ne sui jeo mie pucele;
A tuz jurs mes serai ancele.
Jeo ne soi pas que fust issi,
Ainz quidoue aveir mun ami;
Entre nus celisum l'afaire,
Ja ne l'oïsse aillurs retraire.
Mieuz me vendreit murir que vivre!
Mes jeo ne sui mie delivre,
Ainz ai asez sur mei gardeins
Vieuz e jeofnes, mes chamberleins,
Ki tuz jurz heent bone amur
E se delitent en tristur."

("Alas," she said, "what can I do?
Must I be married? How can I?
I am no longer a virgin,
I'll have to be a servant all my life.
I didn't know it would be like this;
rather I thought I could have my love,
that we could keep it secret between us,

that I'd never hear it bruited about.
Now I'd rather die than live,
But I'm not even free to do that,
Since I have guardians all around me,
Old and young; my chamberlains,
Who hate a noble love,
And take their delight in sadness.")

(133–46)

Like Lanval, she looks for the place where lovers can be free from slander and intrusion, imagining that this is how she thought things should be, that love is a private matter, "celisum" and "entre nus." And like Marie herself in the "Prologue," she knows that the envious are always present, armed with gossip and savoring the suffering of the wise and noble. Marie perseveres, as the *Lais* themselves illustrate; some force drives her on and protects her from the bite of the curs who can never really stop her from revealing, one after the other, these children of her imagination and learning. Oddly, the girl here enjoys some similar success. She keeps the secret of her motherhood into her marriage, for though she fears being discovered as less than a virgin, we never hear report of the husband's discovery. The lady has somehow mastered the art of concealment. Like the open door in "Guigemar," this is one of Marie's oddly magical moments, and so somehow the lover's secret is safe, safe with Marie and safe with us, allowing Milun and his lady to continue the affair, employing at this point the hidden letters. The whole plan ends, finally, in reunion, unity and family—vital, creative, and redemptive principles that flourish in the wake of the sterile, jealous husband's death. Marie is not writing allegorically; the lovers do not merely represent the writer, but both lover and poet face similar trials in their aspirations to live free, to create, and to survive the onslaught of the envious who live to undo the renown and the happiness of others.

As the lovers engage in this combat, we witness continuous images of sealing and secretiveness: Milun writes the first letters and "sis seela" (161), hiding them in the feathers ("E dedenz la plume musciê") (164). Thus his lover extracts it and opens the seal: "Ele en ad la seel bruise (226)," completing the secret process of communication.[17] The scene recalls the mutual knotting and locking of their private bodies by the lovers in "Guigemar," as the lovers here too control the private spaces of intimacy by sealing and unsealing secrets. Even seemingly incidental exposition in "Milun" reveals the language of secrecy, as the very tone and texture of the poem reflects a struggle against exposure and confinement. Milun's messenger who brings the girl the swan claims as his pretense that he wants to show his respects so that he will not be "desturbez" (187) while visiting in the country. The porter then brings him in "in such a way that he wasn't seen or disturbed by anyone," "Celui ameine en teu maniere / Que de nului n'i fu sceüz, / Desturbez ne aparceüz" (200–202), just as Guigemar's lady escapes her room and heads for the ship "undisturbed" (677 and see above). A girl opens the door to the chamber to let the porter in, an image opposed to the scene in "Equitan" where a girl holds the door fruitlessly against the seneschal as he discovers the king with his adulterous wife. Marie tends to describe all the processes of love as spatial negotiations, a series of articulated movements that lead to freedom and love for those who can master the art of concealing and revealing. And the entire process mediated by the swan leads in fact to many intimate encounters between the lovers because nothing can stop love:

> Nuls ne poet estre si destreiz
> Ne si tenuz estreitement
> Que il ne truisse liu sovent.

> (They met together several times.
> (No one can be so closely constrained
> or so closely guarded
> that he can't find a way out.))

(286–88)

Marie here recognizes a force that has nothing to do with *mesure* or with *caritas*. My argument here thus supports Spence's historical hypothesis that "[w]hat we now call courtly love—which Marie and her contemporaries were engaged in exploring—developed at least in part as a response, an answer, a solution even to the growing court vice of envy" ("Double Vision" 267). This force, call it anachronistically "courtly love" or not, breaks through all barriers of restraint and confinement. With what result in "Milun"? This extramarital love, sanctioned in Marie's moral economy, brings forth not a jeweled box but a good son, and when father and son are reunited, Marie makes a family out of the revealed secret, as the *lai* moves toward order, family, and an open and just love. Milun, just as Muldumarec does in "Yonec," reports to his lover that she holds his life in her hands (237–38). Yonec's mother fails, sadly, to protect her lover and must await distant but sure revenge, dying herself, nonetheless, when it is at hand. "Milun," as a companion piece to "Yonec," depicts a similar struggle but one that yields greater success. In opposition to the tragic failure of the hawk, the delightful feathers of the swan keep both murder and tragedy away: Milun lives, and, unlike in "Yonec," the son here need not kill his mother's husband to unite his parents, for the husband conveniently dies. Despite these differences in degree, in both *lais,* the mastering of space and secrecy brings forth final justice against the enemies of love and ensures the perpetuity of family, embodied in two strong sons, loyal to their amorous parents and sworn enemies of the envious. Like Marie's many *lais* themselves, these children, swords in hand if needed, could not stay hidden for long.

After twelve poems in which lovers combat or utilize enclosed spaces in their quest for love and safety, Marie ends the whole affair by putting all three lovers from "Eliduc," the final *lai*, behind sacred walls, where presumably they will be safe from all the dangers at hand and no longer be a bother to poet or reader. But before they reach safe haven, they participate in adventures of love and space that allow Marie to recapitulate the *Lais'* themes of secrecy, slander, envy, adultery, and privacy, all informed by the paradoxical imperative to at once conceal and to reveal. As Eva Rosenn rightly observes, "[I]ssues of concealment and revealment provide a recurrent theme throughout the *Lais*," and "[s]ecrets are at the heart of ten of the twelve *Lais*" (226). These issues run through the prologues and all the *lais* because the good and noble, once others hear of their happiness or fame, become vulnerable to the envious machinations of others. To reveal one's own worth is to expose oneself to attack, but worth is difficult to conceal.[18] Accordingly, "Eliduc" opens by echoing Marie's own troubles in the "Prologue," for the accomplished knight, like our talented poet, is attacked by envy and slander:

> Pur l'envie del bien de lui,
> Si cum avient sovent d'autrui,
> Esteit a sun seignur medlez
> E empeiriez e encusez,
> Que de la curt le cungea
> Sanz ceo qu'il ne l'areisuna.
>
> (But envy of his success,
> which often happens among people,
> caused trouble between him and his lord.
> He was slandered and accused
> until the lord sent him away from his court
> without a formal accusation.)

(41–46)

But "Eliduc" is not only the story of a man dishonored, recalling, in addition to Marie herself, "Lanval" and "Bisclavret," but also the story of a man with two loves, both noble, beautiful, and as he is, deserving of happiness. To put the problem into spatial terms, too many doors are open for Eliduc. In the absence of a *Jaloux* and with his mistress's father encouraging the love (see 492ff.), the married Eliduc thus becomes his own worst enemy. Marie intentionally paints him and herself into a corner: without prison walls and a tormented or closely guarded woman, in "Guigemar," "Yonec," and "Milun," and without the evil treachery that dooms foolish lovers as in "Equitan" or "Bisclavret" ("Laüstic" more innocently works its own justice), this situation in "Eliduc" is difficult to adjudicate by Marie's standards.

And yet, as in the other *lais*, the drama here revolves around secrets concealed and revealed, and such imagery and vocabulary saturates the text. For example, when Guilliadun becomes interested in Eliduc, she sends a chamberlain who approaches the knight "a cunseil" ("in secret") (404); when he returns with news of her suit, she commands him, "nel me celer" ("don't hide anything from me") (419), for though she acted secretly, she wants nothing hidden from herself. But things *are* hidden, for Guilliadun "ne saveit pas que femme eüst" (584) ("didn't know he had a wife"), and, at the same time, Eliduc hides the very affair from his own wife to whom he has promised fidelity and return. The *lai*, then, is a complex game of concealing and revealing. The great truth of love must be revealed, but all revelations, like Marie's own expression of art, bring vulnerability and danger to their "author." Since Eliduc does keep the affair chaste, he is always only on the verge of sin. And yet, with two noble loves, Eliduc is trapped in an unhealthy concealment, and he must "behave very secretly" ("Mut se cuntient sutivement") (717). He makes his entourage pledge and swear "De tut sun afaire celer" (758) ("to keep the whole affair secret"), and as he returns to Guilliadun, "Ne voleit mie estre veüz / Ne trovez ne recuneüz" (765–66) ("he didn't want to be seen, / or found or recognized"). As she plays with the concealed and the revealed, Marie offers us many such pregnant situations, and thus by this final *lai* we know that this is not the kind of secret that can remain hidden under a rock or in a swan's feathers for twenty years. According to the private laws of the heart that Marie has been forging, all these lovers have just claims. What can be done with them?

Before the finale, one odd option presents itself when Guilliadun seems to die at sea, shocked from learning Eliduc's secret. His men prepare to dig a grave for her, a final, private resting place, but "Mes il les fist ariere traire" (922) ("he made them hold"), for he wants to see how he might "le liu eshaucier/ U d'abbeïe u de mustier" (927–28) ("glorify a place with an abbey or a church"). That is, he wants to construct a more elaborate tomb, to create worthier, memorial space, so he can mourn perpetually: "Sur vostre tumbe chescun jur / Ferai refreindre ma dolur" (949–50) (each day on your tomb / I shall make my grief resound). The proposed tomb continues Marie's fixation on memorial space; it recalls that of "Deus Amanz," where place and time remember the two dead lovers, and also the tomb of "Yonec," where tragedy and justice converge, and finally the jeweled box of "Laüstic," that *lai's* elaborate shrine to lost love. Yet it is not this lai's fate to end in such an enclosure, and Eliduc's delay luckily defers the dénouement until all can find shelter in Marie's final, glorious construction, the *Lais's* last enclosure, the sacred space behind the walls of the cloister.[19] Guildeluec first takes the veil; then Marie describes Eliduc's preparation for himself and Guilliadun:

> Pres del chastel, de l'autre part,
> Par grant cunseil e par esgart
> Une eglise fist Elidus.
> De sa terë i mist le plus
> E tut sun or e sun argent;
> Hummes i mist e autre gent
> De mut bone religïun
> Pur tenir l'ordre e la meisun.
> Quant tut aveit appareillé,
> Si nen ad puis gueres targié:
> Ensemble od eus se dune e rent
> Pur servir Deu omnipotent.
> Ensemple od sa femme premiere
> Mist sa femme que tant ot chiere.
> El la receut cum sa serur
> E mut li porta grant honur.
> De Deu servir l'amonesta
> E sun ordre li enseigna.
> Deu priouent pur lur ami
> Qi'il li feïst bone merci,
> E il pur eles repreiot.
>
> (Near the castle, on the other side,
> after great care and deliberation

Eliduc founded a church
To which he gave most of his land
And all his gold and silver.
To maintain the order and the house,
He placed his men in it, and other people,
Devout in their religion.
When he had prepared everything,
he delayed no longer;
with the others he gave and rendered himself up
to serve almighty God.
With his first wife he placed the wife whom he so cherished.
She received her as her sister
And gave her great honor;
She encouraged her to serve God
And instructed her in her order.
They prayed to God for their friend —
That He would have mercy on him —
And he prayed for them.)

(1153–73)

Marie's decision is a crafty one here, confusing and perhaps ironic in its implications, an act that undoes all the picaresque trials of love in "Eliduc" and in all
the *Lais*. If the chaste cloister and mutual prayer are the best safe haven for the
conflicting claims of love, why recount love's trials at all, unless to display love's
folly? But in other *lais*, love brings marriage, happiness, and children, in the spirit
of natural justice. The cloister is the final, but not the authoritative option, Marie's
way of playfully escaping, like Lanval, pulling the world in after her and her lovers, entering a safe, sacred space beyond both romance and reproach.

As Marie builds toward this artfully ambiguous climax in "Eliduc," she leaves us
with a number of questions. What makes things work in the *Lais*? What sort of
moral or romantic universe has Marie created? Does her treatment of slander, surveillance, and confinement reflect how Marie saw marriage or poetry in the twelfth
century — or both? Whoever she may have been, was she trying to undermine the
social paradigms and institutions of marriage in favor of some notion of what we
might call "romantic love," based on private feelings, the secrets of the heart, as
revealed by the noble lovers of the *Lais*, beyond the reach of fathers, husbands,
and all forces of envy and joylessness? Mikhaïlova calls this "amour *absolu*," arguing that "Marie de France plaide pour un amour pur et naturel qui doit être la
seule loi justifieé dans le monde" (152). Yet in "Equitan" and "Laüstic" we see that
"free love" is constrained by violence when necessary. Marie was aware that some
lovers deserve a world free of envy, where, in Lanval's quotable formulation, "U
nuls püist aveir s'amie / Sanz repreoce e sanz vileinie" (165–66).[20]
   Further, how does her work here relate to the rest of her corpus? How can we
connect the drama of conceal and reveal to the world of craft and reason offered
in the *Fables* or in the mystical, visionary adventures into the unknown in the
Espurgatoire Seint Patriz? This latter is interesting, for it is itself a work about the

revelation of secret places of torment and of joy, the inner sanctums of divine justice, concealed from sinners but revealed to the penitent. As "Eliduc" ends with the building of a cloister, this poem features the Saint's erection of an abbey at the sight of his revelations. This abbey is well sealed and becomes the entryway for many who come to witness the truth of St. Patrick's preaching. We recognize here the spatial vocabulary we know so well from the *Lais:*

De mur l'enclost, portes i fist,
e bone fermeüre i mist,
pur ceo qu'um n'i peüst entrer,
se par lui nun, ne la aler . . .
El tens seint Patriz, par licence,
pristrent li plusur penitence.
Quant il esteient absolu,
si vindrent la u li us fu.
Enz entrerent seürement.
Mult sufrirent peine e turment
e mult virent horrible mal
de la dure peine enfernal;
aprés icele grant tristesce
virent grant joie e grant leesce.
Ço qu'il voldrent cunter e dire
fist seinz Patriz iluek escrire.

(He closed it with a wall and made gates,
And placed good locks on them,
So that one could not go or enter there
Without his permission . . .
In the time of Saint Patrick,
Many entered with permission, and did penance there.
When they were absolved of their sins,
They came to the place where the gate was,
And entered securely.
They suffered great pain and torment,
And witnessed much of the horrible agony
Of bitter infernal pain;
After this great sorrow,
They witnessed great joy and happiness.
Whatever they wished to recount and tell,
Saint Patrick had written down on the spot.)
(*Espurgatoire* 343–46 . . . 351–62)

And here, too, in the *Espurgatoire,* just as in the *Lais,* we see that the spatial drama creates narrative, for the Saint and the canons who follow him write down what the visitors witness, "pur edifiér altre gent / e qu'il n'en dutassent niént" (431–32) ("to edify other people and to leave no doubts about purgatory"). These stories thus recall the *Lais* themselves, which will sharpen the minds and the morals of those who hear, interpret, and gloss them throughout time. These striking connections between the *Lais* and the *Espurgatoire* clearly display that space and the complex drama of entering, sealing, and revealing is central to an understanding of Marie, her moral universe, and her art, whether her subject be chivalric love or divine justice. I hope in this chapter to have sparked future study of these thematic and imagistic relations in these two poems about different kinds of "revelations."

Finally, how does our study relate to critical understanding of Marie specifically as a woman and as a woman writer?[21] I have resisted this particular focus here, but I hope to have shown that in whatever gendered or political context we want to embrace Marie, any understanding of the *Lais* must consider Marie's deep treatment of space and secrecy in love. As lovers flee from spaces of confinement and seek places of privacy and freedom, the artificial and natural landscapes, including ships, towers, chambers, tubs, tombs, rocks, birds, and cloisters, all open and close as good lovers require. As if animated by Orpheus's song, or, should we say, Marie's, they themselves move to serve love and to combat envy. How can lovers ensure that the natural and artificial landscape will support their cause, and what has Marie shown us about space, secrets, and the search for privacy in the *Lais*? In part, she shows that those who can master the paradox of concealing and revealing, who can most artfully modulate the two, will thrive and find safety and freedom from envy. As I noted, Marie will often report that the story at hand must be told, that some force is driving her on to reveal the past and to succeed as a learned artist. In her surrogates she replays the drama of her own struggle, punishing the envious *gangleür* and *losengier*, who pry and penetrate, and rewarding the lovers who hide what they must but persevere to reveal the great truth of love, which, like Marie's own "escïence," is a gift from God that emboldens lovers to brave slander, surveillance, time, shame, and death as they seek freedom, privacy, and peace. When all else fails or is exhausted and the priorities of love become nebulous, the sacred walls to the community of heaven on earth are always there to receive the weary lover, who, like an aging troubadour, hears the divine calling.

Writing a "final word' on Marie is difficult, for it is impossible to decide whether to end on a note celebrating concealment or perhaps revelation, *celer* or *mostrer*. Marie's playfulness has shown us that we should not be too bold in any claim to have unlocked the mystery of the *Lais*. Whenever we try to do so, we are thwarted, because Marie's moral, ethical, and gendered frameworks are offered "oscurement," leaving us the obligation of supplying the "surplus" as best we can. Thus, though I hope to have revealed something of her art, I would argue that Marie, finally, seals herself in a private space of art and imagination that we have not yet penetrated.[22] And yet, as master of *celer* and *mostrer*, she has at the same time revealed all the *Lais*, just as promised, in defiance of her envious enemies, and has forged for herself not an open, public love, nor a husband and a child, but rather a place in literary history as heir to the "custume . . . as ancïens" ("Prologue" 9). For like a noble man, a gentile woman, and a worthy love, a wise poet and her "escïence" will not stay hidden for long.

Notes

1. All references to Marie are to the Rychner edition, and all translations, except where noted, are from Hanning and Ferrante. For a basic and thorough introduction to Marie's literary culture and themes, see Mickel and see Burgess; concise studies of Marie, with emphasis on her status as a woman writer, are offered by Ferrante ("French Courtly Poet" and *To the Glory* 195–204); see also here Sankovitch. For a concise historical survey of awareness and attitudes toward Marie, see Maréchal 1–21. Linda Georgianna is currently working on Marie's relations to history, truth, and historiography in preparation for the forthcoming "The Literary Cultures of Early England" (*Oxford English Literary History,* Vol. 1, Georgianna and K. O. O'Keeffe). After composing this chapter, I attended her presentation "Marie de France and the *Aventures* of History" on 25 October 2003 at a conference in honor of Robert W. Hanning, held at Columbia University.

2. On Marie's "Prologue," see Spitzer's influential study of its exegetical dimensions; see Robertson and see Leupin on the same subject and also on the "inexhaustible readership of the future" (241). See Rosenn on the relations of Marie's obscurity to male literary tradition; on textual and editorial problems in relation to meaning and translation, see Burch; and see Bloch 61. See also Cowell, who, in studying "Deus Amanz" specifically, highlights the importance of secrecy to lovers in the *Lais;* his excellent point complements my arguments in this chapter: "['Deux Amanz'] thematizes a desire for silence, or at the very least for strictly guarded private communication. . . . [This creates] a seeming fundamental contradiction between Marie's Pro[logue] and its use of the Parable of the Talents on the one hand, and the content of many of her tales on the other" (341).

3. See Augustine, *De Doctrina,* especially 6.7, and Boccaccio, *Genealogia* 14.12 et passim.

4. As Spence puts it. "All the tales, it can be argued, are about envy and the problems that stem from it" (*Texts and the Self* 127 and note); on publicity and on the audience's participation in it, see Sturges, who studies the characters' need for symbols and interpretive skills, 94–100: "Publicity, we learn over and over again in the tales themselves, can destroy the love-relationship" (94). See also Spence, "Double Vision," for an important and useful study of envy and love in the context of Patristic and vernacular conceptions of "invidia."

5. In his study of "Deus Amanz," Cowell notes the ways in which the *Lais* often recapitulate the drama of particularly female authorship, offering that "Deus Amanz" "is not the only one of Marie's narratives which can be read as the story of the origin of her texts" (339).

6. Though Spence discusses "Guigemar" when making this observation, her idea applies perfectly to "Fresne," where the slandering neighbor repents, now cured of her envy, when happily reunited with her daughter; see "Fresne" 465 ff. But the issue is complex: Spence elsewhere, discussing "Eliduc," not "Guigemar," writes that "aside from this *lai,* however, *caritas* does not play a large part in Marie's work" ("Double Vision" 265). Her ultimate position might found in her comment that there is in Marie a love that is a "*tertium quid* between *caritas* and *invidia*" ("Double Vision" 268) Spence is not interested in secret spaces per se but in the relations among text, self, and reality; thus "Guigemar," is, for example, "clearly the story of the self as a duality which, discovered in the transgressive space outside the court and within the body, is played out in the vernacular written text" (*Texts and the Self* 131). And elsewhere: [Marie] "explores a space in which the causes of envy, the increasingly visualized and reified world, can be manipulated in a different setting to produce different results. This new found land is the land of love, its means of expression, the written text, and its inhabitants, the individual or self. The model the written word offers speaks to the elevation of the signifier and its new visibility which, in turn, reflects a similarly autonomous understanding of the self" ("Double Vision" 275–76).

7. See Curtis's study of the oddly casual violence that pervades the *Lais,* committed by both villainous and heroic characters.

8. My interest in this topic was initially sparked by observing the use of space in the plastic arts, specifically the Metropolitan Museum of Art's *Casket, with Scenes from the Romances* (17.190.173), discussed in the Metropolitan Museum's *Secular Spirit* 26, no. 10, with an

illustration. The fourteenth-century ivory depicts various scenes of privacy, fortification, and surveillance, including one panel of Mark observing Tristan and Isolde. See Barnet for further study of such objects, especially the chapters, "Popular Romances Carved in Ivory" and "Secular Objects and the Romance Tradition," which includes discussion of the Metropolitan's *Casket with Scenes from La Châtelaine de Vergi*, recounting thirteenth-century romance about love, secrecy, and death. Such works provide compelling analogues to the *Lais* and invite further interdisciplinary study.

Mikhaïlova provides a compelling analysis of space, openings, and closures in the *Lais*, often focusing on the boundaries and passages between the social, court world and the "other" world of the marvelous. In the first half of her essay (145–49), Mikhaïlova examines water, forests, windows, and prisons as spaces of boundary and transgression; she is particularly insightful about the ambivalence of space in the *Lais*, and my chapter here hopes to complement some of her fine insights: "La clôture de l'espace est associée à une situation tragique, sans issue, et l'ouverture se présente comme la solution, l'evasion, l'élan vers l'imaginaire. Mais en dehors de cette connotation qui relève d'une symbolique humaine universelle, l'espace dans les *Lais* apparaît ambivalent. Ainsi, à côté de l'espace clôturé comme prison, recontre-t-on également le traitement de la fermeture comme asile, repliement, cachette, lieu de protection de la vie, de l'amour ou d'un secret. Inversement, a côté de l'ouverture-libération, on trouve l'ouverture-chute, l'ouverture-trahison ou déchire-ment" (147). The rest of her essay explores the complex, geometric structure of the *Lais*, relating the themes of openings and closures generally to Marie's narrative art and language, which she sees reflecting a movement, "vers les une ouverture d'ordre plotonicien" and "vers valeurs transcendantales comme l'amour absolu, l'art et la foi dans l'éternal" (153). Mikhaïlova does not study envy, privacy, and control per se but rather the power of words as they variously activate the amorous drama: "L'univers des *Lais* est un monde de la porole, d'une parole ambivalente: dite, entendue ou écrite, elle peut tuer, mettre fin à l'amour et à la vie, mais aussi engendrer l'amour, le prolonger, le sauver" (155).

9. I omit a study of the fascinating "Chievrefoil," which has drawn much commentary; see Spence, "Double Vision" 270ff. and n.18.

10. On the ways "Guigemar" and "Eliduc" thematically frame the collection and on themes of love and social integration in these *lais*, see McCash, "The Curse of the White Hind." For a study of love in "Guigemar," as it relates specifically to the notion of *surplus* established in the "Prologue" and as it reflects Maris's complex Ovidianism, see Adams.

11. See Bloch's use of this passage in his study of how to read "Guigemar" in relation to Marie's complex and even eroticized "programme for the writing and reading of medieval litera-ture," (67) in her "Prologue." Bloch studies the relations between the poet and the lovers in the *lai* and explicates the complex imagery of knots, pleats, and the unfolding of narra-tive; he offers a dramatic and important assessment (though much different from mine) of Marie's relation to her creations: "the poet, in composing, does to the lovers exactly what the jealous husband does to his wife and her lover: she betrays by revealing, and thus destroys at the very moment she creates"(73).

12. On this notion of *privitee*, a Chaucerian theme of interest and importance to readers of Marie, see Hanning.

13. Mikhaïlova notes the importance of the hollow stone and of the king's inner chambers; see 148.

14. The translation is my own with help from Professor M. Roy Harris.

15. For a study of family, parentage and female narratology in the *lai*, see Freeman, "Changing Figure."

16. Freeman sees "Laüstic" reflecting Marie's concerns as a female artist in the "Prologue" and sees the encased bird as a layered symbol that encloses and sanctifies the events of the tale and the characters: "This final object engenders the narratives that retell its origins . . . until finally sealed in the *lai* entitled *Laüstic*" ("Poetics of Silence" 871). Following Freeman, Pickens studies the chasse and notes its relations to the creation of the story itself (144).

See also Mikhaïlova: "L'impossibilité de vivre l'amour charnel mène à la sublimation d'un amour qui s'efface au profit de la beuté, de l'art, à la pérennite de l'Amour" (153).

17. The lady here calls a serving girl for assistance, and the text is ambiguous as to who detaches the letter and who opens it. I believe the meschine detaches the letter but that the "ele" of 226 refers to the lady, the subject of "ad brusié."

18. See Matthew 25:14–32 and consider Rosenn's comment that Marie is beginning the "Prologue" "with an allusion to the parable of the talent" (225). Working from Brian Stock, Rosenn is interested in how the *Lais* "can be seen . . . as a reaction to the social strategies of containment that would deny [Marie] access to the power of speech" (227). See also Wilson and McLeod on the parable as it relates to authorship, responsibility, and dynamic reciprocity, specifically developed by Marie in "Lanvall" and "Yonec," which the authors study comparatively as "male and female fantasies of love" (3).

19. On the relations between religious houses and heaven, see Duby 38ff. See Mikhaïlova 153 for a survey of critical reactions to this religious moment in "Eliduc."

20. On the varieties and complexities of love in the *Lais*, see the thorough survey by Burgess in chapters 6–7, "Women in Love" and "The Vocabulary of Love" (100–178); among Burgess's several solid conclusions is the stark observation that "life for those lovers able to enjoy each other's company is one of constant delight" (178). For a useful study of Marie's women in twelfth-century, sociological context, seeing her treatment of women as "profoundly sympathetic and pragmatic" (107), see McCash, who concludes, however, that "Marie is not a reformer" ("Images of Women" 108).

21. For treatments of Marie's gendered literary consciousness, see Freeman, "Poetics of Silence" 878; Pickens 135; Rosenn 225; Arden 215; Sankovitch 10; and Ferrante, "French Courtly Poet" 67.

22. Mikhaïlova's conclusion is noteworthy here, concerning Marie's rhetorical play: "Cette dynamique de la parole . . . symbolise enfin le côté ouvert, infini de la glose, auquel tous les nouveaux venus apporteront un surplus de sens" (157).

Works Cited

Adams, Tracy. "'Arte Regendus Amor': Suffering and Sexuality in Marie de France's lai de Guigemar." *Exemplaria* 17.2 (2005): 285–315.

Arden, Heather. "The Lais of Marie de France and Carol Gilligan's Theory of the Psychology of Women." *Maréchal* 213–23.

Augustine. *De Doctrina*. Trans. D. W. Robertson Jr. Indianapolis: Bobbs-Merrill Educational, 1958.

Barnet, Peter, ed. *Images in Ivory: Precious Objects of the Gothic Age*. Princeton: Detroit Institute of the Arts and Princeton UP, 1997.

Bloch, R. Howard. "The Medieval Text—'Guigemar'—as a Provocation to the Discipline of Medieval Studies." *Romanic Review* 79 (1988): 63–73.

Boccaccio, Giovanni. *Genealogia Deorum Gentilium*. Trans. Charles G. Osgood. Indianapolis: Liberal Arts, 1930.

Burch, Sally L. "Prologue to Marie's Lais: Back to the Littera." *AUMLA: Journal of the Australasian Universities Language and Literature Association* 89 (1998): 15–42.

Burgess, Glyn S. *The Lais of Marie de France: Text and Context*. Athens: U of Georgia P, 1987.

Cowell, Andrew. "Deadly Letters: 'Deus Amanz,' Marie's 'Prologue' to the Lais and the Dangerous Nature of the Gloss." *Romantic Review* 88.3 (1997): 337–56.

Curtis, Renée L. "Physical and Mental Cruelty in the Lais of Marie de France." *Arthuriana* 6.1 (1996): 22–25.

Duby, Georges, ed. *A History of Private Life*. Vol. 2, Revelations of the Medieval World. Cambridge: Belknap P of Harvard UP, 1988.

Ferrante, Joan. "The French Courtly Poet: Marie de France." *Medieval Women Writers*. Ed. Katharina M. Wilson. Athens: U of Georgia P, 1984. 64–89.

———. *To the Glory of Her Sex: Women's Roles in the Composition of Medieval Texts*. Bloomington: Indiana UP, 1997.

Freeman, Michelle A. "The Changing Figure of the Male: The Revenge of the Female Story-teller." *Maréchal* 243–61.

——. "Marie de France's Poetics of Silence: The Implications for a Feminine Translatio." *PMLA* 99.5 (1984): 860–83.

Hanning, R. W. "'Parlous Play': Diabolic Comedy in Chaucer's Canterbury Tales." *Chaucer's Humor: Critical Essays*. Ed. Jean E. Jost. New York: Garland, 1994. 295–319.

Leupin, Alexandre. "The Impossible Task of Manifesting 'Literature': On Marie de France's Obscurity." *Exemplaria* 3.1 (1991): 221–42.

Maréchal, Chantal, ed. *In Quest of Marie de France: A Twelfth-Century Poet*. Lewiston, N.Y.: Edwin Mellen, 1992.

Marie de France. *Fables*. Ed. and trans. Harriet Spiegel. Toronto: U of Toronto P, 1987.

——. *Les Lais de Marie de France*. Ed. Jean Rychner. Paris: Champion, 1983.

——. *The Lais of Marie de France*. Trans. Robert Hanning and Joan Ferrante. Durham: Labyrinth, 1978.

——. *Saint Patrick's Purgatory*. Ed. and trans. Michael J. Curley. Binghamton: Medieval & Renaissance Texts & Studies, 1993.

McCash, June Hall. "The Curse of the White Hind and the Cure of the Weasel: Animal Magic in the *Lais of Marie de France*." *Literary Aspects of Courtly Culture*. Selected Papers from the Seventh Triennial Congress of the International Courtly Literature Society. Ed. Donald Maddox and Sara Sturm-Maddox. Rochester: Boydel and Brewer, 1994. 211–19.

——. "Images of Women in the Lais of Marie de France." *Medieval Perspectives* 11 (1996): 96–112.

Metropolitan Museum of Art. *The Secular Spirit: Life and Art at the End of the Middle Ages*. New York: Dutton, 1975.

Mickel, Emanuel J., Jr. *Marie de France*. New York: Twayne, 1974.

Mikhaïlova, Miléna. "L'espace dans les Lais de Marie de France: lieux, structure, rhétorique." *Cahiers de Civilisation Médiévale* 40 (1997): 145–57.

Pickens, Rupert. "Marie de France and the Body Poetic." *Gender and Text in the Later Middle Ages*. Ed. Jane Chance. Gainesville: UP of Florida, 1996. 135–71.

Pope, Alexander. "An Essay on Criticism." *Critical Theory Since Plato*. Ed. Hazard Adams. Fort Worth: Harcourt Brace Janovich, 1992.

Robertson, D. W. "Marie de France, *Lais*, Prologue 13–15." *Modern Language Notes* 64 (1949): 336–38.

Rosenn, Eva. "The Sexual and Textual Politics of Marie's Poetics." *Maréchal* 225–42.

Sankovitch, Tilde. "The French Woman Writer in the Middle Ages: Staying Up Late." *Essays in Medieval Studies* 7 (1990): 1–12.

Spence, Sarah. "Double Vision: Love and Envy in the Lais." *Maréchal* 262–94.

——. *Texts and the Self in the Twelfth Century*. Cambridge: Cambridge UP, 1996.

Spitzer, Leo. "The Prologue to the Lais of Marie de France and Medieval Poetics." *Modern Philology* 41 (1943): 96–102.

Sturges, Robert S. *Medieval Interpretation: Models of Reading in Literary Narrative, 1100–1500*. Carbondale: Southern Illinois UP, 1991.

Wilson, Katharina, and Glenda McLeod. "Wholism and Fusion: Success in/of the Lais of Marie de France." *Arachne* 5.1 (1998): 3–30.

Kenneth Bleeth

Chaucerian Gardens and the Spirit of Play

Approaching the Garden of Mirth, the narrator of the *Romaunt of the Rose* observes that "sich solas, sich joie and play, / I trowe that nevere man ne say, / As was in that place delytous."[1] In its various grammatical forms, "play"—a rendering of *deduit, deduire,* or *jouer* in Guillaume de Lorris's *Roman de la Rose*—appears sixteen times in the 1,705 lines of Fragment A of the *Romaunt*. The narrator's favored word for characterizing life in the garden, it denotes a variety of activities—walking about, singing, dancing, making love—that have as their single goal the fulfillment of personal pleasure. As students of the subject have observed, play takes place within carefully prescribed limits of time and space—"temporary worlds within the ordinary world," in Johan Huizinga's phrase (10; cf. Caillois 67; Fink 24)—from which threatening realities are excluded and within which illicit or impossible desires may be satisfied. The *Romaunt* garden functions as just such a "magic circle" (Huizinga 11). The portraits of the 'vices'—Envy, Poverty, Villainy, Hate, and so on—painted on the outside of the garden wall represent unseemly qualities banished from the exclusive paradise of love; Sorrow, who "roughte lytel of playing" (341) is depicted as a spoilsport whose gloom might ruin the party: "For whoso sorouful is in herte, / Him luste nat to play ne sterte" (343–44). Inside the garden, sexual pleasure is exempted from moral strictures: after dancing their "karoles," the elegant denizens of Mirth's garden retire "undir the trees to have her pley" (1318), where the grass is thick and soft as velvet, "on which men myght his lemman leye / As on a fetherbed to pleye" (1421–22). When Dame Idleness, the garden's gatekeeper, identifies herself to the poem's youthful narrator, we are

reminded that entry into this enclosure is a sign of privilege, available only to
those with the leisure that wealth and rank make possible:

> "Lo, sir, my name is Ydelnesse;
> So clepe men me, more and lesse.
> Ful myghty and ful riche am I,
> And that of oon thyng namely,
> For I entende to nothyng
> But to my joye and my pleying."
>
> (592–97)

It has been argued that life in Mirth's garden embodies a male adolescent's sexual
fantasies (Poirion 79–80; Spearing 198). But it figures forth a cultural fantasy as
well, for even as the French nobility was experiencing an erosion of its worldly
power and prestige, Guillaume offered his readers an imaginative space in which
play served as a confirmation of a social identity that was increasingly being
threatened by political and economic realities.[2] In Daniel Poirion's succinct formulation, "Le *Roman de la Rose* nous dit comment la cour se rêve" (tells us how
the court dreams itself to be) (83).

My subject is Chaucer's response to this dream of aristocratic self-fashioning
within a garden setting. First, however, I want to look briefly at another series
of literary pleasure parks, which, like Chaucer's, draw their decor and their thematic associations from Guillaume's *Roman*, but which employ these traditional
topoi to quite different ends. In the author's epilogue to *The Decameron*, Giovanni
Boccaccio takes up the charge that he has written with excessive license, said
things unsuitable for virtuous ladies to hear or speak. He answers his detractors
by invoking the dramatic context of his tales: the stories were told "neither in
a church . . . nor in the schools of philosophers . . . [but in] gardens, in a place
intended for pleasure."[3] The gardens that serve as the setting for the *Decameron*
entertainments are a world of art seemingly closed off from the everyday world,
an alternative reality where special rules obtain. For the ten young people who
make up the *brigata*, the everyday world is the plague-ravaged city of Florence. As
Glending Olson has shown, the move from city to garden can be understood as
part of a well-documented regimen for countering the effects of the plague—both
the physical dangers and the accompanying emotional anxieties—with recreation
and fresh air (*Literature as Recreation* 164–83, 196–204). But the activities of the
young men and women keep the plague at bay in a less immediately practical
sense as well. The gardens and country estates to which they retreat are the site
of what Giuseppe Mazzotta calls "the game of utopia" (40), the ordered exercise
of the imagination that can repair the moral and social dissolution of the city
they have left behind and even, Mazzotta suggests, seems to reverse the effects
of the Fall (42). To be sure, there are hints that the Edenic security of the gardens
is an illusion—at one point we are told that anyone meeting the youthful court-
iers would say that "either these people will not be conquered by death, or they
will die happy."[4] But the irony remains a delicate one, casting only a fleeting
shadow over Boccaccio's confident belief that within art's ludic boundaries, one

can recover something like the "onesto riso e dolce gioco"—the honest laughter and sweet play—that Dante named as the experience of the earthly paradise (*Purg.* 28.96).

As the probable author of Fragment A of the *Romaunt,* Chaucer began his writing career within the *hortus conclusus* of courtly making, addressing an audience whose participation in a privileged textual community was marked by a shared taste for play and game (Minnis 293–302, 305). Laura Howes has suggested that in the *Book of the Duchess* and the *Parliament of Fowls,* the narrator's entrance into a garden represents his acquiescence to the conventions of writing a certain kind of courtly narrative (36–38). But even in his early dream-visions, Chaucer displays some intermittent discomfort with aspects of these conventions, an uneasiness that becomes more pronounced in his later poetry; in particular, he shows himself to be decidedly less sanguine than Boccaccio about the possibility of creating self-sufficient realms of play within the greater world. The gardens I will examine—those in *Troilus* and the *Knight*'s, *Merchant*'s, and *Franklin*'s *Tales*—function differently within their respective poems, but in each case the garden scene is framed by events that expose the simplifications and illusions that attend the cultivation of pure play when it is removed from the pressures of history and the contingencies of communal discourse. In a critique of what he sees as a false dichotomy between "play" and "reality" in the work of Huizinga and Roger Caillois, Jacques Ehrmann argues that "the interior occupied by play can only be defined by and with the exterior of the world, and inversely . . . play viewed as exterior is only comprehensible by and with the interior of the world" (42). What occurs in the gardens of the *Roman* and its numerous French and Italian progeny can be adequately accounted for by Huizinga's notion of play as situated outside of everyday life (34); the framed gardens in *Troilus and Criseyde* and the *Canterbury Tales,* on the other hand, need to be understood in the light of Ehrmann's revision of Huizinga's paradigm. For Chaucer, inside and outside exist in a reciprocal relation; the garden scenes in *Troilus* and the *Tales* ask us to reexamine the notion that the realm of play can be clearly distinguished from a normative reality "out there" and to recognize that play "cannot . . . be isolated as an activity without *consequences*" (Ehrmann 42; Lanham 42–43).

A retreat into play lies at the center of a pivotal episode in Book 2 of *Troilus and Criseyde.* Criseyde, having heard Pandarus's pleading of the lovesick Troilus's case, retires to her "closet" (2.599); from a window in this private room she glimpses Troilus riding through the street, fresh from his victory over the Greeks. The sight of the battle-stained warrior fuels within Criseyde a debate between awakening desire and fear of love's constraints; in a state of characteristic irresolution, "now hoot, now cold . . . bitiwixen tweye" (2.811), she puts off a definitive decision and turns her attention elsewhere: "she rist hire up, and wente hire for to pleye" (2.812). The scene of Criseyde's play is an elegant garden attached to her house, part of the poem's careful rendering of intimate domestic spaces. Chaucer emphasizes both the garden's privacy—it would be walled, and, as Barry Windeatt suggests (193), facing away from the street—and the security it provides for Criseyde at a moment of painful uncertainty in her life. Although the poem's opening episode had depicted Criseyde as an isolated figure in a hostile city (e.g., 1.97–98), the passage under consideration shows her surrounded by a substantial ménage: accompanied by her three nieces and an unspecified number of female attendants, she walks "arm in arm" (2.823) along the sanded pathways and among the turf-topped benches. The pleasure generated by Criseyde's activities is foregrounded in the narrator's comment on her movements and those of her companions, who "up and down ther made many a wente . . . / To pleyen that it joye was to see" (2.815–17).

The communal play among the members of Criseyde's household culminates in a musical interlude, a "Troian song" sung by "Antigone the shene" (2.824–25).[5] It has been argued that, in responding point by point to her misgivings about love, the song works at the level of half-apprehended feelings to persuade Criseyde that "ther is no peril inne" (2.875; Borthwick 232–35; Howard 183). But the circumstances of the song's creation and performance—composed by an unidentified Trojan lady, sung by Criseyde's niece—deflect its relevance to Criseyde's immediate dilemma, her need to choose between love and "libertee" (2.773). Antigone's song is at once an oasis of calm in the midst of emotional turmoil and a demonstration of play's capacity to defer thoughts of futurity (Fink 21–22), just as the garden seems to offer physical seclusion from "th'assege" (2.123) that so distresses Criseyde. The larger design of the work, however, reveals both the fragility of the poem's enclosed spaces and the provisionality of its lyric moments of suspended time. The walled garden lies within the walled city of Troy, itself surrounded by the warring Greeks, who, we are told, "biseged" the city "al aboute," and "shetten"—shut in—"hem of Troie" (1.148–49). As Lee Patterson has argued, the "private [in *Troilus and Criseyde*] stands wholly apart from and seeks to efface the public" (*Chaucer* 107). But the public realm of events makes its presence felt in a variety of ways, among them the poem's representation of physical space. As the series of ever-widening enclosures implies, Criseyde's inner world cannot finally be isolated from the forces of history, any more than the walls of Troy can keep the city from falling. The parallels that exist between Criseyde's personal circumstances and the fate of the city itself, although they refuse to coalesce into a neat pattern of cause and effect (Patterson, *Chaucer* 113–14), unsettle profoundly the binarism of private versus public, inside versus outside.

Like Criseyde's retreat, Emily's garden in the *Knight's Tale* seems initially to exist as an enclave of personal autonomy and control within the poem's larger world of history, politics, and masculine desire. Emily is introduced into the tale almost as an afterthought, as part of Theseus's homeward procession following his victory over the Amazons and his marriage to her sister Hippolyta (1[A].864–71). When we next see her, however, Emily is located squarely within her own space:

> This passeth yeer by yeer and day by day,
> Till it fil ones, in a morwe of May,
> That Emelye, that fairer was to sene
> Than is the lylie upon his stalke grene,
> And fressher than the May with floures newe—
> For with the rose colour stroof hir hewe,

> I noot which was the fyner of hem two—
> Er it were day, as was hir wone to do,
> She was arisen and al redy dight,
> For May wole have no slogardie anyght.
> The sesoun priketh every gentil herte,
> And maketh it out of his slep to sterte,
> And seith: "Arys, and do thyn observaunce."
> This maked Emelye have remembraunce
> To doon honour to May, and for to ryse.
> Yclothed was she fressh, for to devyse:
> Hir yelow heer was broyded in a tresse
> Bihynde hir bak, a yerde long, I gesse.
> And in the gardyn, at the sonne upriste,
> She walketh up and doun, and as hir liste
> She gadereth floures, party white and rede,
> To make a subtil gerland for hire hede;
> And as an aungel hevenysshly she soong.
>
> (I[A].1033–55)

Emily's ordered freedom within the enclosure of her garden is visible partly in her actions—wholly absorbed in her ritual "observaunce" to May, she gathers flowers at her pleasure—and partly in the shape of the passage itself: "Till it fil ones" signals a new subject, the body of the description is rich in repetition and internal cross-reference (the flowers Emily picks for her garland are of the same color as those to which she previously has been compared), and the detail of her angelic singing harmoniously rounds off a framed and stylized whole. In both shape and content, the account of Emily's Maying would appear to exemplify the essential characteristics of the play world as set forth by Eugen Fink: "[I]t possesses its own internal space and time . . . [and] never merges into the continuum of space that we inhabit in real life" (24).

Yet such a merging of discrete spaces is precisely what occurs as we read on, and discover that the very line that had appeared to provide so firm a sense of closure is in fact the first element of a couplet:

> And as an aungel hevenysshly she soong.
> The grete tour, that was so thikke and stroong,
> Which of the castel was the chief dongeoun
> (Ther as the knyghtes weren in prisoun
> Of which I tolde yow and tellen shal),
> Was evene joynaunt to the garden wal
> Ther as Emelye hadde hir pleyynge.
>
> (I[A].1055–61)

Once again, the ordering of the verse imitates the physical disposition of the scene: a shared rhyme and a shared wall join the garden to the tower where Palamon and Arcite are imprisoned by Duke Theseus. Having at first envisaged Emily's *locus amoenus* as a self-sufficient world, we discover that (as in *Troilus*) this seemingly isolated space turns out to be part of a more inclusive structure.

Once brought together, prison and pleasance begin to reveal unexpected connections. Inside the tower, Emily's "pleyynge" is grimly parodied in the activities of
the unhappy Palamon: she rises with the sun "as was hire wone to do" and roams
"up and doun" in the garden singing "as an aungel"; Palamon, "as was his wone,
by leve of his gayler" (I[A].1064), arises on the same sunny morning and roams "to
and fro" in his gloomy cell "compleynynge of his wo" (I[A].1071–72). And when
Palamon at last catches sight of Emily, the two spaces are intertwined:

> And so bifel, by aventure or cas,
> That thurgh a wyndow, thikke of many a barre
> Of iren greet and square as any sparre,
> He cast his eye upon Emelya,
> And therwithal he bleynte and cride, "A!"
> As though he stongen were unto the herte.
>
> (I[A].1074–79)

Evoked with memorable concreteness, the tower window serves as an ominous
frame through which the young knights' aggressive gazing constructs Emily as an
object of desire. The composite image—a double exposure in which the barred window is superimposed on the lady in the garden—sets into motion the transformation of garden into prison that V. A. Kolve has described in *Chaucer and the Imagery
of Narrative* (103–4). Kolve's analysis also underscores the oddly static quality of the
Knight's narration: Emily's vernal garden is recalled in the grove where Arcite goes
"to pleye" (I[A].1503) and "doon his observaunce to May" (I[A].1500) and where
the cousins fight their battle; the grove, in its turn, becomes the site of Theseus's
amphitheater and its tournament in the "lusty seson of . . . May" (I[A].2484) and
then reappears as the setting for Arcite's funeral, with its "wake-pleyes" (I[A].2960),
or funeral games.[6] As the private space of the garden is subsumed in the ubiquitous
mirrorings and repetitions that make up the poem's grand design, so, too, is Emily's
freedom—embodied most vividly in her self-pleasing springtime ritual—gradually constrained by and absorbed into the Knight's public world of masculine competition, chivalric ceremony, and Athenian politics.[7]

Although Palamon addresses her as Venus (I[A].1101–2), Emily's garden play
identifies her as a devotee of Diana, the "chaste goddesse of the wodes grene"
(I[A].2297) to whom she later prays for deliverance from sexual entanglements.
In contrast, "play" in the *Merchant's Tale* almost always connotes sexual activity,
either actual or imagined; the broad semantic range exhibited by the word in the
Romaunt has been narrowed to the *instabilis ludus*—the perverse play—that Alanus
de Insulis personifies as Jocus, born of the adultery of Venus and Antigamus (cols.
455, 459–60). "It is no fors how longe that we pleye," January announces to May
on their wedding night, invoking what he believes to be the church's sanction for
his leisurely lovemaking, "for we han leve to pleye us by the lawe" (IV[E.].1835,
1841). When January moves his bedroom out of doors, he also moves beyond the
licensed couplings of the marriage couch, or so the Merchant hints in a vulgar-
ized echo of the *Romaunt*'s delicate figure of playing on grass "as on a fetherbed":
"thynges whiche that were nat doon abedde, / He in the gardyn parfourned hem

and spedde" (IV[E.].2051–52). January's employment of the image of paradise to describe the joys of marriage in general and the anticipated pleasures of his wife's "yong flessh" in particular (IV[E.].1418; cf. 1265, 1332, 1642–47, 1822) prepares us for the use to which he puts his garden; when he passes through its locked gate, the walled *pleasance* merges with May's body as the *locus* of the aging knight's play: "swich deyntee [he] hath in it to walke and pleye, / That he wol no wight suffren bere the keye / Save he hymself" (IV[E.].2043–45). Examined in the light of theories of play, January's obsessive surveillance of his garden can be understood as an attempt to satisfy thwarted desires for control; play, according to Jean Piaget, "is a deliberate denial of what we perceive to be reality. In play the child assimilates the world, controls it by making it in imagination what he wants it to be."[8] Piaget's account of children's play is strikingly close to what the Merchant tells us about January's method of choosing a wife: he first constructs "inwith his thoght" (IV[E.].1586) an impossibly ideal mate, and then peremptorily rejects alternative suggestions:

> For whan that he hymself concluded hadde,
> Hym thoughte ech oother mannes wit so badde
> That inpossible it were to repplye
> Agayn his choys . . .
>
> (IV[E.].1608–10)

The reflexive construction—"he hymself concluded hadde"—tells us not only that January has made a decision, but also that he has shut out reality, enclosed himself in a "heigh fantasye" (IV[E.].1577) of marital bliss that will take material form in his *hortus conclusus* (cf. "Concluden"). Even as January attempts to remake the world to his own specifications, however, a series of deflationary references to or versions of play reminds us of the consequences of the knight's wish to insulate his playground from the life that lies outside it. Alluding to the moralists' distinction between irresponsible *ludus juvenilis* and mature wisdom, his brother Justinus pointedly warns him that "it is no childes pley / To take a wyf withouten avysement" (IV[E.].1530–31).[9] And May, observing his antics on their wedding night, "preyseth nat his pleyyng worth a bene" (IV[E.].1854); the demure bride of January's imagination, it would appear, already has her own opinion about what might constitute satisfactory male sexual performance (Hansen 260). Finally, May devises her own game (complete with finger signals designed to apprise her lover of her intentions) which she puts into action by stirring up January's desire to "pleye" within his walled garden (IV[E.].2135–36). May's elaborate scheme for cuckolding her blind husband culminates in what she describes as a "strugle" (IV[E.].2374) with a man in a tree—an episode that travesties both the ludic eroticism of the *Romaunt* and the events of Genesis 3.[10] Where the ordered play of the *Decameron* tale telling serves as a way of recovering a prelapsarian world, January's—and then May's—debasement of the decorum of play has the opposite result: it produces a parodic imitation of the Fall.

Among the features of the *Merchant's Tale* that reappear in the Franklin's Breton romance is a paradisiacal garden, initially represented as an alternative to the fearsome coastal rocks that Dorigen imagines as endangering her seafaring husband's ship. Hoping to draw her mind away from this frightening landscape, Dorigen's friends "shopen for to pleyen somewher elles" (V[F].897); they lead her through "places delitables" (V[F].899)—an exact rendering of *loci amoeni* (Burnley 94–95)—"where they dauncen and they pleyen" (V[F].900), and on a May morning move to an elegant garden equaled only by the "verray paradys" (V[F].912), where they "pleye hem al the longe day" (V[F].905). It is the Franklin's insistent evocation of play as the garden's "governing mood—and mode" (Kolve, "Rocky Shores" 172) that, even more than its formal artifice, link this *pleasance* with its precursor in the *Roman de la Rose*. Like its model, the Franklin's garden is a space apart, devoted wholly to pleasure and seemingly exempted from the cares and responsibilities of the world that lies beyond its boundaries. It is thus a fitting site for Dorigen's promise "in pley" (V[F].988) to the squire Aurelius that she will love him best if he removes the rocks from the coast of Brittany. In the probable source of the *Franklin's Tale*—the fourth *questione d'amor* in Boccaccio's *Filocolo*—the task devised by the married lady for her unwelcome suitor (that he produce a flowery garden in winter) is *una sottile malizia* (a subtle trick) designed to get rid of him once and for all (*Filocolo* 396). In Chaucer's poem, we are not told explicitly why Dorigen makes her bargain with Aurelius; given the tale's preoccupation with "the power of the fictive, the fantastic, and the wish-fulfilling" (Patterson, "'What Man Artow?'" 128), however, it is not surprising that critics have understood Dorigen's vow as expressing simultaneously two impossible and incompatible desires. The first, articulated by Dorigen in her earlier address to "Eterne God" (V[F].865), is that the rocks that threaten her husband's return might miraculously disappear. The second is the wish to take a lover, a forbidden fantasy that may be indulged (and thus perhaps defused) only within the garden's "magic circle" of imaginative play.

For Dorigen, such play is a temporary truancy from reality, safely buffered by a reminder (directed at Aurelius, but also at herself) that neither eventuality—the disappearance of the rocks or her own unfaithfulness to her husband—will ever come to pass: "For wel I woot that it shal never bityde" (V[F].1001).[11] In the person of Aurelius, however, "the rhetoric of the courtly garden becomes total fantasy and escape" (Berger 140). Indeed, the lovelorn squire's interpretation of Dorigen's meaning—that her "no" really signifies "perhaps"—is shaped by the associations of aristocratic play in a springtime setting. Just as the garden itself is said to be created by "craft of mannes hand" (V[F].909), so the male prerogatives embedded in the conventional romance plot construe the lady as always willing to be wooed; as Susan Crane observes in her remarks on this scene, "[t]here is no vocabulary of refusal" for women in the literature of courtship (65).[12] When he confronts Dorigen to claim his reward for making the rocks vanish, Aurelius invokes the garden both as a reminder of and the place for the fulfillment of her promise: "in a gardyn yond, at swich a place, / Ye woot right wel what ye behighten me" (V[F].1326–27). And after she reveals her dilemma to her husband, Arveragus sends her to the garden to keep her tryst with the squire, and Dorigen—albeit reluctantly and tearfully—obeys. As the tale nears its conclusion, however, Chaucer abandons the plot set in motion by the earlier interchange in the *locus amoenus*. Headed for their rendezvous in the garden, Aurelius encounters Dorigen in a public space, "amydde the toun, right in the quykkest strete" (V[F].1502–3). Touched by her misery and by her husband's insistence that his wife keep her *trouthe*, he releases Dorigen from her vow—and the garden drops out of the tale, along with Aurelius's daydream of an adulterous liaison.

In the garden's fate—its initial glamorous appearance in May giving way to the implied destruction of its greenness by winter frost (V[F].1250–51) and then to its ultimate disappearance—we may see reflected something of the tale's attitude toward play. Harry Berger, Jr. (whose remarkable commentary on the tale argues implicitly that its subject is the uses and abuses of play) suggests that the Franklin grants "qualified approval" (148) to the illusions of human rhetoric, but that after allowing these fictions a full but temporary display, moves us from the private to the public, from the pleasure-principle to the sterner demands of *trouthe*. In contrast to the narcissistic self-indulgence of his earlier monologues, Aurelius's final conversation with Dorigen embodies communicative speech and empathetic listening; it prepares us for his subsequent exchange with the magician, and for the famous question—"Which was the mooste fre?" (V[F].1622)—with which the Franklin concludes his story. The Franklin's *demande* both concerns and exemplifies what Anne Middleton calls "high play" ("New Men" 22): the spirit of social conviviality that may include "the courtly game of ideal talk" (44) but expands this class-specific activity to include a broader and more heterogeneous audience. In his capacity for such play, the Franklin makes an implicit case for literature as a form of shared discourse rather than (quoting Middleton again) as a "privately constructed world answering to singular desires" ("War" 131). That the denouement of the *Franklin's Tale* occurs not in a courtly pleasance but in a crowded city street tells us something about the Franklin—it is the sort of place where he might conduct his business—but also something about his creator. In locating the *Decameron* storytelling in a series of secluded villa gardens, Boccaccio permits his elegant young aristocrats temporarily to withdraw from history and to assert their own mastery through aesthetically pleasing entertainments.[13] Chaucer, on the other hand, places his diverse company of pilgrims on a busy highway. In so doing, he at once provides a stage for the complex and often unruly social play that characterizes the Canterbury contest and signals his poetry's continuous engagement with the world.

Notes

1. *The Romaunt of the Rose*, lines 487–89, *Riverside Chaucer*, 692. Chaucer's works are cited by line number from this edition. I wish to thank Kevin Gustafson and Lee Patterson for their helpful comments on this chapter.

2. On the "aristocratic privileging of play" as a social marker, see Patterson, *Chaucer* 53.

3. "[N]on nella chiesa . . . né ancora nelle scuole de' filosofanti . . . ma ne' giardini, in luogo di sollazzo" (*Decameron* 960). On this passage, see Olson, "Rhetorical Circumstances" 211–12.

4. "[E] chi scontrati gli avesse, niuna altra cosa avrebbe potuto dire se non: 'O costor non saranno dalla morte vinti o ella gli ucciderà lieti'" (*Decameron* 783).

5. Nolan comments on Antigone's song as a "form of play" (240). On the relation of song and play in the late Middle Ages, see Olson, "Toward a Poetics" 230–37.
6. On Arcite's funeral as play, see Leicester 358.
7. An illumination in a fifteenth-century manuscript (Vienna, Natl. Lib. ms. 2617, fol. 53) of a French translation of Boccaccio's *Teseida* (Chaucer's primary source for the *Knight's Tale*) links the lovers' amorous gaze with Emily's fate. The bas-relief in the space above the tower window depicts an armed warrior falling off his horse in battle—presumably a proleptic reference to the fatal consequences of Arcita's glance, and hence to Palemone's winning of Emilia. The detail in the bas-relief, obscure in the reproductions in Howes (fig. 6) and Kolve (*Chaucer* fig. 37), is clearly visible in a photograph of the manuscript page.
8. Piaget, summarized by Kendrick 36. Cf. Fink: "Man enjoys here [i.e., in the realm of play] an almost limitless creativity, he is productive and uninhibited because he is not creating within the sphere of reality. The player experiences himself as the lord of the products of his imagination" (24–25).
9. See, for example, Francis 287.
10. The Merchant's echoes of Genesis 3 have often been noted. See, for example, Jager 241–98; Howes 101.
11. On the implications of Dorigen's separation of play from reality in this scene, see Lynch 548 and Edwards 235.
12. Cf. Ferster 163: "The garden may also be a source of Aurelius's expectation that Dorigen is approachable: Ladies who walk in gardens are available as lovers."
13. Cf. Taylor 65: "[Chaucer's] busy urban setting . . . locates the *Decameron*'s utopian social agenda precisely as pastoral."

Works Cited

Alanus de Insulis. *Liber de planctu naturae*. Patrologia Latina 210: cols. 430–82.

Berger, Harry, Jr. "The F-Fragment of the Canterbury Tales: Part II." *Chaucer Review* 1 (1966): 135–56.

Boccaccio, Giovanni. *Decameron*. Ed. Vittore Branca. Vol. 4 of *Tutte le Opere di Giovanni Boccaccio*. Gen. ed. Vittore Branca. Milan: Mondadori, 1976.

———. Filocolo. Ed. Vittore Branca. Vol. 2 of *Tutte le Opere di Giovanni Boccaccio*. Gen. ed. Vittore Branca. Milan: Mondadori, 1967.

Borthwick, Sister Mary Charlotte. "Antigone's Song as 'Mirour' in Chaucer's *Troilus and Criseyde*." *Modern Language Quarterly* 22 (1961): 227–35.

Burnley, J. D. "Chaucer's Art of Verbal Allusion: Two Notes." *Neophilologus* 56 (1972): 93–99.

Caillois, Roger. *Man, Play, and Games*. Trans. Meyer Barash. New York: Free, 1961.

Chaucer, Geoffrey. *The Riverside Chaucer*. Gen. ed. Larry D. Benson. 3rd ed. Boston: Houghton, 1987.

"Concluden." *Middle English Dictionary*. Ed. Hans Kurath et al. Ann Arbor: U of Michigan P, 1957.

Crane, Susan. *Gender and Romance in Chaucer's Canterbury Tales*. Princeton: Princeton UP, 1994.

Edwards, Robert R. "Rewriting Menedon's Story: Decameron 10.5 and the Franklin's Tale." *The Decameron and the Canterbury Tales: New Essays on an Old Question*. Ed. Leonard Michael Koff and Brenda Deen Schildgen. Madison: Fairleigh Dickinson UP, 2000. 226–46.

Ehrmann, Jacques. "Homo Ludens Revisited." Trans. Cathy and Phil Lewis. *Game, Play, Literature*. Ed. Jacques Ehrmann. Yale French Studies 41. New Haven: Eastern, 1968. Rpt. Boston: Beacon, 1971. 31–57.

Ferster, Judith. "Interpretation and Imitation in Chaucer's Franklin's Tale." *Medieval Literature: Criticism, Ideology & History*. Ed. David Aers. New York: St. Martin's, 1986. 148–68.

Fink, Eugen. "The Oasis of Happiness: Toward an Ontology of Play." Trans. Ute and Thomas Saine. *Game, Play, Literature*. Ed. Jacques Ehrmann. Yale French Studies 41. New Haven: Eastern, 1968. Rpt. Boston: Beacon, 1971. 19–30.

Francis, W. Nelson, ed. *The Book of Vices and Virtues*. Early English Text Society, o.s. 217. London: Oxford UP, 1942.

Hansen, Elaine Tuttle. *Chaucer and the Fictions of Gender.* Berkeley: U of California P, 1992.

Howard, Donald R. "Experience, Language, and Consciousness: *Troilus and Criseyde,* II, 596–931." *Medieval Literature and Folklore Studies: Essays in Honor of Francis Lee Utley.* Ed. Jerome Mandel and Bruce A. Rosenberg. New Brunswick: Rutgers UP, 1970. 173–92.

Howes, Laura L. *Chaucer's Gardens and the Language of Convention.* Gainesville: UP of Florida, 1997.

Huizinga, Johan. *Homo Ludens: A Study of the Play-Element in Culture.* London: Routledge, 1949.

Jager, Eric. *The Tempter's Voice: Language and the Fall in Medieval Literature.* Ithaca: Cornell UP, 1993.

Kendrick, Laura. *Chaucerian Play: Comedy and Control in the Canterbury Tales.* Berkeley: U of California P, 1988.

Kolve, V. A. *Chaucer and the Imagery of Narrative: The First Five Canterbury Tales.* Stanford: Stanford UP, 1984.

——. "Rocky Shores and Pleasure Gardens: Poetry vs. Magic in Chaucer's Franklin's Tale." *Poetics: Theory and Practice in Medieval Literature.* Ed. Piero Boitani and Anna Torti. Cambridge: Brewer, 1991. 165–95.

Lanham, Richard A. *Literacy and the Survival of Humanism.* New Haven: Yale UP, 1983.

Leicester, H. Marshall, Jr. *The Disenchanted Self: Representing the Subject in the Canterbury Tales.* Berkeley: U of California P, 1990.

Lynch, Kathryn L. "East Meets West in Chaucer's Squire's and Franklin's Tales." *Speculum* 70 (1995): 530–51.

Mazzotta, Giuseppe. *The World at Play in Boccaccio's Decameron.* Princeton: Princeton UP, 1986.

Middleton, Anne. "Chaucer's 'New Men' and the Good of Literature in the Canterbury Tales." *Literature and Society.* Ed. Edward W. Said. Baltimore: Johns Hopkins UP, 1980. 15–56.

——. "War by Other Means: Marriage and Chivalry in Chaucer." *Studies in the Age of Chaucer: Proceedings, No. 1, 1984: Reconstructing Chaucer.* Ed. Paul Strohm and Thomas J. Heffernan. Knoxville: New Chaucer Society, 1985. 119–33.

Minnis, A. J. *The Shorter Poems.* Oxford Guides to Chaucer. Oxford: Clarendon, 1995.

Nolan, Barbara. *Chaucer and the Tradition of the Roman Antique.* Cambridge: Cambridge UP, 1992.

Olson, Glending. *Literature as Recreation in the Later Middle Ages.* Ithaca: Cornell UP, 1982.

——. "Rhetorical Circumstances and the Canterbury Storytelling." *Studies in the Age of Chaucer: Proceedings, No. 1, 1984: Reconstructing Chaucer.* Ed. Paul Strohm and Thomas J. Heffernan. Knoxville: New Chaucer Society, 1985. 211–18.

——. "Toward a Poetics of the Late Medieval Court Lyric." *Vernacular Poetics in the Middle Ages.* Ed. Lois Ebin. Studies in Medieval Culture 16. Kalamazoo: Medieval Institute, 1984. 227–48.

Patterson, Lee. Chaucer and the Subject of History. Madison: U of Wisconsin P, 1991.

——. "'What Man Artow?': Authorial Self-Definition in The Tale of Sir Thopas and The Tale of Melibee." *Studies in the Age of Chaucer* 11 (1989): 117–75.

Piaget, Jean. *Play, Dreams, and Imitation in Childhood.* Trans. C. Gattegno and F. M. Hodgson. New York: Norton, 1962.

Poirion, Daniel. *Le Roman de la Rose.* Paris: Hatier, 1973.

Spearing, A. C. *The Medieval Poet as Voyeur: Looking and Listening in Medieval Love-Narratives.* Cambridge: Cambridge UP, 1993.

Taylor, Karla. "Chaucer's Uncommon Voice: Some Contexts for Influence." *The Decameron and the Canterbury Tales: New Essays on an Old Question.* Ed. Leonard Michael Koff and Brenda Deen Schildgen. Madison: Fairleigh Dickinson UP, 2000. 47–82.

Windeatt, Barry. *Troilus and Criseyde.* Oxford Guides to Chaucer. Oxford: Clarendon, 1992.

Landscape, Power, Identity

Gregory B. Kaplan

Landscapes of Discrimination in *Converso* Literature

In medieval Spanish letters, references to landscapes are often employed in order to reinforce the social dimension of a text. For example, the rise in popularity of the cult to the Virgin reverberates in Gonzalo de Berceo's thirteenth-century collection of miracles, *Milagros de Nuestra Señora* (*Miracles of Our Lady*), which opens with the author situated in an allegorical garden that evokes the divine salvation gained through Marian devotion. During the fourteenth and fifteenth centuries, a profusion of literary references to the sea parallels a growing interest in maritime activity and foreshadows Spain's rise as a naval power during the Renaissance.[1] At the same time, these types of allusions are not restricted to works that present a positive outlook. Landscapes in allegorical works such as the anonymous "Dança general de la Muerte" (*General Dance of Death*) (late fourteenth–early fifteenth century), and the Marqués de Santillana's *Doctrinal de privados* (*Doctrines of the Favorites*) (c. 1453), convey the general pessimism produced by outbreaks of the Black Plague and the economic and political crises that affected Castile during the 1400s. Landscapes also inform texts that depict another tragic occurrence of the late Middle Ages, namely, the solidification after the founding of the Spanish Inquisition of a socioreligious barrier between Christians with a Jewish lineage (*conversos*, or New Christians) and those of pure ancestry (Old Christians). Although the Holy Office was brought into existence in order to eliminate heterodoxy by seeking out and punishing heretics, previous legal and social discrimination against *conversos* contributed to the creation of an atmosphere in which all converts were viewed with skepticism, regardless of whether they were actually practicing Judaism in secret. As a result, all *conversos* lived in fear of the consequences of being accused of heresy by the Inquisition. In response to their predicament, several *converso* writers employed allusions to landscapes as components of allegories that metaphorically allude to their inferior status and to the institution that prevented their assimilation into the Old Christian community.

In 1391, a wave of pogroms swept through Spain, effectively initiating the demise of a Jewish community that had existed on the Iberian peninsula since the beginning of the common era. The origins of this hostility may be traced to a rise in Spanish (and European) anti-Semitism during the mid-thirteenth century, an animus that intensified in the 1300s during outbreaks of the Black Plague and periods of economic difficulty, crises for which the Jews were often blamed. The situation reached its flash point in 1391, when violence erupted in cities throughout Spain. Although Jewish communities had been able to survive previous attacks, the severity and national scope of these pogroms resulted in the conversion (willingly or by force) of thousands of Jews to Christianity. Between 1412 and 1416, after another surge in anti-Semitism, thousands more became Christians.[2]

For the next thirty years, many *conversos* took advantage of their newly acquired status by rising to prominence in political and clerical spheres and in the retinues of the nobility. However, this social freedom began to evaporate after the onset of another economic crisis inspired an insurrection in Toledo in 1449.[3] Although this insurrection was grounded in popular resentment of royal tyranny, it quickly acquired a social motivation (in part due to the fact that the event was provoked by a *converso* municipal treasurer and tax collector, Alonso Cota), and existent anti-Semitic sentiment became directed toward the *conversos* of Toledo. In time, political harmony was restored to the city. The *conversos* of Toledo, however, were forced to endure the promulgation of the Sentencia-Estatuto, the first purity-of-blood statute. The Sentencia-Estatuto marked the onset of legal discrimination against *conversos* based on the conviction that they were heretical and inferior Christians. As such, the *conversos* of Toledo were deemed ineligible for service in civil or ecclesiastical office.[4]

The imposition in Toledo of a legal division between Christians threatened to place *conversos* throughout Castile in a precarious position due to the detrimental effect that the insurrection of 1449 had on the symbiotic relationship between the *conversos* and the monarchy.[5] During the early 1400s the prosperity of many *conversos* (especially those in royal service) was tied to the stability of the government of King Juan II of Castile (r. 1406–54). However, the Toledo insurrection represented a serious challenge to royal authority. The perpetrators threatened to align themselves with Prince Enrique if the *conversos* were not expelled from the city, and the king, after first condemning the Old Christian rebels, eventually acquiesced by pardoning the same Old Christians and by sanctioning the provisions of the Sentencia-Estatuto.[6]

In spite of the king's actions, the violence of 1449 was not repeated during the following decade, perhaps because an organized national movement did not yet support localized anti-*converso* sentiment. The agenda for such a movement was formulated by Alonso de Espina, a Franciscan monk and royal confessor to King Enrique IV of Castile (r. 1454–74), in the *Fortalitium Fidei* (1460) (Fortress of the Faith). Espina advocated a purification of Christian Spain by elaborating a plan that foreshadowed the events of the following decades: the *conversos* were to be subject to an Inquisition in order to weed out the heretics, and the Jews were to be expelled from Spain. King Enrique did not delay in responding to the *Fortalitium Fidei*. In 1461, he issued a request to Pope Pius II for the establishment of a Castilian inquisition.[7] Although the king failed to act on the papal bull he received, he did sanction a nonpapal episcopal inquisition during the 1460s.[8] This further deterioration of the relationship between the *conversos* and the monarchy coincided with repeated outbreaks of anti-*converso* violence and the promulgation of additional purity-of-blood statutes.[9]

For a brief period after the death of King Enrique, the new monarch, Queen Isabel the Catholic (r. 1474–1504), appeared to be working toward improving relations between Old and New Christians by "order[ing] a public campaign of religious education" (Rubin 186) in order to instruct the *conversos* in Christian doctrine. Her ascension to the throne also signified an end to the pogroms that had occurred during her predecessor's reign. However, the formal enactment in 1480 of the papal bull requested by Queen Isabel (and her husband, King Ferdinand of Aragon [r. 1479–1516]), which authorized the Inquisition controlled by the Spanish crown, permanently alienated the *conversos* from Old Christian society. While the Holy Office was entrusted with the task of identifying and punishing only those who were true heretics, the prevalence of anti-*converso* sentiment and the existence of purity-of-blood statutes enhanced the skepticism with which *conversos* were viewed by Old Christians and ensured that any *converso* could easily become the object of slanderous remarks. Cases brought against *conversos* based on false accusations were not uncommon, and many were launched against wealthy individuals in order to augment the coffers of the Inquisition, which, although never much more than solvent, financed itself entirely from confiscations of *converso* property during its first century of existence. Abuses became so rampant that a reform of the institution took place during the early 1500s.[10] Moreover, a variety of minor infractions, including random practices that may have been followed out of habit by *conversos* who were not crypto-Jews (such as changing bedclothes on Saturday and abstention from certain foods), aroused suspicion among the inquisitional authorities. *Conversos* charged with heresy could find themselves in a hopeless situation. The identity of an accuser remained anonymous and the accused was not informed of the nature of the charge. As a result, accused individuals often "went for days, months and even years without knowing why they were in the cells of the tribunal" (Kamen, *Spanish Inquisition* 177).

Allegories composed by three *converso* writers during the 1490s, Diego de San Pedro's *Cárcel de amor* (*Prison of Love*), Rodrigo Cota's *Diálogo entre el Amor y un Viejo* (*Dialogue between Love and an Old Man*), and Fernando de Rojas's *Celestina* (*The Celestina*), are permeated by a despondency and sense of alienation that respond to the arbitrary legal climate generated by the Inquisition. Allegory, as Chandler Rathfon Post writes, "crystallizes a more or less abstract idea by presenting it in the concrete form of a fictitious person, thing, or event" (3). The "abstract idea" manifested in these works, the experience of living in early inquisitional Spain, is "crystallized" through the characterizations of the protagonists, whose actions and words (including references to landscapes) allude to the inferior socio-religious status imposed on the *conversos*.

The action in Diego de San Pedro's *Cárcel de amor* (1492) (*Prison of Love*), a work that is recognized as the best example of the Spanish sentimental novel, takes place sometime between 1483 and 1492 (Deyermond xli–xlii). The story commences when the character called "auctor" (author) encounters Leriano the male protagonist, as the latter is being led to the "Cárcel de Amor," a symbol of the suffering caused by his affection for Laureola, the daughter of the king of Macedonia. Auctor agrees to visit Laureola on behalf of Leriano, and during the exchange of epistles that follows, Laureola displays sympathy toward his suffering. This inspires Leriano to travel to Macedonia, whereupon he is falsely accused of having a clandestine affair with Laureola. The king, believing that his daughter is guilty, induces Persio, the accuser, to publicly challenge Leriano. Although Persio is defeated in combat he continues to plot against Leriano, and the king, wrongly convinced that his own honor has been damaged, imprisons Laureola and condemns her to die. After several failed attempts to convince the king of Laureola's innocence, Leriano rescues Laureola and Persio is killed. However, even upon learning that Persio's accusations are untrue, and after officially exonerating Leriano and Laureola, the king prohibits Leriano from returning to the court until Persio's relatives have forgiven him. After Laureola decides not to see him in order to avoid any further controversies, Leriano dies of despair after providing a lengthy defense of women (a manifestation of the pro-feminism typically found in the Spanish sentimental novel).

Francisco Márquez Villanueva (*"Cárcel de amor"*) posits that the political conflicts in *Cárcel* constitute a *converso* reaction to the arbitrary juridical system of the Inquisition and the royal support of the institution. Márquez Villanueva's theory is supported by several components of San Pedro's plot. Perhaps the most explicit example is found at the conclusion of the combat between Leriano and Persio. Although the medieval tradition of settling disputes by public combat was no longer in vogue in Spain by the time *Cárcel* was composed, San Pedro's reluctance to provide an extended description of "esto que parece cuento de historias viejas" (117) (that which seems like an old fashioned story) indicates that he assumed that his audience would be familiar with the nature of these events.[11] This familiarity would have naturally included the expectation "in accordance with ancient belief . . . [that] the will of God . . . allow the victory of that party which was in the right" (Smith 138, n. 3533). Indeed, the depiction of the battle prepares the reader for such an outcome:

> sabiendo el rey que estavan concertados en la batalla, aseguró el canpo, y señalado el lugar donde hiziesen y ordenadas todas las cosas que en tal auto se requerían segund las ordenanças de Macedonia, puesto el rey en un cadahalso, vinieron los cavalleros cada uno aconpañado y favorecido como merecía; y guardadas en

igualdad las honrras dentramos, entraron en el canpo; y como los fieles los dex-
aron solos, fuéronse el uno para el otro, donde en la fuerça de los golpes mostraron
la virtud de los ánimos, y quebradas las lanças en los primeros encuentros, pusi-
eron mano a las espadas. . . .

(knowing that the combatants had agreed to the duel, the king secured the field
of combat, and once that detail and all others required by Macedonian law had
been arranged, and once the king was situated on the podium, the knights entered
accompanied by their retinues; after they had received the king's approbation they
charged at each other, whereupon each one displayed courage, and after they had
broken their lances in their first encounter, they withdrew their swords. . . .)[12]

(San Pedro 117)

Leriano then proceeds to cut off Persio's right hand, which leaves the latter
defenseless and ready to accept his fate: "Haz lo que has de hazer, que aunque
me falta el braço para defender no me fallece coraçón para morir" (San Pedro 117)
(Do what you must, for although I lack my right arm to defend myself, I do not
lack the courage to die). However, rather than let divine justice take its course,
which would rectify the situation inasmuch as Leriano is in the right, the king
is convinced by Persio's relatives to intervene at this crucial point in the battle
and spare his life. This instance of random arbitration is incomprehensible to
Leriano, who is unable to "pensar por qué el rey tal cosa mandase" (San Pedro
118) (understand why the king ordered such a thing), and he seeks an explanation
for the king's partiality:

si por ventura lo consentiste por verte aquexado de la suplicación de sus parientes,
cuando les otorgaste la merced devieras acordarte de los servicios que los míos
te hizieron, pues sabes con cuánta costança de coraçón cuántos dellos en muchas
batallas y conbates perdieron por tu servicio las vidas; nunca hueste juntaste que
la tercia parte dellos no fuese.

(if by chance you consented because you were moved by the pleas of his relatives,
when you granted them mercy you should have thought of the services that my
own [relatives] have performed for you, for you know in your heart how many of
them have lost their lives in battle in your service; indeed, there has never been an
occasion on which at least a third of your army has not been comprised of them.)

(San Pedro 120)

In his commentary on this passage, Márquez Villanueva observes:

Tan dura acusación de la ingratitud regia hacia los *suyos* sorprende por no re-
sponder a ninguna previa exigencia o necesidad funcional del argumento. Y la
frase final está ahí para dejar bien en claro que el término *parientes* ha de entenderse
en el sentido más lato.

(Such a harsh accusation of royal ingratitude toward his (own) [relatives] is surprising because it does not correspond to any previous passage or fit within the
context of the plot. And the last phrase is included in order to indicate clearly that
the term *relatives* should be understood in a broader context.)

(*"Cárcel de amor"* 194)

Marquez Villanueva's reference to a "sentido más lato" (broader context) should be understood to suggests that Leriano's accusation is an allegorical allusion to the arbitrary and discriminatory practices of the recently established Inquisition. A closer examination of the text reveals how this allusion informs the outcome of the battle between Leriano and Persio. San Pedro instills the setting with references to all the elements necessary for a just resolution of the conflict: the battle is sanctioned by the king, and if Persio were killed according to the rules of combat, his guilt would be proven. However, the description of the confrontation contrasts with the manner by which it concludes. Instead of justice, prejudice and haphazard legislation prevail as a metaphor for the judicial system of the Inquisition and the monarchy that permitted the Holy Office to discriminate against the *conversos*. The latter theme is enhanced by San Pedro's portrayal of the king as a tyrannical figure who refuses to exhibit compassion toward a daughter whose innocence has been proven for fear of "amanzillar la fama de los pasados y la onrra de los presentes y la sangre de los por venir; que sola una mácula en el linage cunde toda la generación" (San Pedro 132) (damaging the reputation of [my] ancestors, the honor of those who are living, and the bloodline of [my] descendants; for even a small blemish in one's lineage does damage to an entire generation).

In a lengthy poem most likely composed a few years after *Cárcel, Diálogo entre el Amor y un Viejo* (*Dialogue between Love and an Old Man*), Rodrigo Cota, another *converso* writing during the 1490s, includes landscapes in an allegory that again responds to the treatment of the *conversos,* albeit from a different perspective. Although one might argue that, in *Cárcel,* the bias displayed by the king toward Leriano suggests that the latter is a New Christian, there is no explicit evidence in the text that Leriano (or any of the other characters) is a *converso.* San Pedro's allegory alludes to the methods of the Inquisition without engaging in this type of direct association, perhaps a reflection of the fact that he was never actually brought before the tribunal. Cota, however, did have personal contact with the Holy Office. In spite of his attempts to assimilate into the Old Christian community, Cota was charged (apparently unjustly) with heresy sometime between 1497 and 1499 and may have spent time in prison before he was most likely acquitted.[13] This episode was one of several encounters with anti-*converso* persecution that haunted the poet throughout his lifetime. The Inquisition also punished several close relatives, and Cota, while a young boy, undoubtedly witnessed his father's role in inciting the Toledo rebellion of 1449.[14]

The plot of *Diálogo* involves a debate between two characters — Amor (Love) and Viejo (Old Man) — concerning whether or not Amor has the capacity to rekindle Viejo's youthful passion. Although Viejo at first refuses to accept the promises made by Amor, he is eventually persuaded that, with Amor's help, he can once again experience physical pleasure. However, immediately after the two protagonists embrace Viejo realizes that he has been tricked. After being chastised by Amor for believing that he had the ability to love again, Viejo is abandoned and closes the poem by contemplating his miserable state.

In a previous study ("Rodrigo Cota's 'Diálogo'"), I discuss Cota's poem as a "*converso* lament," that is, a type of allegory that recalls the discriminatory atmosphere of early inquisitional Spain. According to my interpretation, the contempt demonstrated by Amor (who represents an Old Christian) toward Viejo (who represents a *converso*) symbolizes the refusal by Old Christians to accept their New Christian coreligionists. Aside from the evolution of this relationship, upon which I will elaborate below, a number of previously identified passages in the poem reinforce this interpretation by alluding to the ideologies that prevented *conversos* from attaining honor, exposed them to the severity of inquisitional persecution, and socially classified them as inferior Christians. Moreover, when certain aspects of the work are considered against the backdrop of Cota's own plight—such as the fact that Cota was, like his literary character, called "el Viejo" ("the Elder")—the allegory takes on a personal dimension by evoking Cota's own confrontation with the Spanish Inquisition.

An examination of Cota's references to landscapes complements my previous reading of the poem's allegorical message. The work takes place in the orchard of Viejo, who describes its decayed state in the opening lines:

> La beldad deste jardín
> ya no temo que la halles,
> ni las ordenadas calles
> ni los muros de jazmín.
> Ni los arroyos corrientes
> de bivas aguas notables,
> ni las alvercas, ni fuentes,
> ni las aves produzientes
> los cantos tan consolables.
>
> (The beauty of this garden
> can no longer be found,
> and neither can the neatly trimmed paths,
> or the walls covered with jasmine.
> Also gone are the running streams,
> filled by water teeming with life,
> and the ponds, and the fountains,
> and the birds that once sang
> such soothing songs.)
>
> (Cota vv. 19–27)

In the context of Cota's *converso* allegory, this orchard becomes a symbol of the trajectory of the *converso* experience during the second half of the fifteenth century. Their initial successes prior to the Sentencia-Estatuto are reminiscent of the orchard's once flourishing state whereas its dilapidated condition evokes their change of fortune after the Toledo rebellion of 1449.

The parallel that one might draw between the plight of Viejo's orchard and a postlapsarian Eden enhances the *converso* meaning of Cota's allegory. Although Viejo is not expelled as are Adam and Eve, insofar as it occurs in a garden setting, Viejo's adversity brings to mind the biblical Fall in Genesis (3:22–24). The inversion of this biblical episode was an important theme in medieval Christian typology, a science that analyzed the relationships between myths and prophecies in the Old and New Testaments. This was accomplished by recognizing the manner by which these myths and prophecies are inverted, or as Northrop Frye explains in detail in *The Great Code*, by identifying the transformations of Old Testament types into New Testament antitypes. For typologists, the recuperation of Eden was gained through Christian salvation. According to E. Michael Gerli, "[E]l advenimiento de Cristo no solamente marca la salvación del hombre y cumple con las profecías del Antiguo Testamento, sino que simboliza la repetición invertida de la historia de Adán" (7–8) (the arrival of Christ not only marks the salvation of man and fulfills the prophecies of the Old Testament, it also symbolizes the inverted repetition of the story of Adam). In the aforementioned *Milagros de Nuestra Señora*, Berceo manifests the influence of Christian typology by instilling his allegorical garden with references that "recobra figurativamente el Edén derrochado por Adán y Eva" (Gerli 9) (figuratively recovers the Eden squandered by Adam and Eve).

Exegetic texts like the anonymous *Libro de la infancia y muerte de Jesús* (*Book of the infancy and death of Jesus*) (c. 1200)[15] and *Milagros* by Berceo incorporate figural interpretations of the Eden story in order to emphasize the attainment of Christian salvation. Of course, according to the church this redemption was supposed to be possible for any devout Christian, including Jews who converted to Christianity (as illustrated, for example, by miracle 23 in Berceo's *Milagros*). However, social treatment of the *conversos* during the late fifteenth century contradicted the egalitarian doctrines upon which Christianity had been founded, and each *converso* was in essence considered to be a heretic regardless of his or her actual degree of sincerity as a Christian. Because of their inferior religious status, the promise of Christian salvation would have undoubtedly seemed incongruous to *conversos*. Cota appears to demonstrate an awareness of this incongruity by manipulating the typological inversion of the Eden story. The New Testament antitype seems to be reflected in the promises made by Amor to Viejo, in which the former alludes to a regenerated orchard that might be said to symbolize Christian salvation:

> De verdura muy gentil
> tu huerta renovaré,
> la casa fabricaré
> de obra rica, sotil.
> Sanaré las plantas secas
> quemadas por los friores;
> en muy gran simpleza pecas,
> viejo triste, si no truecas
> tus espinas por mis flores.
>
> (With delightful greenery
> I will renew your orchard,
> I will rebuild your home
> into a rich and elegant place.
> I will revive the dried out plants
> which have frozen to death;

> you commit a great sin,
> sad old man, if you do not exchange
> your thorns for my flowers.)
>
> (Cota vv. 487–95)

However, in the second line of this citation, Cota employs a verb, "renovar" (to renew), that subverts the antitype by speaking to the contradiction between religious doctrines and contemporary social attitudes. Although this subversion might recall the unfulfilled promise of Christian salvation (or Christian equality) for *conversos* in general, the use of the verb "renovar" evokes a particular historical moment during which *conversos* would have felt especially disenchanted with Christian doctrines. Several years prior to the composition of *Diálogo*, this same verb was used by the Catholic Monarchs in a decree directed toward the Jews who had converted in order to avoid being expelled from Spain in 1492. In their decree, which was issued on 6 September 1493, the Catholic Monarchs expressed their desire that these *conversos* renew ("rrenovéys") themselves spiritually after abandoning "las çerimonias e rritos de la ley vieja" (the ceremonies and rites of their former religion) and by "haziendo obras de católicos christianos . . . para que la santa agua del bavtismo sea en vosotros como deue" (performing Christian acts so that the holy water of baptism produce in you the result that it should) (Weill 60). The decree thus implied that *conversos* who assimilated would be treated no differently than Old Christians. However, the complete disregard in this decree of the factors that prevented willing *conversos* from assimilation, namely, the discriminatory practices of the Inquisition and the hostile Old Christian populace, undoubtedly had a disheartening affect on Cota, one of many *conversos* whose attempt to merge into Old Christian society (socially, if not spiritually) met with futility. This aspect of his life was illustrated by his personal struggle with the Holy Office and in a poem composed by another *converso*, Antón de Montoro, in which Cota was warned (vv. 151–60) that he would always be treated as an inferior Christian because of his Jewish lineage.[16]

Although Fernando de Rojas's *Celestina* (*The Celestina*), first published in 1499 or 1500, does not contain a specific reference to the royal decree of 1493, Rojas, like Cota, was undoubtedly aware of the socioreligious impediments faced by *conversos* toward the end of the fifteenth century. The plot of *Celestina* concerns the relationship between Calisto, whose exaggerated behavior parodies the tenets of courtly love,[17] and Melibea, whose refusal to accept Calisto's advances compels the latter to seek the services of an intermediary, Celestina. Celestina eventually succeeds in seducing Melibea, who agrees to a clandestine meeting with Calisto. After they consummate their relationship, Calisto is killed when he falls from the ladder that he had used to reach Melibea's room. Melibea, grief stricken over the accidental death of her lover, commits suicide, leaving her father, Pleberio, to bemoan the tragedy in an extended soliloquy as the book draws to a close.

Celestina is a work that has been interpreted by scholars as a *converso* allegory.[18] As such, Rojas's book shares much in common with Cota's *Diálogo*, a correspondence indirectly suggested by Rojas himself in an introductory epistle in which he claims that his book is actually a continuation of the anonymous first act, written "según algunos dizen . . . [por] Rodrigo Cota" (Rojas 70) (according to some . . . [by] Rodrigo Cota). The textual parallels between the two works suggest that, even if Cota did not compose the first act, Rojas almost certainly relied on *Diálogo* as a source for *Celestina*.[19]

Diálogo and *Celestina* parallel each other superficially and allegorically, correlations that also link both works to San Pedro's *Cárcel*, a copy of which Rojas possessed (Rojas 29). As in *Diálogo* and *Cárcel*, the plot of *Celestina* constitutes an admonition against the perils of worldly love by providing an example of the tragic consequences of surrendering to passion. On a symbolic level, in the tradition of *Diálogo* and *Cárcel*, Rojas depicts the victimization of the *conversos* by the Inquisition.

The literary milieu of *Celestina* reflects the apprehensive soul of the *converso* living with an awareness of the inherent danger that could result from being labeled a heretic, whether or not such an indictment was actually based in fact. On a number of occasions allusions are made to heretical acts committed by Calisto and to his sincerity as a Christian, while in other passages Melibea's "limpieza de sangre" (purity of blood) and "linage" (lineage) are brought into question. In this light, scholars have debated whether the fact that either Calisto or Melibea is of "impure" lineage constitutes the impediment that prevents them from marrying.[20] However, a possible matrimony between the two is never discussed in *Celestina*, and indeed it need not be since marriage is not an objective of the courtly lover that Calisto is meant to parody. Rojas strategically places his discriminatory discourse in a variety of contexts in order to reproduce his contemporary reality, in which individuals could not be trusted and which, from a *converso* perspective, was governed by perturbation. He compels his readers to arrive at their own interpretations concerning a number of passages as a means of drawing them into this anarchic universe. For example, early on in *Celestina*, Sempronio, Calisto's servant, calls his master a "herege" (heretic) (Rojas 92) and accuses him of "blasfemia" (blasphemy) (Rojas 95) for declaring (of Melibea): "Por dios la creo, por dios la confesso, y no creo que hay otro soberano en el cielo aunque entre nosotros mora" (Rojas 95) ("I believe in her as I believe in God, and I say there's no higher sovereign in heaven" [Simpson 6]). As illustrations of the ambiguous tone in *Celestina*, these are terms that may be understood in the context of Rojas's parody of the courtly lover or that may recall those employed in charges leveled at *conversos*. The fact that Sempronio's remark is made as an aside which Calisto does not hear—and when Calisto asks Sempronio to repeat his words he receives a different reply—strengthens the possibility that Sempronio is insinuating that his master is a *converso* by recalling the secret testimony that often incriminated New Christians. However, in this and many other instances the reader cannot be sure of the true meaning of the passage. Sempronio is a deceitful individual and a criminal; he ultimately betrays Calisto and is executed for his part in the murder of Celestina, actions that place his previous accusations into question and that further enlist him with many of the features of witnesses who typically testified before the Inquisition:

The secrecy of testimony against others raised profound questions as to the reliability of witnesses and about the quality of testimony from witnesses who would not ordinarily be accepted because of disqualifying characteristics, including those considered infamous. . . . [T]he very fact that the accused had been charged and arrested at all indicated that sufficient evidence for guilt had already been accumulated on the basis of denunciations from others. . . .

(Peters 92–93)

Whether Rojas's creation of a literary "atmosphere of shared consternation and mutual suspicion" (Gilman, *Spain* 44) was personally motivated by his father's imprisonment (and probable) execution at the stake by the Inquisition (Gilman, *Spain* 45), by the fact that his own Jewish lineage disqualified him from testifying before the Inquisition in 1525 on behalf of his father-in-law, or perhaps by an attempt to speak on behalf of all *conversos* due to a "necessidad que nuestra común patria tiene de la presente obra" (Rojas 69) (need that our country has for the present work), Rojas, like Cota and San Pedro, paints an allegorical portrait of a Spain in which a pervasive mistrust of *conversos* left them exposed to an impartial and chaotic system of injustice. This system is nowhere more graphically depicted than in the series of elegiac references to macabre landscapes in Pleberio's closing lament:

Yo pensava en mi más tierna edad que eras y eran tus hechos regidos por alguna orden. Agora, visto el pro y la contra de tus bienandanças, me pareçes un laberinto de errores, un desierto spantable, una morada de fieras, juego de hombres que andan en corro, laguna llena de cieno, región llena de spinas, monte alto, campo pedregoso, prado lleno de serpientes, huerto florido y sin fruto, fuente de cuydados, río de lágrimas, mar de miserias, trabajo sin provecho, dulce ponçoña, vana esperança, falsa alegría, verdadero dolor.

(Rojas 338)

(When I was young I thought the world was ruled by order. I know better now! It is a labyrinth of errors, a frightful desert, a den of wild beasts, a game in which men run in circles, a lake of mud, a thorny thicket, a dense forest, a stony field, a meadow full of serpents, a river of tears, a sea of miseries, effort without profit, a flowering but barren orchard, a running spring of cares, a sweet poison, a vain hope, a false joy, and a true pain.)

(Simpson 159)

During the early sixteenth century, many New Christians escaped oppression by fleeing to Italy, where they encountered a Jewish community, including some ten thousand Jews who had been expelled from Spain in 1492, which was making a name for itself in tolerant cultural and intellectual centers such as Venice and Rome.[21] *Conversos* arriving in Italy at this time expressed a fascination with the open expression of a religion and culture that was prohibited in Spain, and some reverted to Judaism. In 1528, Francisco Delicado, a *converso* who had sought refuge in Italy, published (anonymously) *Retrato de la Lozana andaluza* (*Portrait of Lozana: The Lusty Andalusian Woman*), a novel in dialogue (like *Celestina*) that depicts the activities of the Italian Jewish and *converso* communities. The story recounts the experiences of Lozana, a *conversa* who, like Delicado himself, hails from Córdoba and establishes residence in Italy. In Rome, Lozana meets other *conversos* who help her enter courtly society, where she becomes a prostitute and healer in the tradition of Rojas's *Celestina*. During the course of her adventures Lozana displays an interest in Jewish culture that recalls the sentiment felt by *conversos* for Italian Jews. This inquisitiveness is also evident in the urban landscapes that inform Delicado's dialogues. Bruno M. Damiani observes that "[t]he stimulating factor in these dialogues is Lozana's curiosity to know the city of Rome, the interest she has in seeing and knowing all that surrounds her" (69). Examples of this "curiosity" (noted by Damiani [69]) occur as Lozana is strolling through the city with her *converso* companion (and pimp), Rampín:

Lozana. ¿Por dó hemos de ir?
Rampín. Por aquí, por Plaza Redonda, y verés el templo de Panteón, y la sepultura de Lucrecia Romana, y el aguja de piedra que tiene la ceniza de Rómulo y Remo. . . .

(Delicado 239)

(**Lozana.** Which way should we go?
Rampín. This way, through the Plaza Redonda, where you'll see the Pantheon, the tomb of Lucretia, the obelisk containing the ashes of Romulus and Remus. . . .)

(Damiani 60)

Lozana. ¿Qué plaza es ésta?
Rampín. Aquí se llama Nagona, y si venís el miércoles veréis el mercado que, quizá desde que nacistes, no habés visto mejor orden en todas las cosas.

(Delicado 241)

(**Lozana.** What square is this?
Rampín. It's called Navona. If you come here on Wednesdays you'll see a market like nothing you've ever seen in all your born days, so orderly and complete in every ware under the sun.)

(Damiani 62)

In time, tolerance in Italy toward Jews and *conversos* who returned to Judaism was tempered by restrictive legislation. Jews were required to wear identifying garments, a Jewish ghetto was created in Venice in 1516, and they were expelled from the Spanish province of Naples two decades later. In order to deal with those considered heretical, including *conversos*, Protestants, and sorcerers, inquisitions were established in a number of Italian cities, beginning with Rome in 1542. Although they were persecuted to a lesser extent than in Spain (Peters 110), Italian *conversos* must have felt a renewed sense of alienation as they witnessed the evolution of the movement that supported these institutions, the Counter Reformation, which had been gaining momentum since the early decades of the sixteenth century. Márquez Villanueva, who considers *Lozana* to be a "fiel documento de la vida conversa" ("El mundo converso" 92) (a faithful document of *converso* life), writes that the contemporary socioreligious climate in Italy could produce, among *conversos*, an "indiferencia . . . ante toda religión organizada"

("El mundo converso" 94) (an indifference toward all organized religion). When seen in this light, Lozana is more than just a curious *conversa;* she is also a personification of the New Christian who had become ambivalent toward any faith, a notion that reverberates in the declaration by Teresa, another *conversa* in Rome, that Lozana is "con los cristianos . . . cristiana, y con los jodíos, jodía" (Delicado 203) ("a Christian among the Christians, a Jew among the Jews" [Damiani 30]).[22]

Although *Lozana* is not an extended *converso* allegory like the other texts considered in this study, this ambivalence is another facet of the *converso* experience in Italy that is evoked metaphorically in the urban landscapes within the work. An example occurs during a conversation between "autor" and his friend, Silvio, concerning the practice by godfathers of bringing gifts to a newborn child:

> **Silvio.** Mirad, aquella garrafa que traen de agua es la que sobró en el bacín cuando se lavaron los que tienen la criatura, y tráenla a casa, y de allí envíanla al tal y a la tal, y ansí a cuantos quieren, y dicen que, por haberse lavado con aquel agua, son compadres, y así envían, quién una cana de raso, quién una de paño, quién una de damasco, quién un ducado o más, y d'esta manera es como cabeza de lobo para criar la criatura. . . .
>
> **Autor.** No se lo consentirían, esto y otras mil supersticiones que hacen, en España.
>
> **Silvio.** Pues por eso es libre Roma, que cada uno hace lo que se le antoja, agora sea bueno o malo y mirá cuánto, que si uno quiere ir vestido de oro o de seda, o desnudo o calzado, o comiendo o riendo, o cantando, siempre vale por testigo, y no hay quien os diga mal hacéis ni bien hacéis. . . .
>
> (Delicado 298–99)

> (**Silvio.** That pitcher they brought in contains the water that was left over when the ones who are taking care of the child washed themselves. First it is taken to their home and from there they send it from one person to another, to as many as they wish. They tell each one to wash himself in that water in order to become a godfather too. Then the godfathers send in their gifts: five feet of satin, a piece of fine fabric of the same length, another just as long of damask, a ducat or two. Each one tries to outdo the others in order to have the honor of raising the child. . . .
>
> **Author.** In Spain they wouldn't stand for such nonsense or for any of the other superstitions that you put up with here.
>
> **Silvio.** Well, that's why Rome is free, because each person can do whatever strikes his fancy, be it good or bad. Here's proof—if someone wants to go through the streets dressed in gold or silk, stripped to the buff or wearing fine shoes, while he laughs or dines or sings on his way, everyone will leave him alone and no one will tell him that he did right or wrong. . . .)
>
> (Damiani 113–14)

According to Silvio, Rome is free. However, as Silvio explains, it is free for those who are indifferent to the world around them, an allusion to the insensibility to religion that developed among *conversos* in Italy.

Between 120,000 and 300,000 *conversos* lived in Spain in the early 1500s. Although a number of them prospered economically as "the new urban middle class" (Gitlitz, *Secrecy* 42), assimilation into the Old Christian community continued to be thwarted by purity-of-blood statutes, which caused "a serious barrier to status mobility" (Kamen, *Inquisition and Society* 121). Strict examinations of lineage prevented *conversos* from occupying university positions and entering religious and military orders (and from possessing the honor associated with such membership). Confronted by the harsh reality that they would always be judged to be inferior Christians because of their Jewish ancestry, *conversos* of the 1500s continued to employ literature as a vehicle of protest, as David Gitlitz observes:

> Many intellectual assimilationist *conversos,* frustrated by a society that hemmed them in and a bureaucracy that seemed to wait perpetually in ambush, gave vent to their angst in literature. It is not at all surprising that the literature of escapism and alienation as well as the theater of social protest of the early Spanish Renaissance flowed largely from *converso* pens. In most of this literature one senses a profound dissatisfaction with the surface pieties of Spanish Catholicism and a concern for the moral rot perceived to be at the heart of Spanish society.
>
> (*Secrecy* 42)

La vida de Lazarillo de Tormes (1554) (*The Life of Lazarillo of Tormes*), the prototype of the Spanish picaresque novel, may be interpreted as an example of this "profound dissatisfaction." The book is narrated by the protagonist, Lázaro of Tormes, who recounts the story of his life, from his youth spent with parents (and a stepfather) who are prosecuted and punished for larceny, to his "education" while serving a series of masters from whom he learns the hypocritical nature of contemporary society and how to survive by his own cunning, to his employment in Toledo as a town crier and his marriage to the maidservant of the archpriest of San Salvador. As he moves from master to master, Lázaro constantly suffers from physical beatings and hunger and is unable to establish himself as a productive member of society. Even after he finds a place for himself as a town crier Lázaro remains a marginal figure and, as such, the object of ridicule by his fellow townspeople, who allege that his wife is the archpriest's concubine.

Scholars have identified themes in the work—such as an explicit anticlericalism (which resulted in the suppression of two chapters by the Inquisition in 1573) and the portrayal of a world filled with deception[23]—that reveal a *converso* subtext and that strongly suggest that *Lazarillo,* which was published anonymously, was composed by a *converso.*[24] Recent sociolinguistic readings by José Faur and Colbert I. Nepaulsingh have shed new light on the *converso* presence in the work. Faur believes that the "central theme of the book. . . . evolves around the determination of Lázaro's mother to integrate with the old Christian society, and to show how this determination eventually passed on to her son" (64).[25] The name given by Antona Pérez (Lázaro's mother) to her first son, "Lázaro" (in English, "Lazarus"), is illustrative of this "determination" insofar as it evokes the resurrection by Jesus of his biblical namesake and by extension Antona's hope that her son will be socially resurrected as a (New) Christian (Faur 63). Lázaro's own struggle to integrate is foreshadowed by the abnormal circumstances of his birth, which he explains in the opening paragraph of chapter 1:

> Mi nacimiento fue dentro del río Tormes, por la cual causa tomé el sobrenombre, y fue desta manera. Mi padre, que Dios perdone, tenía cargo de proveer una moli-

enda de una aceña que está ribera de aquel río, en la cual fue molinero más de
quince años; y estando mi madre una noche en la aceña preñada de mí, tomóle el
parto y parióme allí. De manera que con verdad me puedo decir nacido en el río.

(*La vida de Lazarillo* 100)

(I was actually born in the Tormes River, and that's how I got my name. It happened this way: My father (God rest his soul) was in charge of a mill on the bank of
that river, and he was the miller there for more than fifteen years. Well, one night
while my mother was in the mill, carrying me around in her belly, she went into
labor and gave birth to me right there. So I can really say I was born in the river.)

(Rudder 5)

Lázaro's birth in the Tormes River has been compared to the biblical episode in
which Moses is placed into the Nile River by his mother so that his life might
be spared (Exod. 2:3). According to this interpretation, Lázaro's repetition of his
birthplace at the end of the citation above, "So I can really say I was born in the
river," is meant to create a distance between the birth of Moses in the Old Testament (his Jewish lineage) and his *converso* condition inasmuch as the phrase "con
verdad" (which Nepaulsingh translates as "in truth" [57]) alludes to "*the* truth
through Jesus; so that, on its mythological level, the old (testament) Mosaic text
'in the river' . . . is glossed and made to reveal a new (testament) Christian text 'in
truth . . . born in the river' . . . which refers, again, on the mythological level . . . to
baptism, forced, voluntary, or inherited" (Nepaulsingh 57).

While the setting of Lázaro's birth may distance him from the Jews, his subsequent failure to become a respectable member of his community is a metaphor
for the inability of the *converso* to assimilate into sixteenth-century Christian society because of his Jewish lineage. If Lázaro is indeed a *converso*, then his story,
which he relates to a narratee called Vuestra Merced (Your Grace) in order to
reveal "el caso muy por extenso" (*La vida de Lazarillo* 95) ("all the details of the
matter" [Rudder 4])—the matter being the nature of the relationship between the
archpriest of San Salvador and Lázaro's wife—is an allegorical condemnation of
the social impediments faced by *conversos* in inquisitional Spain, especially the
purity-of-blood statutes that restricted them from possessing honor. This theme
is presented on a number of occasions in the book and is strengthened by the
inclusion of a landscape as a significant component of Lazaro's experiences with
his first master, a blind man. Shortly after they set out from Salamanca in search
of a more profitable place for the blind man to sell prayers and medical advice,
Lázaro and his new master arrive at a bridge to cross the Tormes River:

está a la entrada della un animal de piedra que casi tiene forma de toro, y el ciego
mandóme que llegase cerca del animal; y allí puesto me dijo:

"Lázaro, llega el oído a este toro y oirás gran ruido dentro dél."

Yo simplemente llegué, creyendo ser así, y como sintió que tenía la cabeza par
de la piedra, afirmó recio la mano y diome una gran calabazada en el diablo del
toro, que más de tres días me duró el dolor de la cornada, y díjome:

"Necio, aprende que el mozo del ciego un punto ha de saber más que el
diablo."

Y rió mucho la burla. Parecióme que en aquel instante desperté de la sim-
pleza en que como niño dormido estaba. Dije entre mí: "Verdad dice éste, que me
cumple avivar el ojo y avisar pues solo soy, y pensar cómo me sepa valer."

(*La vida de Lazarillo* 108–10)

(at the edge of this bridge there's a stone statue of an animal that looks something
like a bull. The blind man told me to go up next to the animal, and when I was
there he said, "Lázaro, put your ear up next to this bull and you'll hear a great
sound inside of it."

I put my ear next to it very simply, thinking he was telling the truth. And when
he felt my head near the statue, he doubled up his fist and knocked my head into
that devil of a bull so hard that I felt the pain from its horns for three days. And
he said to me, "You fool, now learn that a blind man's servant has to be one step
ahead of the devil." And he laughed out loud at his joke.

It seemed to me that at that very instant I woke up from my childlike simplicity and I said to myself, "He's right. I've got to open my eyes and be on my guard.
I'm alone now, and I've got to think about taking care of myself.")

(Rudder 8–10)

The rude awakening Lázaro receives, an intellectual rebirth that functions as a
call for him to open his eyes to the cruelty and deception of the world, also serves
as a symbol of his spiritual rebirth as a converted Jew (or a descendant of converts) into a similarly hostile society. This allegorical meaning is revealed when
it is taken into consideration that the episode occurs on what is today called the
"Puente romano" (Roman Bridge), now a pedestrian bridge and still the site of
the "statue of an animal that looks something like a bull" (Rudder 8), an artifact
from pre-Roman times that is located right outside the medieval Jewish quarter of
Salamanca. Unlike Nepaulsingh's reading of Lázaro's physical birth, the fact that
Lázaro's intellectual rebirth takes place at this particular location reinforces his
inferior *converso* status by associating him with the alienated figure of the Jew.

The image of the inferior and ignoble *converso* is perpetuated in Lázaro's dealings with his third master, an arrogant and otiose squire whose "honor" consists of nothing more than a superficial attribute that derives from his outward
appearance (his clothes and his preoccupation with "limpieza" ["cleanliness" or
"purity"], literally the cleanliness of Lázaro's hands and figuratively the purity
of his lineage), rather than virtuous deeds. The squire thus represents the Old
Christian conception of honor as viewed from a *converso* perspective (as the entire
book should be viewed insofar as it consists of Lázaro's personal recollection of
his life). Such honor would have been seen as superficial by *conversos*, whose own
virtuous deeds were of no importance in affording them honor because of their
ancestries.

Like the *converso*, Lázaro is only capable of living in dishonor, an unfortunate
reality reflected in the likely resolution of the aforementioned "matter" that he
attempts to remedy. This outcome is suggested by the archpriest of San Salvador's
ironic declaration that his wife's visits are "muy a tu honra y suya" (*La vida de Lazarillo* 202) ("very much to your [Lázaro's] honor and to hers" [Rudder 99]), by the
frequent gifts bestowed upon Lázaro's wife by the archpriest, and by the fact that

he has the married couple "alquilar una casilla par de la suya" (*La vida de Lazarillo* 201) ("rent a little house right next to his" [Rudder 98]). Just as the *converso* was relegated to a marginal existence, *Lazarillo* ends by intimating that public gossip is based in truth and that Lázaro will be unable to acquire the honor that he seeks by appealing to Vuestra Merced.

Lazarillo closes a chapter on the initial *converso* literary reaction to the social climate created after the establishment of the Spanish Inquisition (and, if the work was actually composed around 1525, as evidence in the text suggests,[26] literature composed by *conversos* who would have also had a personal knowledge of pre-inquisitional Spain). The works heretofore considered participate in this reaction from different perspectives: San Pedro wrote in response to the recent establishment of the Inquisition by the monarchy; Cota, and perhaps Rojas, were personally motivated to respond to the cruelty of the Inquisition, Delicado represents the indifferent *converso* in exile; and the anonymous author of *Lazarillo* depicts the dishonorable existence of *conversos* in early Renaissance Spain. At the same time, these works are linked by allusions to landscapes couched in allegories that possess a common motivation. Well before the formal imposition in 1558 of literary censorship, which criminalized impugnation of the Holy Office, the authors of these works (with the exception of Delicado, who was writing outside of Spain) demonstrate their apprehension at expressing such sentiment by resorting to allegories in order to depict the discriminatory doctrines of an institution that would continue to influence the moral nature of Spain for centuries to come.

Notes

1. For a discussion of these literary references to the sea, see Navarrio González.
2. See Baer (95–243) for a comprehensive review of the period 1391–1414. Netanyahu believes that there were as many as 200,000 conversions after the pogroms of 1391 and that as many as 200,000 additional conversions occurred in the wake of the second wave of anti-Semitism (*Marranos* 235–40). Other scholars lean toward more conservative estimates and posit that there were only around 225,000 *conversos* in the country by 1492 (Domínguez Ortiz 43).
3. See MacKay for a discussion of the inflationary crisis that occurred prior to 1449 (53).
4. For a review of the events of 1449 and the text of the Sentencia-Estatuto, see Benito Ruano (33–81 and 191–96, respectively). For a more recent discussion of the rebellion and its affect on the *conversos,* see Netanyahu (*Origins* 254–712).
5. Although *conversos* throughout Spain faced a similar predicament, the present study will focus on the *conversos* of Castile (including much of northern Spain and Andalusia), the region in which the majority of the *conversos* lived.
6. See Benito Ruano, 74–76, 216–20, 222–23.
7. See Netanyahu (*Origins* 736–40) for more on this request.
8. Baer discusses some of the activities of this episcopal inquisition, headed by the leader of the Jeronimite Order, Alfonso de Oropesa (289–92).
9. For a review of the uprisings in Castile, see MacKay. For more on the purity-of-blood statutes, see Henry Kamen (*Spanish Inquisition: A Historical Revision* 233–42) and Albert A. Sicroff's comprehensive study.
10. See Kamen (*Inquisition and Society* 53–57).
11. Whinnom speculates that this knowledge of public combats would have derived from readings of novels of chivalry (San Pedro 117 n. 119).
12. Unless otherwise indicated, all translations of Spanish literary and critical texts are my own.

13. See Kaplan ("Subverting a Critical Myth").
14. For more on the involvement of the Cota family, see Francisco Cantera Burgos 8, 10–11, 42–43, 45, 50–54, 77, 82.
15. See Foster (71–77) for a discussion of the *Libro de la infancia* in this context.
16. For the text of this poem, see Ciceri (164–73). The poem could not have been composed after 1477, the probable year of Montoro's death (Ciceri 15).
17. For a discussion of this facet of *Celestina,* see Martin (71–134).
18. For the most comprehensive study on this topic, see Gilman, (*Spain*).
19. For an enumeration of these similarities, see Castro Guisasola (178–80), and for the most recent studies on the subject, see Martínez and Severin.
20. For example, Rodríguez Puértolas argues in favor of Calisto while Serrano Poncela posits that Melibea is the *conversa.*
21. For a review of the Jewish experience in Italy during the sixteenth century, see Gerber (182–86).
22. On the *converso* presence in *Lozana,* see also Pike.
23. See, for example, Gilman ("Death") and Márquez Villanueva (*Espiritualidad* 30–38, 67–137). Most recently, Gitlitz ("Inquisition Confessions") considers *Lazarillo* to be structurally and thematically influenced by contemporary confessions made before the Holy Office.
24. Américo Castro (50) and Gilman (*Spain* 154) are among several scholars who believe that a *converso* wrote *Lazarillo.*
25. Faur (63–64) believes that this "central theme" constitutes a response the aforementioned decree issued by the Catholic Monarchs in 1493 that encouraged *conversos* to become good Christians.
26. See Ricapito's introduction to his edition of the text (*La vida de Lazarillo* 11–24) for a review of the polemic.

Works Cited

Baer, Yitzhak. *A History of the Jews in Christian Spain.* Vol. 2. Philadelphia: Jewish Publication Society, 1961.

Benito Ruano, Eloy. *Toledo en el siglo XV: Vida política.* Madrid: Consejo Superior de Investigaciones Científicas, 1961.

Berceo, Gonzalo de. *Milagros de Nuestra Señora.* Ed. Michael Gerli. 5th ed. Madrid: Cátedra, 1991.

Cantera Burgos, Francisco. *El poeta Ruy Sánchez Cota (Rodrigo Cota) y su familia de judíos conversos.* Madrid: de Madrid, 1970.

Castro, Américo. *La realidad histórica de España.* 2nd ed. Mexico, D.F.: Porrúa, 1962.

Castro Guisasola, F. *Observaciones sobre las fuentes literarias de La Celestina.* 1924. Madrid: Consejo Superior de Investigaciones Científicas, 1973.

Ciceri, Marcella, ed. *Antón de Montoro: Cancionero.* Intro. and notes by Julio Rodríguez Puértolas. Salamanca: de Salamanca, 1991.

Cota, Rodrigo. *Diálogo entre el Amor y un Viejo.* Ed. Elisa Aragone. Florence: Felice Le Monnier, 1961.

Damiani, Bruno M. *Francisco Delicado.* New York: Twayne, 1974.

——, intro., notes, and trans. *Portrait of Lozana: The Lusty Andalusian Woman.* By Francisco Delicado. Potomac, MD: Scripta Humanistica, 1987.

"Dança general de la Muerte." *Poesía crítica y satírica del siglo XV.* Ed. Julio Rodríguez Puértolas. 3rd ed. Madrid: Castalia, 1984. 43–70.

Delicado, Francisco. *Retrato de la Lozana andaluza.* Ed. Claude Allaigre. Madrid: Cátedra, 1994.

Deyermond, Alan. *Diego de San Pedro: Cárcel de amor.* Ed. Carmen Parrilla. Barcelona: Critica, 1995.

Domínguez Ortiz, Antonio. *Los judeoconversos en la España moderna.* Madrid: Mapfre, 1992.

Espina, Alonso de. Fortalitium Fidei. Lyon, 1511.

Exodus. *Pentateuch and Haftorahs.* Ed. J. H. Hertz. London: Soncino, 1958. 203–406.

Faur, José. *In the Shadow of History: Jews and Conversos at the Dawn of Modernity.* Albany: State U of New York P, 1992.

Foster, David William. *Christian Allegory in Early Hispanic Poetry.* Lexington: UP of Kentucky, 1970.

Frye, Northrop. *The Great Code: The Bible and Literature.* New York: Harcourt Brace Jovanovich, 1982.

Genesis. *Pentateuch and Haftorahs.* Ed. J. H. Hertz. London: Soncino, 1958. 1–202.

Gerber, Jane S. *The Jews of Spain: A History of the Sephardic Experience.* New York: Free, 1992.

Gerli, E. Michael. "La tipología bíblica y la introducción a los Milagros de Nuestra Señora. *Bulletin of Hispanic Studies* 62.1 (1985): 7–14.

Gilman, Stephen. "The Death of Lazarillo de Tormes." *PMLA* 81 (1966): 149–66.

———. *The Spain of Fernando de Rojas: The Intellectual and Social Landscape of La Celestina.* Princeton: Princeton UP, 1972.

Gitlitz, David. "Inquisition Confessions and Lazarillo de Tormes." *Hispanic Review* 8 (2000): 53–74.

———. *Secrecy and Deceit: The Lives of Crypto-Jews.* Philadelphia: Jewish Publication Society, 1996.

Kamen, Henry. *Inquisition and Society in Spain in the Sixteenth and Seventeenth Centuries.* Bloomington: Indiana UP, 1985.

———. *The Spanish Inquisition.* New York: New American Library, 1965.

———. *The Spanish Inquisition: A Historical Revision.* New Haven: Yale UP, 1998.

Kaplan, Gregory B. "Rodrigo Cota's 'Diálogo entre el Amor y un Viejo': A 'Converso Lament.'" *Indiana Journal of Hispanic Literatures* 8 (1996): 7–30.

———. "Subverting a Critical Myth: Rodrigo de Cota and the Spanish Inquisition." *Journal of Unconventional History* 8.3 (1997): 49–66.

Libro de la infancia y muerte de Jesús (Libre dels tres reys d'Orient). Ed. Manuel Alvar. Madrid: Consejo Superior de Investigaciones Científicas, 1965.

MacKay, Angus. "Popular Movements and Pogroms in Fifteenth-Century Castile." *Past and Present* 55 (1972): 33–67.

Márquez Villanueva, Francisco. *Espiritualidad y literatura en el siglo XVI.* Madrid: Alfaguara, 1968.

———. "Cárcel de amor, novela política." *Revista de Occidente.* 2nda época. 14 (1966): 185–200.

———. "El mundo converso de La Lozana andaluza." *Archivo Hispalense* 171–73 (1973): 87–97.

Martin, June Hall. *Love's Fools: Aucassin, Troilus, Calisto and the Parody of the Courtly Lover.* London: Tamesis, 1972.

Martínez, Salvador. "Cota y Rojas: contribución al estudio de las fuentes y la autoría de La Celestina." *Hispanic Review* 48 (1980): 37–55.

Navarrio González, Alberto. *El mar en la literatura medieval castellana.* N.p.: de la Laguna, 1962.

Nepaulsingh, Colbert I. *Apples of Gold in Filigrees of Silver: Jewish Writing in the Eye of the Spanish Inquisition.* New York: Holmes and Meier, 1995.

Netanyahu, Benzion. *The Marranos of Spain: From the Late XIVth to the Early XVIth Century.* New York: American Academy for Jewish Research, 1966.

———. *The Origins of the Inquisition in Fifteenth Century Spain.* New York: Random House, 1995.

Peters, Edward. *Inquisition.* Berkeley: U of California P, 1989.

Pike, Ruth. "The Conversos in La Lozana Andaluza." *Modern Language Notes* 84 (1969): 304–8.

Post, Chandler Rathfon. *Mediaeval Spanish Allegory.* Cambridge: Harvard UP, 1915.

Rodríguez Puértolas, Julio. "El linaje de Calisto." *Hispanófila* 33 (1968): 1–6. Rpt. in *De la Edad Media a la edad conflictiva.* Madrid: Gredos, 1972. 209–16.

Rojas, Fernando de. *La Celestina.* Ed. Dorothy S. Severin. 6th ed. Madrid: Cátedra, 1992.

Rubin, Nancy. *Isabella of Castile: The First Renaissance Queen.* New York: St. Martin, 1991.

Rudder, Robert S., intro. and trans. *The Life of Lazarillo of Tormes.* NY: Frederick Ungar, 1973.

San Pedro, Diego. *Obras completas, II: Cárcel de amor.* Ed. Keith Whinnom. 2nd. ed. Madrid: Castalia, 1983.

Santillana, Marqués de. "Doctrinal de privados." *El Marqués de Santillana: Obras.* Ed. Augusto Cortina. 6th ed. Madrid: Espasa-Calpe, 1980. 83–98.

Serrano Poncela, Segundo. "El secreto de Melibea." *Cuadernos Americanos* 17 (1958): 488–510.

Severin, Dorothy S. "Cota, His Imitator, and La Celestina: The Evidence Reexamined." *Celestinesca* 4 (1980): 3–8.

Sicroff, Albert A. *Los estatutos de limpieza de sangre: Controversias entre los siglos XV y XVII.* Trans. Mauro Armiño. Madrid: Taurus, 1985.

Simpson, Lesley Byrd, trans. *The Celestina.* By Fernando de Rojas. Berkeley: U of California P, 1955.

Smith, Colin, ed. *Poema de mio Cid.* Oxford: Clarendon, 1972.

La vida de Lazarillo de Tormes. Ed. Joseph V. Ricapito. Madrid: Cátedra, 1983.

Weill, J. "Note sur les maranes d'Espagne." *Revue des Études Juives* 87 (1929): 59–61.

Kari Kalve

"Truthe is therinne"
The Spaces of Truth and Community
in Piers Plowman *B*

Holi Chirche tells Will that Truth is in the "tour on a toft" ("Prologue" 14), seemingly the same place as the "castel" (1.4) from which she has just emerged. When she later tells Will to seek Truth, why does he not just walk across the field of folk and enter that "tour"? It is virtually the only desirable inside space in *Piers Plowman*, and although Will spends the poem searching for Truth, he never gets to Truth or the tower. That tower of Truth appears to be heaven, a place Will can only reach after death; his task is to find Truth on earth. Will's search is unsuccessful, and the characters in the poem often seem farthest from Truth when they are inside something—inside Mede's bower, in a tavern, or in an exclusive group. When Will seems closest to Truth, he is usually not in a specific place, or he is on a road, in a field, or in some amorphous space that seems to have no relationship to inside or outside. Truth may be "therinne" (1.12), but the inside spaces described in the poem's earthly world are almost entirely harmful, closing people off from community and from spiritual interaction. In the most positive moments of the poem, the distinctions between inside and outside almost seem to dissolve, suggesting that these distinctions should be broken down. The work of the social and spiritual institutions, associated with so many of the buildings and spaces in the poem, must be done openly, even though such openness inevitably leads to difficulties.

Scholars tend to ignore the spatial relationships throughout the poem, doubtless in part because the setting for the poem's actions is so much less prominent than the actions themselves. The opening lines of the poem are as precisely located as any medieval dream vision, but once the narrator falls asleep, all sleeping and waking places rapidly lose any sense of specificity, with the exception of the potentially biographical section in the C-text (C.5.1108).[1] The barn of Unity receives more detailed description than any other building or enclosed space in the poem, yet the construction of the barn is described only allegorically. The other description of the process of building in the poem occurs when Kynde shows Will that birds build better nests than anything produced by masons or other craftspeople (B.11.344–49). Although the poem demonstrates such little regard for the form of buildings, it seems quite concerned with the physical relationship of people to each other, in particular with the limitations and dangers of interior spaces, withdrawn from more open places in which a community can work, learn, eat, and pray together as a group.

Examining the differences between private and unrestricted space in this poem and between inside and outside generates a new angle from which to examine the poem's attitude toward community and specialization. It would seem that a poem with such distrust of being inside or of entering interior spaces would also oppose any set of workers—priests, knights, millers—carrying out their duties without at least the contribution of observers who can keep the inside group from fraud. In my thinking about space and buildings in literature, I have also been interested in the way a text's representations of the relationship between insides and outsides can reveal perspectives on subjectivity;[2] here I can only begin to analyze the connection between spatial representation and *Piers Plowman*'s attitudes toward subjectivity by analyzing the poem's concept of "indwelling" as an internal relationship between a believer and God. The main focus of this essay, however, is the social ramifications of the concrete descriptions of enclosed spaces such as buildings, and of characters entering or exiting those spaces.

This visionary poem's strong visual images are either precise and focused visual guides to aid a reader's understanding of theological ideas or vivid story elements, such as the field of folk, which are not described with background detail or much spatial information. Those metaphorical, detailed images, such as the tree of charity described by Anima (16.4 ff)[3] or the dunghill covered with snow compared to "ypocrisie in Latyn" (15.111–16), strain the limits of visual representation while engaging the reader's visual imagination; they demand the labor of the reader's mind. As C. David Benson has observed, the easily visualized action scenes "are rarely located in a recognizable space" (28). Readers can imagine the scenes without noticing that spaces are rarely described; the reader almost never even knows whether a character is indoors or out. Unlike many medieval poems, which pay attention to the surface texture of their settings, there are no extensive descriptions of buildings. The one extensively illustrated manuscript of *Piers Plowman*, a manuscript of the C-text, Bodley Douce 104, does not have the elaborate architectural frames of much medieval painting and has few representations of buildings at all, with only a pulpit at 47r, a lectern at 41r, and a rough illustration of a castle at 34r, presumably the Castle of Truth, but it is such a schematic drawing that it could be a city or a castle or a gate (see Scott and Pearsall, for facsimile illustrations). The poem's language contains very little reference either to the concrete inside and outside of any building or to the concept of insides and outsides. Virtually everything seems to take place in a space that is neither inside nor outside, and yet not a borderland either. It takes place in a dream world that rejects the world of insiders and the world of outsiders and creates a space of collective action, sometimes communal. Often these collective spaces are marked by some boundaries, though not usually enclosed within a building—and sometimes space is simply shared by a group of disparate people.

Will wanders through many spaces, and apparently goes inside some buildings, yet he is never described as inside or as in the act of entering a building or an enclosure. The few buildings referred to, with the partial exception of the barn of Unity, seem formless, and the two most clearly delineated spaces with groups of people inside are hell, stormed by Piers as Jesus, and the tavern that Gloton (Glutton) stops in instead of going to church. The inside of these two spaces are sites of danger and sin; coming out from the inner space is what matters to the poem's progress toward Truth or to the exiters' salvation. Even when the characters are presumably inside a home or public building, it is an uncomfortable stopping place, unless the people within have something to hide. It seems, for example, that leaving the protected, presumably interior space of the banqueting scene in passus 13 is necessary for the continued learning of Will, Conscience, and Patience. They leave behind both the Doctor of Divinity's twisted learned speeches and Will's anger at that sort of speech, and they search for Do-Wel on the road as "pilgrymes" (13.216).

Far more important to Langland than the inside of buildings is the inside of people—their hearts. Yet even while the poem suggests nurturing an inward relationship with God, it seems that mental interiority is problematic, as is any group of insiders that denies access to other Christians, closing itself off while making decisions that pertain to those outside the privileged space as well as to insiders. Will seems to be given the task to teach about Truth by Holi Chirche in part because he is not an insider, not a scholar who knows the theological discourse and so able only to talk with other scholars. She tells Will: "Lereth it thus lewed men, for lettred it knoweth" (1.136). While *Piers Plowman* must be the product of an extremely learned man in Latin scholarly traditions (Kerby-Fulton 529), the poem contains many critiques of scholarship. What seems to be criticized in particular is that study which takes one away from other humans into one's own mental space, or study which, by increasing one's own material benefit, separates one from others, such as the friars Will meets as he looks for Do-wel, the "men of grete witte" (8.9) who can only define Do-Wel in a circular fashion for Will. They have knowledge, but it only serves to separate them further from those around them.

Will's opening view of the field of folk establishes the relationship between inside and outside which will pertain for the rest of the poem: worthy inside spaces are virtually nonexistent on earth; earthly inside spaces are mostly to be avoided. The home of Truth, presumably heaven, is closed off from humans. It seems to have a distinct inside, since "Truthe is therinne" (1.12), but that may be only from the desiring vantage point of fallen, living humans—Will and the readers. Since the poem never reaches heaven, much less Truth, neither Will nor the readers can know whether the inside/outside dichotomy so important on earth also pertains in heaven. There are a very few architectural images of heaven in the poem, and those familiarly suggest that heaven is an inner space—the inside of a castle, church, or tent. Indeed, one of the most common Latin quotations in *Piers Plowman* is "domine, quis habitabit in tabemaculo tuo," "Lord, who shall dwell in your tabernacle," from Psalm 14 of the Vulgate (Alford). There is no question that being inside the Lord's tabernacle offers the highest reward; to be inside, here, is a powerfully positive image, yet no building in the poem represents that tabernacle, other than the unreachable "tour."

More immediate to this poem than the physical space of heaven—which is never described although frequently mentioned—is a human's inner relationship with heaven and with God. The architectural and psychological images of heaven in *Piers Plowman* are well analyzed by Mary Clemente Davlin in "Tower and Tabernacle," where she shows that even through its architectural metaphors the poem depicts an image of heaven as a nonvisual state of "being with and in God" (107). Here "in" does not describe a physical place but the notion of "indwelling," taken from John and quoted in *Piers Plowman,* in which the loving believer "dwells in God and God also dwells in the person" (Davlin 105). Holi Chirche sends Will to find Truth within himself and among other people.

Although *Piers Plowman* represents heaven primarily as a metaphorical state of dwelling, the poem also represents a search for Truth through a material, concrete world. Several scholars have argued that Will's search turns its back on the social and physical world; one of the more useful of these arguments has been made by Mary Carruthers in her *Search for St. Truth.* Carruthers asserts convincingly that *Piers Plowman* "is an epistemological poem, a poem about the problem of knowing truly" (10). Yet this epistemological search is shaped by the visual and physical descriptions, which maintain their social and material relevance even while they convey several allegorical meanings. As Anne Middleton argues in "The Audience and Public of 'Piers Plowman,'" the poem maintains "parallel interests in both individual understanding and penance on the one hand, and social and historical analysis and reform on the other" (110). Langland's poem has powerful visual and thematic connection to the material world, and it is worth noticing what the poem does *not* describe as well as the material settings and objects that it does. As scholars examine the characters and ideas in the poem, we should also examine the verbal structures along with the physical structures which they describe.

Carruthers suggests that the poem's "structural fluidity" contributes to the lack of importance of the physical representation of Will's search (23). "Structural fluidity" is an apt phrase for both the structure of the poem and the structures presented within Will's dreaming and waking world, and this phrase could also apply to the descriptions of structures in several other medieval texts. That spatial structural fluidity needs to be noted and explored. The physical structures in this poem, the places and buildings, are open to change, which seems to be a virtue. Yet with all the permutations of space and time in the poem, there is at least one constant: inside spaces are perpetually slighted.

The field of folk shows people separated into groups, but strikingly, the imagery presents all the groups in the same field, presumably outside. No buildings are described within the earthly realm in this early section until we meet Mede, a dangerous character who seems to work primarily indoors. Even the lawyers and dishonest priests, notoriously members of groups who benefit from the exclusivity of their professions, are in the same outdoor field as the food sellers, the King, and beggars. Langland's description of the folk moves from those who normally ply their trade outdoors, such as pilgrims, to those who work inside, such as stewards, bishops, and the King. In both groups, there are both honorable and dishonorable professions and workers, and all are outside in one field together, where their labor is visible to each other and those they work for are visible to them. The processes of institutions are open to view.

The first discussion in the poem of an inside space refers to that most sacred space, heaven, with the reference to St. Peter's role as guardian of the gate of heaven ("Prologue" 100). Peter has the power "to close and to shette, / And to opene it to hem and hevene blisse shewe" ("Prologue" 105–6). Peter is also given the cardinal virtues to help humans, and the poem then plays on that noun "cardinal" by referring to the cardinals in Rome who have taken on some of Peter's power by appointing the pope, his successor. Roman cardinals, who "presumed" to have that power ("Prologue" 108), seem secondary to cardinal virtues in this passage rather than embodying them, thus suggesting that the holy space of heaven is more conceptual and less physical than the court at Rome. Langland hints at a satirical critique of the papal curia, saying, "I kan and kan naught of court speke moore" ("Prologue" 111). As James Simpson points out in "The Constraints of Satire in 'Piers Plowman' and 'Mum the Soothsayer,'" this phrase plays on two "different senses of the verb 'connen,' and can be translated 'therefore I know how to, and am not able to, speak more of the papal court'" (13). Even the most spiritual court on earth would seem to contain the hint of flawed political processes, although the narrator does not explicitly pass such a judgment. Peter guards the entrance to the only inside space in the "Prologue," another metaphorical space with the same referent as the "tour on a toft" ("Prologue" 14)—the Kingdom of God.

From the courts of heaven and Rome, the "Prologue" turns to the earthly King's court and to earthly, British, government. "Court" in Middle English, as today, could refer both to the physical location of a ruler and his close followers—usually a building—and to the group constituted by the ruler with his followers and advisers. Here, the word "court" is not used, but the poem seems to bring in the King and his entourage as a parallel to the papal court. The King and "Knyghthod" ("Prologue" 116), however, are described as entering the field among the other folk, visible to the watching narrator, and working with and among "the Commune" (115) to create a functioning community. In this vision, all work together with no physical separation among those with different roles. The "Prologue" takes a visual and metaphorical leap when, once a dispute threatens this harmony among the different estates, the focus of the poem switches to an anxious group of rats running in, apparently representing Parliament. These rats do not interrupt the scene previously described; rather, they replace it. To describe a dispute among rats, the narrator must be closer to the scene than he was before, bringing the readers with him to a less dispassionate distance from the action. I suspect this shift does not seem major to most readers; however, this has seemed to be an allegorical field from the beginning, one in which rats and a cat may easily bring new perspectives to the question of how to create a civil society. Perhaps the sense of this field as a place of serious play makes the fact that all of its life takes place outdoors also less prominent. Yet after turning over the interpretation of this dream of a "route of ratons" ("Prologue" 199) to his readers ("Prologue" 209–10), the narrator's dream returns to an extremely broad view of the field as a whole. He is able to see the activities of a broad variety of workers, from barristers to tavern keepers, all together in the field, reminding his readers that they are all outdoors together. No group has its own place separate from the others.

I have dwelt so long on the "Prologue" because, although after leaving Holi Chirche Will appears to leave the field of folk, in some ways he stays outside in it for the rest of the poem, outside among all of the workers and leaders and priests. Open, public space becomes the default mode of the poem, with internal and private spaces usually being specifically mentioned. Holi Chirche tells him that the field is a "maze" (1.6), that Truthe is in the "tour" rather than the field, and that most of the people in the field do not even care about heaven, so it seems the seeker for Truth would go elsewhere. Yet when Holi Chirche walks away and Will is left to watch Mede's wedding, he is back among some of the same people from the field of folk. Many readers would probably also agree that he seems to wander in a "maze" for the rest of the poem, not in vain, but not reaching his stated goal.

The poet's use of space during the actions centered around Mede exemplify the lack of description of public spaces and the danger of inner, private rooms within the world of this poem. The narrator's first view of Mede is across the field, as a contrast to Holi Chirche, yet soon all of the activity centered around Mede seems to be taking place inside halls in court buildings. The "moothalle" is never described (4.135), and characters are never described as entering it, but when Theologie convinces Mede and her followers to go to London with Cyvyle and they all join with the King's court, they are presumably inside, since Mede moves back and forth between the assembled people and an inner room, that is, a room beyond the public rooms of a building.

Mede herself enters the most private of inside spaces. When she is first described, she is standing in the field, but then the narrator shifts his view to all the folk surrounding her. After this, Mede is no longer among the group—the "route," as the narrator calls her followers (2.62), reminding the reader of the rats in the "Prologue." Instead, Mede has to be brought from her inner chamber out to the assembly: Favel "fette hire out of boure" (2.65). Private rooms are still relatively new in the late fourteenth century and still cause some concern among poets concerned with social relationships. Later in this poem, Study comments on rich people avoiding the public halls and resorting to private rooms to eat: "elenge is the halle," she asserts about the public halls (10.96), spaces she argues are made for eating: "maad for meles" (10.101). She claims the halls are lonely so that rich people can avoid eating around poor people, presumably to avoid giving food away, to avoid guilt, and to be more comfortable around only other wealthy and high-ranking people.

Readers could argue that Study is not necessarily a reliable authority, but Mede's use of a private room, a bower, marks both Mede and the private space as dangerous to the social good, confirming Study's concerns. Mede works for her own benefit and corrupts those around her: she is just the kind of person who needs to go off by herself to a private room in order to advance her deceitful activities. Here Mede emerges from one to be married to Fals; later she retreats into one at the King's court. She is joined in this latter "chambre" by a variety of clergy members (3.10), where she makes promises to them that engage them in a secretive and indebted relationship with her. After promising wealth to these clerks and to the Mayor in return for their spiritual and civil forgiveness of those who are overfond of money, she is led to the King's private room, another "boure" (3.103). Again, this room seems to be a site of dangerous activity, as the King suggests Mede should marry Conscience. When Conscience arrives, he speaks to the entire council and others, a large number of people, thus suggesting that the activity has moved without comment into a more public space again, with the King's council and many other figures observing and sometimes participating in the debate between the King and Conscience over this potential marriage. What brings Mede down is the presence of the public, the "commune" (4.166), who are able to witness the judgment by Reason and the potential loss of Law if Mede does indeed marry Conscience. The King makes the decisions, but the public nature of this discussion helps guide him in avoiding a disastrous outcome.

Study's complaint about the growth of private rooms occurs in the context of her speech against covetousness, and the other character with an inner room in this poem is Coveitise, who uses his private rooms for similarly dishonest goals and that same monetary gain that Mede seeks. He explains to Repentaunce that he stores his best products there in order better to deceive his customers: "The beste ale lay in my bour or in my bedchambre" (5.218). Keeping the ale hidden allows Coveitise's wife secretly to water down the ale his customers buy after they have tasted the unadulterated ale from the same barrel. Again, private space creates a greater possibility for antisocial and illegal activity.

The other allegorical sins in this section of the poem do not have their own private rooms, but some of them show the potential problems associated with different sorts of interior spaces. Wrathe lives in a cloister and sows disharmony among friars and among nuns whose convent he has also worked in. Wrathe's stories vividly evoke the emotions that can fester and flare in small communities when anger begins to hold sway. Some scholars believe Langland spent some time as "part of a monastic literary community" (Kerby-Fulton 530); this experience may have aided in creating the animation of this passage. Wrathe describes his spreading of destructive gossip as vomiting inside the cloister (5.179), constructing a picture of a highly unpleasant enclosed space. While the enclosure does not create Wrathe, it does offer fertile ground in which Wrathe's evils may grow.

The most vivid interior space visited in this poem is the tavern frequented by Gloton. The poem does not describe the building or its decor, but readers do learn what is sold inside, who spends time in this tavern, and the games Gloton plays while there. The remarkably lively scene creates a more specific small community than readers have seen before in *Piers Plowman,* apparently because the space is sufficiently defined to allow most of its visitors to be named, if still first in terms of their profession, such as "Clement the cobelere" and "Bette the Bocher" (5.320, 323). This greater intimacy and the playfulness in the Tavern show how appealing such a comfortable inner space can be, but its influence causes sin. This space, and the woman who runs it, has drawn Gloton away from his path to the church for repentance, and he gets unattractively drunk while there. Once again, an inner space is associated with sin and with poor guidance, and no character enters a church. So far in the poem, up to the middle of passus 5, the only spaces characters are described inside are the dangerous and dishonest private rooms—bowers, chambers, and a bedroom—the unhappy cloisters that nurture anger, and a tavern that inspires gluttony. No one aside from Holi Chirche has yet made it inside a church, let alone Truth's tower. The other settings of the poem's actions are not described as indoors. Some are described as outdoors and others are merely seen as public spaces.

The poem does not describe the inside of hell, nor do its main characters enter there, but the action of the poem does approach its entrance nearer than that of heaven. When Piers jousts with the devil in Jesus' arms, Jesus does approach the gates and let out the residents trapped inside. The hell that Jesus approaches in passus 18 is the ultimately negative space in the poem, and contains some reminiscence of the "dongeon" in the "dale" contrasted with the "tour" in the opening vision of the poem ("Prologue" 15, 14): it is lower, it is surrounded by a field, and it is a type of fortified building. Below the earth, the narrator envisions another broad field, in which Mercy, Truthe, Pees, and Rightwisnesse can walk from the four compass points to meet each other outside the gates of hell. So although the dreamer along with Jesus has "descendit ad inferna" (18.111), that space down below is not all hell. Hell only seems to refer to the central fortified space that Lucifer and the other demons (another "route" [18.405]) try to protect from Jesus' powerful light. Jesus says he will enter into the gates guarded by Lucifer and the other "Dukes of this dymme place" (18.320), but the predominant image is of the gates of hell breaking and of those Jesus loves emerging from hell. Jesus' death and his harrowing of hell in passus 18 may be the most beautiful and dramatic in the poem. In Jesus' triumph over Lucifer, light triumphs over darkness, life over death, and coming out of an enclosed space becomes part of that triumph. The poem does not show these saved souls proceed into heaven; readers are led to imagine them liberated rather than newly enclosed. With this association of liberation with salvation, heaven again seems like a place that would not follow the earthly model of enclosure to mark those saved as inside.

But what of the buildings which for so many readers today signify the Middle Ages, which dwarfed other medieval buildings, which created large interior spaces and which framed or formed countless medieval images? What about cathedrals and churches? Not only are no churches described in *Piers Plowman,* almost never does a character get into one, and when one does, with the notable and destructive exception of Sire Pentrans-domos entering the barn of Unity as I will analyze below, the entrance into the space is never described. After the King has narrowly avoided abandoning law to Mede's will, he and his court head to church — "to the kirke wente" — and the dreamer wakes up, presumably while they are still on their way; the characters are not described entering the church (5.1–3). The preposition "to" could mean "into" in Middle English, so the description of the King and his knights going "to" the church could mean that they went "into" the church. The ambiguity of the phrase is itself significant, however, as is the avoidance of a preposition or verb that would more clearly signify the act of entrance. The King's court may or may not cross the threshold of the church within the poem; the ambiguity indicates the overall difficulty of making such an entrance within this poem. None of the confessing sinners, including Gloton, reach a church to make their confession. The waking narrator finally goes to church after dreaming about the harrowing of hell, but he is not described entering the church or as "in" the church, so this space also remains undescribed in the poem. These churches seem to be such large spaces with large congregations that, for example, the narrator can fall asleep during the offering (19.1–6). Here, as throughout the poem, the space matters less than the activities that go on within it. Churches are described less as places in themselves than as homes for the rites of the Christian community.

The most obviously useful, good building in the poem is the barn of Unity. Built under the direction of Grace and with the blood of Christ as the mortar, this building represents the church on earth, a home for those who believe in Christ and who try to live according to Christ's law. Piers realizes he needs a barn to store the fruit of his plowing, that fruit being the believers who flourish from hearing Christ's word, as in the parable of the sower in Mark 4. Grace gives the cross, the crown of thorns, Christ's baptismal water and blood to make this building, roofs it with Holy Writ, and names it "Unite-Holy Chirche on Englissh" (19.330). The barn is ready for the harvest, but the only character shown entering this building becomes its downfall. Before that character arrives, others enter the barn of Unity for protection but we do not see them enter, and by the time they are inside it, the barn is seriously besieged and therefore not a place that sustains community or comfort. When Pride and others come to mislead Christian believers, Conscience is led by Kynde Wit to turn the barn of Unity into a fort, with a moat around it and other fortifications. Yet this very process reveals the connections of the community beginning to break down, perhaps adding to the members' delay in entering the barn of Unity and the lack of security they find within. Conscience exhorts the group to go into the barn when Antecrist attacks them forcefully (20.75), and though at this point the poem does not describe the action of folks entering the barn, at a later point in the passus the narrator comes "to Unitee" (20.213). At this point, Conscience, his followers, and the narrator appear to be inside Unity since they are "bisegede" by Antecrist's troops (20.215), and sieges take place against groups within fortified spaces.

This holy and metaphorical building represents a bond among Christians that seems to be valued throughout the poem, yet even this space provides no lasting shelter for its occupants. The gatekeepers allow hospitality to best their watchfulness and let in "Sire Penetrans-domos" (20.341), also known as "Frere Flatterere" (20.324): "Thus thorugh Hende-Speche entred the frere, / And cam in to Conscience and curteisly hym grette" (20.355–56). Fewer than fifty lines from the end of the poem a character is finally described as entering and coming into an enclosed space, and this entry brings down the safety of that building. By this stage in the poem it seems inevitable that some force will break apart any struggling community, but one would think it would be better not to let in someone with the name "Sir Enterer- or Piercer-of-Homes" at a time when one's walls and fortifications are necessary. Will has earlier praised the person who can pierce "the paleys of hevene" as one who will be saved, not one who wants to destroy heaven (10.459), but Will's expertise could be doubted, and this visitor enters an earthly building, much more easily destroyed than a heavenly space. Indeed, the friar's presence in the barn of Unity creates an entry for the besieging deadly sins, as Sire Penetrans-domos brings with him the discord and the private monetary reward that destroys this community and the safety of its building, just as Mede destroyed community with her secretive payments and secretive spaces. Sire Penetrans-domos enters an innocent communal space, unlike Mede's secretive bowers or Gloton's tavern, but this carefully described entry, like their entries into spaces with more potential for corruption, creates the possibility for the moral downfall of a large group. Because this friar has entered Unity, bringing with him private payments, the characters searching for Truth and virtue must leave the barn. The poem ends in the same sort of space as it began, with characters searching through a formless, outdoor area.

I am not arguing that Langland felt people should give up shelter or only live in large groups in barns; although concerned with the daily struggle to be a Christian in the world, this poem does not give such concrete advice as where to live or what to eat—and if it did, the advice of this notoriously inconsistent narrative could very well be contradictory. Yet the poem's position on private rooms is unusually unambiguous for *Piers Plowman:* they allow too easily for sin and deception. And the minimal discussion of buildings, the absence of security in any inside space, as well as the greater importance of community rituals rather than communal spaces, also suggest a remarkably consistent analysis of the limitations and dangers to private space and to the figurative consequences of being "inside."

Even when Will and those around him are within a building with public spaces and honorable occupants, leaving that space can bring growth and greater good. Some of the beneficial action of the poem does seem to take place within buildings, as at the King's court, mentioned above. Dame Study sends Wit to find Clergie (Clergy) in or near an allegorical court reminiscent of the path to Truth that Piers initially described to those who instead plowed his field (10.159–69); Clergie and Scripture appear to live together in this court. Will exits these places through the vagaries of his dream: he wakes up from one and falls into a deeper dream in the other, but in both cases the dream moves him because he has reached the end of his learning in that spot. The well-known banqueting scene takes place within the court of Conscience and though that seems to fit the definitions of a good interior space, it also can only be a stop along the way for Will and even for Conscience.

The dinner party at the court of Conscience outlines some concerns and actions that will appear again when Conscience fortifies and administers the barn of Unity, just as that later section reflects and expands Piers's initial plowing scene. Traugott Lawler in "Conscience's Dinner" draws the connection between these two scenes of Conscience offering food or housing to all guests (101). Lawler argues that although Conscience first leaves his own court and later leaves the barn of Unity, he is not merely escaping:

> Conscience's two pilgrimages may seem like escapes, or at least releases: in an indoor, confined place—his court the barn of Unity—the pressure builds until it impels him outward. Instead they might be seen as expressions of faith and hope, and of an active will.
>
> (103)

Having looked at the ambivalent nature of "indoor, confined place[s]," Lawler's division between a release and an expression of an active will seems less to mark a difference than a correspondence. To be enclosed may obscure one's faith and hope and therefore limit one's will.

At first it seems that an invitation to dine with Clergie at the court of Conscience offers Will a great opportunity to learn and move forward on his quest. Will arrives to find more guests, including an unknown friar who turns out to love good food more than he loves following his own preaching. Will himself is not shown entering the hall in which the group dines; instead Patience, the character who will lead Will and Conscience back out to a larger pilgrimage, is invited into this interior hall from his waiting place also "in the paleis" (13.29). Although Will and Patience are allowed into this relatively interior and private space, Will's sense that he and Patience are marginalized makes him angry. Patience responds to Will's anger and to the discussion of how to do well leads him to call for others to join him on his way out of this palace and into the larger world. Simpson argues that this departure "could not be more spectacular as an act of social and institutional disruption" ("Desire" 237). Conscience's court is safe for those who are within it, but there are still those outside who need the benefits of the love about which Patience has preached. This inside space may not be dangerous, but it is exclusive. Patience, Conscience, and Will need to take their learning from this effete interior dinner out among larger numbers of people.

I have not yet mentioned one crucial edifice in the poem: the "castel that Kynde made" (9.2), the human body. This structure receives the most physical description of any in the text and is the least ambiguous. Humans need their bodies in order to protect their spirits, this tale by Wit suggests, and the body has been well constructed—"wittily" and "craftily"—to perform its protective function well (9.4–5). This may seem surprising in a world where sin is found in carnality, but here the flesh and its senses are commanded by "Inwit" (9.18). As with other edifices, however, the body has an external enemy, the devil as "*Princeps huius mundi*" (9.8). This external enemy, if allowed in, will sabotage the body's defenses and use them against the spirit, turning those same defenses into the entry points for sin.

This image of the body as castle provides an excellent entry to an analysis of the concept of the indwelling of God in *Piers Plowman*. In the course of describing the threats to and defenses of the body, Wit quotes a standard passage from John about indwelling: "Qui manet in caritate, in Deo manet &c." ("who dwells in charity, dwells in God" 9.64a). In 1 John the passage continues "and God in him"; the quotation evokes that continuation by its etcetera. This metaphor of the body as castle attaches that mutual dwelling to a mental and verbal picture of a public place. This image of the body as an accessible space, inhabited by one's spirit and by God, is akin to Bruce Harbert's analysis of the collective nature of Langland's spirituality:

> The journey that matters to Langland is the inner journey, into oneself and toward the discovery of the indwelling God. But for all his interiority Langland does not have a privatised spirituality. Not for him the lonely imaginative journey to a distant time and place: he prays in crowds. . . .
>
> (69)

Will prays in crowds, and the palace of flesh should be able to protect itself without withdrawing from all outside influence. In *Piers Plowman,* to house God and to dwell within God does not lead to a closed off interiority. This dwelling for God replaces other physical structures in the manner that Piers gives his directions to Truth's house. If Will and the other seekers have Grace's aid and follow Piers's instructions, "Thow shalt see in thiselve Truthe sitte in thyn herte" (5.606). It may seem that the believer searching for Truth leaves one sort of interior for another, one's own body. Yet, as I have shown, the interior of one's own body seems less enclosed and less distinct from a community of believers than does the interior of buildings. The relationship between inside and outside one's body is intriguingly less vexed than other relationships between inside and outside in this poem. This relationship may be less vexed because God made the body, and also, this poem suggests, because humans know God from sources both within and outside of their bodies.

Piers Plowman's well-populated world contains few buildings, but Langland builds his own tower with this poem, a tower of words. Just as the tower changes with each re-vision, indeed, with each scribal copy, so the truth inside is never final, never Truth, always changeable earthly approximations. Similarly, any building or earthly shelter within the poem only approximates the safety and glory of God's tabernacle, the palace of heaven. No church in the poem, not even the barn of Unity, becomes the "herberwe" that holy church is said to be (10.402–5), but that shelter may exist in the rites of the church and among the community of people who make up the church instead of the building. Whenever the poem represents an interior space, an external space also exists, and there is tension between the two. Often an interior space is one of deceit, but the exterior space is not automatically the better space. The barn of Unity, for example, offers safety and community for a while, and even the dishonest friar in Conscience's court contributes to a thoughtful spiritual discussion which has things to teach Will. But the tension between inside and outside of any space on earth or in hell, aside from the human body, eventually puts too much pressure on the inside for it to maintain its strengths. The tension comes from those who are outside and who want to enter, and from those who are inside who want to take sinful advantage of their privacy.

In the course of rejecting private space and the status of insiders, *Piers Plowman* may seem to argue for the equal participation of any person in shaping political policy or theological beliefs. Yet for Langland, political and religious institutions should shape that participation. As Simpson argues in "Desire and the Scriptural Text," Langland's imagery and hermeneutic strategies have radical consequences for the church, and, I would add, for the state. "Leaving a place of physical or institutional enclosure causes the type of social and institutional disruption" (Simpson 237), yet this potential disruption does not outweigh the need for those institutions; it calls for their profound reform. Langland values the collective aspect of open spaces as well as he values the rites that create a public and ritual space for actors from different parts of society. Instead of outside space as the key opposition to inside, Langland opposes communal space to inside space. Ralph Hanna has argued that "[a]lliterative poetry may, more than most Middle English poetic forms, suppress alternate voices, but its fiction—ideologically poised against claims of clerical exclusivity—is for utter inclusiveness and communal unity" (503). The spatial openness in this poem supports this social inclusivity, inclusivity also called for by Augustine in *The City of God:* "for as long as this Heavenly City is a pilgrim on earth, she summons citizens of all nations and every tongue, and brings together a society of pilgrims" (19.17, p. 946). According to Augustine, no earthly society can provide the "harmonious fellowship" that the heavenly city will provide after human life (19.17, p. 947), yet those who strive for peace and love on earth in order to prepare must attend to social structures: "the city's life is inevitably a social one" (19.17, p. 947). Langland lays out a city in his opening field, and shows the limitations of earthly communities in his final vision. Yet life within the city, a community, is vital to his imagination, and the poem offers suggestions for how to work for that heavenly city on earth, even though it cannot be finally built in Langland's world. The well-intentioned characters in Langland's poem each have a necessary place in a larger social organization, which argues more for revitalizing political and religious institutions than for obliterating them. The individual believer may dwell with God, but such a mutual relationship depends on the foundations of ritual and membership in open institutions. The failure to describe any beneficial crossing from outside to inside throughout this long narrative poem indicates how much the author's imagination was fixed in open, public spaces and suggests the futility of retreating to an interior space for spiritual succor.

Notes

1. The first five passus of the B-text in particular evoke the activities and atmosphere of London, but not with visual specificity; see Barron 93–94 and Pearsall.
2. I have been influenced by Grosz and Dollimore's attention to the boundary between the inside and outside of a subject. Each demonstrates the linguistic and conceptual breakdown

of that binary in Western philosophical writings. Dollimore, focusing on the concept of perversion, includes an analysis of Augustine's inability to locate the source of sin as from within or without the human subject (131–47). Grosz draws on Lacan's extended image of a Mobius strip to show the ways which mind and body, "the inside and the outside of the subject," continually become each other (xii).

3. These and later references are to the B-text, giving the passus number, followed by line numbers.

Works Cited

Alford, John A. *Piers Plowman: A Guide to the Quotations.* Binghamton: Medieval & Renaissance Texts & Studies,1992.

Augustine. *The City of God Against the Pagans.* Ed. and trans. R. W. Dyson. Cambridge: Cambridge UP, 1998.

Barron, Caroline M. "William Langland: A London Poet." *Chaucer's England: Literature in Historical Context.* Ed. Barbara A. Hanawalt. Minneapolis: U of Minnesota P, 1992. 91–109.

Benson, C. David. "*Piers Plowman* and Parish Wall Paintings." *Yearbook of Langland Studies* 11 (1997): 1–38.

Carruthers, Mary. *The Search for St. Truth: A Study of Meaning in* Piers Plowman. Evanston: Northwestern UP, 1973.

Davlin, Mary Clemente, O.P. "Tower and Tabernacle: The Architecture of Heaven and the Language of Dwelling with/in God in the B-Text of Piers Plowman." *Essays in Medieval Studies* 10 (1993): 99–110.

Dollimore, Jonathan. *Sexual Dissidence: Augustine to Wilde, Freud to Foucault.* Oxford: Clarendon, 1991.

Grosz, Elizabeth. *Volatile Bodies: Toward a Corporeal Feminism.* Bloomington: Indiana UP, 1994.

Hanna, Ralph. "Alliterative Poetry." *The Cambridge History of Medieval English Literature.* Ed. David Wallace. Cambridge: Cambridge UP, 1999. 488–512.

Harbert, Bruce. "Langland's Easter." *Langland, the Mystics and the Medieval English Religious Tradition: Essays in Honour of S. S. Hussey.* Ed. Helen Phillips. Cambridge: D. S. Brewer, 1990. 57–70.

Kerby-Fulton, Kathryn. "*Piers Plowman.*" *The Cambridge History of Medieval English Literature.* Ed. David Wallace. Cambridge: Cambridge UP, 1999. 513–38.

Langland, William. Piers Plowman *by William Langland: An Edition of the C-Text.* Ed. Derek Pearsall. Berkeley: U of California P, 1978.

——. *The Vision of* Piers Plowman: *A Complete Edition of the B-Text.* Ed. A. V. C. Schmidt. New York: Everyman, 1987.

Lawler, Traugott. "Conscience's Dinner." *The Endless Knot: Essays on Old and Middle English in Honor of Marie Borroff.* Ed. M. Teresa Tavormina and R. F. Yeager. Cambridge: D. S. Brewer, 1995. 87–103.

Middleton, Anne. "The Audience and Public of 'Piers Plowman.'" *Middle English Alliterative Poetry and Its Literary Background.* Ed. David Lawton. Cambridge: D. S. Brewer, 1982. 101–23.

Pearsall, Derek. "Langland's London." *Written Work: Langland, Labor, and Authorship.* Ed. Steven Justice and Kathryn Kerby-Fulton. Philadelphia: U of Pennsylvania P, 1997. 185–207.

Scott, Kathleen, and Derek Pearsall. Piers Plowman: *A Facsimile of Bodleian Library, Oxford, MS Douce 104.* Cambridge: D. S. Brewer, 1992.

Simpson, James. "The Constraints of Satire in 'Piers Plowman' and 'Mum and the Sothsegger.'" *Langland, the Mystics and the Medieval English Religious Tradition: Essays in Honour of S. S. Hussey.* Ed. Helen Phillips. Cambridge: D. S. Brewer, 1990. 11–30.

——. "Desire and the Scriptural Text: Will as Reader in Piers Plowman." *Criticism and Dissent in the Middle Ages.* Ed. Rita Copeland. Cambridge: Cambridge UP, 1996. 215–43.

Catherine S. Cox

Eastward of the Garden
The Biblical Landscape of Sir Gawain
and the Green Knight

At the culmination of the beheading game in fitt 4 of *Sir Gawain and the Green Knight,* as Gawain, in the role of spectator,[1] observes his own blood glistening upon the snow-covered ground of the Green Chapel—"þe schene blod ouer his schulderes schot to þe erþe. / And quen þe burne seȝ þe blode blenk on þe snawe . . ." (2313–14)—he realizes that, despite the ominous signs of death and burial that surround him,[2] he has somehow survived the Green Knight's blow. Earlier the Green Knight had warned Gawain that being called "recreaunt" would be the price of his failing to show up at the given appointment—"Þerfore com, oþer recreaunt be calde þe behoues" (456)—yet, ironically, in attempting to bolster his courage to make this appearance, he accepts and conceals the Lady's girdle, thereby fulfilling the label's twofold connotations of apostasy and cowardice. Having invested his faith in a deceptively acquired talisman, Gawain must now come to terms with his dishonesty and its discomfiting reflection upon his inner virtue and Christian faith.

Gawain's dilemma can be elucidated by way of the Green Chapel's allusive relationship to the land of Cain's exile, *'erets-nod,* a highly symbolic biblical and narrative space. To be sure, Gawain's own sin is relatively trivial compared to Cain's act of fratricide; nonetheless, the Green Chapel sequence draws off the semantic and exegetical possibilities of Cain's erraticism, in particular, the metaphoric topography of the post-Edenic landscape and its connection to scriptural hermeneutics both authoritative and popular. In this regard, a biblical paradigm of material and figurative exile, articulated by way of the narrative and exegetical texts and traditions of the biblical Cain, informs *Sir Gawain and the Green Knight*'s depiction of Gawain's sin and its consequences, as well as the narrative processes that give life to these and related stories within the time and space of the telling.

I

Notorious and intriguing as a biblical persona and cultural icon, Cain's reputation derives from his status as the exiled perpetrator of the first homicide, subsequent to his parents' own post-Edenic exile, with its intimations of exclusion, mortality, and transgression. A reading of the Cain and Abel (*Qayin* and *Hevel*) episode in the biblical Hebrew, however, shows that the image of the exiled Cain as the original evil murderer, ubiquitous in medieval orthodox Christianity, misses the penitential nuances of the original language. The brief story, a continuation of the Adam and Eve (*'Adam* and *Havvah*) expulsion sequence in the first narrative unit of Bereshit/Genesis,[3] tells us that God accepts Abel's sacrifice of choice firstlings but rejects Cain's offering of the fruits of the earth; Cain, jealous, kills Abel, hides his body, and lies about it to God, asking, "Am I the watcher/keeper of my brother?" (Gen. 4:9).[4] God's stern reprimand curses both Cain and the ground that has received Abel's blood (*damim*) with exile and sterility respectively; to this reprimand, Cain replies with a rather cryptic three-word utterance: *gadol 'avoni minnes'o* (literally, "too great my sin/punishment than to bear/pardon"). Multiple possibilities of literal translation coexist within this single textual expression, and the polysemous ambiguity of the Hebrew is necessarily sacrificed to some degree in rendering the utterance into English, Latin, or another language. Even at its most literal level, a translation will necessarily exclude other literal, as well as connotative, possibilities that both complement and contradict each other.[5]

The Hebrew word *'avon*—etymologically related to *'avah,* something bent or twisted[6]—conveys a pair of semantic options, sin and punishment, necessarily and inextricably linked. And *neso',* to bear or to pardon, is used in its infinitive mode, eliding altogether the identity of its agent.[7] The utterance therefore foregrounds the ambiguities of situation and expression. In context, Cain's logical response to God's stated sentence could well be a declaration that God's intended punishment is perhaps excessive, or that Cain knows himself to be too weak to sustain himself in exile: "My punishment is too great to bear." Construed as a question—"Is my sin too great to be forgiven?"—the utterance is overtly penitential, signifying a repentant sinner's cautious attempt to ascertain God's intentions with an underlying plea for forgiveness. In statement form, "My sin is too great to be forgiven," it signifies Cain's willingness to acknowledge the magnitude of fratricide as sin, while expressing his fear that he will be denied the opportunity to atone.

St. Jerome, in his Vulgate translation of the *Hebraica veritas*, the "Hebrew truth," as he respectfully terms the Hebrew Bible source text,[8] offers a somewhat tortured rendering of Cain's utterance, capturing the essence of sin and punishment: "Maior est iniquitas mea, quam ut veniam merear" (my iniquity is greater than that I might merit forgiveness) (Gen. 4:13).[9] Perhaps partly owing to the polysemous ambiguity of *'avon,* Jerome uses the somewhat ambiguous term *iniquitas*—literally "imbalance" or "inequality," though conventionally associated with the Christian concept of "sin"—to convey *'avon*. But he elides the problem of literal polysemy with *veniam*, "forgiveness" or "pardon." Having become familiarized with Jewish exegetical methods during his ten years of Hebrew study with the Palestinian rabbis, Jerome frequently draws off rabbinical exegesis to help determine word choices in his Latin translation;[10] it is not surprising, then, to find a midrash that supports Jerome's rendering of *'avon* as *iniquitas* with the additional clarification of *veniam*. In *Bereshit Rabbah,* the collection of midrashim on the first book of the Hebrew Bible composed primarily in the third and fourth centuries but based on more ancient oral traditions,[11] Cain considers his father's transgression in Eden and declares his own sin (*hatta't,* "error" or "sin") more heinous: "My father violated a light precept and was expelled from the Garden of Eden . . . how much greater then is my sin!" (22.11). Jerome's translation reflects this midrash's emphasis on the magnitude and degree of Cain's sin even as it elides some of the ambiguity of the original. A medieval reader familiar only with Jerome's rendering, then, would miss the ambiguous polysemy of the Hebrew's interconnected semantic options.

Indeed, patristic commentary on Jerome's Vulgate—the foundation of medieval orthodox Christianity's scriptural exegesis—expands upon this emphasis and even distorts it. St. Augustine in *De civitate Dei,* for example, asserts that the perverted and benighted Cain acted with envy and malice aforethought, and that "[q]uo modo autem significauerit etiam Iudaeos, a quibus Christus occisus" (indeed, he also symbolizes the Jews, by whom Christ was slain) (15.7).[12] Interestingly enough, in attempting to explain the significance of Cain's Hebrew name as well as those of other Genesis personae, Augustine must rely upon unnamed—and at times obviously inaccurate—lexical sources, since he himself has no Hebrew facility; hence Augustine's use of "we are told," "so they say," and similar tags (15.17), not unlike the *Sir Gawain and the Green Knight* narrator's claims, "as I in toun herde," "þe bok as I herde say" (31, 690), which infuse *Sir Gawain* with a similar ironic distance between assertions of authority and the accuracy of what is reported, though in *Sir Gawain*'s case, the irony seems deliberate. Such extreme associations as those of Augustine are hardly atypical; as John Hood notes in his recent study of Jewish texts and Christian traditions, "The spectacle of some of the greatest minds in European history devoting their lives to the systematic misinterpretation of ancient texts is truly one of the wonders of intellectual history" (3). In seeking to supply christological glosses to all aspects of the Old Testament, Augustine and other typologically motivated exegetes disregard the penitential undertones of the Cain story to foreground instead the archetypal murderer motif.[13] Popular treatments of the Cain story in early Christian and medieval lore thus tend to associate Cain with Judas and the apocalyptic Antichrist, as famously rendered, for example, in the Feast of Corpus Christi's *Killing of Abel* pageant, the Ninth Circle of Dante's *Inferno,* and the cathedral art at St. Denis.

But this image of Cain as archetypal sinner, so distorted in typological renderings, is only part of Cain's exegetical history. For, as Jerome and the later Christian Hebraists—including Andrew of St. Victor and Nicholas of Lyre, as well as the anonymous Hebrew scholars employed by the English Dominican Nicholas

Trevet and other Christian clerics in Westminster and Lambeth[14]—understood, scriptural interpretation in the Hebrew textual traditions is a continuous, discursive process that seeks to open new lines of inquiry with complementary and often contradictory readings of texts and traditions. As Beryl Smalley notes in her landmark study, "Altogether, the Christians made a sound bargain when they studied Hebrew, with Jewish thought and tradition. They got some good grain, even if it came to them mixed with a lot of chaff" (364). Thus we find, for instance, that *Bereshit Rabbah* offers, in close proximity to the midrash cited a moment ago, an exegetical anecdote appended to the biblical story:

> Adam met Cain and asked him, "How did your case go?" "I repented and am reconciled," [Cain] replied. Thereupon Adam began beating his [own] face, crying, "So great is the power of repentance, and I did not know!" Forthwith he arose and exclaimed, *A Psalm, a song for the Sabbath day: It is a good thing to make confession unto the Lord.*
>
> (22.13)[15]

In this instructive conversation, Cain serves as the originary exemplar of the power of repentance, from which his father, Adam, as well as those who read or hear this midrash in context, might learn.

II

This multifaceted and ambiguously penitent "Cain" who inhabits the *'erets-nod* underlies the *Gawain*-poet's understanding not only of sin, punishment, and repentance but also, in relation to written and oral texts and traditions, their conflated signification through verbal and material signs. For *Sir Gawain and the Green Knight*'s poetics, I shall argue, are based upon its intertextual and intercultural engagement with not only Christian but also Jewish exegetical modes. Different accounts of the same story emerge as the written text—with "lel letteres loken" (35), as the narrator describes his own purported romance source text—is interpreted in conjunction with subjective lines of exegetical discourse—as "herde" and told "with tonge" (31–32), that is, the oral traditions that complement, contradict, and communicate the original text. Just as the narrative persona of the *Gawain*-poet claims to draw off source texts both written and heard in order to retell this story of "Arthurez wonderez" (29), so too the poet himself works from within and without both Christian and Jewish, Hebrew and Latin, source texts and traditions.[16]

A text obsessed with the problems and methods of signification and hermeneutics, *Sir Gawain and the Green Knight* manifests Cain's ambiguous *'avon* in Gawain's wearing of the green girdle—a flexible, bending, twisting knot, a signifier of ambiguous referents. This aspect of signification in *Sir Gawain and the Green Knight* is further connected to the Cain story through the green girdle's evocations of the notorious "mark" or "sign" of Cain: we learn in the Hebrew text that, to assuage Cain in the aftermath of his anguished expression of guilt, the LORD puts an *'ot* (a sign, mark, or letter) on Cain, lest anyone who meets him should kill him (Gen. 4:14–15). In its Hebrew context, the *'ot* is inscribed upon Cain as a very public sign of the lord's protection, even if it serves the subsidiary function of identifying Cain as a former sinner. It therefore, at least implicitly, affirms God's acceptance of Cain's repentance. Hence the amelioration of the stated original punishment: the ground that received Abel's *damim* is still unavailable to Cain for continuing his original occupation of agriculture, but God reduces the twofold punishment of agricultural sterility and ceaseless wandering to agricultural sterility in a context of innovative urban development, as Cain will found the first city, Enoch (4.17).

In this regard, the biblical narrator's descriptions of Cain's interim and ultimate destinations convey the spiritual and epistemological symbolism of Cain's exile. After receiving the lord's *'ot*, Cain, we're told, leaves the presence of the lord and settles in the land of Nod (*be'erets-nod*), east of Eden (4.16). The Hebrew word *nod* (wandering), used to identify the location of Cain's exile, not only supplies the geographical locale that the literal level of the story requires—or at least the illusion thereof—but also, and ultimately more important, signifies a spiritual state of exile which, while mitigated by repentance, precludes the full restoration of the original bond. *Nod,* as Jerome interprets in his etymological commentary *Hebraicae Questiones in Libro Geneseos,* "est instabilis et fluctuans ac sedis incertae" (is unstable and fluctuating and of uncertain foundation); more than a literal place-name, it signifies disjunction and turmoil, "expletur sententia dei, quod huc atque illuc uagus et profugus oberrauit" (as expounded by the sentence of God, for here and there, in different directions, wandering and exiled, Cain roamed about) (4:16). This label of simultaneous disjunction and conjunction conveys as well the epistemological mode of trial and error, a "wandering" of sorts, necessitated by his being expelled from the agricultural environment from which his fruits of the soil were previously derived.

The punitive aspect of Cain's exile figures prominently for Augustine, who, in his *Confessions,* uses the concept of exile as a metaphor for spiritual and epistemological disjunction, *in regione dissimilitudinis* (in a region of unlikeness) (7.10). In her analysis of Augustine's metaphor, Margaret Ferguson pithily describes the textual traditions of exile literature: "delineations of an allegorical landscape of exile, a landscape of the mind in which the generically erring soul, fallen into matter or sin, wanders with such cohorts as Satan, Cain, and the Prodigal Son" (846). Dante, whose influence upon the *Gawain*-poet is perhaps obvious, reiterates the Augustinian ontology of erring in the opening lines of the *Commedia:* "Nel mezzo del cammin di nostra vita / mi ritrovai per una selva oscura, / che la diritta via era smarrits" (Midway on the journey of our life, I found myself in a shadowed forest, for the straight way was lost) (1.1–3); Dante's subsequent image of demarcation in the *Purgatorio,* "contro al cieco fiume" (against the blind/hidden river) (1.40), seems to correspond as well to *Sir Gawain and the Green Knight's* Green Chapel and its demarcation: "Þe borne blubred þerinne as hit boyled hade"; "When he wan to þe watter, þer he wade nolde" (2174, 2231).[17] But while Dante occupies an Augustinian landscape not unfamiliar to the *Gawain*-poet and his readers, Gawain inhabits a biblical landscape as much Hebraic as it is patristic in its paradoxical conflation of sin and punishment, disjunction and conjunction: *'erets-nod.*

Gawain's desolation, like Cain's, is inextricably bound to issues of significa-tion. Only Cain himself knows the full story behind the *'ot*, including the extent of his own culpability and contrition therein. Accordingly, the *'erets-nod* label corre-sponds to the spiritual and mental disjunction already effected by and expressed through the sinner's blasphemous, perhaps desperate, deflection of blame in the face of his own obvious culpability. For, like his notorious parents, Cain too ini-tially attempts to evade detection and responsibility by implicitly attributing his own error (*hatta't*) to God. Just as Adam had earlier asserted that God should share the blame for Adam's own transgression—"The woman whom *you* put with me, she gave to me from the tree and I ate" (Gen. 3:12; emphasis added)—so too Cain impugns God's own role in failing to protect Abel: "Am I the watcher/keeper of my brother?" (4:9).[18] Gawain echoes this blaming gesture in his claim to the seemingly omnipotent Green Knight that he, Gawain, inadvertently played Adam to the Green Knight's Lady's Eve: "Bot hit is no ferly þaȝ a fole madde / And þurȝ wyles of wymmen be wonen to sorȝe; / For so watz Adam in erde with one bygyled" (2414–16).[19]

Gawain's appeal to the authority of Christian exegetical tradition—which, fol-lowing St. Paul's reading, posits "Eve" as seductress and originary sinner—pro-vides a familiar and perhaps effective point of comparison in relation to the chris-tological *felix culpa* motif of the tripartite Haudesert temptation sequence. The Hebraic connotations of conflated discourse and desire (*havvah*)[20] in the Edenic transgression sequence, however, would seem to align Gawain more closely with Eve (*havvah*) than with Adam; the lexical hybridization discernible in *havvah* sug-gests an internal debate of conscience and desire which, I would argue, *Sir Gawain and the Green Knight* replicates in Gawain's own ethical and spiritual dilemma, itself projected outward in the embodied form of his own desire, the Lady. The superficially Eve-like Lady thus more closely resembles the Vulgate's proverbial temptress—"aliena quae verba sua dulcia facit" (the strange woman who makes her words sweet) (Prov. 7:5)[21]—since it is the life-bearing properties with which her words, *verba dulcia*, temporarily invest the girdle that entice Gawain to com-promise his *trawthe*.

Further, in connection with *Sir Gawain and the Green Knight*'s intertextual semi-otics, the girdle exchange at the chapel sequence foregrounds the poem's concern with identity categories and the underlying ideological assumptions that they betray. Frequently misunderstood in medieval orthodox Christianity as a sign of punitive exile and of God's disapproval, the sign or mark of Cain effectively inscribes his status as "Other." Augustine, for instance, notoriously remarks in his oft-cited Christmas sermon (no. 201) that Jews should be marked, "velut Cain accipiente signum" (like Cain, assenting to a sign), in order to serve the Augustin-ian doctrine of witness: "ut ejus fidei cujus inimici sunt, ubique testes fieri cogeren-tur" (that they might be compelled to become witnesses in all places to the faith that they hated).[22] In associating a collective "Other" with the sinful legacy of Cain, Augustine thereby affirms their subordinate status in the larger Christian hegemony. Hence in *De civitate Dei*, Augustine sets forth the *terrena civitas* (earthly city) founded by Cain in marked contrast to the *civitas Dei* (city of God) derived from typological renderings of the shepherd Abel's Christ-like blood sacrifice.[23] This originary locus of civilization's *iniquitas* is echoed in the opening stanzas of *Sir Gawain and the Green Knight* in conjunction with an ambiguously Augustinian rendering of the founders' motif: "Where werre and wrake and wonder / Bi syþes hatz wont þerinne / And oft bothe blysse and blunder / Ful skete hatz skyfted synne" (16–19). Ultimately the poem will evade closure deceptively with a return, full circle, to the Augustinian "blisse and blunder" dichotomy that foregrounds not only the inherently unstable and divisive reality of civilization and culture but also the patristic transformation of the multivalent Hebraic Cain into an unambiguous figure of unmitigated evil, a sign whose meaning is "loken."

Sir Gawain and the Green Knight's self-reflexive exploration of the superficial certainty promised by "loken" signs demonstrates of course that such meanings are neither fixed nor fully understood.[24] In this regard, the green girdle, itself an ambiguous signifier, reiterates the connotations of Cain's *'ot*, uniting the Edenic and post-Edenic symbolism as it foregrounds a discursive resemblance between bending, twisting signifiers of ambiguity and desire. This "syngne of . . . surfet" (2433), as Gawain himself describes it, signifies Gawain's "surfet" of sinful dishonesty as well as the "surfet" of his punishment or penance.[25] Within a Christian environment—of this earth, not the otherworldly realms of Divine Justice—Gawain wears the "bende of . . . blame" (2506) appropriately in the spirit of Christian *contrapasso*, deriving from the biblical *lex talionis* and the *mida keneged mida* (measure for measure) rabbinical principle as an expression of appropriately analogous or antithetical punishment.[26] His willingness to atone, to undergo the "penaunce" alluded to earlier by the Green Knight at "þe poynt of [his] egge" (2392)—but fulfilled only now in Gawain's public display of the girdle—evinces Gawain's intense inner sense of guilt as well as his desire to make amends both to the Green Knight and, by extension, to God: "I biknowe yow, knyȝt, here stylle, / Al fawty is my fare. / Letez me ouertake your wylle / And efte I schal be ware" (2385–88). Repented and reconciled, Gawain truly learns that such is the power of repentance.

III

It is fitting, then, that the penitential encounter at the Green Chapel should be situated in proximity to a burial mound—the "balȝ berȝ bi a bonke" (2172)—since its allusive connotations of the *'adam/'adamah* bond set forth in the Genesis creation and expulsion sequence—"And the lord God formed the human (*'adam*) from dust of the ground (*'adamah*)," " . . . you [will] return to-the-ground (*'el-ha-'adamah*) since from it you were taken" (Gen. 2:7, 3:19)[27]—so aptly correspond to the symbolic death of the formerly unenlightened and cowardly Gawain whose sin, however trivial, proves instructive and ultimately life changing. Exegetical excursuses of the *'adam/'adamah* bond, from the biblical sages to medieval scholars, enrich these associations: "Þenne al rypeȝ and roteȝ þat ros vpon fyrst, / And þus ȝirnes þe ȝere in ȝisterdayez mony" (528–29), the *Gawain*-narrator observes, an echo of the *lekol zeman* (to everything a time) theme of the biblical sage Qohelet: "all come from the dust and all return to the dust" (Eccles. 3:1, 3:20).

We might recall, then, in context that at the moment of Gawain's anguished expressions of contrition, the Green Knight, in declaring him absolved of whatever debts he might have incurred to Bertilak, discursively creates for him a new identity: "I halde þe polysed of þat ply3t and pured as clene / As þou hadez never forfeted syþen þou watz fyrst borne" (2393–94). The Green Knight's language, while accommodating the medieval orthodox Christian problem of what Augustine deems *peccatum originale* (original sin)[28] — Gawain is deemed not sinless per se, but rather as sinless as a newborn — nonetheless links absolution with a symbolic death and rebirth. In this regard, Gawain's symbolic rebirth is not unlike that associated with baptism, the liturgy of which allows the subject to temporarily transcend cultural categories and to elide the problem of identity. In St. Paul's famous citation, "Non est Iudaeus, neque Graecus: non est servus, neque liber: non est masculus, neque femina" (There is neither Jew nor Gentile: there is neither slave nor free: there is neither masculine nor feminine) (Gal. 3:28).[29] The egalitarian fantasy proposed by the baptismal language is obviously not pragmatic or realistic; in the real world, no society could ever be completely free of identity categories. But Paul's words, like the Green Knight's proposed symbolic renewal, offer a tantalizing possibility of change. Temporarily liberated from the tyranny of normative expectations and the imposed cultural categories in which he uneasily resides, Gawain finds an opportunity for a self-determined subjectivity. Gawain, of course, cannot negate categories and expectations, but he can choose at this juncture how to position himself within their range; after a brief foray into misogynistic Christian tradition,[30] he elects to do so by bearing the "bende of . . . blame" (2506) as an identity marker, which, overlapping the scar that testifies to the Green Knight's blow, conveys publicly Gawain's otherwise private reconciliation and shame.

Because identity is performative — constituted by discursive signs, utterances, and gestures and governed by place and circumstance[31] — it is subject to the interpretive biases and agendas of those who witness its construction and performance. Gawain's identity is of course challenged throughout his adventures, first by the Lady, who questions his reluctance to affirm Gawain's amorous reputation ("Bot þat 3e be Gawan hit gotz in mynde," "Sir, 3if 3e be Wawen, wonder me þynkkez" [1293, 1481]), then by the Green Knight, who declares in response to Gawain's flinching, "Þou art not Gawayn" (2270).[32] Gawain is repeatedly measured against the Arthurian code and the aggregate reputation of its devotees; though ultimately the code, and the court, will be divided against itself owing to its incompatible directives of vengeance and *pite*, Gawain is nonetheless compelled to prove himself a worthy member of that community, or at least to show that he is able to play that part. Like the Green Knight/Bertilak, Gawain is able to shape his identity, if not his form; but unlike the Green Knight/Bertilak, who claims allegiance to Morgan's absolute power,[33] Gawain must make his own decisions in the context of somewhat inconsistent and discordant cultural codes.

A material marker with metaphorical resonance, then, the chapel "ber3" (2172) foregrounds the uneasily interconnecting textual and ideological traditions upon which *Sir Gawain and the Green Knight* draws. In terms of the discursive and the performative, the Green Chapel figuratively corresponds to the biblical landscape between Eden and Enoch, the '*erets-nod* of Cain. An indeterminate and transitory location, the Green Chapel's parameters are figuratively delineated by narrative subjectivity and constituted by the discourse of repentance. It is almost as if Gawain enters into, experiences, and departs from a wholly discursive dimension, as materially insubstantial as the shimmering mirage that appears in response to his prayer to the Virgin Mary, and as fleeting as the words uttered within it: "Þat holde on þat on syde þe haþel auysed, / As hit schemered and schon þurȝ þe schyre okez"; "Þat pared out of papure purely hit semed" (771–72, 802). It is within this (re)configured biblical landscape that Gawain is repented and reconciled. But bearing his penitential marker, his own '*ot*, he returns to an iconic locale whose legend, history, and epic self-identity seem almost self-perpetuating; while the material locale of Camelot has remained the same, Gawain is himself so changed that any restoration of his past relationship to it is impossible.

To Arthur's knights, then, Gawain's penitential "syngne" (2433) instead affirms their own well-intended but ultimately unsustainable "broþerhede" (2516). The penitent Gawain who returns to the court bearing the "bende of . . . blame" (2506) is therefore regarded by the court not as a humble penitent with a lesson to convey but as an exemplar of the court's own chivalric/Christian code(s). Even as Gawain exhibits a sign of penitential renewal, corroborated by the story he tells, his figurative exile from the Arthurian court's normative expectations affects how the court reads Gawain's sign. As in fitt 1, where the Green Knight's visit is dismissed uncritically and largely shrugged off with a laugh, so here the court dismisses Gawain's story with a laugh and appropriates his "syngne" — "þe court als / Laȝen loude þerat and luflyly acorden / Þat . . . / Vche burne of þe broþerhede, a bauderyk schulde haue" (2513–16) — thereby denying Gawain both the authority of his own experience and the right to tell that story. Predisposed to locate signs of affirmation and to protect the egalitarian fantasy of the "Round Table" and its demonstrative communal unity, this "broþerhede" simply will not allow Gawain to mark himself as Other. Ironically, though, the court's self-constructed communal unity symbolically excludes the penitential Gawain himself, whose singular sign of humility is appropriated as a sign of collective pride.

On the level of intertextual and cultural poetics, the court's appropriation of Gawain's "syngne" (2433) replicates the uneasily contiguous biblical textual traditions upon which *Sir Gawain and the Green Knight* draws: Jewish and Christian, the Old and the New. In their quest for unambiguous certainty — for signs whose meaning is "loken" — the Arthurian knights co-opt and replace the polysemous connotations of Gawain's "syngne" or '*ot* with a Christianized *signum* of common, unambiguous meaning: "stad and stoken," "stif and stronge" (33–34). Such a hermeneutic gesture is hardly unique to this group, as seen in the typological renderings of the Cain and Abel story, representative paradigms of typological enterprise. In the manner of such exegetes, then, the court erases Gawain's narrative by subsuming it, symbolically rejecting the Old even as it uses it as a foundation for its claims of supersession, the New, in the form of a Christian "broþerhede" whose origin and legitimacy are always already a given and whose claim to identity manifests itself within the larger panorama of Christian history. In effect, the court subjugates the legitimacy of the literal, carnal, proper, and Old in favor of its own imposed sense of the figurative, spiritual, improper, and New.[34] Like Friar John of Chaucer's *Summoner's Tale,* who so famously imposes his own gloss in the absence of a recognized text—"I have no text of it as I suppose, / But I shal fynde it in a maner glose" (1919–20)[35]—the Arthurian knights impose their own gloss upon Gawain's text without first understanding, or even acknowledging, its autonomy and legitimacy prior to their act of reconfiguration and subsumption.

Just as Gawain's arrival at the Green Chapel leaves him initially "Debatande with hymself quat hit be myȝt" (2179), so readers of *Sir Gawain and the Green Knight* are invited to participate in the text's semiotic and hermeneutic conundrums. From *Sir Gawain and the Green Knight*'s treatment of the Hebrew and Vulgate discrepancies and the critical and popular receptions of those texts and their authoritative interpretive traditions, we see perhaps that the *Gawain*-poet effectively marks an exegetical impasse as he and his poem grapple with issues of religious tradition and cultural identity. In this regard, the poem—and the poet—would seem to articulate an overtly orthodox, yet subtly subversive, Christian hermeneutics. For, ultimately rejecting the simplistic dichotomizing that it superficially appears to endorse, *Sir Gawain and the Green Knight* instead invites us to consider the ways in which the text informs, and is informed by, necessarily contiguous but ultimately divided traditions.[36]

Notes

1. On Gawain as spectator and the poet's ocular hermeneutics, see Stanbury 96–115 and 116–40: "details of the landscape are carefully controlled and presented as they might be seen by the fictional travelers, a technique of spatial focusing that centers sensory experience and also its understanding and interpretation on the spectator in the text" (119). On sanguineous observation, cf. Dante's Jacopo: "e li vid' io / de le mie vene farsi in terra laco" (and there I saw from my veins a pool form on the ground) (*Purg.* 5.83–84). The life-blood trope is a *topos* of both classical and biblical texts; see, for example, *Aeneid* 2, 4, 10 and Metamorphoses 6; Genesis 9:4–6, Leviticus 17:11–14, Numbers 35:33.

2. While critics of *Sir Gawain and the Green Knight* remain divided as to the significance of the chapel description and its connotations both familiar and obscure, Carson makes an etymological case for the *chapel* label's signifying both the familiar sense of devotional space as well as a more archaic sense, that of a combat locale. On the significance of the *chapel* and *lawe* in *Sir Gawain and the Green Knight,* see Prior 104–17, who describes the chapel as "a strange conflation of visual and verbal images with conflicting interpretations" (105); see further Elliot (43–63 and 89–92), who considers possible English place locations as site models; on seasonal *topoi* and their Christian connotations in *Sir Gawain and the Green Knight,* see Pearsall and Salter 119–60; and on literary space in medieval literature, see the overview in Howes 1–13.

3. The Bereshit sequence of the Hebrew Bible begins with the creation account and concludes with the genealogies preceding Noah (Gen. 1:1–6.8)—the familiar chapter divisions are of medieval Christian origin and do not always coincide logically with the narrative's organic divisions; the two expulsion stories—Adam and Eve, Cain and Abel (2:4–5.1)—are linked internally by the *vav* conjunction and *toledot* narrative markers. On the continuity of this sequence, see Sarna 30–31. The Cain and Abel episode, Genesis 4:1–26, figures most prominently in my analysis.

4. Translations my own here and throughout, except where noted otherwise for comparative purposes. On sibling rivalry and its problems in Genesis narratives, see Greenspahn 111–40; Quinones 23–40.

5. For example, *JPS Hebrew-English Tanakh* translates the line as "My punishment is too great to bear!"; Fox, in "The Five Books of Moses," renders it, "My iniquity is too great to be borne!"; Sarna, *JPS Torah Commentary*, offers, "My sin is too great to be forgiven" and "Is my sin too great to be forgiven?" as alternatives.

6. Etymological material discussed here and throughout is based upon the etymological entries in the Brown, Driver, and Briggs lexicon; as well, I have consulted Klein.

7. The narrator of *Sir Gawain and the Green Knight* uses the same infinitive strategy to elide agent: "And bi trewe tytel þerof to telle þe wonder" (480).

8. While Jerome articulates great respect for the *Hebraica veritas* owing to its significance for Christianity, he notoriously describes its vocalization as "grunnitus suis et clamor asinorum" (the grunting of a pig and the braying of an ass) (*In Amos* 5.23). On Jerome's attitudes toward his Hebrew source materials, see Simon 212–16; Hood 14–18; Smalley 20–22; Horbury 200–25.

9. Translations of biblical and patristic Latin texts my own here and throughout.

10. On Jerome's Hebrew study, see Sparks 510–41; Horbury 200–225; Hood 15–18.

11. An insightful discussion on midrash as exegetical mode is provided by Boyarin, *Intertextuality*; of the vast bibliography available, a few studies of particular relevance include Hartman and Budick; Fishbane 1–21. A more general overview keyed to biblical passages in sequence is provided by Kugel, and a highly theoretical treatment in Rojtman.

12. Augustine develops this anti-Judaic perspective further in his *Tractatus Adversus Judaeos*, in which he accuses the Jews of distorting the Old Testament prophecies so as to deny Christ.

13. On typology's centrality to medieval Christianity, see Charity; Auerbach 11–76. While the findings of typology might seem contrived or glib, Paxson, however, argues that Christian exegetes were as likely to use typology as a method of exploration as they were to locate what they wished to find.

14. See Smalley 149–85 and Dahan 81–104. Manuscript evidence suggests that numerous Christian Hebraists, owing largely to the influence of Andrew of St. Victor, were studying and writing in England, France, and Spain during the twelfth through fourteenth centuries, both as interested scholars of exegetical methods and as Christian apologists in the polemical debates; it is not unreasonable to deduce that the *Gawain*-poet might have been familiar with their work, especially given the notoriety of the Disputations of 1240 (Paris) and 1263 (Barcelona), as well as the widespread circulation of such texts as the *Pugio Fidei*, a compilation of rabbinic texts with christological glosses provided by the Dominican convert/apostate Raymond Martini. See also Grabois; Hood 19–37; Krauss 68–90; Berger; Chazan 67–85; Hailperin 103–34; Saltman 357–59. Bibliography on Jewish/Christian medieval cultural relations is vast; see, for instance, Narin van Court; Cox, "Neither Gentile Nor Jew"; Shapiro 43–88; Grayzel; Mark Cohen.

15. It is important to keep in mind, however, that no single midrash trumps any other, and that the repentant Cain coexists alongside the fiendish murderer in the *Bereshit Rabbah* sequence; see Boyarin, *Intertextuality*, on the intertextual and dialogical aspects of midrash.

16. Because no known evidence identifies the author of *Sir Gawain and the Green Knight*, analyses must confine themselves to what his texts convey within the historical possibilities of fourteenth-century English culture. I use "his," for instance, based on the likelihood of male authorship, although no evidence directly supports my assumption (curiously, the most vociferous positivists take this as a given even as they reject other similarly circumstantial assumptions about authors and authorship in medieval England). As well, I make what I consider a necessary distinction here between the *Gawain*-poet and *Sir Gawain and the Green Knight*'s narrator, the latter a fictive persona who makes his presence known throughout (e.g., 24, 27, 31, 624).

17. The water-as-marker imagery in *Sir Gawain and the Green Knight* is not unlike the image in *Pearl*, where it serves as a "deuyse" (139); see also Prior 104–5.

18. Blasphemy in the form of the sinner blaming God for the sinner's own sin is a central motif in the two interrogation sequences. See the compelling analysis by Fewell and Gunn; see also Trible, who notes, "Neither God nor the woman has tempted the man, and yet he implicates them both with his guilt" (119).

19. The woman-as-sinner motif of Christian renderings of the Fall exonerate Adam from temptation while paradoxically insisting that Eve is the originary sinner; see St. Paul's notorious (mis)reading of 1 Timothy 2:14, which provides a template for later exegetes, and commentary in Bal 104–30. The Genesis narrative itself gives no indication that it is any more Eve's fault than Adam's, and Jerome's Vulgate accurately reproduces the sense of the Hebrew text, in which the man is described as *'immah* (with her, in proximity to her) (Gen. 3:6). On Christian motifs in *Sir Gawain and the Green Knight*, see the oft-cited studies by Benson; Mills; Haines; Phelan.

20. On *havvah* and its puns in the Hebrew Bible, see Kimelman. While the Haudesert temptation sequence is obviously patterned on Christian readings of the Genesis transgression account—in which Eve is blamed for humankind's Fall—Gawain's admissions of culpability indicate that Gawain and the *Gawain*-poet know better than to simply brush off Gawain's guilt as simple seduction, even if St. Paul's misreading, above, provides an authoritative text for Christianity's antifeminism; see also Cox, "Genesis and Gender," and *Judaic Other*.

21. On the gender dynamics at work in the Hebrew text of the *nokriyya* (stranger or outsider, *aliena*), see Camp.

22. See also commentary in Mark Cohen 30–51; Baron 96–106. On the story of Cain as the type-story for biblical expressions of the "Other," see Schwartz, especially 77–97.

23. The governing structure of Augustine's *De civitate Dei* is the typological asymmetry of Cain and Abel, the latter anticipating Christ's sacrifice and the former associated with that which is ignorant, Jewish, and demonic. See especially 15.7–17 on the hidden meanings of Abel's death and the attribution of *terrena civitas* to the earthly city founded by Cain and Cain's symbolic association with the Jews.

24. Much has been written on the importance of signification as both theme and method in *Sir Gawain and the Green Knight*; see, for example, Shoaf, "Syngne of Surfet" and *Poem as Green Girdle*; Hanna; Fisher; Heng; Scala.

25. On the significance of error in relation to semiotics and epistemology in general, see Evans 1–26.

26. Dante coins the label "contrapasso" to describe the divine quid pro quo of justice fictionalized in his *Commedia*, where it is uttered by Bertran de Born in canto 28 of *Inferno*—a decapitated precursor, perhaps, of the Green Knight—"Cosi s'osserva in me lo *contrapasso*" (Thus one sees in me the *contrapasso*) (142). The Latin term *contrapassum* on which it is based is from St. Thomas Aquinas's *Summa theologiae*, itself indebted to the biblical explication of *lex talionis* (Exod. 21), the Aristotelian concept of ethical justice set forth in the *Nicomachean Ethics* and the rabbinical *mida keneged mida* (measure for measure) principle discussed by Maimonides, whose *Guide for the Perplexed* motivated Aquinas to produce a Christian rendering of Aristotelian logic. Maimonides explores the epistemology of erring in connection with God's words to Cain apropos of *hatta't* (error, sin) in the *Guide* 3.23.

27. Gawain's proximity to death and the burial mound that symbolizes it perhaps calls to mind as well Rashi's commentary that God made humankind of soil gathered from all four directions—north, south, east, west—so that anywhere a person dies the ground will receive the body in burial; on Christianity's familiarity with Rashi's commentary in the Middle Ages, see Hailperin 103–34.

28. The phrase *peccatum originale* appears in Augustine's *De continentia* 3.8; he develops the concept in greater detail in *De civitate Dei* 13–14. See also commentary by Schreiner 135–86; Jeremy Cohen offers a critique of Augustine's concept and its development in Aquinas's Summa in conjunction with the treatises of the apostate/convert Raymond Martini, *Pugio fidei*; see also Chazan.

29. On the political pragmatism of the Pauline formulations, see Boyarin, *Radical Jew* 13–38; Hall 67–84. Briggs considers the performative aspects of the Pauline formulations; I consider the significance of the Pauline performative to late medieval and early modern gender and religion in "Neither Gentile Nor Jew."

30. On the notorious "anti-feminist diatribe," see, for instance, Fisher, who argues that Gawain's diatribe is an attempt to distance himself from the Lady; Heng, who notes the

irony of the power shift; Haines, who argues that the speech is deliberately in jest (123). In any case, the speech intensifies the ironic gap between Gawain's knowledge of the Bible and the poet's, since none of the listed men is actually deceived: Samson, Judges 13–16; Solomon, 1 Kings 3, 10–11; David, 2 Samuel 11–12.

31. Butler, *Gender Trouble* 134–37; see also *Excitable Speech*. Butler's theoretical interrogations of identity politics and cultural categories, which inform my own thinking, are insightfully applied to late medieval texts by Dinshaw ("Kiss" and "Chaucer's Queer Touches").

32. On secrecy and identity in *Sir Gawain and the Green Knight,* see Lochrie, who notes of Gawain's revelations, "his telling is but another reflex of the secrecy that conditions all sin . . . the only truth to be said about Gawain is the one that he and other characters have uttered throughout, that he is not Gawain" (52); see also Stanbury: "we know and see what Gawain sees; we watch as others watch him, returning his evaluative look" (112).

33. On the significance of Morgan, see Dinshaw ("Getting Medieval"), who argues that the men of the story "are actually tokens in a plot between women—a shadowy but terrifying plot of intensely desired vengeance between Morgan la Faye and Guenevere" (149); Fisher also makes a case for Morgan's significance in dictating the Green Knight's actions. See also Kamps, who traces the poetic implications of incest and the Arthurian tradition; and Margherita on paternalistic and maternalistic subtexts, 137–51.

34. "Old" and "New" pertain most overtly to the appropriation and renaming of the Hebrew Bible ("Old Testament") by adherents of Christianity to signify its subordinate relationship to their "New Testament"; on these labels in Jewish and Christian traditions, see Levenson. Related binarisms include Jewish vs. Christian, feminine vs. masculine, and flesh vs. spirit, with the subordinate terms often conflated in opposition to the patristic norm, largely deriving from Pauline theology (see esp. 2 Cor. 3:6ff). Bibliography on these associations is vast; see, for instance, on the flesh/feminine correspondence in orthodox medieval Christianity, Bynum; and on the Jewish/carnal association, Boyarin, *Carnal Israel,* especially 1–60; I consider the Christian formulations of feminine/letter and their patristic histories in "*Pearl*'s 'Precios Pere.'"

35. On the ubiquity of "glossing" as an exegetical enterprise and literary trope in medieval culture, see the historical survey provided by Hanning; Besserman 138–59.

36. A portion of this paper was presented as "The Hebrew Truth and *Sir Gawain and the Green Knight*" at the annual meeting of the Northeast Modern Language Association, in Pittsburgh, 17 April 1999.

Works Cited

Auerbach, Erich. "Figura." *Scenes from the Drama of European Literature.* Minneapolis: U of Minnesota P, 1984.

Augustine. *Confessions.* Patrologia Latina 32: cols. 659–868.

——. *De civitate Dei.* Ed. Bernardus Dombart and Alphonsus Kalb. Corpus Christianorum, Series Latina, 48. Turnholt: Brepols, 1955.

——. *Sermon 201.* Patrologia Latina 38: cols. 1031–33.

——. *Tractatus Adversus Judaeos.* Patrologia Latina 42: cols. 51–67.

Bal, Mieke. *Lethal Love: Feminist Literary Readings of Biblical Love Stories.* Bloomington: Indiana UP, 1987.

Baron, Salo Wittmayer. *A Social and Religious History of the Jews.* 2nd ed. New York: Columbia UP, 1967.

Benson, Larry D. *Art and Tradition in* Sir Gawain and the Green Knight. New Brunswick: Rutgers UP, 1965.

Berger, David. "Mission to the Jews and Jewish-Christian Contacts in the Polemical Literature of the High Middle Ages." *American Historical Review* 91 (1986): 576–91.

Besserman, Lawrence. *Chaucer's Biblical Poetics.* Norman: U of Oklahoma P, 1998.

Biblia Hebraica Stuttgartensia. Ed. Karl Elliger and Wilhelm Rudolph. Stuttgart: Deutsche bibelgesellschaft, 1977.

Biblia sacra iuxta vulgatam Clementinam. 4th ed. Ed. Alberto Colunga and Laurentio Turrado. Madrid: Biblioteca de Autores Cristianos, 1965.

Boyarin, Daniel. *Carnal Israel: Reading Sex in Talmudic Culture.* Berkeley: U of California P, 1993.

———. *Intertextuality and the Reading of Midrash.* Bloomington: Indiana UP, 1990.

———. *A Radical Jew: Paul and the Politics of Identity.* Berkeley: U of California P, 1994.

Briggs, Sheila. "'Buried with Christ': The Politics of Identity and the Poverty of Interpretation." *The Book and the Text.* Ed. Regina M. Schwartz. Cambridge: Blackwell, 1990. 276–303.

Brown, Francis, S. R. Driver, and Charles Briggs, eds. *A Hebrew and English Lexicon of the Old Testament.* Trans. Edward Robinson. Oxford: Clarendon, 1951.

Butler, Judith. *Excitable Speech: A Politics of the Performative.* New York: Routledge, 1997.

———. *Gender Trouble: Feminism and the Subversion of Identity.* New York: Routledge, 1990.

Bynum, Caroline Walker. *Fragmentation and Redemption: Essays on Gender and the Human Body in Medieval Religion.* New York: Zone, 1991.

Camp, Claudia V. "Woman Wisdom and the Strange Woman." *Reading Bibles, Writing Bodies: Identity and the Book.* Ed. Timothy K. Beal and David M. Gunn. New York: Routledge, 1997. 85–117.

Carson, Angela. "The Green Chapel: Its Meaning and Its Function." *Studies in Philology* 60 (1963): 598–605.

Charity, A. C. *Events and Their Afterlife: The Dialectics of Christian Typology in the Bible and Dante.* Cambridge: Cambridge UP, 1966.

Chaucer, Geoffrey. *The Riverside Chaucer.* Gen. ed. Larry D. Benson. 3rd ed. Boston: Houghton, 1987.

Chazan, Robert. *Daggers of Faith: Thirteenth-Century Christian Missionizing and Jewish Response.* Berkeley: U of California P, 1989.

Cohen, Jeremy. "Original Sin as the Evil Inclination: A Polemicist's Appreciation of Human Nature." *Harvard Theological Review* 73 (1980): 495–520.

Cohen, Mark. *Under Crescent and Cross: The Jews in the Middle Ages.* Princeton: Princeton UP, 1994.

Cox, Catherine S. "Genesis and Gender in Sir Gawain and the Green Knight." *Chaucer Review* 35 (2001): 378–90.

———. *The Judaic Other in Dante, the* Gawain *Poet, and Chaucer.* Gainesville: UP of Florida, 2005.

———. "Neither Gentile Nor Jew: Performative Subjectivity in The Merchant of Venice." *Exemplaria* 12 (2000): 359–83.

———. "Pearl's 'Precios Pere': Gender, Language, and Difference." *Chaucer Review* 32 (1998): 377–90.

Dahan, Gilbert. *The Christian Polemic Against the Jews in the Middle Ages.* Trans. Jody Gladding. Notre Dame: U of Notre Dame P, 1998.

Dante Alighieri. *The Divine Comedy.* Ed. Charles Singleton. Princeton: Princeton UP, 1970–73.

Dinshaw, Carolyn. "Chaucer's Queer Touches / A Queer Touches Chaucer." *Exemplaria* 7 (1995): 75–92.

———. "A Kiss is Just a Kiss: Heterosexuality and Its Consolation in Sir Gawain and the Green Knight." *Diacritics* 24 (1994): 205–26.

———. "Getting Medieval: Pulp Fiction, Gawain, Foucault." *The Book and the Body.* Ed. Dolores Warwick Frese and Katherine O'Brien O'Keeffe. Notre Dame: U of Notre Dame P, 1997. 116–63.

Elliot, Ralph W. V. *The* Gawain *Country: Essays on the Topography of English Alliterative Poetry.* Leeds: U of Leeds, 1984.

Evans, G. R. *Getting It Wrong: The Medieval Epistemology of Error.* Leiden: Brill, 1998.

Ferguson, Margaret. "Saint Augustine's Region of Unlikeness: The Crossing of Exile and Language." *Georgia Review* 29 (1975): 842–64.

Fewell, Danna Nolan, and David M. Gunn. "Shifting the Blame: God in the Garden." *Reading Bibles, Writing Bodies: Identity and the Book.* Ed. Timothy K. Beal and David M. Gunn. New York: Routledge, 1997. 16–33.

Fishbane, Michael. *The Exegetical Imagination: On Jewish Thought and Theology.* Cambridge: Harvard UP, 1998.

Fisher, Sheila. "Taken Men and Token Women in Sir Gawain and the Green Knight." *Seeking the Woman in Late Medieval and Renaissance Writings.* Ed. Sheila Fisher and Janet E. Halley. Knoxville: U of Tennessee P, 1989. 71–105.

Fox, Everett, trans. "The Five Books of Moses." *Schocken Bible.* Vol. 1. New York: Schocken, 1995.

Grabois, Aryeh. "The Hebraica Veritas and Jewish-Christian Intellectual Relations in the Twelfth Century." *Speculum* 50 (1975): 613–34.

Grayzel, Solomon. *The Church and the Jews in the Thirteenth Century.* Rev. ed. New York: Hermon, 1966.

Greenspahn, Frederick E. *When Brothers Dwell Together: The Preeminence of Younger Siblings in the Hebrew Bible.* Oxford: Oxford UP, 1994.

Hailperin, Herman. *Rashi and the Christian Scholars.* Pittsburgh: U of Pittsburgh P, 1963.

Haines, Victor Yelverton. *The Fortunate Fall of Sir Gawain: The Typology of Sir Gawain and the Green Knight.* Washington, D.C.: UP of America, 1982.

Hall, Sidney G. *Christian Anti-Semitism and Paul's Theology.* Minneapolis: Fortress, 1993.

Hanna, Ralph. "Unlocking What's Locked: Gawain's Green Girdle." *Viator* 14 (1983): 298–302.

Hanning, Robert W. "'I Shal Finde It in a Maner Glose': Versions of Textual Harassment in Medieval Literature." *Medieval Texts and Contemporary Readers.* Ed. Laurie Finke and Martin Shichtman. Ithaca: Cornell UP, 1987. 27–57.

Hartman, Geoffrey, and Saul Budick. *Midrash and Literature.* New Haven: Yale UP, 1985.

Heng, Geraldine. "Feminine Knots and the Other *Sir Gawain and the Green Knight." PMLA* 106 (1991): 500–514.

Hood, John Y. B. *Aquinas and the Jews.* Philadelphia: U of Pennsylvania P, 1995.

Horbury, William. *Jews and Christians in Contact and Controversy.* Edinburgh: T. & T. Clark, 1998.

Howes, Laura L. *Chaucer's Gardens and the Language of Convention.* Gainesville: UP of Florida, 1997.

Jerome. *Hebraicae Quaestiones in Libro Geneseos.* Ed. Paulus de Lagarde. Corpus Christianorum, Series Latina, 72. Turnholt: Brepols, 1959.

———. *In Amos Prophetam Libri Tres. Patrologia Latina* 25: cols. 989–1096.

JPS Hebrew-English Tanakh. Philadelphia: Jewish Publication Society, 1999.

Kamps, Ivo. "Magic, Women, and Incest: The Real Challenges in Sir Gawain and the Green Knight." *Exemplaria* 1 (1989): 313–36.

Kimelman, Reuven. "The Seduction of Eve and the Exegetical Politics of Gender." *Women in the Hebrew Bible.* Ed. Alice Bach. New York: Routledge, 1999. 241–69.

Klein, Ernest. *A Comprehensive Etymological Dictionary of the Hebrew Language.* New York: Macmillan, 1987.

Krauss, Samuel. *The Jewish-Christian Controversy from the Earliest Times to 1789.* Ed. and rev. William Horbury. Tubingen: J. C. B. Mohr, 1995.

Kugel, James L. *Traditions of the Bible: A Guide to the Bible as It Was at the Start of the Common Era.* Cambridge: Harvard UP, 1998.

Levenson, Jon. *The Hebrew Bible, the Old Testament, and Historical Criticism: Jews and Christians in Biblical Studies.* Louisville: Westminster, 1993.

Lochrie, Karma. *Covert Operations: The Medieval Uses of Secrecy.* Philadelphia: U of Pennsylvania P, 1999.

Maimonides. *Guide for the Perplexed.* Trans. M. Friedlander. New York: Dover, 1956.

Margherita, Gayle. *The Romance of Origins: Language and Sexual Difference in Middle English Literature.* Philadelphia: U of Pennsylvania P, 1994.

Midrash Rabbah. Gen. ed. H. Freedman and Maurice Simon. English trans. 10 vols. 3rd ed. London: Soncino, 1983.

Mills, M. "Christian Significance and Romance Tradition in Sir Gawain and the Green Knight." *Modern Language Review* 60 (1965): 483–93.

Narin van Court, Elisa. "Socially Marginal, Culturally Central: Representing Jews in Late Medieval English Literature." *Exemplaria* 12 (2000): 293–326.

Patrologiae Latina Cursus Completus, Series Latina (Patrologia Latina). Ed. J. P. Migne. Paris: Migne, 1844–64.

Paxson, James J. "A Theory of Biblical Typology in the Middle Ages." *Exemplaria* 3 (1991): 359–83.

Pearl. The Poems of the Pearl Manuscript. Ed. Malcolm Andrew and Ronald Waldron. Berkeley: U of California P, 1978. 53–110.

Pearsall, Derek, and Elizabeth Salter. *Landscapes and Seasons of the Medieval World*. London: Paul Elek, 1973.

Phelan, Walter S. *The Christmas Hero and Yuletide Tradition in* Sir Gawain and the Green Knight. Lewiston, N.Y.: Edwin Mellen, 1992.

Prior, Sandra Pierson. *The Fayre Formez of the* Pearl *Poet*. East Lansing: Michigan State UP, 1996.

Quinones, Ricardo J. *The Changes of Cain: Violence and the Lost Brother in Cain and Abel Literature*. Princeton: Princeton UP, 1991.

Rashi. *Commentary on the Torah*. Sapirstein edition. Brooklyn: Mesorah Publications, 1995.

Rojtman, Betty. *Black Fire on White Fire: An Essay on Jewish Hermeneutics*. Berkeley: U of California P, 1998.

Saltman, Avrom. "John of Salisbury and the World of the Old Testament." *The World of John of Salisbury*. Ed. Michael Wilks. Oxford: Basil Blackwell, 1984. 343–59.

Sarna, Nahum. *The JPS Torah Commentary: Genesis*. Philadelphia: Jewish Publication Society, 1989.

Scala, Elizabeth D. "The Wanting Words of *Sir Gawain and the Green Knight:* Narrative Past, Present, and Absent." *Exemplaria* 6 (1994): 305–38.

Schreiner, Susan E. "Eve, The Mother of History: Reaching for the Reality of History in Augustine's Later Exegesis of Genesis." Genesis 1–3 in *The History of Exegesis: Intrigue in the Garden*. Ed. Gregory Allen Robbins. Lewiston, N.Y.: Edwin Mellen, 1988. 135–86.

Schwartz, Regina M. *The Curse of Cain: The Violent Legacy of Monotheism*. Chicago: U of Chicago P, 1997.

Shapiro, James. *Shakespeare and the Jews*. New York: Columbia UP, 1996.

Shoaf, R. A. "The 'Synge of Surget' and the Surfeit of Signs in Sir Gawain and the Green Knight." *The Passing of Arthur: New Essays in Arthurian Tradition*. Ed. Christopher Baswell and William Sharpe. New York: Garland, 1988. 152–69.

———. *The Poem as Green Girdle: Commercium in* Sir Gawain and the Green Knight. Gainesville: UP of Florida, 1984.

Simon, Marcel. *Verus Israel: A Study of the Relations Between Christians and Jews in the Roman Empire, AD 135–425*. Trans. H. McKeating. New York: Littman, 1986.

Sir Gawain and the Green Knight. Poems of the Pearl *Manuscript*. Ed. Malcolm Andrew and Ronald Waldron. Berkeley: U of California P, 1978. 207–300.

Smalley, Beryl. *The Study of the Bible in the Middle Ages*. Notre Dame: U of Notre Dame P, 1978.

Sparks, H. F. D. "Jerome as Biblical Scholar." *The Cambridge History of the Bible. Vol. 1, From the Beginnings to Jerome*. Ed. P. R. Ackroyd and C. F. Evans. Cambridge: Cambridge UP, 1970. 510–41.

Stanbury, Sarah. *Seeing the* Gawain-*Poet: Description and the Act of Perception*. Philadelphia: U of Pennsylvania P, 1991.

Trible, Phyllis. *God and the Rhetoric of Sexuality*. Philadelphia: Fortress, 1978.

Sylvia Federico

The Place of Chivalry in the New Trojan Court
Gawain, Troilus, and Richard II

Despite the geographical and dialectical distance between them, *Sir Gawain and the Green Knight* and Chaucer's *Troilus and Criseyde* are often linked together under the rubric of "Ricardian Poetry." According to J. A. Burrow's influential discussion, Ricardian poetry shares not only a moment in time but also certain elements of style, genre, and topic (2). Missing from the list of characteristics that define the term "Ricardian," however, is the consideration of Richard II himself. This chapter seeks to refocus our examination of the Ricardian moment by considering how aspects of its literary achievement are specifically related to contemporary views of Richard II and the central problematics of his reign. *Sir Gawain and the Green Knight* and *Troilus and Criseyde* are especially Ricardian in their explorations of the intersections of historical place and chivalric identity, two of the main issues of concern in the chronicles of the late fourteenth century. These texts identify martial failure as a central element of Richard's rule and further assert a relationship between the misdirection of knightly prowess and the physical site of its occurrence: the bedroom is where Ricardian chivalry is lost. Moreover, through their allusions to historical place, the poems and the chronicles characterize the Ricardian moment as one of new Trojan deviance.

The idea of chivalry and many of its defining practices underwent significant changes in the later fourteenth century. Recent scholarship has demonstrated, for instance, how one of the foundational elements of chivalric culture—the sworn feudal relationship—was eroded and ultimately replaced by new models of affiliation, and how such changes in practice were attended by changes in the way the chivalric ethos was defined and described.[1]

Coincident with the shifting meanings and underlying relationships of Ricardian chivalry is the absence of large-scale, successful war efforts during the period, coupled with the "absence of crusading . . . from the center of national military enterprise" (Middleton 120). His Scottish and Irish campaigns notwithstanding, Richard was seen as a military failure in comparison with his father, the Black Prince, and, more especially, in relation to his grandfather, Edward III. Unlike Edward, who had painstakingly developed support for the war with France—and thus political support for himself—Richard embarked on a quest for peace. His efforts culminated in a truce, and in his second marriage to the young Princess Isabel. But the virtues of peace were construed by Richard's detractors as symptoms of the failures of warriors; as many chronicle accounts have it, in Richard's court, a chivalric knight was not a fighting knight. Instead, the king was said to surround himself with his friends and favorites, with ladies, and with foreigners.[2] Thomas Walsingham, for example, notes disparagingly that Richard's coterie consists of

> knights of Venus rather than knights of Bellona, more powerful in the bedchamber than on the field, more vigorous with words than with weapons, quick in speaking but slow to perform the acts of war.

(2: 156)

As the language of this comment suggests, Richard and his circle were thought to have substituted domestic pleasures for properly chivalric behaviors. Ricardian knights are still vigorous and powerful, but this energy is misdirected toward the wrong place, the bedroom rather than the field, and deployed in the wrong way, with language rather than deeds.

The split between the symbols and actions of proper knighthood is further noted in complaints about Richard's dealings with the Order of the Garter, a society founded by Edward III in 1348. The order's knights, whose motto appears at the bottom of the manuscript page at the end of *Sir Gawain and the Green Knight*,[3] were men selected for their long tenure and success in battle. Once again, however, Richard's attempts at securing a chivalric reputation went awry, as his election of his friend, Robert de Vere, to the order in the early 1380s was seen as a premature elevation of a young man at the expense of more established and experienced soldiers like Richard, earl of Arundel. Indeed, de Vere became the first known degradation from the order when he was removed following his appeal of treason in the Merciless Parliament in 1388 (Collins 173). The king's friends and favorites were especially unpopular with the political commentators of his day, and his decisions to raise them to positions of high status much resented. De Vere was particularly reviled, a point exacerbated when Richard made him duke of Ireland, thus opening himself to charges that he was sharing the regality of kingship (Mitchell 118).[4] Richard's chivalric impulses, as these examples suggest, were not necessarily incorrect so much as they tended to settle in the incorrect places.

Ricardian chivalry was located not in the fields of France but in the pleasures of his court, which featured frequent games, feasts, and musical and literary entertainments. Here, too, he was criticized. The Monk of Evesham, for example, writes that the king was

> "prodigious with gifts," extravagant in dress and faint-hearted in war . . . he often spent "half the night up carousing with his friends and indulging himself in other unmentionable ways."

(Saul 447)

Such pleasures of court life were not always confined to interior spaces or even to the space of London but, rather, were mobile; the king sponsored a number of tournaments (although he apparently did not joust in them himself) and traveled with his entire entourage for such important feasts as Christmas.[5]

The extramartial quality of Richard's brand of chivalry is complicated by his attachment to the history of Troy. Perhaps following the model of his father-in-law, Charles IV (1316–1378) of Bohemia, Richard took an interest in mythic Trojan history and in his own role as a descendant of a long line of Trojan and post-Trojan heroic figures.[6] He and one of his close associates, Nicholas Brembre, referred to London as "new Troy" on separate occasions.[7] Seen one way, reference to the city of Troy, with its fabled stylishness, wealth, and beauty, would of course flatter London by association. And the history of Troy, more broadly, would invoke warfare and conquest—the traditional aspects of chivalric pursuit. In the context of Ricardian chivalry, however, allusions to Troy reflected poorly on the king and his court; instead of noble grandeur and knightly valor, Richard's appeals to Trojan history reinforced the reputation of his court as one of foreignness, arrogance, treachery, deceit, and sexual perversion—all the other characteristics of ancient Troy that attend its glory.

Ricardian court culture haunts the chivalric spaces inhabited and visited by the titular characters of *Sir Gawain and the Green Knight* and *Troilus and Criseyde*, pulling them back from proper knightly pursuits and directing them instead toward deviant identities. Both poems present us with images of chivalric identity that fail. Gawain sets off on a quest as an idealized Christian knight, armed with his symbolic shield, but returns to court with the profoundly pained awareness that he is unable to uphold that ideal. Troilus, despite his role as Troy's second most important defender, ends up shamed, heartbroken, and questioning the purpose of all human endeavor. Chivalric pursuit, in both instances, leads to a crisis, even a disintegration, of identity.

Troy is kept at a distance in both texts, invoked and set aside in the opening stanzas. In this way, Troy both is and is not a proper place: we may think of it instead as a mythic place that travels great distances in time, and in narrative, to characterize its "new" inhabitants. The Trojan qualities of Gawain and Troilus not only undo themselves as individuals but also implicate the society they represent. Like Richard II's alleged moral lapses, the private moral failures of Gawain and Troilus suggest themselves as symbols of public crises of cultural identity.

The setting of *Sir Gawain and the Green Knight* is announced as postwar: the siege has ended and Troy has been lost. Of course, from a British perspective the fight has been won, and the poem shows the peace that was finally established

after Aeneas's descendant, Brutus, settled the island. Arthur's court is one of leisure and entertainment, of feasts and games. This is not the chivalric society of
fighting men, but of men at sophisticated, refined play. Christmas tournaments
and jousts are followed by fifteen days of singing, dancing, gift giving, and kissing
games. The ritualized pleasures of the court include the expectation of disruption
by adventure: Arthur will have a wonder before he will eat. But the king misrec-
ognizes the nature of the Green Knight's visit; it is not designed for his personal
entertainment, but to question and challenge the bravery and, ultimately, the
masculinity of his court.

The Green Knight's awe-inspiring physicality is extramasculine: gigantic in
height, thick of limb, with a full head of hair and a big beard. And his taunts are
specifically directed at the masculine pride of the king and his men, such as when he
asks, with Arthur in plain sight, "wher is . . . / Þe gouernour of þis gyng?" (224–25),
and when he derides the entire company as so many "berdlez chylder" (280).[8]

The Green Knight's challenge exposes Arthur's court of peace and leisure as
one of boyish, less than fully masculine, pleasures. His offer of a beheading game,
initially just a surprising diversion for the holiday feast, becomes a threat of cas-
tration in light of what is at stake: the reputation of the defenders of the realm. The
poem reiterates this threat to masculinity once Gawain arrives at Bertilak's castle.
Ladies, feasts, entertainments, and gift giving prevail here as well, striking a parallel note with Arthur's court. And the exchange of winnings game revisits the
Christmas kisses of a year earlier, only this time Gawain kisses the lord. Gawain
does not seem especially bothered or troubled by playing kissing games with
Bertilak; they are but the logical extension of the sexual gaming at Arthur's court.
Kissing Bertilak "full savorly" is a boy's game and one way of being chivalric in
post-Trojan Britain.

Gawain is disgusted with himself upon return from the Green Chapel, specifically because he has broken his *trawthe*. As Green writes, he sets off "bearing the image of a pentangle on his shield 'in bytoknyng of trawþe' (626) and
returns wearing a green girdle as 'a tokyn of vntrawþe' (2509)" (4). Instead of
noble Gawain, he is fallen Gawain, as treacherous and deceitful as his Trojan
ancestors. This deeply wounding acknowledgment of his flaw is the result of his
personal confrontation with the split definition of chivalry: he thought he was on
a serious quest and that he was a knight ready to face death for his king. Instead,
he was the entire time part of a court game that compromised his sense of himself
as a true knight and a warrior and further exposed Arthur's court as a group of
foolish children, not fighting men. This last point is made clear at the end of the
poem, when the knights of the Round Table reject Gawain's interpretation of his
fault and insist instead that his tale contributes to the glory of their reputation.
The knights do not recognize that their brand of chivalry has unmanned them.[9]

The larger context of the poem, as announced in the opening stanzas, is
the *translatio imperii*—the translation of empire from the ancient world. From
Aeneas through Brutus to Arthur, and implicitly on to his own unnamed lord,
the *Gawain*-poet creates a historical continuum of individual failure and political
dysfunction.

Troilus and Criseyde also engages the fall of Troy, but like *Sir Gawain and the Green Knight,* Chaucer's poem focuses not on knights at war but on a knight at court. The narrator insists that he writes only of Troilus's "sorrow in loving," and while we are made to understand that Troilus continues to fight while in love, that is not what we actually see. Instead, images of Troilus insistently invoke his courtly, nonmartial, even feminine, persona. He writes and sings, faints and swoons, and he resists sexual consummation. By the time he and Criseyde finally have established a sexual routine, Troilus's martial exploits are less notable than his courtly practices:

> In suffisaunce, in blisse, and in singynges,
> This Troilus gan al his lif to lede.
> He spendeth, jousteth, maketh festeynges.
>
> (3.1716–18)

Comforted by love, Troilus becomes distracted from the war and shifts his attention to leisure.

Troilus's name means "little Troy," and thus Criseyde's undoing of him in the private sphere of amorous relations has public and political consequences. When and how he goes, so goes the city. Based on this connection, Chaucer—like Guido delle Colonne before him and Henryson after him—blames Criseyde for causing the fall of Troy, although he does so reluctantly. But this causal trajectory, however muted by Chaucer's sympathetic narrator, is like that which blames Helen instead of Paris as the root of the problem: it is the ruse by which we are distracted from the preexisting condition of Trojan sexual deviance. Troilus's feminine behavior in the realm of love only serves to highlight the feminine quality of the Trojans in the first place.

Even before the affair begins, when the poem is careful to point out that he fights Greeks as one of the best knights in Troy, Troilus is a compromised masculine figure. An elaborate description comes in book 2, as he returns to the city on a wounded horse after a long day's battle. His shield and helmet are dented, his clothes torn and bloody:

> So lik a man of armes and a knyght
> He was to seen, fulfilled of heigh prowesse,
> For bothe he hadde a body and a myght
> To don that thing, as wel as hardynesse;
> And ek to seen hym in his gere hym dresse,
> So fressh, so yong, so weldy semed he,
> It was an heven upon hym for to see.
>
> (2.631–37)

This lovingly detailed description, in which Troilus is admired by a sexually appraising gaze, is reminiscent of those of young women in courtly verse. His is a body on self-conscious display, not a body in action; as Gayle Margherita has written, Troilus here is the feminized object of the chivalric gaze (117–18). Chaucer's description shows how easily decorative trappings can take precedence over, and even substitute for, the deeds of war; Troilus's wounds are in this context less the result of battle than the cause for self-display.

The ultimate sign of Troilus's failure, however, is his willingness to trade in women—that other aspect of Trojan deviance famous for initiating the destruction of the city. Noble Troilus has sunk to the level of Pandarus when he offers his friend one of his own female relatives as a pledge of his faith:

> "And that thow knowe I thynke nought ne wene
> That this servise a shame be or jape,
> I have my faire suster Polixene,
> Cassandre, Eleyne, or any of the frape—
> Be she nevere so fair or wel yshape,
> Tel me which thow wilt of everychone,
> To han for thyn, and lat me thanne allone."
>
> (3.407–13)

Troilus has not only betrayed the women he offers his friend, he has betrayed the chivalric ethos of Troy's nobility. Hector articulates the idealized version of Trojan chivalric values when, in response to the request to trade Criseyde for Antenor, he declares that "we usen here no wommen for to selle" (4.182). The other, deviant, version of Trojan chivalry, however—that which permits Paris to take Helen—is articulated in Troilus's offer as well as in the parliament's decision. Despite Hector's protest to the contrary, Criseyde, a woman and a civilian, is traded for a prisoner; the "noyse of the peple" (4.183) demands a transgression of masculine, chivalric norms that ultimately will destroy and also define the Trojan nation.

While Richard II is never accused in the chronicles of having transgressive relationships with or dealings in women, he and the members of his court party nevertheless were rumored to be sexual deviants. Rather than the license with women that prevails between men in the definition of old Trojan chivalry, Richard's new Trojan knights are notorious for their associations among themselves. Walsingham (2:148), for example, speculates that de Vere resorted to black magic to gain ascendancy over the king, and that the two shared "obscene intimacies" (*familiaritatis obscoenae*). Henry Knighton more generally calls Richard's favorites "the seducers of the king" (*seduxerant regem*) (*Knighton's Chronicle* 404–5), but Adam of Usk finally names the king's "sodomies" (*sodomitica*) when he lists the causes of the deposition in his chronicle (*Chronicon* 29). Ricardian chivalry, during and after Richard's reign, was seen as inappropriately unmasculine. Like *Sir Gawain and the Green Knight* and *Troilus and Criseyde*, these chronicle accounts speak to the consequences of a definition of chivalric practice that fails to engage in appropriately masculine, fighting behavior. Knights who don't fight run the risk of losing the battle for their masculine identity as well as their physical, bodily integrity.[10]

The importance in these texts of the bodies of Gawain, Troilus, and Richard II, and especially the way their bodies function as symbols of the realm, underscores a point made recently by Edward S. Casey: that place is defined and recognized by the lived body. Working from Maurice Merleau-Ponty, Casey discusses how "the lived body is itself a place [and] . . . constitutes place, brings it into being" (235). Gawain's nicked and girdled body, for instance, not only reinforces the impression that the whole of Arthur's court is a site of shame, but further calls the Arthurian space into narrative existence. Similarly, Troilus's battle finery, his clever arrangement of wounded flesh and metal, is a specific physical display that means for, and even creates, general Trojan deviance. And Richard II, finally, is a political aberration whose failed chivalric body defines his historical reputation: excused in youth, subject to correction in maturity, and ultimately deserving of usurpation.

As these three figures make clear, the personal and private "failure" of the chivalric body has implications for larger, public concerns with the body politic. The brand of chivalry associated with Richard II, and reiterated in Gawain and in Troilus, cannot be part of a national narrative univocally proud of its own history. Like the myth of Troy, and its continuation in the myth of Arthurian Britain, Ricardian new Troy must also be subject to censure, even destruction. *Sir Gawain and the Green Knight* and *Troilus and Criseyde* narrate the nation[10] and offer figures for the disastrous body of the king himself, but they also offer appraisals of a national culture that is based on heroic bodies. On the one hand, the desirability of chivalry is questioned in the texts, as neither Gawain nor Troilus is a suitable defender of its ethos. On the other hand, however, these Ricardian poems betray a desire for chivalry and for a return to a mythical time and place in which its ethos led not to the destruction but to the assertion of a cultural identity. The absence of representation of a properly chivalric body, in other words, calls forth its presence. In this way, the arrival in 1399 of the idealized knightly body of Henry of Lancaster is both a remedy for Ricardian failure and a fulfillment of its place in history.

Notes

This chapter was presented in a shorter form at the 1999 International Congress of Medieval Studies in Kalamazoo, Michigan.

1. Strohm (108) notes that as part of this redefinition sworn vassalage was replaced with a variety of more supple forms of "attractive, shorter-term arrangements, including vassalage for cash payment; sworn brotherhood; short-term retention; household service; liveries of cloth, hats, hoods, collars, signs, or badges." And Green (xv) argues that the emergence of a new sense of "trouthe," one of the more important terms in the discourse of chivalry, can be located "firmly in the reign of Richard II."

2. Among the inhabitants of Richard's court was Janico Dartasso, a Navarrese esquire of the household who was one of about fifteen companions who were with the king when he arrived at Conway castle in August 1399. Janico was "something of a minor chivalric celebrity," according to Walker (32).

3. Collins notes the traditional version of the founding of the Order of the Garter in 1348: Edward III, to defend the honor of a lady whose garter had fallen to the ground, retrieved it before the mockery of the assembled company. He then attached it to his own leg, defiantly pronouncing the words later to be inscribed on the insignia, and claimed that forthwith he would institute an order of knights to bear the device. Collins suggests, however, that the motto (*Honi soit qui mal y pense,* or "Shame to the one who thinks evil of it") may have more to do with Edward's assertion of his claim to France than with the story of the lady (159).

4. Richard's attachment to de Vere is further noted in a record of his odd behavior at his friend's funeral, when he fondled and put rings on de Vere's fingers: " . . . curavitque thecam cypressinam, in qua corpus, balsamo delibutum, jacuit, aperire, faciem considerare, digitos contrectare; qui, ut fertur, ditati fuerunt annulis aureis pretiosis, cum corpore terrae tradendis. Demonstravitque dilectionem defuncto publice, quam impenderant prius vivo" (*Annales* 184–85; cited by Stow 91).

5. Bennett, 18–19, details the movements of Richard and his court in the late 1380s and 1390s.
6. Charles was apparently so taken with the idea of his supposed descent from Dardanus, founder of Troy, that he lined the walls of the royal reception hall in his castle at Karlstein, near Prague, with his mythic ancestors' portraits (Tanner 97–98). Saul (83–95, 346–49, 450) discusses the relationship between Richard and Charles IV, Anne of Bohemia's father.
7. For Richard II's use of the term "la neuf Troie" at the Smithfield tournament of 1390, see Lindenbaum (10). Walsingham (2: 174) describes Nicholas Brembre's desire to rename the city.
8. After all, as Dinshaw asks, "What's more chivalric than homosexual relations, often troubling the borders of knightly terrain?" (127).
9. Fisher (129) notes that *Sir Gawain and Green Knight* tries to revise Arthurian history "to demonstrate how the Round Table might have averted its own destruction by adhering to the expectations of masculine behavior in Christian chivalry."
10. I mean to refer here to the concept as articulated by Bhabha (142), that "representation of the nation [is] a temporal process" occurring as "the language of culture and community is poised on the fissures of the present becoming the rhetorical figures of a national past."

Works Cited

Annales Ricardi Secundi. Johannis de Trokelowe: Chronica et Annales. Ed. Henry T. Rile. Rolls Series. London, 1866.

Bennett, Michael J. "The Court of Richard II and the Promotion of Literature." *Chaucer's England: Literature in Historical Context.* Ed. Barbara Hanawalt. Minneapolis: U of Minnesota P, 1992. 3–20.

Bhabha, Homi K. *The Location of Culture.* London: Routledge, 1994.

Burrow, J. A. *Ricardian Poetry.* London: Routledge, 1971.

Casey, Edward S. *The Fate of Place.* Berkeley: U of California P, 1997.

Chaucer, Geoffrey. *The Riverside Chaucer.* Gen. ed. Larry D. Benson. 3rd ed. Boston: Houghton, 1987.

Chronicon Adae de Usk, 1377–1421. Ed. and trans. Edward Maunde Thompson. London: Henry Frowde, 1904.

Collins, Hugh. "The Order of the Garter, 1348–1461: Chivalry and Politics in Later Medieval England." *Courts, Counties and the Capital in the Later Middle Ages.* Ed. Diana E. S. Dunn. New York: St. Martin's, 1996. 155–80.

Dinshaw, Carolyn. "Getting Medieval: Pulp Fiction, Gawain, Foucault." *The Book and the Body.* Ed. Dolores Warwick Frese and Katherine O'Brien O'Keefe. Notre Dame: U of Notre Dame P, 1997. 116–63.

Fisher, Sheila. "Leaving Morgan Aside: Women, History, and Revisionism in *Sir Gawain and the Green Knight.*" *The Passing of Arthur: New Essays in the Arthurian Tradition.* Ed. Christopher Baswell and William Sharpe. New York: Garland, 1988. 129–51.

Green, Richard Firth. *A Crisis of Truth: Literature and Law in Ricardian England.* Philadelphia: U of Pennsylvania P, 1999.

Knighton's Chronicle, 1337–1396. Ed. and trans. G. H. Martin. Oxford: Clarendon, 1995.

Lindenbaum, Sheila. "The Smithfield Tournament of 1390." *Journal of Medieval and Renaissance Studies* 20 (1990): 10–15.

Margherita, Gayle. *The Romance of Origins.* Philadelphia: U of Pennsylvania P, 1994.

Middleton, Anne. "War by Other Means: Marriage and Chivalry in Chaucer." *Studies in the Age of Chaucer: Proceedings* (1) 1984: 119–33.

Mitchell, Shelagh. "Richard II: Kingship and the Cult of the Saints." *The Regal Image of Richard II and the Wilton Diptych.* Ed. Dillian Gordon, Lisa Monnas, and Caroline Elam. London: Harvey Miller, 1997. 115–24.

Saul, Nigel. *Richard II.* New Haven: Yale UP, 1997.

"Sir Gawain and the Green Knight." *The Poems of the* Pearl *Manuscript.* York Medieval Texts, 2nd series. Ed. Malcolm Andrew and Ronald Waldron. Berkeley: U of California P, 1979.

Stow, George. "Richard II in Thomas Walsingham's Chronicles." *Speculum* 59 (1984): 68–102.

Strohm, Paul. *Social Chaucer.* Cambridge: Harvard UP, 1989.

Tanner, Marie. *The Last Descendant of Aeneas: The Hapsburgs and the Mythic Image of the Emperor.* New Haven: Yale UP, 1993.

Walker, Simon. "Janico Dartasso: Chivalry, Nationality and the Man-at-Arms." *History* 84 (1999): 31–51.

Walsingham, Thomas. *Historia Anglicana.* 2 vols. Ed. Henry Thomas Riley. Rolls Series 28. London, 1863. Rpt. New York: Kraus Reprint, 1965.

Robert W. Hanning

Before Chaucer's *Shipman's Tale*
The Language of Place, the Place of Language
in Decameron *8.1 and 8.2*

Several scholars in recent years have considered Chaucer's debt to *Decameron* 8.1 and 8.2. As an indirect contribution to that discussion, but also to give the two *Decameron* novelle the independent attention they deserve, this chapter will compare and contrast them via quasi-independent analyses, with a view to examining how two versions of the same story (long known to folklorists as "the lover's gift regained") offer quite different evocations of place and of the signi-fying potential of language, and how they mediate to their audience divergent cultural preoccupations which, I believe, would have been obvious to, and shared by, that audience.[1]

Underlying my reading of these novelle is my conviction that the *Decameron* (like the *Canterbury Tales* after it) mediates a broad range of such preoccupations. That is, quite aside from whatever *intentions* its author may have had in cre-ating the *Centonovelle*, its major *cultural work* as a verbal system is to present, and represent, to its first audience issues of significance, and the anxieties that frequently accompany them, in partly disguised and displaced versions. I must put this claim in a bit of context. Following Raymond Williams and Anthony Giddens, I believe that imaginative language and the creativity that underlies it play a varied but constitutive role in the ongoing, albeit nonteleological, evolution of social processes and systems. Although Williams, in his influential study *Marx-ism and Literature*, gives a distinctly mixed blessing to the concept of mediation applied to the cultural function of literature by the Frankfurt school, this is the term I have chosen to describe the process by which various kinds of personal and collective experience pass through the grid (itself an ever-changing system) of established discourses and literary forms to become a "literary" expression of the fears, aspirations, anxieties, pleasures, and strategies of social existence within the systems that frame that existence.[2]

In particular, the cultural work of the *Decameron* consists, at least in part, in its response and relationship to the three major mediated systems that shaped and dominated the civilization of late medieval Europe: the institutional Catholic Church, secular government, and international commerce. Response, because many Boccaccian novelle deal inventively with these mediated systems, individually and in their complex interaction, exploring both the consequences of involvement with them and the opportunities and risks of manipulating them for personal advantage. Relationship, because the *Decameron* is itself an example of a multiply mediated system: a collection of oft-told tales reconceived and transmitted to its readership through a fictionalized narratorial position, with the further mediation of a framing fiction in which an ad hoc community tells the tales to each other.[3]

It's my contention that the particular form taken by the *Decameron* fits it, and thus its readers, for a multileveled cultural engagement with the claims, complexities, and problems of hegemonic structures, be they ecclesiastical, governmental, or commercial. The representations of such structures—and of their impact on issues of status and gender—in *Decameron* novelle offer occasions for contemplating both structures and issues from an intellectual or emotional distance. This distancing or mediating effect, part of the overall pleasure we take in fictions or imaginings, creates the possibility (and here we can only speak hypothetically) for attaining perspectives on cultural problems otherwise difficult or impossible to achieve in the "real world" and thus, perhaps, the potential as well for less anxious, more calculated responses—of acceptance, manipulation, or resistance—to mediated systems as they are experientially encountered.

The most obvious distinction between the two *Decameron* novelle here under discussion is their setting: 8.1 in Milan, 8.2 in the Tuscan countryside. The contrasting spatial frames reflect divergent narrational concerns and strategies. Urban anxieties about gender and commercial relations percolate near the surface of 8.1, only marginally obscured by the tone of righteous indignation it directs at its female protagonist for subordinating her chastity to financial considerations. By contrast, the rural location of 8.2 allows its narrator to indulge freely in stereotypes about village and peasant culture that, as David Wallace has recently demonstrated (*Chaucerian Polity* 126, 136), patronize country denizens and implicitly offer their inferiority as a justification for Florence's exploitation of the *contado* and poor treatment of its residents.[4] Nonetheless, within this comprehensive, racist discourse about country folk (for such it is, anticipatory of the "shuffling darky" and *Amos 'n' Andy* stereotypes prevalent until recently in "white" America) can be distinguished specific cultural concerns about two rural constituencies, each associated with a specific locus: the parish clergy, established in the orbit of the church building and its immediate surroundings, and the peasantry, placed in their fields and humble dwellings. And looming in the background is yet another place, the city itself, evoked here for its legal and economic power over the countryside, and thus contributing to what might be called the novella's bad conscience about its chosen strategy of representation. The note of idealization—of soft pastoral, as it were—in the denouement of 8.2 can be understood, I believe, as a not wholly successful attempt to appease or muffle its conscientious impulse.[5]

In *Decameron* 8.1, Gulfardo, a German mercenary stationed in Milan, loves Madonna Ambruogia, wife of his friend, the rich merchant Guasparruolo Cagastraccio. She replies to his request for sexual favors with a demand for two hundred gold florins. His desire turned to scorn by Ambruogia's placing a price on her body, Gulfardo borrows the two hundred florins from Gasparruolo and, when the merchant is away on business, gives them to her in the presence of a third party whom he brings to the assignation, saying that she is to give them to her husband when he returns. Ambruogia accepts the money, assuming that the words accompanying it are intended to trick Gulfardo's companion, and after the latter's departure takes the mercenary to bed. After Gasparruolo returns, Gulfardo tells him in the presence of his wife that he has returned the loan through her since he could not use it as he intended; given the witnessed words of Gulfardo, she has no choice but to agree and hand the two hundred florins to her husband.

Like so many other *Decameron* novelle, 8.1 is a tale of trickery—a *beffa* (cf. Mazzotta, 66–67, 190); its teller, Neifile, says that after a day devoted to the "beffe fatte dalle donne agli uomini" ("tricks played by women upon men"), she will now recount "una fattane [i.e., a *beffa*] da uno uomo a una donna" (670.2) ("one which was played by a man upon a woman" [551]).[6] In this case, as in several other *Decameron* novelle, the primary weapon of deception in the battle of the sexes is language (as opposed, e.g., to hiding lovers in closets, communicating with them via strings hanging out windows, bribing maids to take one's place for a beating, or pretending there is a stone that makes one invisible). Paradoxically, the plot turns on the deployment of words which deceive by meaning exactly what they say. The result is to make the place and resources of language in both gender and commercial relations, as well as in writer-reader transactions, a central concern of this novella.

Echoing the traditional restraints placed more on female than on male desire in Mediterranean patriarchal society (cf. Goursonnet), Neifile presents her story as, in effect, an exemplum of just punishment for a woman who, failing "la sua castità come la sua vita guardare" ("to guard her chastity with her life") besmirches it—and not even owing to "le . . . forze grandissime" ("the powerful forces") of love (which an earlier novella [6.7] had shown to be grounds for lenient judgment), but "per prezzo" ("for monetary gain"), thus showing herself "esser degno del fuoco" (670.3) ("deserv[ing] to be burnt alive" [552]). Neifile's *saeva indignatio* at Madonna Ambruogia—whom she slightingly refers to as a "donna, anzi cattiva femina" (671.9) ("lady, or strumpet, rather" [553])—saturates and frames the tale; at its conclusion, she relates, the latter must return to her husband "il disonesto prezzo della sua cattività" ("the ill-gotten proceeds of her depravity"); Gulfardo is pronounced *sagace* ("sagacious") in his trickery, while his victim is denounced as *avara* ("rapacious") (673.18; 554). Gulfardo himself is said to feel disgust for "la viltà di lei la quale egli credeva che fosse una valente donna" (671.8) ("the lack of decorum [of one whom he] had always thought of . . . as a perfect lady" [553]), and the other members of the *Decameron* brigata share Neifile's opinion: all, men and women alike, deride Ambruogia as "la 'ngorda Melanese" (674.2) ("the covetous Milanese lady" [554]).[7]

Behind all this righteous moralizing, however, lie multiple anxieties. The political dimension of the novella has already drawn some attention: the fact that Ambruogia is the female form of the name of Milan's patron saint suggests that she represents Milanese "rapacity" (Wallace, *Decameron* 86; Ferreri, 200). In which case her frustrated sexual/business relationship with Gulfardo (even though it has payment going in the wrong direction) expresses the hope that Milan's extensive reliance on mercenaries (such as the famous English *condottiere*, John Hawkwood) to extend its rule over other city-states, including Florence — that is, its being "in bed" with foreign forces of violence — will in the end lead to its being "screwed" and cheated.

However, I think that 8.1 embodies more palpable anxieties about gender and commercial relations, specifically about female encroachment on male pre-rogatives in a mercantile urban world from which, as JoAnn McNamara has recently documented, women had been increasingly excluded during the com-mercial revolution in high and late medieval Europe.[8] Seen from this perspective, Ambruogia's commercial initiative — selling her body for money — is much more than merely morally transgressive. First, it upsets gender relations by regarding Gulfardo as a source of commercial, rather than emotional and sexual, satisfac-tion: she agrees to accept him as her lover in return for cash because "ricco uomo era," and "ella avesse per alcuna sua cosa bisogno di fiorini dugento d'oro" (671) ("He was well off and she wanted to buy something for herself [for] two hundred gold florins" [552–53]).[9] But it also marks her attempt to free herself from finan-cial dependence on her well-to-do merchant husband and, worse still, in effect places her in unauthorized competition with him (cf. McNamara, 152–53) as an entrepreneur of a commodity — her own sexuality — that by the standards and logic of a patriarchal society should be under his exclusive control (not to say for his exclusive use). Moreover, it blurs important social distinctions: between a prostitute (a woman of minimal, indeed despised status) and the wife — and thus the prized possession — of a respectable merchant,[10] and between public and private spheres, that is, between the male-dominated *loci* of commerce and money lending and the household places of conjugal domesticity, centered on the bed-chamber, over which, as Leon Battista Alberti's norm-laden *Libri della famiglia* makes clear (207–11), the bourgeois wife exercised day-to-day control, but which she was expected to keep for her husband as a haven of order, tranquility, and (especially) chastity.[11]

Ambruogia's offenses against all these patriarchal hierarchies and prescrip-tions are summed up in her behavior when Gulfardo brings her the money she has demanded as a precondition to his enjoying her carnally. As she takes the two hundred florins she has made the price of having sex with Gulfardo, and before she leads him into her *camera* ("bedroom") to consummate the deal, the merchant's wife mimics the actions of a careful moneylender seated at his table in the pubic space of the market: in reply to what she believes to be her suitor's fictive command, "'Madonna, tenete questi denari e daretegli a vostro marito quando sarà tornato'" (672.12) ("Here, take this money, my lady, and give it to your husband when he returns" [553]), she says, "'Io il farò volentieri, ma io voglio veder quanti sono'" (672.13) ("I shall see that he gets it, of course, but first I should like to make sure that it is all here" [553]) and then "versatigli sopra una tavola e trovatogli esser dugento, seco forte contenta gli repose" (673.13) ("she emptied the florins out onto a table, and on finding . . . to her great satisfaction that they came to exactly two hundred, . . . she put them away in a safe place" [553–54]) (cf. Ferreri, 204).[12]

Ambruogia's threat to gender hierarchy and spatial order is ultimately thwarted, and punished, through Gulfardo's resort to verbal trickery. But the irony of this trickery, as I have already suggested, is that in a literary form (the *fabliau*) and an environment (commerce) where language traditionally functions (or is seen to function) effectively when used unreferentially—as lies, exaggerations, fictions—in this case language becomes tricky and outwits the would-be subverter of patriarchal norms by meaning precisely what it says. Of course, the *beffa* depends on Ambruogia not realizing this until the moment, after her husband has returned from his business trip, when Gulfardo reports the statement to him, thus coercing her into passing the money to her husband (since there was a witness to her having received the money and since she is in no position to offer a contrary explanation of why she was given it).

Hence, by offering a strong dose of unexpectedly stable meaning, language reverses and "cures" the menacing (to men) errancy from stable gender hierarchy and local signification caused by a woman's introducing commercial language and calculation into her bedroom.

The denouement of 8.1 is not without problems: Gulfardo, in putting Ambruogia in her place, also cuckolds his friend, using money Guasparruolo has loaned him, and even manages to cheat the merchant out of the interest Gulfardo usually pays on such loans (cf. 671.5).

These problematic elements suggest a hierarchy of values embedded in the novella as in the culture it mediates. Neifile (countering but also subscribing to the "racial" stereotyping that, like gender stereotyping, runs through the *Decameron*)[13] characterizes Gulfardo as unusually loyal for a German, in two specific areas: as a mercenary soldier, faithful "a coloro ne' cui servigi si mettea" ("to those in whose service he enrolled") and in credit dealings, where he is a "lealissimo renditore" (671.5) ("scrupulous in repay[ment]" [552]) of monies lent him. That is, he subscribes to a code that underlies male cooperation in matters of war and business. But if all is not fair in war, it appears to be in love, "conoscendo [as Neifile puts it] le sue forze grandissime" (670.4) ("knowing how powerful . . . [the forces of love] are" [552]). Hence the novella tolerates Gulfardo's amorous overtures to his merchant friend's wife (with none of the usual *fabliau* suggestions that the husband is too old, impotent, or preoccupied with his affairs to satisfy his wife in bed) as long as he honors his martial and credit commitments. (The importance of filling the obligations imposed on you by your status and circumstances is underscored by repeated uses of the verb *dovere* throughout the novella; by contrast, the verb does not appear in 8.2.)[14]

Furthermore, a woman in business, profiting from her body, is more of a threat to male hegemony than a man seeking a sexual relationship with another man's wife. In recognition of this fact, the novella transforms Gulfardo's adulterous desire into an instrument for the reassertion of male dominance. His verbal deception of Ambruogia serves a double purpose: first, by stripping her adultery of its intended profit, the trick confirms rather than challenges male control of female sexuality—Ambruogia has surrendered to Gulfardo's importunacy and has nothing to show for it.

Even more ironically, Gulfardo counters Ambruogia's introduction of the language of the market place into the bedroom that should be its polar opposite by the equally inappropriate importation of "un suo compagno di cui egli si fidava molto e che sempre in sua compagnia andava in ciò che faceva" (671.8) ("a companion of his whom he greatly trusted, who was privy to all his affairs" [553]) from the places where such homosocial bonding takes shape into a site of heterosexual encounter. This further invasion of the female sphere (cf. the Ovidian *thalamus*) by male forces transforms an erotic assignation with the wife into a financial transaction with the husband, since the *compagno*, who in another kind of story might have served as a go-between for the lovers, here functions as a witness to the repayment of a debt. The imposition of (we might surmise) the mercenaries' campfire onto the bedroom-turned-marketplace thus puts Ambruogia in the unwanted and unexpected position of becoming Guasparruolo's unsalaried collection agent, accepting on his behalf, carefully counting, and passing on to him the two hundred florins owed him by his debtor (cf. Ferreri, 204). That the novella even countenances Gulfardo's avoidance of the interest ("quello utile" [672.10]) owing on his loan, which it must do to depict his *beffa* as successful, suggests the urgency of its need to squelch Ambruogia's gesture of fiscal autonomy.

The verbal trickery that drives the *beffa* in Neifile's novella deserves another look. As we have seen, what appears to be a deliberately misleading command, uttered merely to hide from Gulfardo's companion what is really happening and therefore lacking in prescriptive force, turns out to be the statement of a contract between Gulfardo and Ambruogia, witnessed by the *compagno* and therefore binding on Ambruogia, however against her will. Because Ambruogia misconstrues Gulfardo's intention in giving this order, and mistakes as well the significance of the presence of a third party, the scam turns out to be on her, not on the friend. The transformation of these words from protective to prescriptive status—from convenient fiction to unavoidable command—effects a rearrangement of forces, from lovers vs. friend (and, at greater remove, husband) to males in league to control the female who seeks transgressive economic power.

This paradoxical situation, in which Gulfardo's language deceives Ambruogia not by what he says but by the context in which he says it, is interestingly anticipated by the summary at the head of the novella, which analogously deceives its reader. In English translation it says, "Gulfardo takes out a loan from Guasparruolo and having agreed with Guasparruolo's wife to be able to lie with her for it [i.e., the amount of the loan] gives it to her. And then in her presence he says to Guasparruolo that he gave it to her and she says it's true" (my translation). As far as it goes, this summary is accurate, but of course by not going far enough it delivers a completely different (and differently surprising) story from the one it introduces.[15] By analogy with other *Decameron fabliaux,* we are betrayed into anticipating some kind of tricky explanation by the lovers that fools the cuckolded husband, or perhaps a guilty confession. Nothing prepares us for the verbal legerdemain practiced by Gulfardo, with the assistance of his friend, at Ambruogia's expense.

The lesson, which the reader and Ambruogia can only learn retrospectively, is that the circumstances in which words are spoken or written, and the expectations with which we receive them, can allow them to fool us and/or us to be fooled. By extension, the lesson of 8.1 is that the "place" of language is often to assist those who can fashion from its potential for equivocation and deception an instrument for maintaining authority and frustrating the desires for agency of those subject to it.

In the second novella of the eighth day, told by Panfilo, the story of Gulfardo, Ambruogia, and Guasparruolo is radically recast. The parish priest of Varlungo, a village in the Florentine *contado,* is a ladies' man, a confirmed seducer of the wives of the parish. He becomes enamored of Monna Belcolore, wife of the peasant Bentivegna del Mazzo, and goes to visit her while her husband is in town on business. She plays hard to get, chiding the padre on his lechery and saying she will only let him have his way with her in return for five *lire,* enough money for her to retrieve her best dress from the *usuraio* (pawnbroker) in town. The priest promises to deliver the money on a later occasion, but Belcolore insists on payment now. In a state of great sexual excitement, the priest offers his cloak as a pledge and Belcolore accepts it. Later, after satisfying his desires, the priest realizes he lacks the wherewithal to pay Belcolore as promised; to get his cloak back, he sends a boy to borrow Belcolore's mortar, then has the child return it after Bentivegna has come home, with instructions to ask for the cloak the priest has left as security for the mortar. Trapped by the presence of her husband and embarrassed by his disapproval of her accepting security of any kind from the priest, Belcolore hands over the cloak, stating via a double entendre that she will never again have sex with the offending cleric. Eventually, by a mixture of threats and cajolery, the priest works out a reconciliation and offers, in lieu of the five *lire,* a small gift. The novella ends with the suggestion that the two will again enjoy sex together.

At first glance, Panfilo seems to adopt a strategy like that of Neifile before him; he begins by announcing his indignation at priests who make parish wives their sexual prey. But whereas Neifile's initial scorn for Ambruogia is carried through the novella single-mindedly, Panfilo's ostensible ire against predatory clerics—a *topos* borrowed from late medieval antifraternal satire, which applied the derogatory Pauline term, *penetrantes domos* (home invaders), to friars who supposedly went about the countryside seducing unwary women[16]—is immediately undercut by the cascade of comically exaggerated similes and metaphors in which he describes their activities: "sopra le nostre moglie hanno bandita la croce, e par loro non altramenti aver guadagnato il perdono di colpa e di pena, quando una se ne posson metter sotto, che se d'Allessandria avessero il soldano menato legato a Vignone" (674.3) (they "have proclaimed a crusade against our wives, and who seem to think, when they succeed in laying one of them on her back, that they have earned full remission of all their sins, as surely as if they had brought the Sultan back from Alexandria to Avignon in chains" [555]). The seriousness of Panfilo's attack is also fatally compromised when he appends to his expressed annoyance that laymen cannot retaliate by taking similar advantage of (wifeless) priests the codicil, "come che nelle madri, nelle sirocchie, nelle amiche e nelle figliuole con non meno ardore, che essi le lor moglie assaliscano, vendichin l'ire loro" (674.4) ("albeit we may vent our spleen against their mothers, sisters, mistresses and daughters with no less passion than the priests display when assailing our wives" [555]).

Panfilo concludes his opening gambit by saying (illogically) that because of (or to illustrate) the offenses and animosities he has just described, he will tell "uno amorazzo contadino, più da ridere per la conclusione che lungo di parole, del quale ancora potrete per frutto cogliere che a' preti non sia sempre ogni cosa da credere" (674.5) ("this tale of country love, more amusing for its ending than conspicuous for its length, from which you will be able to draw a useful moral, namely, that you shouldn't believe everything that a priest tells you" [555]). A wider divergence from Neifile's righteously indignant tone in the preceding novella would be difficult to imagine. The "moral," not to believe priests, is balanced by the note that this is a comic, not serious, exemplum (cf. Goursonnet 117). Above all, the image of gathering fruit, taken together with the description of the subject matter as an "amorazzo contadino" (674.5)—perhaps best rendered, "a ridiculous story of hick love"—makes it absolutely clear that what follows is a tale of stereotyped rustic (mis)adventures.

That is, Panfilo's novella proclaims itself less concerned with clerical abuses and their victims than with offering an amusing (to city folk), because patronizing, depiction of life in the sticks.[17] As I've already suggested, the representation of place in 8.2 reflects the kind of racist stereotyping to which exploiters (in this case the Florentine commune) resort in order to disguise, and to justify, their treatment of the less powerful and marginalized (in this case the Florentine *contado*, which supplied raw materials for the city and cheap, disenfranchised labor for the cloth trade on which its wealth and power were largely based).[18]

Accordingly, the tone adopted for much of the novella might best be characterized as a snicker, and one of its main verbal manifestations is the noun modified by an ending which suggests diminution toward insignificance or exaggeration toward the ridiculous and grotesque. Setting the tone at once, Panfilo inserts into his opening description of epic sexual warfare between ravishing priests and wronged husbands the phrase, "secolari cativelli" (674.4) ("poor dupes" [555]), which makes the latter seem more like wimps than domestic champions, and prepares us for the brief depiction of Belcore's husband as an illiterate simpleton who manifests at the end of the tale a ridiculous respect for the priest who has just cuckolded him. Then comes the already noted "amorazzo contadino," and shortly thereafter we learn that the priest of Varlungo, "come che legger non sapesse troppo, pur con molte buone e sante parolozze la domenica a piè dell'olmo ricreava i suoi popolani" (674–75.6) ("albeit he was none too proficient at reading books, always had a rich stock of good and holy aphorisms with which to entertain his parishioners under the elm every Sunday" [555]). We are clearly intended to derive from this description an image of a grotesque, unintentionally hilarious sermon preached by a barely literate priest to an even more ignorant congregation. And when Belcolore is introduced, Panfilo describes her as "una piacevole e fresca foresozza, brunazza e ben tarchiata . . ." (675.9) ("a vigorous and seductive-looking wench, buxom and brown as a berry" [555]).[19] And so on, through "scarpette" (677.25) ("little . . . shoes" [557]), "frenello" (ibid.) ("silk head scarf" [ibid.]), "Billiuzza" (677.30), "basciozzi" (678.38) ("luscious kisses" [559]), to "gozzoviglia" (680.46) ("guzzle" [560]) and "sonagliuzzo" (680.47) ("pretty little bell" [560]).

The inhabitants of Panfilo's version of the countryside are incapable of finer feelings or sentiments. Like the parish clerk, Absolom, in Chaucer's *Miller's Tale*, the priest of Varlungo woos his distant beloved with distinctly unromantic gifts—garlic, beans, shallots (675.11)—from which, we are surely intended to believe, will come a flatulence quite at odds with (and at opposite ends from) the perfumed sentiments of courtly love (cf. Thompson 205). Indeed, the inhabitants of Varlungo are much given to mangling language, by accident or design. When the priest encounters Bentivegna del Mazzo, the latter is on his way to Florence, where he will seek assistance from an advocate who can, in return for the gifts Bentivegno will give him, help the peasant in a matter of law which he cannot in the least understand, as can be seen from the legal terminology which bubbles out of him in a veritable fountain of malapropisms (676.14; cf. Thompson 205). Later, when Monna Belcolore questions the worth of the cloak the priest offers her as security against the five *lire* she demands as payment for sex with him, the latter responds by praising the garment as "di duagio infino a treagio, a hacci di quegli nel popolo nostro che il tengon di quattragio"—a word play on the sought-after cloth of Douai and the numbers 2 (*due*), 3 (*tre*), and 4 (*quattro*), designed to confuse and impress her, as only a country bumpkin could possibly be impressed.

Within its overall placement in the countryside, the action of the novella distinguishes two other places—church and peasant home. And in delineating these *loci*, 8.2 gives us some access into larger cultural preoccupations beyond the urban, patrician narrator's desire to ridicule his poor country cousins.

Turning first to the church, we must understand it not just as a physical structure but as the signifier in stone (or wood) of clerical authority (and thus of the corruption of authority). Through its portrait of a sex-crazed padre who sings like a braying jackass when sexually aroused by the sight of Belcolore at Mass (675.10), the novella mediates a cultural anxiety about the power given to a none-too-well-trained clergy by the institutional church: first and foremost, their power to save or damn souls thanks to their role as necessary mediators of the sacraments of penance and the eucharist, made obligatory on an annual basis by the Fourth Lateran Council (1215), but also the further power they arrogate to themselves within the parish on the basis of their sacramental functions.

In the comic world of 8.2, the priest of Varlungo is actually treated with some ambivalence. On the one hand, he is portrayed as ready to use his ecclesiastically endowed power for purely personal ends: at the end of the novella he threatens Belcolore with excommunication when she snubs him in her anger at his trick. On the other, his outrageous pursuit of sexual satisfaction with the wives of the parish signals with comic hyperbole an awareness of the dangers to the Christian community of the celibacy imposed on the secular clergy by the reform papacy (still widely resisted by them in Boccaccio's day).[20] When the priest first propositions Belcolore, she asks in mock wonderment, "o fanno i preti così fatte cose?" (677.22) ("do priests do that sort of thing?" [557; translation altered]), and he replies that they do so better than other men, "perché noi maciniamo a raccolta . . ." (677.23) ("because we do our grinding when the millpond's full" [557]). Such a claim—a *topos* of *fabliau* mythology about sexually athletic, because deprived, clerics, couched predictably in rural terms—here contributes to the sense of sexual urgency the celibate priest feels.

Both the elemental force of sexual need and the authority the priest manipulates (and corrupts) to satisfy it are represented by his erect phallus, made much of in the novella (674.6, 678.31, 37). That phallus, which apparently gives pleasure to Belcolore—who has earlier been described similarly as "atta a meglio saper macinar che alcun altra" (675.9) ("better versed in the grinder's art than any other girl in the village" [555])—also ruins her fellow peasant Biliuzza, who, presumably made pregnant by the priest, must go to the city in disgrace and become a prostitute. And as the priest's threat to excommunicate Belcolore later in the novella makes clear, there is an unstated but implied "phallic" element of coercion in his wooing of Belcolore, precisely because of the sacramental and juridical weapons the institutional church has placed in his hands.

More physically tangible than the church, as a place within the rural world of 8.2, is the home of the peasants Belcolore and Bentivegna (whose name means "welcome," an irony given the consequences of his wife's welcoming the hedgerow *penetrans domos* into their home: "O sere, voi siate il ben venuto" (676.17) ("Oh, Father, you are welcome" [557]). Here on her own turf Belcolore is something of an ironist at the priest's expense, as well as a shrewd bargainer (cf. Pomilio 209). Furthermore, the novella modifies its air of patronization by including in its depiction of this place (in what I have referred to as a manifestation of bad conscience) some indications of the hard life of peasants and of the difficult, no-win choices imposed on them by poverty. For one thing, it suggests the subsistence level at which Belcolore and Bentivegna live when it tells us that while the priest is propositioning her, Belcolore "cominciò a nettare sementa di cavolini che il marito avea poco innanzi trebiati" (676.19) ("began to sift a heap of cabbage seed that her husband had gathered earlier in the day" [557]). What induces her to surrender to clerico-phallic exigency is her desire to have at her disposal, after what one must presume to be a considerable interval, clothing in which she can be seen without shame on public occasions. She is thus placed by poverty in a position of bartering her conjugal honor for her dress, choosing between private and public shame. (We might well, in our own idiom, call this novella a tale of "grinding" poverty.)

When Belcolore finally comes to an agreement with the priest to give him what he so desires, she insists on a change of venue of manifold significance: "Sere, andiancene qua nella capanna, ché non vi vien mai persona" (678.37) ("Let's go into the barn, Father. Nobody ever comes near the place" [559]). Her words simultaneously express caution, an implicit unwillingness to besmirch the marriage bed (cf. note 11), and, I believe, her sense that she is sinking below human level ("non vi vien mai persona") by coupling with a stranger in a barn or shed. Belcolore knows the difference between conjugal relations and what the priest has forced upon her by his authority and by her desire to retrieve her good clothes from the pawnbroker.

What the two articulated places within Panfilo's stereotypical countryside — church and peasant's home — have in common is their lack of resources. Just as Belcolore is cajoled into servicing the priest by her desire for sartorial adequacy she cannot otherwise afford, so the priest is forced into playing a cruel trick on Belcolore by his realization that he lacks the means to deliver the reward he promised her: "pensando che quanti moccoli ricoglieva in tutto l'anno d'offerta non valeva la metà di cinque lire, gli parve aver mal fatto e pentessi d'avere lasciato il tabarro e cominciò a pensare in che modo riaver lo potesse senza costo" (679.39) ("it began to dawn on him that all the candle-ends he could muster from a whole year's offerings would scarcely amount to a half of five pounds in value, and he could have kicked himself for being so stupid as to leave her his cloak. So he began to consider how he might retrieve it without having to pay" [559]). Necessity, not wickedness, is the parent of his invention. (Note also that the priest is in the same position vis-à-vis Belcolore that she is vis-à-vis the Florentine pawnbroker, but he gets his clothing back, while she does not — another tangible sign of clerical power in a small polity.)

Functioning as a backdrop to 8.2's mixed pageant of foolishness and poverty in Varlungo is the quintessentially opposing place: the city, Florence. Here again, what I have been calling the novella's bad conscience about its stereotypical representation of country life shows through in the functions it assigns the metropolitan center. It is the place to which the pregnant Biliuzza must go to become a streetwalker after she has been disgraced by the priest at home (cf. McNamara 150; Karras ch. 3). It is also the place to which Belcolore takes the wool she has spun, as a member of an exploited, underpaid rural work force — in one of the few occupations allowed to women, but without the protection of guilds or other associations open to men, and controlled by male entrepreneurs and merchants — on whose labor Florence's cloth industry, the basis of its wealth and prestige, largely depended (McNamara 147–49). And it houses the *usuraio* to whom she has had to pawn her dress.

Finally, Florence is the place to which Bentivegna must travel in search of assistance in dealing with to him incomprehensible litigation. His reliance on a

Florentine lawyer suggests that he may be about to be doubly exploited—by the commune and by his own counsel. Taken together, these details suggest that the city is not a place to which Panfilo's rural residents can look for comfort or relief (cf. Wallace, *Chaucerian Polity* 134–36, on "the city screwing the countryside").

The coexistence within 8.2 of hick-scorning comedy and awareness of rural poverty and urban indifference or exploitation makes for an uneasy reading experience, reflecting mixed feelings and what I have been calling a bad conscience about the state of things in the *contado,* as well as anxiety about the clergy's misuse of its institutional power for personal gain. Does the novella attempt any resolution?

It does, in more than one way. First of all, the comic language of 8.2, which I have argued should register with twenty-first-century readers as colonizing, patronizing, and self-exculpatory on the part of a member of the urban elite intent on presenting a marginalized and exploited rural population as Other, can also be understood as an attempt to suggest that nothing that happens to such folk is really serious and that "we" can all enjoy a good laugh at the expense of the world's (more precisely, the *contado's*) Varlungese priests and peasants (Copland 13). In rhetorical terms, Panfilo's comedic representation of the world of 8.2 constitutes a conscience-soothing *color* imposed on a tale of seduction and betrayal; the heroine's name, "bel colore," can thus be said to expose the narrator's game.[21]

Right at the center of the novella's comic coloring is its extensive use of a language of sexual metaphor, euphemism, and double entendre (Porcelli 86–89; Pomilio 207–8). This verbal register domesticates and recuperates, even as it records, transgressiveness. For example, when the priest of Varlungo visits parish wives whose husbands are away from home, he comes "portando loro della festa e dell'acqua benedetta e alcun moccolo di candela talvolta infino a casa, dando loro la sua benedizione" (675.7) ("bringing them fairings and holy water and a candle-end or two, and giving them his blessing" [555]). In the course of this series, the language of sacramentals becomes more and more suggestive in the context of the priest's reason for visiting: holy water stands for semen, candles for the phallus, giving benediction for the sex act itself. Even as the passage communicates the priest's misuse of the church's beliefs and rituals, it manages to render that abuse amusing and almost harmless, even suggesting, perhaps, that sexual pleasure is itself a holy act deserving of religious celebration. (In the same vein, the narrator describes the priest's having sex with Belcolore as his "faccendola parente di messer Domenedio" [678.38], "[making] her a kinswoman of the Lord God" [559]).

The sexualization of objects of every day life functions as a central comic strategy of the *Decameron* and is referred to with mock innocence by the narrator in his epilogial apology for his tale collection (960.5). Among the objects particularly mentioned are the *mortaio,* or "mortar," and *pestello,* or "pestle," which figure so prominently in the *beffa* by which the priest retrieves his cloak from, in effect, being in "pawn" to Monna Belcolore. When Belcolore realizes that the priest has swindled her, and that her husband has unknowingly acquiesced in the deception, she angrily tells the priest's emissary, "Dirai così al sere da mia parte: 'La Belcolore dice che fa prego a Dio che voi non pesterete mai più salsa in suo mortaio: non l'avete voi si bello onor fatto di questa'" ("Give the priest this message from me: 'Belcolore says that she swears to God you won't be grinding any more of your sauces in her mortar, after the shabby way you've treated her over this one'"); on receiving this message, the priest instructs his subordinate, "Dira'le, quando tu la vedrai, che s'ella non ci presterà il mortaio, io non presterò a lei il pestello; vada l'un per l'altro" (680.45) ("Next time you see her, tell her that if she doesn't lend me her mortar, I shan't let her have my pestle. It's no use having one without the other" [560]). What starts out as a wife's necessarily coded expression of resistance to further exploitation by her seducer becomes a comic exchange, an indirect *laus veneris,* and a final change rung on the rural metaphor of grinding as a generically appropriate way of signifying the fulfillment of desire among those equally incapable of finer feelings and the courtly language in which to couch them. In effect, the priest and Belcolore buy into the stereotyped view of them propounded by their narrator.[22]

The conclusion of the novella provides a microcosm of its rather complicated and not fully self-consistent understanding of the world of Varlungo, and of the place of language in attempting to occlude its more somber perceptions. Belcolore remains angry at the priest until the wine harvest; after he has threatened her with damnation, they reconcile in a rural feast of new wine and chestnuts and in lieu of the five *lire* owed her, the priest "fece . . . rincartare il cembal suo e appiccovi un sonagliuzzo," leaving Belcolore "contenta" (the last word of the novella) (680.47) ("put a new skin on her tambourine and tricked it out with a pretty little bell" [560]).[23] The patronizing language of comic pastoral returns (*sonagliuzzo*), and with it the idea that peasants like Belcolore can be bought off and satisfied with baubles. But the priest's institutionally supported coercion, and Belcolore's continued deprivation of her wedding clothes (and thus her inability "andare . . . in niun buon luogo" [677.28], "to go . . . anyplace respectable" [557–58; translation altered]) cannot be fully effaced; they provide a criterion for establishing the limits of language's ability to construct an imaginary rural garden of amoral pleasure free of the real toads of poverty and exploitation.

Boccaccio's two versions of "the lover's gift regained" provide an interesting instance of his attraction to telling the same story twice in very different ways, expressing divergent cultural concerns. (Two other examples are the pairings of *Decameron* 10.4 and 10.5 with the thirteenth and fourth *quistioni d'amore* in book 4 of the *Filocolo*.) In this comparative reading of *Decameron* 8.1 and 8.2, I have attempted to suggest the importance of culturally resonant places, and of the language in which they are represented, for the divergent yet complementary significances of these two novelle.

Notes

1. Goursonnet: "La huitième journée du *Décaméron* est ouverte par deux nouvelles qui présentent la particularité d'être construites autour d'un canévas identique et d'aboutir à des résultats totalement différents" (111). See Spargo (*Chaucer's Shipman's Tale*) for a taxonomical study of the tale in its appearance in many forms and languages and Spargo ("Shipman's Tale") for the text of Sercambi's novella based on *Decameron* 8.1. Copland and Thompson compare the two novelle to *The Shipman's Tale,* Heffernan and Beidler 8.1 and

The Shipman's Tale. For separate or comparative analyses of *Decameron* 8.1 and 8.2, see, for example, Pomilio; Goursonnet; Mazzotta (190–92 [8.1]); Sanguineti (143–49); Wallace (*Decameron* 85–86 [8.1]); Baratto (377–79 [8.2]; 395–98 [8.1]); Ferreri [8.1]; Porcelli [8.2]; Forni (69–72 [8.2]); Tateo (195–96).

2. See Williams 95–100, "From Reflection to Mediation."

3. I have discussed this perspective on *Decameron* and the *Canterbury Tales,* and the problems created by late medieval Europe's mediated structures of church, secular governments, and commerce, in "Mediation and the Work of Language in the Decameron and the *Canterbury Tales,*" the Tenth Annual Rossell Hope Robbins Lecture, Medieval Club of New York, November 1999, part of which has been printed in "The *Decameron* and the *Canterbury Tales,*" *Approaches to Teaching Boccaccio's* Decameron, ed. James H. McGregor (New York: Modern Language Association, 2002) 103–18.

4. Cf. Copland, who notes the "shift in social and spiritual level of the characters and a corresponding decorous shift in narrative style" between 8.1 and 8.2 (11).

5. Pomilio insists on the fundamental benevolence and lightness of touch of 8.2's representation of rural society: "Boccaccio . . . ha preso le distanze e si diverte. Ma lo fa con la mano più leggera, senza mai slittare nella crudezza" (208).

6. Italian page and paragraph numbers follow Boccaccio, Branca's edition; translation page numbers follow Boccaccio, McWilliam's translation.

7. Mazzotta, Ferreri, and Porcelli all cite Andreas Capellanus, *De amore,* as the inspiration for Neifile's condemnation of Ambruogia; Mazzotta (192) says that Neifile is upset because "the law of the market has disrupted the fairyland of courtly love," while Wallace (*Decameron* 86), argues that the novella implicates all its characters in the vices of "a world in which all relations are established *per prezzo,*" an argument made at greater length by Ferreri.

8. Wallace (*Decameron* 85–86) notes that "the mercantile society of Trecento Florence frequently expressed the stresses and strains generated by its own volatile and expansionist energies through narratives of gender conflict. . . . The first and last novelle of *Decameron's* eighth day show women entering into . . . the spirit of the market economy."

9. Mazzotta (191) speaks of the "threat to Gulfardo's identity" by Ambruogia's attaching a fixed monetary value to his sexuality; in addition, her demand on him turns her into a mercenary who "deals with him on his own terms."

10. The specter of poor women turning to prostitution as a way of supplementing meager family incomes hangs over such *Decameron* novelle as 7.2 and, as we shall see, 8.2. Cf. McNamara 150; Karras ch. 3.

11. Giannozzo, the elder Alberti, tells his young relatives that when his wife said she hoped to please him, he replied, "'Dear wife, listen to me. I shall be most pleased if you do just three things: first, my wife, see that you never want another man to share this bed but me.' . . . I repeated that she should never receive anyone into that room [the bedroom] but myself. That was the first point. The second, I said, was that she should take care of the household, preside over it with modesty, serenity, tranquillity, and peace. That was the second point. The third thing, I said, was that she should see that nothing went wrong in the house" (Alberti 211). Cf. Wallace: "The whole strategy of [Boccaccio] . . . is to keep women indoors reading his book while men go about their public business" (*Chaucerian Polity* 27).

12. Goursonnet (116 n. 18) calls attention to an illustration in a fifteenth-century manuscript of *Decameron* which "montre d'ailleurs Gulfardo et son ami séparés d'Ambruogia par un comptoir sur lequel elle vérifie, une par une dirait-on, les pièces de monnaie." Ferreri (201) stresses how the two hundred florins, as they circulate through the hands of all the main characters of the novella, define its "termini finanzieri" and "contesto mercantesco."

13. Copland refers to this as "the sort of gratuitous quip that Boccaccio characteristically found irresistible" (11).

14. Ferreri, 201–2, prefers to stress the parallels between Gulfardo and Ambruogia; both, he argues, are to blame for "amore prezzolato . . . che finisce per accomunare i due protagonisti in una sordida avidità."

15. See Trimpi 342 on the historical pedigree of these introductions, stretching back to the *controversiae* debated by Roman rhetoricians. The *Decameron* narrator, in the "Conclusione dell'autore" (962.19), insists that the reader can know what individual novelle have hidden in their breasts by reading what is written on their *fronte,* "per non ingannare alcuna persona"—which is clearly not the case in 8.1.

16. For a history of antifraternal satire, see Szittya; for the warning against false preachers *penetrantes domos,* see 2 Timothy 3:6. The most extensive instance of antifraternal polemic in *Decameron* can be found in 3.7, addressed by Tedaldo degli Elisei to his former mistress (cf. Delcorno).

17. Copland (11–12); Goursonnet (117–18); Pomilio; Baratto (379); Porcelli; and Thompson (209) all stress the comic intent of 8.2's rural setting, wooing, and diction. Copland (12), Thompson, and Pomilio note the good-naturedness of the representation, and Goursonnet speaks of "un univers où les rapports entre individus s'établissent dans une sorte de convivialité souriante" (118)—an interpretation of the novella which the current discussion finds too univocal as well as too positive. Cf. Wallace: "[I]t is difficult for us to grasp or even to think to look for signs of power or intelligence in rural settings: we are all heirs to long traditions of political prejudice in which city-centered standards of *civilitas* are defined against the countryside" (*Chaucerian Polity* 126).

18. Florentines often rationalized, and occluded, their exploitative relations with the *contado* by stigmatizing the *nuova gente,* upwardly mobile residents of the countryside who moved to Florence to advance their condition and, according to the stereotype, did so by marrying into established but impoverished Florentine families (Wallace, *Chaucerian Polity* 17). For a representation of this prejudice, see *Decameron* 7.8.

19. See Pomilio (207–8) and Porcelli (85 and footnote 3) on the novella's use of suffixes and words featuring spellings with *zz,* thereby signaling comic (because socially inferior) rusticity. Copland (15) speaks of the "highly elaborated effusion of comic chatter," but Thompson (208) sees instead "infectious energy . . . conveyed by vivid language [including] many rustic allusions, epithets, and diminutives (especially of the -*azzo,* -*ozzo* group)." For a general consideration of the linguistic register of comic rusticity in *Decameron,* see Branca (xxxiv–xxxix).

20. The priest's portrait "raises the question of priestly continence in a realistic setting, [so that] we come to a greater understanding of why [priestly incontinence] arises" (Thompson 209).

21. On colors, see Trimpi 309–20; the *quistioni d'amore* in book 4 of Boccaccio's *Filocolo* are exercises in colors, and so, for example, is Tedaldo's long speech to his former mistress in 3.7 (cf. note 16), urging her to ignore the counsel of her friar-confessor.

22. Porcelli says, "l'incontro del prete e della Belcolore ha dunque tutte le caratteristiche dell'animalità dei rustici; il macinare in particoli periodi, cioè quando se ne ha la possibilità . . ." (93). Pomilio, responding to the mortar-pestle exchange, praises "l'efficacia metaforica che in fin del conto risolve il tutto in levità" (212); for similar views, see Forni 70–71; Thompson 204–5, 208; Tateo 196. I would argue that this is the effect sought by the narrator, but it may not suffice to efface the problems and anxieties already presented by the novella.

23. Porcelli documents the obscene allusions in all these viands and artifacts (89).

Works Cited

Alberti, Leon Battista. *The Family in Renaissance Florence: A Translation of I Libri della famiglia.* Trans. Renée Neu Watkins. Columbia: U of South Carolina P, 1969.

Andreas Capellanus. *De amore et amoris remedio.* Ed. P. G. Walsh. London: Duckworth, 1982.

Baratto, Mario. *Realtà e stile nel "Decameron."* 2nd ed. Rome: Editori Riuniti, 1993.

Beidler, Peter G. "Contrasting Masculinities in the Shipman's Tale: Monk, Merchant, and Wife." *Masculinities in Chaucer.* Approaches to Maleness in the *Canterbury Tales* and *Troilus and Criseyde.* Ed. Peter G. Beidler. Cambridge: D. S. Brewer, 1998. 131–42.

Boccaccio, Giovanni. *Decameron.* Ed. Vittore Branca. Milan: Mondadori, 1976. Vol. 4 of *Tutte le opere di Giovanni Boccaccio.* 10 vols. 1964–98.

——. *Decameron*. Trans. G. H. McWilliam. 2nd ed. London: Penguin Books, 1995.

Branca, Vittore. "Una chiave di lettura per il Decameron." *Decameron* by Giovanni Boccaccio. Ed. Vittore Branca. 3rd ed. Torino: Einaudi, 1992. vii–xxxix.

Copland, Murray. "The Shipman's Tale: Chaucer and Boccaccio." *Medium Aevum* 35.1 (1966): 11–28.

Delcorno, Carlo. "La 'predica' di Tedaldo." *Studi sul Boccaccio* 27 (1999): 55–80.

Ferreri, Rosario. "Madonna Ambruogia e l'amore prezzolato (*Decameron* VIII 1)." *Studi sul Boccaccio* 21 (1993): 199–206.

Forni, Pier Massimo. *Adventures in Speech*. Philadelphia: U of Pennsylvania P, 1996.

Giddens, Anthony. *Central Problems in Social Theory: Action, Structure and Contradiction in Social Analysis*. Berkeley: U of California P, 1979.

Goursonnet, André. "Deux beffe du Décaméron." *Hommage a Louise Cohen: Langue et littératures italiennes*. Annales de la Faculté des lettres et sciences humaines de Nice, no. 42. Paris: Belles Lettres, 1982. 111–20.

Heffernan, Carol Falvo. "Chaucer's *Shipman's Tale* and Boccaccio's *Decameron* 8.1: Retelling a Story." *Courtly Literature: Culture and Context*. Ed. Keith Busby and Erik Cooper. Philadelphia: J. Benjamins, 1990. 262–70.

Karras, Ruth Mazo. *Common Women: Prostitution and Sexuality in Medieval England*. Oxford: Oxford UP, 1996.

Mazzotta, Giuseppe. *The World at Play in Boccaccio's* Decameron. Princeton: Princeton UP, 1986.

McNamara, JoAnn. "City Air Makes Men Free and Women Bound." *Text and Territory: Geographical Imagination in the European Middle Ages*. Ed. Sylvia Tomasch and Saly Gilles. Philadelphia: U of Pennsylvania P, 1998. 143–58.

Pomilio, Mario. "Il tono basso-realistico del Boccaccio." *Atti del convegno di Nimega sul Boccaccio*. Ed. Carlo Ballerini. Bologna: Pàtron, 1976. 207–14.

Porcelli, Bruno. "Decameron 8.2: un amorazzo contadino da ridere." *Studi e problemi di critica testuale* 50 (1995): 85–94.

Sanguineti, Edoardo. *Lettura del* Decameron. Salerno: Edizioni 10/17, 1989.

Spargo, John Webster. *Chaucer's* Shipman's Tale; *the Lover's Gift Regained*. Folklore Fellows Communications 91, Helsinki, 1930.

——. "The Shipman's Tale." *Sources and Analogues of Chaucer's Canterbury Tales*. Ed. W. F. Bryan and Germaine Dempster. Chicago: U of Chicago P, 1941. 439–46.

Szittya, Penn R. *The Anti-Fraternal Tradition in Medieval Literature*. Princeton: Princeton UP, 1986.

Tateo, Francesco. *Boccaccio*. Roma-Bari: Laterza, 1998.

Thompson, N. S. *Chaucer, Boccaccio, and the Debate of Love: A Comparative Study of* The Decameron *and* The Canterbury Tales. Oxford: Clarendon, 1996.

Trimpi, Wesley. *Muses of One Mind: The Literary Analysis of Experience and Its Continuity*. Princeton: Princeton UP, 1983.

Wallace, David. *Chaucerian Polity: Absolutist Lineages and Associational Forms in England and Italy*. Stanford: Stanford UP, 1997.

——. *Giovanni Boccaccio:* Decameron. Landmarks of World Literature. Cambridge: Cambridge UP, 1991.

Williams, Raymond. *Marxism and Literature*. Oxford: Oxford UP, 1977.

Contributors

WILLIAM R. ASKINS is Professor of English and Humanities at the Community College of Philadelphia. Recent work includes contributions to *Charles d'Orleans in England, Sources and Analogues of* The Canterbury Tales, and *Reading Medieval Culture: Essays in Honor of Robert W. Hanning*.

KENNETH BLEETH is Professor of English at Connecticut College. He has published essays in *Dante Studies, Medium Aevum, Harvard Studies in Language and Literature, English Studies, Chaucer Review, PMLA,* and in the essay collection *Chaucer's Cultural Geography.* He has also edited the chapter on the *Physician's Tale* in *Sources and Analogues of* The Canterbury Tales. Forthcoming is a volume on the *Physician's, Squire's,* and *Franklin's Tales* in the Toronto Chaucer Bibliographies.

MICHAEL CALABRESE, Professor of English at California State University, Los Angeles, is author of *Chaucer's Ovidian Arts of Love* and essays on Abelard and Heloise, the *Canterbury Tales,* Marco Polo, and the Middle English *Cleanness.* One of the editors of the Piers Plowman Electronic Archive and author of "Prostitutes in the C-text of *Piers Plowman,*" Professor Calabrese has also written about masculinity in Boccaccio's *Decameron* and on the politics of reading the *Prioress's Tale.*

LISA H. COOPER is Assistant Professor in the Department of English at the University of Wisconsin–Madison; before taking this position, she was from 2003 to 2005 a post-doctoral Humanities Fellow at Stanford University. Her research focuses on the intersection of medieval narrative and material culture, and she has recently published articles in the *Journal of the Early Book Society,* in *New Medieval Literatures,* and in

Arthuriana. She is currently completing a book titled *Crafting Narratives: Artisans, Authors, and the Literary Artifact in Late Medieval England.*

CATHERINE S. COX is Professor of English at the University of Pittsburgh's Johnstown campus. She is the author of articles on a variety of biblical and medieval texts and topics, and of the books *Gender and Language in Chaucer* and *The Judaic Other in Dante, the Gawain-poet, and Chaucer.*

SYLVIA FEDERICO, Assistant Professor of English at Bates College, is author of *New Troy: Fantasies of Empire in the Late Middle Ages,* in addition to several articles on late medieval literature and culture.

JOHN M. GANIM is Professor of English at the University of California–Riverside. He is the author of *Style and Consciousness in Middle English Narrative, Chaucerian Theatricality,* and, most recently, *Medievalism and Orientalism: Three Essays on Literature, Architecture, and Cultural Identity.* He has also published articles on urbanism and architecture.

ROBERT W. HANNING, Professor Emeritus of English and Comparative Literature, Columbia University, is author of *The Vision of History in Early Britain* and *The Individual in Twelfth-Century Romance,* and co-translator, with Joan Ferrante, of *The Lais of Marie de France.* Professor Hanning is currently completing *Poetics of Deliberation: Prudential Fictions in the* Decameron *and* The Canterbury Tales.

THOMAS J. HEFFERNAN is the Kenneth Curry Professor at the University of Tennessee. He is the author of *Sacred Biography: Saints and Their Biographies in the Middle Ages, The Liturgy of the Medieval Church* (with Ann Matter), and *Sermons and Homilies* (with Patrick Horner). Professor Heffernan's areas of interest are church history, hagiography, historical linguistics, and ancient and medieval biography. His critical edition of the *Passio Sanctarum Perpetua et Felicitatis* is forthcoming from the series Ancient Christian Writers.

LAURA L. HOWES, Associate Professor of English at the University of Tennessee, is the author of *Chaucer's Gardens and the Language of Convention.* She has also published essays on Chaucer's Criseyde, literary landscape in Middle English poetry, the *Miller's Tale,* and *The Book of Margery Kempe.*

KARI KALVE is Associate Professor of English and Associate Academic Dean at Earlham College. She has written about *Piers Plowman* and about American popular culture.

GREGORY B. KAPLAN is Associate Professor of Spanish at the University of Tennessee, specializing in the literature of the Spanish Middle Ages. Recent publications include *The Evolution of Converso Literature* and articles in *Bulletin of Hispanic Studies* and *Hispanófila.*

LAWRENCE WARNER is Lecturer of Middle English at the University of Sydney. He is the coeditor of the *Yearbook of Langland Studies* and has published essays on *Piers Plowman,* Chaucer's *Nun's Priest's Tale,* Geoffrey of Monmouth, Dante, and Obadiah the Proselyte.

Index

Place, Space, and Landscape in Medieval Narrative was designed and typeset on a Macintosh computer system using InDesign software. The body text is set in 9/12 Palatino Linotype and display type is set in Beacon. This book was designed and typeset by Kelly Gray and manufactured by Thomson-Shore, Inc.